The market and beyond

The market and beyond
Information technology in Japan

MARTIN FRANSMAN

*Director, Institute for Japanese–European Studies
and Reader, Department of Economics, University of Edinburgh*

CAMBRIDGE
UNIVERSITY PRESS

Published by the Press Syndicate of the University of Cambridge
The Pitt Building, Trumpington Street, Cambridge CB2 1RP
40 West 20th Street, New York, NY 10011–4211, USA
10 Stamford Road, Oakleigh, Victoria 3166, Australia

First published 1990
Reprinted 1991
First paperback edition 1993

Printed in Malta, at Interprint Ltd

British Library cataloguing in publication data
Fransman, Martin, 1948–
The market and beyond: cooperation and competition
in information technology development in the Japanese
System.
1. Japan. Electronics industries
I. Title
338.4'7621381'0952

Library of Congress cataloguing in publication data
Fransman, Martin.
The market and beyond: cooperation and competition in
information technology development in the Japanese
System / Martin Fransman.
p.   cm.
Includes bibliographical references.
ISBN 0 521 26803 6
1. Electronics industries.   2. Computer industry.   I. Title.
HD9696.A2F7   1990
338.4'7004'0952 – dc20   89-17311 CIP

ISBN 0 521 26803 6 hardback
ISBN 0 521 43525 0 paperback

To my parents, Dee and Elie,
and to Jonathan,
who was also made in Japan

Contents

List of figures	*page*	viii
List of tables		ix
Foreword		xi
Preface		xiii
1 Introduction		1
2 A periodization of the development of the computer and electronic devices industry in Japan, 1948–1979		13
3 The VLSI Research Project, 1976–1980		57
4 The Optical Measurement and Control System Project, 1979–1985		98
5 The High-Speed Computing System for Scientific and Technological Uses Project (The Supercomputer Project), 1981–1989		145
6 The Future Electronic Devices Project, 1981–1990		177
7 The Fifth Generation Computer Project, 1982–1991		193
8 Cooperation and competition in the Japanese computing and electronic devices industry: a quantitative analysis		243
9 Conclusions and theoretical implications		256
Appendix 1 NEC's total quality control		292
Appendix 2 Specialization in industrial and consumer electronics by Japanese electronics companies		294
Notes		300
Bibliography		312
Index		323

Figures

3.1 Research areas in the VLSI Project's joint laboratories   *page* 70
3.2 Joint patents in the VLSI Project   73
3.3 The propensity to share technological knowledge in four technology areas relating to VLSI technology   78
3.4 Japanese market share of memory LSI   83
3.5 NEC's management system for VLSI development   88
3.6 The benefits of alternative forms of government research support   89
3.7 The costs of alternative forms of government research support   95
4.1 The research design for the Optical Measurement Project   108
4.2 The total Optical Measurement System and its subsystems   113
4.3 The funding of the Optoelectronics Joint Laboratory   115
5.1 The supercomputer and its subsystems   155
6.1 A model of joint search   183
7.1 Fifth Generation Project grand design   227
7.2 Some alternatives for government high-technology intervention   230
A.1 NEC's total quality control   292

Tables

2.1 Performance of information technology R & D in Japan, 1970–1981   *page* 50
3.1 Joint patents in the VLSI joint laboratories   75
3.2 Ranking of firms in terms of number of joint patents held with one other firm in the first three laboratories of the VLSI joint laboratories   76
3.3 Inter-laboratory joint patents in the VLSI joint laboratories   77
3.4 Propensity to share knowledge by firms participating in the VLSI Project   79
3.5 Commercializable products which have emerged from the VLSI Project   84
4.1 Japanese semiconductor sales, 1985   100
4.2 III-V compound devices sold in Japan   100
4.3 The subsystems and components and the firms involved in the Optical Measurement project   114
4.4 Membership of the Optoelectronics Joint Laboratory   119
5.1 Supercomputer Project: allocation of research tasks to the participating companies   155
6.1 FED Project: areas of research specialization by the Kansai companies involved in research on three-dimensional devices   184
6.2 FED Project: areas of research specialization by the companies involved in research on superlattices   185
6.3 Diffusion of patents from the Next Generation (Jisedai) Programme   190
7.1 Research areas in Fujitsu in artificial intelligence   223
7.2 Funding the Fifth Generation Project   228
8.1 Intensity of competition between the firms involved in the national cooperative research projects   244
8.2 Danger of knowledge leakage in the national cooperative research projects   246
8.3 Opportunism in the national cooperative research projects   246
8.4 Role of government as a facilitator of national cooperative research   248

8.5 Benefits received from the national cooperative research
     projects   250
8.6 Amount of research occurring in the absence of the national
     cooperative research projects   254
8.7 Evaluation of success of the national cooperative research
     projects   254
9.1 Oriented-basic research areas in five MITI-initiated projects 274
A.1 Size of Japanese and other international electronic/electrical
     companies   295
A.2 Sectoral specialization by major Japanese electronics
     companies   295
A.3 The importance of communications products in the four
     main NTT-supplying companies   298

Foreword

Until recently rather few social scientists took the trouble to visit Japan and to learn about Japanese society at first hand. However, among this small group were such distinguished economists and sociologists as Schumpeter and the Webbs. Even after the Second World War it took a rather long time before people realized that new social, economic and technological developments in Japan merited careful study and analysis. Professor G. C. Allen of London University and Professor Ronald Dore of the University of Sussex were among the few who pioneered comparative research on technical and institutional change in Japan and other industrialized countries.

More recently the achievements of Japanese technology and the closely related performance of the Japanese economy have stimulated much more widespread attempts to explain these achievements. But among all the publications generated by this upsurge of interest in Japan, relatively few are based on careful in-depth research and still fewer have examined the heartland of Japanese technological strength – the mode of organizing and coordinating research and development networks.

In this book Martin Fransman has made an outstanding contribution to our understanding of the Japanese science–technology system. In particular, by his detailed study of some of the major government-sponsored programmes, he has thrown much light on the relationship between government and industry which has been the subject of much controversy and misunderstanding. It is especially gratifying that Martin Fransman's work has led to the establishment of a new research centre at the University of Edinburgh.* It is to be hoped therefore that this study will be the first of many others exploring the sources of Japanese technological strength and the implications for the rest of the world.

Christopher Freeman

Science Policy Research Unit
University of Sussex
October 1989

*Institute for Japanese – European Technology Studies

Preface

In many ways this book began in small machinery firms in the back-streets of Hong Kong; it ended in some of the largest electronics companies in the world in Japan. The studies in both cases (and also other studies done in between in Singapore and Taiwan) were motivated by a desire to better understand the causes of the remarkable economic performances of these Asian countries. It was this desire that soon led to an interest in the process of technical change, a process that I discovered was little analysed or appreciated by my fellow economists.

I am indebted to a large number of people and institutions for assistance in various ways with the writing of this book. The Nuffield Foundation, by granting me a Social Science Fellowship for the academic year 1985–6, provided for a replacement who took over my academic duties. This gave me the opportunity, unfortunately all too rare these days, to read widely, unimpaired by university responsibilities, in the area of technology studies and in other relevant areas such as organisation theory and industrial organisation. During this year I was able to lay the conceptual foundations for the research that I conducted over the following year in Japan. A number of organizations provided support for this research. The British Academy and the Japan Society for the Promotion of Science awarded me a Fellowship that covered the basic costs for myself and my family. The Leverhulme Trust provided a substantial grant for research assistance and related research costs, and the Nuffield Foundation also gave help. I was particularly fortunate to be able to work with an excellent group of Japanese research associates who provided a source of intellectual stimulation as well as research assistance. Our regular Wednesday night meetings at Tokyo University's International Lodge provided ideas as well as more informal discussions. I am therefore deeply grateful to Shoko Tanaka, Ryu Imahashi, Hisanaga Amikura and Yuko Yamashita for all their support.

I must also record my thanks to Professor Ronald Dore who, through his interpretation of things Japanese and his comparative references to Britain, has influenced most British and other international scholars working on Japan. Ron was particularly helpful in providing a number of initial contacts who proved to be of great assistance in my subsequent research in Japan. I am similarly grateful to Professors Yasusuke Murakami and Shumpei Kumon, formerly of the Department of International Relations at Tokyo University, who provided me with a base in their department, generously arranged contacts and meetings for me, and acted as critical commentators on various drafts of my work. Their help was indispensible for my research. Thanks are due too to the late Professor Keichi Oshima and Mr Toshihide Takeshita of Technova who also provided me with a base in their research institute.

I am particularly grateful to numerous individuals in the Japanese companies and government who were extremely generous with their time and information. With the trade war between Japan and her trading partners intensifying even as I conducted my research, the time was in many ways inappropriate to ask penetrating questions about often sensitive areas. It is a tribute, however, to the spirit with which these companies and government organizations have internationalized that, in almost all cases, my interviews were conducted in an extremely frank manner, providing me with the deeper '*honne*' level of information without which an accurate analysis of research cooperation in Japan could not have been undertaken. However, since I undertook to guarantee confidentiality in these interviews, I have decided not to mention here the names of the company and government representatives who provided such important assistance in this research.

Nevertheless, I must acknowledge with deep gratitude the opportunities that I was given to receive collective feedback from groups of officials intimately involved with some of the projects I have analysed in this book. In this regard I am particularly grateful to Dr Kazuhiro Fuchi and Mr Takashi Kurozumi who organised an afternoon meeting in ICOT, the Institute for New Generation Computer Technology, during which I was given detailed comment on a draft of my chapter on the Fifth Generation Computer Project. Likewise, Mr Satoshi Mizuno, Deputy Director-General of MITI's Machinery and Information Industries Bureau, arranged a similar afternoon meeting that gave me the benefit of detailed comment on the first draft of the whole of this book from senior MITI officials closely involved in the Japanese electronics industry. Although none of the individuals mentioned in this preface bears any responsibility for the content, conceptual or empirical, of this book, it is particularly important to stress that the officials mentioned in this paragraph are in no way to be associated with the correctness of my information, analysis and conclusions.

I am also grateful to IBM's Thomas J. Watson Research Center in Yorktown Heights, New York, for information given to me on the reasons behind the decision to significantly de-emphasize research on Josephson junctions in 1983. I must also record my appreciation for help and information given by Dr Clive Bradley and Mr Kerry Pocknell of the Science and Technology section of the British Embassy in Tokyo.

I was also fortunate to be appointed to the NTT Chair of Telecommunications at the Research Center for Advanced Science and Technology (RCAST) at the University of Tokyo for almost four months from July to the end of October 1988. This gave me the opportunity to complete the introduction and conclusion to the present book, benefiting greatly from the comments of my colleagues at RCAST. A special word of thanks is due to Professor Takanori Okoshi, Director of RCAST, and to Professors Kei Takeuchi and Takeshi Hiromatsu of the RCAST division dealing with the relationships among science, technology and industry for their comments and their hospitality. Ikuko Suganuma provided efficient secretarial and other assistance that often went far beyond the call of duty.

Finally, to this list of acknowledgements must be added a personal note. I am grateful to Mihoko Nakayama, who battled gallantly to fit in regular Japanese lessons between numerous interviews and meetings, for her dedication, perseverance and good spirit. I have been particularly fortunate to work with Shoko Tanaka as both a colleague and a kindred spirit. Her comments, observations and support were of great help to me in numerous ways and my debt to her is therefore especially great. My family, Tammy, Judith, Karen and, towards the end of this study, Jonathan, made significant sacrifices on my behalf (which included coping with the unfamiliarity of the Japanese school system in addition to the sometimes long absences of father and husband). Tammy's constant support and faith have been of inestimable importance. Their help was unfailing and has been a *sine qua non* for the present study.

1
Introduction

This book is intended to make a contribution in two broad areas. The first is a detailed study of the major Japanese cooperative research projects in the area of computing, related electronic devices and optoelectronics. These include the VLSI Research Project, 1976–80; the Optical Measurement and Control System Project, 1979–85; the High Speed Computing System for Scientific and Technological Uses Project (The Supercomputer Project), 1981–89; the Future Electronic Devices Project, 1981–90; and the Fifth Generation Computer Project, 1982–91. It is believed that the present study is the most detailed analysis of these projects available.

The second area to which this book contributes, relates to the conceptualization of the process of technical change and its relationship to economic change. Based on the analyses of the above projects and on the historical chapter which reconstructs the policy alternatives facing the Japanese companies and government in the computing and related electronic devices industry in the postwar period, the final chapter of this book explores some of the key analytical concepts that are necessary to analyse the process of technical change in what is referred to as the Japanese Technology-Creating System.

The book throws light on a number of issues which have emerged in academic and policy-oriented analyses and debates. To begin with, the complexities surrounding the process of research cooperation between competing firms are examined in detail. It is widely believed in many Western circles that in Japan there is a substantially higher propensity for competing companies to cooperate in research. The present study, however, shows that Japanese corporations are just as cautious as their Western counterparts in entering into cooperative research agreements. It is significant in this connection that there are only two examples of spontaneous research cooperation between the largest competing Japanese industrial electronics companies, that is research cooperation agreed in the absence of facilitating measures taken either by government or a large procurer. Research cooperation, however, has brought significant benefits to this Japanese industry and the present study shows in detail how important has been the role of the Japanese government and Nippon

Telegraph and Telephone (NTT) in bringing about such cooperation.

Secondly, this study contributes to the analysis of research cooperation by introducing a twofold classification based on the degree of sharing of the knowledge created under the cooperative research project. This study accordingly distinguishes between coordinated in-house research, where the research is performed inside the participating companies but the research activities of the companies are coordinated, and joint research in joint research facilities, where the companies send researchers to joint laboratories. In the latter case the degree of cooperation is significantly greater since there is a joint creation and sharing of knowledge. The present study reveals, however, that as a result of the strong degree of competition between the industrial electronics corporation in Japan, it is coordinated in-house research, rather than joint research in joint research facilities, that has been the dominant form of organization for the cooperative research projects.

Thirdly, this study throws light on the vexed question of government–industry relations and industrial policy in Japan. Two poles of the debate on this question can be clearly distinguished: the one concluding that the industrial policy of the Japanese government has had an important effect on the economic performance of the country,[1] and the other arguing that little causal significance is to be attributed to government activities in accounting for this performance.[2] However, no consensus is yet in sight to resolve the contradictory conclusions arrived at by these two sets of writers. It is significant that such seasoned observers of the international economic scene as Eads and Nelson (1986, p. 245) conclude, regarding the debate on the effects of industrial policy in Japan, that:

this dispute represents problems of where to draw the line . . . By defending the issue one way, one scholar is able to see vast influence; by changing the definition, another concludes quite reasonably that the extent of influence is substantially less. But even more worrisome, it suggests how scholars debating the question of what the Japanese government does in the way of support for its high technology industries could appear to be talking past each other.

The present book makes its contribution to the industrial policy debate by focusing primarily on the development of a number of core information technologies and analysing the contribution to the development of these technologies made by the Japanese companies, by government officials (including Ministry of International Trade and Industry (MITI) policy-makers and researchers in government research laboratories such as the Electrotechnical Laboratory (ETL)), and by the universities. By so doing, it is sometimes possible to pose the counter-factual question regarding what would probably have happened in the absence of various government measures, and to provide what seem to be reasonable answers to this question. While many writers have concluded that such counter-factual questions by definition cannot be resolved,[3] the present study, by tracing the development of specific technologies, suggests that significant progress can be made in tackling these questions.

Fourthly, and finally, this study makes a contribution to the conceptual analysis of technical change and its relationship to economic change. One way in which a contribution is made is through the development in this book of a conceptualization of the Japanese Technology-Creating System consisting of a number of institutions and forms of organization (including market processes) which together influence the process of technical change, namely the acquisition, assimilation, creation, and diffusion of technologies. As the present book shows through the analysis of the cooperative research projects and the history of the Japanese computing and electronic devices industry, it is meaningful to view the major Japanese institutions and forms of organization which have had an impact on technical change as constituting a system, the components of which have interacted to influence the evolution of technologies. In view of the complexity of this system, no attempt is made here to summarize the conclusions reached, and the reader is referred to the final chapter of this book.

Another way in which a conceptual contribution is made is through the development of the concept of 'bounded vision'. This concept, again emerging from the detailed analyses of cooperative research projects and the history of the industry, suggests that different kinds of organization have different limitations on the field of their 'vision', that is their ability to perceive the importance of various areas of science and technology and to make serious attempts to assimilate and develop these areas. For example, the field of vision of for-profit corporations is determined largely by their existing activities in product and factor markets, in production, and in R & D and by their need in the short to medium term to generate satisfactory profits. The resulting bounded vision implies that new technologies emerging from neighbouring areas where the corporation does not have current activities are likely to take some time to penetrate the corporation's field of vision. Furthermore, the corporation is unlikely to 'see' scientific and technological research areas to which a significant degree of commercial uncertainty attaches. The need to generate satisfactory profits in the short to medium term therefore further bounds the vision of the corporation, contributing in some cases to a degree of 'short-sightedness'. One example is the creation of technologies for 'the day after tomorrow' where the degree of commercial uncertainty is frequently great. In view of their bounded vision, corporations often tend to underinvest in the creation of such technologies.

The existence of such bounds on the vision of for-profit corporations implies that a complementary or compensating role may be played in a national technology-creating system by other forms of organization which have different constraints on their vision. In the Japanese System examples are the role played by government research institutes like the Electrotechnical Laboratory of MITI or the Electrical Communications Laboratories of NTT, and the role played by universities. Another example is the government-initiated cooperative research projects analysed in this book which bring together in one coordinated project the different bounded visions of the various participating organizations. These cooperative forms of organization, it is argued, have played a significant role, complementing that of the private corporations and contributing to the ability of the Japanese System to rapidly develop and commercialize new technologies.

These are some of the specific contributions made by the present book. There are, however, a number of more general concerns that have informed the present study and these are clarified in the following section.

Some general concerns

The ultimate concern of this book is the causes of the wealth of nations, more specifically, the causes of different economic performance among nations. A fundamental tenet of this book is that these causes relate intimately to the process of technical change, that is the acquisition, assimilation, creation, and diffusion of new technologies. This argument is in line with that of Adam Smith who, in the first page of *The Wealth of Nations*, emphasized the importance of the development of machinery and the emergence of a category of workers whose job is 'not to do anything, but to observe everything', workers who in the division of labour in the modern corporation are referred to as R & D researchers.

However, there are two broad themes that thread their way through Adam Smith's work. One, already referred to here, came out of an interest in the process of production and the way in which it was organized. It was this interest that led to the famous analysis of the pin factory. There was, however, a second theme which dominated Adam Smith's thinking, and this was his analysis of the market process, the workings of the so-called Invisible Hand.[4]

In the present book Adam Smith's first theme is followed, with less emphasis given to his second theme, thus reversing his priority ordering. In this sense the present book is in line with several well-known recent books whose titles reveal their concerns with important phenomena that lie beyond the market, phenomena that must be analysed if the complex process of economic change is to be understood. These books include Oliver Williamson's *Markets and Hierarchies* and Alfred Chandler's *The Visible Hand*.

What in the present case is the justification for insisting on the need to go beyond the market in analysing the process of technical change? Surely the market, as the 'place' where the products and services of competing firms meet one another and vie for the attention and choice of purchasers, exercises a crucial influence on the process of technical change in these firms? In insisting on the need to go beyond the market, it must be stressed, the present book does not argue that market processes are unimportant as determinants of the process of technical change: quite the contrary. The market process, as is documented in detail in the present book in the analysis of the cooperative research projects and the history of the Japanese computing and electronic devices industry, is a crucial source of *pressure*, *incentive* and *information*, all of which have a central bearing on the process of technical change. The first of these influences on technical change, for example, has been summarized in a memorable paragraph from Schumpeter (1966, pp. 31–2):

... capitalist economy is not and cannot be stationary. Nor it is merely expanding in a steady manner. It is incessantly being revolutionized *from within* by new enterprise, i.e. by the intrusion of new commodities or new methods of production or new commercial opportunities into the industrial structure as it exists at any moment. Any existing structures and all the conditions of doing business are always in a process of change. Every situation is being upset before it has had time to work itself out ... Possibilities of gains to be reaped by producing new things or by producing old things more cheaply are constantly materializing and calling for new investments. These new products and new methods compete with the old products and old methods not on equal terms but at a decisive advantage that may mean death to the latter. This is how 'progress' comes about in capitalist society. In order to escape being undersold, *every* firm is in the end compelled to follow suit, to invest in its turn and, in order to be able to do so, to plow back part of its profits, i.e. to accumulate. Thus, everyone else accumulates.

The market process also provides incentives for entrepreneurs and corporations to innovate in the attempt to generate sufficient revenues over costs to earn attractive rates of return on investment. Furthermore, the market is also an important source of information, not only with regard to prices and quantities, but also qualities, concepts and ideas which may constitute important inputs for innovation. Why then the need to go beyond market?

There are several reasons for the necessity to go beyond the market, while analysing the effects of market processes. The first is that, while many (but by no means all) of the pressures, incentives and information flows which constitute the motive force for technical change originate in market processes, they do not fully determine the ensuing process of technical change, its form, characteristics and evolutionary direction. Technical change does not follow directly, or automatically, from market processes. Forms of organization and institutional practices exert further influences, shaping the process of technical change. It is therefore necessary that these forms of organization and institutional practices be carefully analysed. Such an analysis constitutes one of the major preoccupations of the present book where particular attention is paid to the process and effects of research cooperation. In undertaking the analysis it becomes apparent that the organizations and institutions analysed, frequently have their own historical and national specificity, and in some cases this specificity may constitute an important part of the explanation of differing national economic performances.

A further reason for the need to go beyond the market is that under some circumstances the market, as a form of organizing the allocation of resources, does not necessarily provide adequate guidance for resource allocation. One case in point, stressed in the present book, is the creation of new technologies for 'the day after tomorrow'. In this case a significant degree of uncertainty is often associated with research with the consequence that firms, acting and interacting in the absence of government intervention, may not invest socially desirable amounts in innovation. One example, analysed in detail in the present book, is the instance of Josephson junction. The importance of uncertainty and the ways in which it has been dealt with in the Japanese System are examined in each of the chapters in this book and a synthesis is presented in the final chapter.

A third and related reason for going beyond the market is that market processes, by which is meant here the actions and interactions of private corporations without government measures to influence the outcome, are limited by the bounded visions of for-profit corporations. The significance of this point emerges strongly in the detailed empirical analyses in the present book.

A fourth reason is that market processes do not tend to generate an appropriate amount of research cooperation. As noted in this book, there are only two minor instances of spontaneous research cooperation, arranged by competing private corporations without the assistance of government or a large procurer, involving the major Japanese industrial electronics companies in the post-war period. This is explained through an analysis of the transactions costs involved in the private establishment of research cooperation, the most important of which arise from attempts to minimize knowledge leakage between competing firms. It is here that government and large procurers such as NTT have played important roles, economizing on transactions costs and increasing the amount of research cooperation undertaken in the Japanese System.

For all these reasons it is concluded that an analysis of technical change and its relationship to economic change necessitates the examination of phenomena that lie beyond the market, while including the study of the effects of market processes. In undertaking such an analysis in the present book, the conceptualization of a Japanese Technology-Creating System has proved helpful which synthesizes the influences of market processes and other institutions and forms of organization, including government intervention, on the process of technical change.

The proof of the pudding is in the eating. An extremely important question, with substantial economic, political, and social consequences, relates to the different economic performance of different countries and the reasons for these differences. If it is accepted that the ability to adopt and create new technologies is a central determinant of these differences, then it remains to establish how best to analyse these processes of technical change. The approach adopted in the present book provides one way forward. It is an approach that stresses the importance of an analysis of institutions, forms of organization and history. If it has provided greater understanding of the ways in which technical change has taken place in Japan, it will have served its purpose.

An overview

In view of the detail and complexity of the material in this book, an overview is presented in this section in order to highlight the major issues and arguments.

In the following chapter, chapter 2, the history of the computer and electronic devices industry in Japan in the postwar period is recreated. At the beginning of this period, Japanese researchers, in the midst of a society coming to grips with the legacy of war and picking up the pieces as part of the process of reconstruction, began to acquire and assimilate the new information technologies such as computers and transistors that were being developed in other Western countries. By the late 1970s, however, Japanese companies started to dominate world markets for memory semiconductors, and Japanese computers competed effectively with IBM computers in terms of processing cost and speed. These two sharply contrasting snapshots of the comparative state of the Japanese computer and electronic devices industry pose a number of important and complex questions.

At the most general level the question is: how was Japan able to catch up, and in a number of areas achieve a dominant position in this industry? In turn, this question poses a number of more specific questions. For example, to what extent were private Japanese companies responsible for these achievements? What role was played by the measures taken by the Japanese government which were intended to influence this industry and what relative importance should be attached to the different measures? How great was the contribution made by Japanese universities?

A number of important points emerge in tackling these kinds of questions in chapter 2. The first is that, rather than a single type of organization being responsible for the major achievements of this industry, significant complementary roles were played by different kinds of organization. Accordingly, the roles played by competing and cooperating private companies, by government research laboratories, by government planners and by universities are distinguished and their various contributions analysed. This in turn suggests the notion of a *system* comprised of different types of organization which play complementary roles in the development of specific technologies. In the present book this system is referred to as the Japanese Technology-Creating System, or the Japanese System. This system, it is important to stress, is technology-specific. In the Japanese context, for instance, the system of organizations which has been responsible for the development of industrial electronic technologies is fundamentally different from that involved in the development of consumer electronic technologies. More specifically, the Japanese government played a significantly smaller role in the development of these consumer technologies. The second point to emerge is that as a result of the evolution of the Japanese System over time, a historical periodization is necessary.

In chapter 2 three periods are distinguished. In the first period, lasting from 1948 to 1959, it was government research laboratories such as MITI's Electrotechnical Laboratory (ETL) and NTT's Electrical Communications Laboratories (ECL) and the universities, rather than the private corporations, that took the lead in acquiring, assimilating, and creating the new information technologies. The reasons for the failure of the private corporations, involved primarily in the areas of telecommunications and heavy electrical equipment, to decisively enter the emerging information technology field in this period are analysed in detail. During this period, therefore, a central role was played by non-profitmaking organizations in speeding the entry of the Japanese System into the area of information technology.

However, by the beginning of the second period, from 1960, with a wider market beginning to emerge for computers and related electronic devices, the locus of research activity moved decisively to the private corporations. Government measures (which are closely examined in chapter 2), nevertheless, played an important supportive role. With the technology gap between Japan and other Western countries beginning to widen, the Japanese corporations, with the exception of Fujitsu, entered into technology agreements with American companies. At the same time the Japanese government, attempting to deepen the technological capabilities of Japanese corporations, initiated a number of cooperative research programmes. These programmes raise a number of important questions. Was government intervention necessary for cooperative research to take place? In view of the benefits of cooperative research (which are closely analysed), why did the private Japanese corporations, all of which lagged behind and faced a common threat from the American leaders, not take it upon themselves to establish cooperative research agreements? How far did research cooperation go, did competing corporations jointly create and share technological knowledge or was their cooperation more limited than this? What effect did government intervention have on the diffusion of technological knowledge among the industrial electronics corporations? These and other questions are examined in detail.

The third period, from 1970 to 1979, began with a crisis for policymakers in the corporations and in government provoked by two causes: the great waves created by IBM with the introduction of its System 370 which threatened to overwhelm its American, European and Japanese rivals; and the increasing external pressures to liberalize both trade and foreign investment in Japan in the computer and electronic devices industry. How did the Japanese System cope with this crisis and with IBM's great leap forward which led to the exit from the computer market of leading American firms such as RCA, General Electric, and TRW? How important were the measures taken by the Japanese government and how would the Japanese corporations have coped in the absence of these measures? These issues are considered and answers provided.

By the end of this period, the technology gap between Japanese companies and their Western competitors had in most areas been closed and in some, such as memory semiconductors, the Japanese had begun to establish a firm lead. At the same time the research priorities established for Japanese researchers began to change. As followers, the Japanese were able to learn by observing the world leaders. This reduced some of the uncertainty and obviated the need for much original research. However, having reached the international technology frontier, it was now necessary for the Japanese System to undertake a greater amount of this kind of research. As a result, a new emphasis was given to what may be referred to as 'oriented basic research'. This, in turn, posed a number of important questions. Firstly, how would the Japanese System deal with those areas of oriented basic research where there was a significant degree of uncertainty? This question presents a dilemma since there is a strong tendency for for-profit companies to avoid making investments in areas where significant uncertainty attaches to the obtaining of adequate rates of return. Yet it is in these companies that the bulk of research is located. Left to their own devices it was likely that the private Japanese companies would not invest as much as was desirable in areas where there was an important amount of uncertainty.

Another question related to the issue of research cooperation. MITI officials were aware of the potential benefits of inter-firm cooperative research. These benefits could be particularly significant in areas of oriented basic research which do not result in immediately commercializable outputs and where, accordingly, competing firms might be expected to find common ground which could serve as the basis for research cooperation. However, the Japanese industrial electronics companies showed no inclination to enter spontaneously into cooperative research agreements without government encouragement. Accordingly, how could the potential benefits of research cooperation be realized in practice?

A further question related to the diffusion of technological knowledge. From MITI's point of view with its objective of improving the longer-term performance of the Japanese economy, it was desirable that new technological knowledge be spread as widely as possible amongst the Japanese companies that could commercialize this knowledge, both at home and abroad. The companies, however, had a vested interest in monopolizing the technological knowledge they had created in order to increase thereby the returns that they were able to appropriate from this knowledge. How would the dilemma that this conflict of interest posed be resolved within the Japanese System? All of these questions are analysed in chapter 2.

The present book is largely concerned with the questions that are posed in the preceding paragraphs. In order to analyse these issues a number of the major government-initiated cooperative research projects in the area of computers and electronic devices are examined in great detail with a chapter being devoted to each. These include the VLSI Research Project, 1976–80; the Optical Measurement and Control System Project, 1979–85; the High Speed Computing System for Scientific and Technological Uses Project (the Supercomputer Project), 1981–89; the Future Electronic Devices Project, 1981–90; and the Fifth Generation Computer Project, 1981–90. These projects are examined in chapters 3 to 7. In chapter 8 a quantitative analysis is provided of many of the issues surrounding research cooperation based on a questionnaire survey answered by four of the major Japanese industrial electronics companies.

In tackling the complex question of oriented basic research MITI policy-makers faced four possible options:

(1) no government intervention, leaving the amount and the areas of oriented basic research to be decided by the private companies;
(2) isolated in-house research, intervening to increase oriented basic research and possibly influencing the priority areas of such research, but without making any attempt to coordinate the research done by the recipients of government resources;
(3) coordinated in-house research, intervening to increase the amount, and influence the areas, of oriented basic research while coordinating the research of government resource recipients, but without insisting that the research be undertaken in joint research facilities;
(4) establishing joint research in joint research facilities.

In the computer and electronic devices industry MITI attached particular importance to a combination of options (3) and (4), although option (2) was also used, for example, by the granting of research-related tax incentives.

Options (3) and (4), however, raised a number of complex problems. For example, how would priority areas for research be selected? Who would make the major selection decisions? How could the effective participation of the private Japanese companies be secured given that these companies competed strongly in the related product markets? This question was particularly important since *oriented* basic research had obvious and intended implications for the longer-run competitiveness of these companies. What precisely should the role of government be in facilitating such cooperative research? Other questions related to the appropriate design of the research project. For example, to what extent should the project concentrate on the development of 'enabling technologies', leaving it to the companies to develop commercializable prototypes. To what extent and in what detail should the end-product of the research be specified and produced as part of the research output? Further issues concerned the choice between options (3) and (4). What were the costs and benefits of these two options? To the extent that option (4) was to be preferred on the grounds of the greater degree of joint production and sharing of knowledge created in joint research facilities, how was this option to be reconciled with the greater degree of inter-firm knowledge leakage that choosing this option implied? These and other related questions are examined in detail in these six chapters.

The four alternatives faced by MITI policy-makers also provide a useful framework for an evaluation of the net social benefits of these projects. In conducting such an evaluation it is necessary to ask not only about the social costs and benefits associated with the project, but also how these costs and benefits compare with those that might have been realized had one of the other options been chosen. While it is not possible to conduct a quantitative evaluation of this kind, the methodology forces a consideration of the *alternative* forms of organization and ways of using the resources that could have been chosen. Each of the projects examined in this book is evaluated in this way.

In the concluding chapter, chapter 9, a synthesis is provided of the major issues raised and analysed in this book. With regard to the determinants of the long-term economic performance of a national system it is shown that an important distinction must be drawn between technical change for 'tomorrow' and for 'the day after tomorrow'. As is increasingly well understood, the Japanese System has excelled in producing the 'downstream' incremental technical changes for 'tomorrow'. These changes, which have included product and process innovations, have in many cases significantly increased the international competitiveness of Japanese products. It is shown that behind these technical changes have been important organizational innovations which have facilitated the mobilizing of flows of information which in turn have been used as an input for technical innovation. However, it is less well understood that the Japanese System has also been efficient in the production of technical change for 'the day after tomorrow'. Such change presents complex problems for national systems largely as a result of the inherent and irreducible uncertainty involved in long-term technical change. For example, for-profit companies tend to avoid investing in innovation in areas where high degrees of uncertainty threaten the chances of earning adequate rates of return. This suggests the concept of 'bounded vision' according to which the 'vision' of for-profit companies is constrained by their profit making objectives. This concept is elaborated in chapter 9 where an analysis is also provided of the ways in which other kinds of organization have compensated for the bounded vision of for-profit companies in creating technical change for 'the day after tomorrow'. In the Japanese System effective ways of facilitating research cooperation have also evolved, whereby strongly competing companies are brought together for research purposes. Similarly, ways have been found of diffusing technological knowledge more widely among competing industrial electronic companies. These strengths of the Japanese System are analysed in depth in this final chapter.

2

A periodization of the development of the computer and electronic devices industry in Japan, 1948–1979

1948–1959: Government research institutions and universities take the lead

The development of the first transistors and computers in the United States in the latter 1940s aroused great research interest in Japan after only a very short time lag. Makoto Kikuchi (1983), for example, recounts the excitement in some of the laboratories of MITI's Electrotechnical Laboratory that greeted the first public announcements in the United States of the invention of the transistor. Around 1950 in the United States 'there was already a mountain of information accumulating about transistors... On countless occasions, the center director [in the Electrotechnical Laboratory], Sakuji Komagata, would get together with my boss, Dr George Michio Hatoyama, with Dr Kubo from the University of Tokyo and researchers from NEC, Toshiba and other companies, to "decode" this material' (p. 27).

The rapidity with which transistor and computer technologies were acquired from the United States and Europe and reproduced in Japan was largely a function of the substantial capabilities that had been built up in the country since the 1920s in government research institutions, universities and private companies. These capabilities were developed as part of the process of constructing key infrastructural industries such as electricity generation and transmission and telecommunications. Significant government assistance was given to these industries from the time of their establishment and even higher priority was accorded to them during the militarization of the 1930s, the war years, and the immediate postwar period of reconstruction. Although the technological capabilities of these industries still lagged behind those of the world's leaders by the 1950s, enough had been learned to facilitate a fast and successful assimilation of the cluster of new technologies that heralded the arrival of the information technology age.

In the case of computers, however, it is important to note that *the earliest research tended to be done, not in the private companies, but rather in government research institutions and universities.* The fruits of this research were then transferred to the companies with a short time lag.

The 'failure' of the companies with an interest in electronics to develop the new information technologies as rapidly as the government research institutions and universities was understandable. In the late 1940s and early 1950s their major markets and corresponding technologies were growing at a fast rate largely as a result of government-initiated reconstruction programmes. The new information technologies at this stage had little impact on these markets and there was a high degree of uncertainty regarding their future commercial importance. This was particularly so in the case of the computer where a profitable mass market only began to develop from the early 1960s.

The private companies that came to dominate the field of industrial electronics in Japan were in the early 1950s divided into two main groups. On the one hand were the companies that had tended to specialize in the production of telecommunications equipment. These firms included Nippon Electric (NEC), Fujitsu, Hitachi and Oki. They had developed a close relationship with the Ministry of Communications and its successor from 1952, the Ministry of Post and Telecommunications. From 1952, with the formation of Nippon Telegraph and Telephone as a distinct organization charged with responsibility for the maintenance and development of the telecommunications network, these four firms became the main members of NTT's group of supplying firms, known as the Den Den family. The second group of companies comprised those which were involved in the production of heavy electrical equipment. The three major firms in this group were Hitachi, Toshiba, and Mitsubishi Electric. Only Hitachi was a significant member of both groups.

From the end of the war and through the 1950s the first group of companies benefited greatly from a number of telephone expansion programmes initiated by the Ministry and NTT. The main ones during this period were the three-year rehabilitation programme from April 1946 to March 1949, and the five-year programmes from October 1953 to March 1958 and from April 1958 to March 1963. In addition, the outbreak of the Korean War in 1950, and the expansion of radio broadcasting and television in the early 1950s, further stimulated the activities of these companies. Similarly, the second group of companies was a major beneficiary of government infrastructural investment in the electrical power area. In the early 1950s four industries were designated as strategic industries by MITI and given substantial government funding through the Japan Development Bank. These were electrical power, shipbuilding, coal and steel with about 23 per cent of all investment in the electrical power industry coming from the Japan Development Bank.[1] In May 1952 Japan was formally admitted to the IMF and World Bank and in the autumn of 1953 the World Bank made its first loan to Japan, a 40.2 million dollar loan for the building of thermal electricity generating plants.[2]

The expansion in the late 1940s and the first few years of the 1950s in the areas of telecommunications and electrical power generation and transmission, largely as a result of government-initiated programmes, meant that the members of both groups of companies were at the time not particularly interested in diversifying their activities into the area of computing.[3] This is clear, for example, in the case of Fujitsu, currently the largest computer manufacturer in Japan and the only one amongst the Japanese computer producers which opted to develop its own computing technologies in the early 1960s rather than enter into a technology agreement with an American partner as the other firms did. In 1935 Fuji Electric, which was part of the Furukawa *zaibatsu* which included firms such as Furukawa Electric and Yokohama Rubber, established Fuji Tsushinki (Fuji Telecommunications) which would specialize in the production of Siemens' telephone switching equipment. (In 1967 Fuji Tsushinki changed its name to Fujitsu.) In December 1949, in the midst of a severe economic recession, the Japanese government established an Industrial Rationalization Review Board and in 1950 a research fund was established to encourage research in mining and manufacturing technology. Taiyu Kobayashi, then Manager of the Technical Development Department of Fuji Tsushinki (henceforth to be called Fujitsu), successfully applied to this fund for a research grant and used part of it to develop the company's first computer, the FACOM 100 (<u>F</u>uji <u>A</u>utomatic <u>Com</u>puter). Completed in 1954 this was a relay-based computer. Kobayashi's personal interest in computers had been aroused by a military communications system he had helped to build for the wartime defence of Tokyo, but his company continued for some time to attach a low priority to computers. Kobayashi, who was later to become Chairman of the Board of Fujitsu, records that in 1954, the year that the FACOM 100 was completed, 'the bulk of the money we had available for this project came from the MITI subsidy program for mining and industrial research. We were still being treated like a stepchild by Fujitsu and consequently received very little in the way of a development budget' (T. Kobayashi, 1986, p. 36). As this statement makes clear, research on computing would have started much later in Fujitsu were it not for the MITI funding.

A more positive company attitude to computers had to wait until 1959 when Kanjiro Okada, who had been President of Furukawa Electric but had been ousted in a realignment, became President of Fujitsu. Until 1960 Fujitsu's computers were manufactured in a wing of a factory which produced communications equipment.[4] It was only in 1960 that a new electronics department and factory were established in Fujitsu to specialize in the production of computers. Okada became President towards the end of 1959. In that year twenty-six computers were produced in Japan but by the following year the number had increased to sixty-six.[5] However, despite the rapid increase in computer production and demand in Japan, the majority of Fujitsu's board were cautious about the future of the computer industry, preferring to accord priority to telecommunications where the long-term and relatively certain relationship with Nippon Telegraph and Telephone (NTT) guaranteed reasonable profits. As Kobayashi was later to recall, in the late 1950s,

Our first order of business was a plan to construct a new factory devoted to computers. I was to devise the plan and present it to the Board of Directors. President Okada aside, most of the directors as yet had no understanding of computers. Regardless of the merits of our plan, because we were still viewed with the bias accorded a stepchild, we could expect a predictably sour response... As might be expected, more than half of the directors preferred a more cautious course of action which dealt with known quantities. Rather than attempting some unknown... *if we stuck to contract work for Nippon Telegraph and Telephone, it had the advantages a long steady relationship offers, as well as the prospect of assured profitability.*[6]

However, around 1959–60, 'Okada disregarded the advice of the directors set in their old ways. He quickly picked a number of young men like our computer group and assigned them to important positions in the company... Fujitsu was now clearly committed to computers' (T. Kobayashi, 1986, pp. 44–5).

The other companies that were later to constitute the main members of Japan's industrial electronics industry were even slower than Fujitsu to diversify into the area of computers. They depended more than Fujitsu on computer technology developed initially in government research institutions and universities and transferred subsequently to the companies. As will be documented in more detail later, it was only in 1958 that NEC and Hitachi introduced their first commercial computers based on models designed in MITI's Electrotechnical Laboratory and NTT's Musashino Laboratory, part of its Electrical Communications Laboratories. Accordingly, it was government research institutions and universities in Japan which pioneered the earliest research in the computer industry rather than the private companies which, confronted with uncertainty regarding the future commercial prospects for this industry, took a longer time to diversify into computers.

If uncertainty constrained the ability of the for-profit Japanese corporations to become the first acquirers and assimilators of computer technology, why were the government research institutions and universities quicker to develop an expertise in this area (and by so doing to speed the entry of the corporations into the computer market)? An answer to this important question requires a closer analysis of the most important of the government research institutions in the field of computers, namely MITI's Electrotechnical Laboratory (ETL) and NTT's Electrical Communications Laboratories (ECL).[7]

Before 1948 ETL and ECL were part of one laboratory. The establishment of this laboratory goes back to 1876 when the Telegraph Insulator Laboratory was set up under the Ministry of Industrial Affairs. In 1891 the laboratory was reorganized under the Ministry of Communications and until 1948 it retained the link with this Ministry. In 1948 the laboratory was again reorganized, part of it keeping the communications link and becoming part of NTT when the latter was established in 1952: at this time the laboratory was renamed the Electrical Communications Laboratories (ECL). This laboratory was concerned primarily with communications-oriented light electronics. The other part became a major laboratory in the Agency for Industrial Science and Technology (AIST) which was established under the Ministry of International Trade and Industry in 1948. AIST was established to fulfil three main purposes: (1) to consolidate institutes from a number of ministries; (2) to administer the Japan Industrial Standard; and (3) to provide assistance in order to strengthen the technological level in Japanese industry. In 1970 this second laboratory was renamed the Electrotechnical Laboratory (ETL). Immediately after its incorporation into AIST it concentrated on research on energy conversion and energy conservation technologies. With the advent of the new information technologies, beginning with the transistor and the computer in the late 1940s, ETL soon came to specialize in these technologies and played an important role in developing technological capabilities in these areas in Japanese firms.

In analysing the role played by ETL and ECL in the early development of the information technology industry in Japan it is necessary to understand their specific structures which conditioned their functioning. The main aim of ETL was to undertake research in areas that were likely to be of longer-run benefit to Japan's industrial development. As part of the powerful Ministry of International Trade and Industry, ETL's budget was allocated independently of the financial performance of the private companies which it served. This meant that ETL could select research areas without taking account of the short to medium-term commercial pay-off. On the other hand, since one of MITI's overall briefs was to ensure Japan's longer-run international competitiveness, ETL's research agenda was to some extent constrained by this pragmatic general objective. ETL's structure, therefore, ensured that its decisions regarding the allocation of resources to technological research were relatively uninfluenced by short to medium-term profitability considerations.[8] The 'vision' of ETL was therefore bounded by fundamentally different determinants from that of the private companies where expectations about profit implications were given a significantly greater weight in their calculations.

Under these structural conditions it was hardly surprising that in the early uncertain stages of computer development it was organizations like ETL rather than the private Japanese companies, preoccupied with expanding activities in profitable areas such as telecommunications and electrical power generation and transmission, which took the first steps in the acquisition and assimilation of the relevant computer technologies.[9]

The case of NTT's ECL bore some similarities to that of ETL, as well as showing some significant differences. The most important similarity was that decisions regarding research specialization in ECL were also relatively independent of considerations of short and medium-term profitability (although this began to change after privatization of NTT in April 1985). This meant that like ETL, ECL was also able to develop technologies at a time when they might not have appeared commercially attractive to private firms.[10] For this structural reason ECL was another government research institution which made an early entry into the new field of computers, as will shortly be seen. However, unlike ETL, the research agenda of ECL was shaped by the anticipated needs of the telecommunications network. As a result there was some divergence between the research done in the two institutions. Nevertheless, since the field of telecommunications converged increasingly with those of electronics and computing, there was a significant degree of overlap in the research of ETL and ECL.

Like ETL and ECL the Japanese universities shared a relative insensitivity to commercial considerations in their choice of research agenda. Furthermore, their research brief was not restricted by a concern with longer-term international competitiveness which meant that their research could range more widely in areas of basic research. Under these different structural constraints Japanese universities made a number of important contributions to early computer research in the country.[11] For example, in the 1930s Tohoku University established an Electrical Communication Research Laboratory which specialized in more basic telecommunications research. After the war, researchers at Tohoku University worked with their colleagues at NEC to develop this firm's first commercial computer based on the parametron. This model, the NEAC-1101, was introduced in 1958.[12] Similarly, Tokyo and Kyoto universities engaged in computer research, the former collaborating with the Toshiba Corporation in a not very successful attempt to jointly develop a computer. However, a potentially important contribution was made at Tokyo University with the invention of the parametron in 1954 by Eiichi Goto, then a postgraduate student at the university. The parametron, a logic circuit, consisted of a small magnetic core, coils and capacitors, and applied a parametric excitation principle. In the mid 1950s the parametron was thought to have important and widespread application. As will be seen later, ECL developed at this time a parametron-based computer, the Musashino-1, which was subsequently transferred to a number of Japanese corporations, while ETL was pursuing research on transistor-based computers. At the same time research was undertaken in the firm that was to become Fanuc (a subsidiary of Fujitsu), currently the largest supplier of numerical control systems for machine tools and robots, on parametron-based numerical control. The first electronic switching system introduced by ECL in the mid 1950s used parametrons. However, as the reliability of transistors increased it soon became apparent that parametrons could not compete with them in operation speed and reliability and accordingly parametrons were eventually dropped in favour of transistors in applications areas.

The first computer built in Japan was the ETL Mark I, a relay computer completed in 1953. In building this computer ETL researchers were able to draw on a long and fruitful tradition of research in Japan in the area of circuit design theory. Whether or not this research was as internationally advanced as has been claimed,[13] it is clear that the design of the first Japanese computer did not involve a complete reproduction of ideas originating in the United States and Europe.

A year later, in 1954, ETL introduced its second computer, the ETL Mark II, an improved relay computer. This was in the same year that Fujitsu brought out its first computer, the FACOM 100. Although there is some dispute about the existence and extent of cooperation between researchers in Fujitsu and ETL, it appears that Fujitsu did receive some assistance from the ETL research on the Mark I and II.[14]

Towards the end of 1954 Dr Wada and others in ETL made the decision to develop a transistorized computer, the ETL Mark III. This also required further development of transistors since at that time the performance of transistors was not satisfactory and relays remained the most reliable device. At the end of 1954 an electronic computer research group was established in the circuit section of the electronics division of ETL under the direction of Shigeru Takahashi. However, the development of the Mark III, Japan's first transistorized computer, was temporarily held back by the appearance of the parametron which some researchers thought might be superior to transistors for use in computers. Tests undertaken in ETL, however, suggested that the prospects for the transistor were better and accordingly ETL's computer research continued in this direction. Nevertheless, an agreement was reached between officials of MITI and NTT whereby the former would concentrate its research on the development of transistors and transistor-based computers while the latter would emphasize parametrons and parametron-based computers. *In this way the Japanese Technology-Creating System was able to cover both options, acquiring and assimilating foreign technology while at the same time developing indigenous alternative technology.*[15]

In December 1954 Sony, at the time a small postwar electronics factory, made its entry into the world electronics market with its transistorized radio. At this stage there were three main commercial producers of transistors: Sony, Kobe Industry and Hitachi.[16] ETL tested the transistors of all three companies and found the Hitachi products to be most suitable for the Mark III. In July 1956 the ETL Mark III was completed. At the same time further research continued in ETL under Makoto Kikuchi to improve the performance of Japanese transistors.

The Mark III, Japan's first transistorized computer, was in fact its second electronic computer. The first, the FUJIC, was produced a few months earlier in March 1956 by Fumio Okazaki from the Fuji Film company. This small computer, the first in Japan to use vacuum tubes (the earlier models being based on relays), was built in order to assist with the task of lens design. The FUJIC was the only computer built in Japan in the 1950s which did not benefit from government research and financial assistance. However, it was not technically advanced and was never produced for the commercial market.

While the first parametron computer was developed at Tokyo University in 1956, the important Musashino-1, NTT's first parametron computer, was introduced by ECL in March 1957, shortly before the completion of the ETL Mark IV. The architecture of the Musashino-1 was based on that of Illiac-1 of the University of Illinois. The link between Japanese research and the University of Illinois was cemented by the research done at the university by a number of Japanese researchers, including Hideo Aiso and Masao Kato, who went on to play important roles in the development of the ETL Mark IV and the Musashino-1 respectively.[17] NEC's NEAC 1101, its first trial computer, drew on the technology developed for the Musashino-1 and formed the basis for the NEAC 1102 which NEC produced jointly with Tohoku University.[18]

The Musashino-1 technology was similarly transferred to Fujitsu and Hitachi who, together with NEC, were part of NTT's Den Den family of supplying firms. Fujitsu's FACOM 201 was based on the Musashino-1 which also provided the basis for the FACOM 202, another parametron computer. Fujitsu had taken orders for the FACOM 202 from the School of Physical Sciences and the Industrial Science Institute at Tokyo University and from Toyota Motor Corporation. At the same time as producing parametron-based computers Fujitsu was also manufacturing computers using relays and transistors. At this stage it was still unclear which of these alternative technologies was preferable. However, while the FACOM 201 and 202 were Fujitsu's first commercial computers and about thirty of them were ultimately produced, there were significant technical problems with these parametron-based models. Accordingly, the decision was made in Fujitsu to switch to transistors.[19]

In November 1957 the ETL Mark IV was completed, a more sophisticated transistorized computer than the Mark III which used junction transistors. Although somewhat less sophisticated than the computers that were being produced in the United States at the time, the Mark IV technology was actively transferred to most of the main Japanese computer-producing firms and became their first commercial transistorized computer. NEC, for example, obtained Mark IV technology and used it as the basis of the NEAC 2201 which was introduced in 1958. The good relationship between NEC and Dr Wada, head of the electronics division of ETL, smoothed the informal agreement to transfer the technology. NEC sent one engineer to ETL where the circuit designs for the Mark IV were scaled up for the larger commercial computer produced by NEC. ETL staff also went to NEC to assist in the technology transfer process. No payment was made by NEC to ETL for the technology supplied, since one of the main objectives of ETL was to aid the strengthening of technological capabilities in Japanese firms. In similar fashion, Mark IV technology was also transferred to Hitachi, where it became the basis for the HITAC 301, and to Matsushita. In 1959 NEC developed its NEAC 2203 which was based on a refinement of the Mark IV technology. The following year this computer was used in an on-line, real-time seat reservation system sold by the company to an Osaka-based private railway company.

However, not all the technology used in the Mark IV was indigenously developed. For example, the Japanese firm Hokushin which produced the magnetic drum for the Mark IV had a technology agreement with the British firm Ferranti. Furthermore, the Mark IV was not transferred to any Japanese company that requested it. For instance, Mitsubishi Electric, despite its strong ties with the Mitsubishi group of companies and the political influence of this group, was apparently refused access to the Mark IV technology.[20]

From the present account it is clear that research done in government institutions such as ETL and ECL speeded the entry of Japanese corporations into the computer market. These corporations, as mentioned, were initially involved in areas such as telecommunications and electrical power equipment and until around 1957–8 were not particularly interested in diversifying their activities into the computing area. As the computer market began to expand from the late 1950s, however, and the interest of the corporations grew, so their entry into this new field of activity was greatly facilitated by the research that had already been done in ETL, ECL and the universities. The latter institutions, therefore, played their role in the Japanese Technology-Creating System by ensuring that steps were taken to develop technological capabilities in Japan in the area of computing despite the initial luke-warm response of the corporations that only later would become interested in diversifying into this new field. The situation around

1957 is summarized in the following extract from an interview held by the present author with a senior member of the Japanese computing establishment:

> Informant: The Japanese companies had more research money [than ETL]. But even NEC did not provide good measuring equipment... ETL had much better equipment than NEC. The gap between ETL and the private sector was very large.
> Fransman: So at that time ETL was much more sophisticated, both in terms of staff and equipment?
> Informant: That is right.
> Fransman: Was that because the companies were not giving much priority at the time to the computing area?
> Informant: Yes.
> Fransman: NEC was doing quite well then financially, were they not?
> Informant: Yes, but even NEC always came to ETL to check their equipment and then asked their manager to make the necessary purchase.
> Fransman: Was that because they did not have much experience in this field, rather than because of budgetry constraints?
> Informant: I think so.

However, if the Japanese corporations were slower than government research institutions to begin research in the computing area, by what year might it be concluded that these institutions had established computing as a priority area for research? In the case of ETL there is some evidence to suggest that from 1953 or 1954 computing had become a priority area beginning to rival energy research. As noted earlier, in 1953 the ETL Mark I was completed and in 1954 the ETL Mark II, an improved relay computer, was introduced. 1954 was also the year that ETL first established its electronics division consisting of three sections specializing in circuits, components and electronic measurement devices. Dr Kikuchi, who at the time was engaged in research on transistors, and Dr Komamiya, who had developed the ETL Mark I, were moved from the physics division to the new electronics division and they were joined by some researchers from ECL. Some idea of the priority that was given to computers and the related area of transistors at this time can be gained from an examination of the relative importance of the electronics division in terms of number of researchers and budget. In 1954 the division had 50 researchers, or about 11 per cent of ETL's total of 452 researchers. However, in the financial year 1954, 15 million yen, or about 7 per cent of ETL's total budget, was allocated to the ETL Mark II. Added to the 20 million yen that went to the transistor laboratory, this meant that around 17 per cent of the total ETL budget in 1954 went to research on the Mark II and transistors. The progress made by the new information technologies in ETL was partly the result of the important support given by Dr Goto, Director General of ETL and Dr Wada who became head of the electronics division in 1954 and who was a vociferous proponent of the electronics industry in Japan.[21]

ETL officials were also apparently behind the Electronics Industry Promotion Special Measures Law (number 171 of 11 June 1957) proposed by MITI.[22] During the first half of the 1950s MITI had taken the decision to nurture (*ikusei*) a number of designated industries which included steel, electric power, shipbuilding and chemical fertilizers. In the latter half of the 1950s a number of additional industries were added which included synthetic textiles, plastics, petrochemicals, automobiles, machinery[23] and electronics.[24] According to the 1957 law on electronics, provision was made for subsidized loans to be given by semi-governmental financial institutions such as the Japan Development Bank to assist with the costs of R & D and capital investment. However, the absolute funding made available by government in this way, excluding the financing of government research institutions such as ETL, was not particularly large. By 1961 the total subsidy for R & D on computers amounted to under one million US dollars.[25] However, MITI's assistance to the Japanese computer industry did not only take the form of funding and direct assistance through technology transfer. MITI also took the initiative in encouraging the major firms in the computer industry to set up an association which would help to formulate and articulate the common needs and interests of the industry and in this way the Japan Electronic Industry Development Association (JEIDA) was established in 1958. As a bridge between the industry and MITI and NTT, JEIDA came to play an important role in the policy-making process in the computer and electronics industries.

1960–1969: Developing national capabilities on the basis of imported technology and domestic cooperative research programmes

From 1957 when the first commercial computers were produced in Japan, there was a rapid increase in the number of computers manufactured in the country. While in 1957 there were 3 computers of all sizes made in Japan, by 1962 this number had increased to 308. Over this six-year period the annual growth rate of computers produced did not fall below 117 per cent.[26] The message was clear: Japan was rapidly developing a substantial domestic market for computers.

By 1961 the development philosophy was firmly in place on the basis of which the computer and related electronic devices industry would be carefully nurtured so that with the passage of time it might come to play an important role in both the Japanese and international economies. The policy regime derived from this philosophy had already been elaborated and applied to a number of other industries. The outlines of this regime were therefore clear. The computer and electronic devices industry merited inclusion as a strategically selected industry because it fulfilled the twin criteria laid down by MITI: the income elasticity criterion and the productivity increase rate criterion. According to the first criterion the demand for the output of the industry must increase more than the average for the economy as a whole as income rises, while the second criterion stipulated that productivity in the industry must increase more rapidly than the average. The first criterion had been in use in MITI from at least about 1953 when it formed part of the discussions surrounding the so-called Okano Plan which amongst other things suggested the building-up of the heavy and chemical industries.[27] By 1963 both criteria had been firmly established in MITI as tools for selecting industries for special promotion.[28]

In passing, it is worth noting that these criteria were by no means uncontroversial. Built up pragmatically over the years,[29] the two criteria used by MITI contradicted the conventional concept of comparative advantage. This concept, in both its Ricardian and Heckscher-Ohlin versions, which hypothesize respectively different technologies and factor endowments for the trading partners, assumes that productivity remains constant. It suggests that under an optimal trade and industry policy regime only those industries should be developed which enjoy a (*static*) comparative advantage. This would have ruled out many of the heavy, chemical, machinery and electronics industries which were promoted in Japan in the 1950s and 1960s since most of them were far from being internationally competitive. The second criterion used by MITI in the selection of industries for promotion, the 'productivity increase rate criterion', is particularly interesting because, in sharp contrast to the concept of comparative advantage, it requires an *ex ante* judgement regarding the productivity rate increases that will in the future be realized in the industry in question. Since such increases cannot be rigorously predicted, the door is open for 'rational inconsistencies of opinion' regarding whether particular industries should be promoted in defiance of static comparative advantage. Such inconsistencies of opinion were at the heart of differences between MITI and the Bank of Japan in the 1950s over whether the automobile industry merited protection and promotion.[30]

Be this as it may, it is clear that MITI officials, whether implicitly or explicitly at the time, or in retrospect, rejected the concept of comparative advantage as a principle for shaping trade and industrial policy. As Yoshihisa Ojimi, himself the author of the 1960 trade liberalization plan and a subsequent vice-minister at MITI, put it:

There was a great outgrowth of industries that depended on low wage labor during the pre-war period and the post-war period of transition when Japan was plagued by shortages in capital. At the same time, these industries enjoyed an advantage from the viewpoint of the theory of comparative advantage... Should Japan have entrusted its future to the development of those industries characterized by the intensive use of labor?... If Japan had adopted the simple doctrine of free trade and chosen to specialize in this kind of industry, it would have sentenced its population to the Asian pattern of stagnation and poverty. The Ministry of International Trade and Industry decided instead to promote heavy industries that require intensive employment of capital and technology, industries such as steel, oil refining, petrochemicals, automobiles, aircraft, all sorts of industrial machinery, *and electronics, including electronic computers.* In terms of the comparative cost of production, these industries should be the most inappropriate for Japan. From a short-run, static viewpoint, promoting their development would seem to conflict with economic rationalism, but from a long-range viewpoint, these are precisely the industries where the income elasticity of demand is high, technological progress is rapid, and labor productivity rises fast.[31]

However, while the rejection of the concept of comparative advantage was later to be criticized by some economists,[32] MITI took steps in 1961 to increase the protection extended to the computer industry. In an extensive revision of its tariff schedule in 1961, 'Japan raised, through the tariff negotiations under GATT, tariff rates on quite a few manufactures such as machinery, heavy electric machinery, *computers,* and some agricultural products... in exchange for the reduction of tariff rates on certain other commodities.'[33] This was done in the same year that important concessions were made under American pressure and the import of textiles was liberalized.[34] Two of the seven principles which informed the 1961 tariff revision had particular relevance for the computer industry. The first principle was: 'To set the tariff rates low on those goods which cannot be produced domestically, or on those goods [for] which the potential domestic supply is limited and has no possibility of... expansion in the future, and to set the tariff rates high on those goods [for] which the potential domestic supply is elastic, and [which] are or will be competing with imports from foreign countries.' The second principle was: 'To set the tariff rates high on the products of those industries which have a good prospect of development in the future, and especially on the products of newly establishing industries.'[35]

According to the regulations computers were classified as an import quota item. This meant that MITI approval was required on a case-by-case basis if a user wished to purchase an imported computer. In practice, however, it was relatively easy to get MITI's approval for imports if 'similar' domestically produced computing goods and services were unavailable.[36] Nevertheless, in the government sector, which formed a significant proportion of the market in the early years of the computer industry, rules and regulations made it more difficult to buy foreign computers.[37] Although calculations have not been made of effective rates of protection and effective rates of subsidy for the Japanese computer and electronic devices industry in the 1960s as they have for some other countries,[38] it seems clear that the Japanese government's protection and promotion measures in this industry contributed significantly to insulating Japanese producers from more efficient international competition. In this way conditions of greater market certainty were created for Japanese computer producers compared to what would have existed in the absence of these measures. In turn this facilitated the investment in skills, equipment, and innovation that was necessary for the Japanese corporation to diversify their activities and enter the computer market.

In addition to protecting the domestic market for Japanese producers of computers, MITI also took steps to subsidize the financial costs involved in selling computers. As a result of the high unit cost of computers (and perhaps also users' lack of familiarity with computers) it was common practice for users to rent rather than buy their computer. In the absence of government intervention this would have placed a burden on the computer producer as a result of the adverse cash flow implications and the possibility that the user would return the computer before paying its full price. In order to cope with this problem the Japan Electronic Computer Company was established in 1961 under MITI guidance.

The role of the Japan Electronic Computer Company (JECC) is to buy computers from the manufacturers and rent them to users. If a user returns the computer to JECC it must be repurchased by the manufacturing company at its depreciated value. In order to cover such expenses the companies are allowed to set a fixed percentage of their income aside in the form of a tax-free reserve fund. While JECC is owned jointly by the computer manufacturing companies, it has also received significant loans at subsidized rates from the Japan Development Bank. JECC's activities have also had wider implications for the development of the Japanese computer industry. For example, sales through JECC were contingent on a minimum proportion of the value of the computer being produced domestically and this proportion was increased over time. Furthermore, JECC's sales might also have had the effect of limiting price competition between Japanese computer producers.

The Japanese computer market was also controlled in a number of other ways. The Foreign Exchange and Foreign Trade Control Law of 1949 gave government complete control over the allocation of foreign exchange and this was used in order to regulate imports of goods and technology. In this way selected industries could be given priority treatment. The Foreign Capital Law of 1950 controlled the acquisition by foreign companies of assets in Japan, including the sale of their technology to Japanese companies. Foreign companies wishing to acquire assets in Japan had to be granted a licence by a committee set up under the Law. The control over foreign exchange remained an important policy instrument for MITI until 1 April 1964 when Japan joined the IMF as a full member and foreign exchange rationing through MITI-controlled budgets ceased.[39]

Control over the activities of foreign companies in Japan was also used by MITI in an attempt to strengthen the domestic computer manufacturing companies. A notable example is the case of IBM, which first opened a subsidiary, Nihon Watson Tokei Kaikei Kikai, in Japan in 1937, and which established IBM Japan as a 100 per cent-owned subsidiary in 1950. As a yen-based company IBM Japan was formally outside the control of the legislation aimed at foreign companies. However, MITI officials were determined not to allow this to interfere with their attempts to strengthen the domestic computer manufacturers. As Shigeru Sahashi, who became Deputy Director of the Heavy Industries Bureau of MITI (which controlled the electronics industry) in June 1957, and Director of the powerful Enterprises Bureau in July 1961, bluntly told IBM Japan: 'We will take every measure possible to obstruct the success of your business unless you license IBM patents to Japanese firms and charge them no more than a 5 per cent royalty.'[40] MITI got its way and in 1960 IBM agreed to give access to its patents to Japanese computer-producing firms. However, the right of access negotiated by MITI was of no particular significance for Japanese companies since no mechanism was included in the agreement for the active transfer of technology from IBM. In effect the Japanese companies only obtained the right to scrutinize IBM's patent applications with legal impunity but since such applications typically contain only a small subset of the total amount of knowledge that is needed to make full use of the technology, this right was of limited use.[41] Further support for this conclusion comes from the technology agreements entered into from 1961 between Japanese companies and American computer producers (with the exception of IBM) as will shortly be documented.

Partly as a result of the measures taken by the Japanese government to protect and promote the Japanese computer industry, but partly also as a result of the improvement in Japanese-made computers following on the technology agreements concluded with a number of American computer producers and the computer research programmes established by MITI, the share of the Japanese market held by Japanese companies increased dramatically. From about 18 per cent of the market in 1961, the Japanese share increased to 54 per cent in 1966 and remained at around that level to 1982. In 1966 Hitachi held the largest part of the Japanese market amongst Japanese producers with a share of 16 per cent, while NEC and Fujitsu came second and third with 15 and 10 per cent respectively.[42]

By 1961 it was clear that despite the productive steps that had been taken to develop the Japanese computer industry, a substantial technology gap remained, particularly in relation to American computer producers. The decision was therefore taken by MITI and the Japanese firms to enter into technology agreements with American producers. Accordingly, Hitachi, with the largest share of the Japanese computer market amongst the Japanese firms, was the first to enter into an agreement with an American firm, signing with RCA in May 1961. This was followed by Mitsubishi Electric which entered into an agreement with TRW in February 1962, NEC which concluded its agreement with Honeywell in July 1962, Oki which set up a joint venture with Sperry Rand in September 1963, and Toshiba which signed with General Electric in October 1964.

Alone amongst the Japanese computer producers, Fujitsu did not at this stage enter into a technology agreement with a foreign firm. Taiyu Kobayashi, who played an important role in the establishment of computer production in Fujitsu from the 1950s, suggests that it was only from 1960 or 1961 that Fujitsu became committed to computers. By this time the other Japanese computer producers had already entered into negotiations with prospective American technology partners. Fujitsu also actively pursued the possibility of a technology link with an American firm. As Kobayashi, who became Chairman of the Fujitsu Board in 1981, later recalled: 'Like many other Japanese businesses at the time, we gave serious consideration to introducing advanced European and American technology. It was, of course, the easiest method of obtaining such technology.' In view of the negotiations that had already been started by the other Japanese companies, Fujitsu made overtures to IBM.

It turned out, however, that when negotiations to introduce IBM technology were conducted, IBM flatly refused to consider technology transfers unless they were given 100 per cent capital participation. This was 'IBM's world policy'. Of course, there was no way that Fujitsu was going to become a wholly-owned subsidiary of IBM. This meant that independent development was now the only route open ... although that path was not an easy one.[43]

In 1962 Fujitsu Laboratories was established through a merger of a number of research and development sections which were under the control of separate technical divisions. This was the first Japanese laboratory specializing in computer research and development.

It is necessary to point out, however, that the concluding of technology agreements with American companies was not an indication of the failure of Japanese attempts to develop domestic technological capabilities in the area of computing. The import of foreign technology and the building of local technological capabilities should not be seen as alternatives but should rather be viewed as complementary policies. Indeed the ability of Japanese computer-producing companies to enter into technology agreements with their American partners and to successfully assimilate this technology was a function of the capabilities they had already developed in the computing field. While it is true that by 1961 there was a substantial (and perhaps even growing) gap between Japanese and American computer capabilities and that the import of American computer technology was an effective and rapid means of narrowing this gap, the import strategy itself was possible only as a result of the substantial domestic computer capabilities that had already been accumulated. In this sense the earlier steps taken by both the Japanese computer-manufacturing companies and by MITI to develop domestic capabilities in this area laid the foundation for the later measures which jointly resulted in the closing of most, if not all, of the technology gap by the late 1970s.

In addition to facilitating the import of foreign technology under its guidance, MITI also helped to establish a number of important cooperative research programmes which further strengthened Japanese computer capabilities. In 1960 MITI established the Five Year Programme for the National Production of Electronic Computers which amongst other things made provision for the setting up of a research association of firms that would receive government assistance. In 1962 the so-called FONTAC project was launched under MITI guidance with the Electronic Computer Technology Research Association charged with the coordination of the project.[44] The aim of the project was to reduce the technology gap by increasing speed and memory capacity in Japanese computers. The project was under the overall leadership of Fujitsu with NEC and Oki as the other participants. Under the agreed division of labour Fujitsu was to develop a large computer while NEC and Oki were to produce smaller satellite computers. MITI provided 1.16 million US dollars to the project from 1962 until 1966 when the project ended. Hitachi, which was developing its own computer system and which by a small margin held the largest share of the domestic market amongst the Japanese firms, decided not to participate in this project.[45]

The FONTAC project was the first of a number of MITI-initiated cooperative research projects of which at least one has been in existence from 1962 to the present day. In general terms the FONTAC project set the pattern for many of the projects that were to follow. For the purposes of the cooperative research project the member companies agree to specialize in selected, non-overlapping areas. Although MITI makes a financial contribution, an important proportion of the total research costs are borne by the participating companies. While in the earlier years MITI funding tended to be given in the form of a conditional loan (*hojokin*), in later years the ministry moved to a system of contract research (*itakuhi*) where it, rather than the companies as in the former case, retained all resulting intellectual property rights. Accordingly, the FONTAC project was based on a conditional loan from MITI. It is important to note, however, that there was until 1976 no significant case of research being done jointly by the companies which participated in these MITI-initiated projects. Rather the research was done in-house with minimal communication with the other companies involved. As will be analysed in detail later, the VLSI Project 1976–9 was the first one in which joint research was undertaken in joint research facilities. *It would be wrong, therefore, to suggest that before 1976 there was a significant degree of sharing of knowledge between the competing firms which participated in these MITI-initiated projects.* Rather the boundaries between the firms were distinct and tightly defined in terms of flows of research information.

The FONTAC project was particularly important for Fujitsu which as we have seen relied on its own technological capabilities. Fujitsu was one of the last of the Japanese computer producers to introduce a transistorized computer, although it produced the first Japanese relay-based commercial computer. In 1961 Fujitsu held 10 per cent of the Japanese computer market compared to 16 per cent for Hitachi and 15 per cent for NEC. In view of the technology gap that existed *vis-à-vis* the United States and Europe, exports did not provide a viable option for increasing output. This left the local market. However, Fujitsu's relatively late entry into the transistorized computer market proved to be an obstacle in those instances where competitors had already established long-term 'obligational' relationships with important computer users. A case in point was Nippon Telegraph and Telephone (NTT). As Fujitsu's Taiyu Kobayashi later recalled:

Nippon Telegraph and Telephone is one of Fujitsu's main customers – primarily for telephone switching equipment. We also ... tried to sell them computers ... however, they had an unwritten policy that worked against us: regardless of how hard we strove, as a manufacturer late to the market we were not able to displace NEC which was there first. A friend of mine at Nippon Telegraph and Telephone told me: 'If you want to obtain a lion's share of the orders from us, you have to become the undisputed leader, so well known in markets outside NTT's sphere of influence, that everyone will be asking why we are not buying Fujitsu equipment.'[46]

It was therefore important for Fujitsu that the company should rapidly upgrade its computers on the basis of its own research. The research done under the FONTAC project proved to be important for Fujitsu for it led to the development of the computer architecture on which the company based its 230 series which remained in use until the 1970s.

In 1964, half-way through the FONTAC project, the computing world was shaken by IBM's introduction of its System 360 which used hybrid integrated circuits. This system (in the design of which Gene Amdahl played a significant role) constituted a significant breakthrough in computer architecture, facilitating an important reduction in both the size and the cost of mainframe computers. The Japanese computer companies, like their American counterparts who also competed with IBM, took immediate steps to upgrade their computers in line with System 360. Hitachi, NEC and Toshiba, which had technology agreements with RCA, Honeywell and General Electric, introduced new products that were compatible with IBM's System 360. In autumn 1965 Fujitsu began to modify its 230 series with research that was to lead in 1968 to the FACOM 230–60, an integrated circuit-based computer influenced by System 360. The FACOM 230–60 was later regarded in Fujitsu as a 'strategic turning point'[47] for the company. While in 1965 Fujitsu was third to NEC and Hitachi (which held the first and second largest shares respectively of the Japanese market amongst Japanese companies), by 1968 Fujitsu had moved to first place largely as a result of the success of the FACOM 230–60. In 1968 computer revenues for the first time exceeded revenues from the company's communications division.[48] The first sale of the FACOM 230–60 was to Kyoto University and Taiyu Kobayashi later recalled both the significant teething troubles that existed with this first computer (for which the university was compensated by a low price which did not leave Fujitsu with much profit) and the strong competition that occurred for the important university market for computers.[49] Subsequently NTT and the Dai-Ichi Kangyo Bank, which had and still has close financial ties with Fujitsu and the Furukawa group of companies, bought the FACOM 230–60.

MITI also played a role in developing integrated circuit capabilities in Japanese companies. In 1962 NEC built the first experimental Japanese integrated circuit based on planar technology that it had acquired from Fairchild. MITI made a significant contribution to the diffusion of integrated circuit technology in Japan when in the middle 1960s it forced NEC to sublicense the planar technology to other Japanese companies.[50] Without this external pressure, the tendency would have been for NEC to try and monopolize this new technology. Furthermore, in 1964 MITI gave a relatively small grant to six companies (Fujitsu, Hitachi, NEC, Toshiba, Mitsubishi Electric and Oki) for the development of specialized integrated circuits for computers. By the end of 1965 (a year of major economic recession in Japan) Fujitsu, Hitachi and NEC had announced the development of computers containing several integrated circuits.

By 1965 it had become apparent that the main focus of computer research had shifted sharply from government research institutions and universities (where, as was seen above, the emphasis lay from the early to the late 1950s) to the Japanese companies. In 1963, having failed with the parametron computer, ECL developed the CM-100 transistorized computer. However, this lagged somewhat behind the work being done in the companies. In 1965 ETL completed the Mark VI, its last computer architecture developed entirely in-house. Henceforth ETL concentrated on cooperation with the Japanese companies in the national research and development projects that were established under MITI auspices.

By the end of 1964 it had become clear that a major effort was required if Japanese companies were to remain in the computer market and strengthen their position. In 1964, as noted, IBM introduced its System

360 and in the same year this system was used for the Tokyo Olympic Games and was also purchased by a number of major banks. Also in 1964 General Electric of the United States acquired Machines Bull, the largest French computer manufacturer, thus indicating the difficulties that Europe was having in maintaining an independent presence in the computing area.[51] Events such as these, in particular the introduction of System 360, made it obvious that steps needed to be taken to strengthen the Japanese computer industry. This led to a series of important discussions amongst interested parties in both the government and private sectors in Japan, the outcome of which was reflected in MITI's important 1966 Electronics Industry Deliberation Council report. This report for the first time identified computers as the most important factor in Japan's long-term economic growth. The report established three objectives for government policy. The first was to strengthen domestic computer capabilities, the second was to increase the Japanese share of the domestic computer market, while the third was to increase the profitability of Japanese computer manufacturers.[52]

In response to the first objective MITI established the Very High Speed Computer System Project which lasted from 1966 to 1972 (VHSCS). This project was under the overall technical leadership of ETL which also provided some of the more basic research input. Amongst the companies it was Hitachi that took the lead. The other companies involved in the project were Fujitsu, NEC, Toshiba and Oki. Under the VHSCS project Hitachi, Fujitsu and NEC developed the hardware for a time-sharing computer system similar to the IBM 360/67 introduced in 1965, while Toshiba and Oki built peripheral equipment. The general aim of the project was to improve the technology for high-speed computing. As a result of their work ETL researchers had concluded that memory capability was a major constraint on high-speed performance. They therefore proposed that one important objective of the VHSCS project should be to improve memory technology. In addition, improved high-speed semiconductor logic circuits were required.[53] Through a process of negotiation between ETL and the member companies it was agreed that NEC would specialize in the development of memory devices and that Hitachi, in addition to playing a major role in the design of the mainframe computer, would concentrate on the logic circuits.[54] The VHSCS project made an important contribution to the development of computer capabilities in the member firms. For example, it is likely that NEC's superiority in the area of memory devices (NEC is now the world's largest producer of semiconductor in general and memory devices in particular) can be traced to the company's specialization in memories from the time of the VHSCS project. The Japanese companies that had technology agreements with American partners introduced some of the VHSCS-derived technology into their computers. For instance, Hitachi's

8700/8800 computer system which was introduced in 1973 drew both on RCA as well as VHSCS technology. Similarly, Fujitsu used VHSCS technology to further upgrade its 230 series.[55]

It is clear, however, that the VHSCS project was primarily involved in 'catching up' research rather than in producing new 'frontier' technology. This much is implied by an analysis of patent data. MITI contributed a total of about 10 billion yen to the VHSCS project to which must be added the additional expenditure made by the companies in connection with their research on the project.[56] This compares with a MITI contribution of about 22 billion yen on the Pattern Information Processing System (PIPS) project, 1971–1980, which is considered in more detail below.[57] While the VHSCS project resulted in a total of only 39 patents, the figure was 365 for the PIPS project.[58] This strongly suggests that while the VHSCS project was more concerned to increase the technological capability in the Japanese computer-producing companies by drawing on the international stock of technological knowledge, the PIPS project was aimed at more basic research issues. Indeed, in discussing the PIPS project we shall see that there is further evidence for this conclusion.

The VHSCS project was the second major MITI-initiated cooperative research project. Since the VHSCS project is commonly credited with making an important contribution in developing computer capabilities in Japanese firms it is worth posing a number of fundamental questions about this project (even if definitive answers to these questions might prove difficult to provide).

To begin with, further questions might be asked about the benefits supposedly provided by the VHSCS project. To ask an extreme question: what difference would the absence of the VHSCS project have made to the Japanese computer industry? Although this is a counter-factual question and therefore inherently difficult to answer, it is perhaps possible to give a general answer to this question. It is likely that the Japanese computer producers would have continued to strengthen their capabilities without this project. Two factors lend support to this conclusion. In 1966, as will be recalled, Japanese producers accounted for about 54 per cent of the Japanese computer market largely as a result of the efforts of MITI to protect and promote the Japanese computer sector. This meant that Japanese computer producers enjoyed relatively attractive and certain prospects in the domestic computer market, although the fact that there were a relatively large number of producers and that there was strong competition between them did add difficulties. Furthermore, all the computer producers, with the exception of Fujitsu, had, as noted, entered into technology agreements with American firms while Fujitsu was able to develop and depend on its own capabilities. In the absence of the VHSCS project it is therefore likely that these producers would have continued to deepen their capabilities. Nevertheless, it is likely that computer capabilities would have been strengthened at a slower rate without the project. Some uncertainty would have attached to the outcome of the research (although the fact that Japanese computer producers at this stage were still catching up in technologies they had already been developed would have reduced the degree of uncertainty involved), with the implication that the producers are unlikely to have invested as much in the research as in the event they did through the VHSCS project. In other words, the uncertainty would have reduced the expected returns to investment in this research thus tending to reduce the amount actually invested. In this way the VHSCS project is likely to have speeded up the acquisition of technological capabilities in the Japanese computing industry.

Further important questions are raised by the form of research cooperation inherent in the design of the VHSCS project. For example, under an alternative design MITI could have announced that it was making the same sum of 10 billion yen available in the form of subsidies to Japanese firms undertaking research and development aimed at increasing the speed of mainframe computers (and perhaps even specifying the inclusion of research on memory and logic circuits) but without attempting to coordinate the research.[59] In the event, however, and as in the case of the FONTAC project as well as other computer-related projects undertaken after VHSCS, MITI chose a project design that gave it a direct role in the selection of specified and non-overlapping research areas for the participating companies and in the coordination of the companies' research.[60] What difference did this particular design for the VHSCS project make?

In answering this question the first point that must be made is that there was in effect very little sharing of technological information among the private companies that participated in the VHSCS project[61] although there was a greater flow of information between ETL on the one hand and the companies on the other. As competing entities the Japanese companies were highly reluctant to share their technological knowledge and it was only from 1976 with the establishment of the VLSI project under a special set of circumstances (which will be analysed in detail below) that the companies were prepared to share knowledge through joint research undertaken in joint research facilities. Evidence to support this important conclusion comes from the analysis of patent data. Of the thirty-nine patents that were produced by the VHSCS project none are joint patents involving inventors from two or more different companies. Therefore, to the extent that patents provide a reliable indication of the degree of joint research of the kind that leads to the creation of patentable knowledge, it may be concluded on the basis of the patent analysis that there was little or no such joint research. Of course, this patent analysis does not take account of the existence of other forms of knowledge sharing (such as those which do not lead to the creation of patentable knowledge). However, the interviews referred to in note 61 confirm that in practice there was little or none of the latter kind of knowledge sharing. It may accordingly be concluded that the VHSCS project did not yield benefits resulting from the sharing of technological knowledge.[62]

If the design of the VHSCS project was such that it did not yield substantial benefits from the sharing of knowledge among the participating companies, it is likely that it did produce benefits arising from economies of specialization. As a result of the VHSCS project and the others like it, it is probable that a greater degree of specialization among Japanese computer-producing companies took place than would have occurred in the absence of these projects (although it must be admitted that it is very difficult to provide irrefutable evidence for this conclusion). Since, however, the allocation of MITI resources for these projects was contingent on the acceptance by the companies of a process of specialization, this conclusion does seem reasonable. Furthermore, there is evidence that in some instances companies relied on other participants for technology which the latter had developed under the VHSCS project. For example, Flamm (1985, p. 7-67) notes that 'Fujitsu did purchase NMOS storage devices from NEC for use in the DIPS-1 computers it built for NTT,[63] and NEC's chips used VHSCS technology.' However, this should not be taken to imply that the companies actually specialized along the lines indicated by their research roles in the MITI projects and completely avoided research overlap. Here it must be recalled that the firms were all actual or potential competitors in the field of computers and therefore would have made strategic calculations regarding the importance of the technology in question. In general, the more strategically significant the firm judged the technology to be from the point of view of its longer-run competitiveness, the more likely it would have been for the firm to do the related research itself even where this research was not funded by MITI or where it overlapped with the research of other companies. For this reason a substantial degree of research overlap was inevitable. Nevertheless, in the case of 'non-strategically significant' research, or in the instance where one company developed a substantial technological advantage, it is likely that the design of the VHSCS project resulted in a greater degree of specialization than would otherwise have occurred. It is therefore likely that the VHSCS project provided national benefits in the form of economies of research specialization.

A further set of important questions arises in connection with the social benefits derived from the diffusion of technological knowledge. As a contract research project (*itakuhi*) the technological knowledge created under the VHSCS project belonged formally to MITI, rather than to the companies themselves. In principle, as owner of the knowledge, MITI is able to diffuse it as it sees fit. Again in principle, this should lead to the wider diffusion of the knowledge than would result if the same stock of knowledge were owned by the participating private companies, since MITI, unlike the companies, has an interest in diffusing the knowledge as widely as possible in order to assist in attaining the national goal of industrial growth. On the other hand, the companies, interested in private profitability and market share, have an interest in restricting the outflow of their technological knowledge to the extent that such outflows are expected to negatively impinge on their objectives. For these reasons the design of the VHSCS project and others like it ensures in principle a greater 'socialization' of technological knowledge than would occur if the ownership of the intellectual property rights were vested in the participating private companies.

In these projects MITI has in practice claimed ownership of both the patents *and the know-how* that have resulted. The latter refers to important but non-patentable knowledge that has been produced under the project. However, it is likely that the significant degree of tacitness inherent in both patentable and non-patentable technological knowledge limits the effective degree of appropriation of this knowledge by MITI. Even if the participating firm which created the knowledge were willing to transfer this knowledge to MITI, its ability to do so would be limited by the constraints on expressing the entire stock of knowledge in an explicit form. As a result, a smaller knowledge set would be transferred to MITI than was created by the firm under the project. The rest would remain in the effective possession of the firm thus giving it a possibly important advantage (depending on the relevance of the knowledge which remains tacit) over the other firms to which MITI might want to transfer the knowledge. Furthermore, for obvious reasons firms might in some cases be unwilling to give the knowledge to MITI. In these cases the tacitness inherent in the knowledge would limit the ability of MITI to effectively possess the knowledge it legally owns.

For these reasons the effective 'socialization' of the technological knowledge created under the project will be limited. It is, however, possible to give a statistical account of the diffusion of patents held by MITI under the VHSCS project. On 31 March 1987 there were sixty-eight patents that had been generated under the VHSCS project which were available to be licensed through MITI. By the same date seven, or 10.3 per cent, of these patents had been licensed out. A total of two firms had purchased these licences.[64] These figures tend to confirm the conclusion that there has been only a relatively limited 'socialization' of the knowledge generated as a result of the VHSCS project. Even if both the firms that purchased licences were not the original creators of the technologies concerned, this still implies that at least three out of five firms that participated in the VHSCS project did not license any of the technology that was created. Furthermore, the figures imply that some 90 per cent of the patents generated under the project were not licensed. For these reasons it would be wrong to argue that the VHSCS project resulted in a significant diffusion of computer-related technology.

To summarize, therefore, it may be concluded that the VHSCS project produced the following social benefits: an increase in the rate of acquisition of computer-related technological capabilities; an increase in the economies of specialization; and a possible, though limited, increase in the diffusion of computer-related knowledge. The VHSCS project did not achieve a significant sharing of technological knowledge among the participating firms whose boundaries remained relatively impermeable in terms of inter-corporate information flows. Against these social benefits must be weighed the social costs of the project including the financial costs to both MITI and the participating companies and the time devoted by their employees to the project.

By 1969, when reference was first made in MITI to the strategic importance of the so-called 'knowledge-intensive industries',[65] Japan boasted a relatively robust domestic computer industry. To be sure, there was still a fairly wide technology gap between the Japanese companies and the American leaders in the world computer market as would be dramatically revealed in the opening year of the following decade. Nevertheless, the Japanese computer industry had acquired sufficient technological capabilities to survive the many shocks that were to come. The relatively healthy state of this industry was the result of the coordinated efforts of both the Japanese companies and various government agencies.

Although, as was seen, in the 1950s it was government institutions such as ETL and ECL and universities that took the lead in the development of national computing capabilities, by the end of the 1960s the main thrust came increasingly from the Japanese computer producers. However, government agencies continued to play an important role in facilitating the development of the computer industry. This can be illustrated by several examples. Without the infant industry status that was accorded this industry it is doubtful whether the Japanese companies, originally involved in other areas such as telecommunications and heavy electrical equipment, would have diversified into computing, or if they did, would have survived in the face of the substantial technology gap that existed relative to the world leaders. Government research funding, which was well targeted to areas where there seemed to be a high pay-off to research, helped to compensate for the firms' inherent tendency to underinvest in areas of research where there was an important degree of uncertainty. Government-initiated cooperative research projects also made significant contributions as has just been shown. Here it should be recalled that it was not only MITI and ETL, but also NTT and ECL, that were important for the development of the Japanese computer industry. Although NTT 'backed the wrong horse' with the parametron and the parametron-based computer, its role in this instance in the Japanese Computer Technology-Creating System was to help cover alternative technologies which, given the uncertainty that existed at the time, might in the longer run have proved to be superior. From this point of view NTT's work with the parametron might be seen as having improved the chances of adequate longer-run performance of the Japanese System as a whole, rather than as a failure. From 1968 with the increasing interest in time-sharing computing and with NTT's initiation of the DIPS computer project in conjunction with Fujitsu, Hitachi and NEC, NTT made an important contribution to the development of large-scale computer technology in Japan. The DIPS project, which is analysed in more detail in the present author's research on telecommunications, [66] also drew on technology created under the VHSCS project. Lastly, government also assisted the development of the Japanese computer industry by helping to create new organizations which served the interests of the industry as a whole. Examples during the present period include the Japan Information Processing Development Centre (JIPDEC), which was originally created in 1967 to train computer personnel and which, as will later be seen, played an important role in the establishment of other computer-related research projects such as the Fifth Generation Computing Project, and the Information Technology Promotion Agency, the latter established in 1970 to promote software research. Japan therefore entered the 1970s with a fairly robust domestic computer industry.

1970–1979: Between the devil (IBM) and the deep blue sea (liberalization)

As was shown earlier, by 1960 Japan had come under growing American pressure to liberalize international trade. This led in 1961 to an extensive revision of the Japanese tariff schedule. However, while import restrictions were reduced in some areas such as textiles, they were increased in other areas, such as computers, which were treated as infant industries. Nevertheless, the pressures to extend the liberalization of international trade continued and by 1970, with Japanese computer producers holding around 50 per cent of the domestic computer market, the Japanese government had been forced to concede a significant degree of liberalization in this market by 1976.[67] As Welke (1982, p. 39) notes, 'The Japanese computer manufacturers wanted the liberalization to begin much later and proposed April 1977 for the start of import decontrol.' Nevertheless, despite the concession it was clear that MITI was not about to abandon the Japanese computer producers to the harsh winds of international competition until they were ready to stand comfortably on their own two feet. Fujitsu's Taiyu Kobayashi (1986, p. 94) remarks that in 1971 the Japanese computer manufacturers 'in competition with IBM still faced a wide gap in technological development and international marketing strength. Because of the strategic importance of computers the industry was excluded from the liberalization up to [1971]. Even after this, however, the government exerted every effort to protect and nurture domestic computer manufacturers.' The pressures to liberalize international trade in computers, however, were growing and had eventually to be accommodated. In 1972 some of the quotas on computer peripheral equipment were removed and from December 1975 quantitative restrictions on the imports of mainframe computers were eliminated. By 1979 the tariff rates on mainframes and peripherals/terminals were 10.5 per cent and 17.0 per cent respectively.[68] At the same time as liberalization increased so, as some Japanese economists noted,[69] the dominant ideology in Japan changed to become more favourably disposed towards free trade.

The coming inevitability of liberalization of computer trade posed serious problems for both MITI officials and the computer-producing companies in the early 1970s. As if to underscore the substantial technology gap that remained between Japanese producers and the leading company in the field of computers (to say nothing of the marketing gap), IBM in 1970 introduced its System 370. With its virtual memory, System 370 represented a significant step beyond IBM's System 360 and caused as much trouble for the company's American competitors as it did for the Japanese producers.

In April 1970 Honeywell acquired the computer division of General Electric and made the decision to adopt General Electric's architecture. This presented difficulties for Toshiba, which had had a technology agreement with General Electric since October 1964, and for NEC which had signed an agreement with Honeywell in July 1962 and which, prior to the latter's adoption of General Electric's architecture, had been working with Honeywell on a new architecture. As a result of these changes Toshiba developed a closer relationship with Honeywell and this in turn led to closer connections with NEC as will later be seen. Furthermore, in September 1971, largely as a result of System 370, RCA decided to abandon mainframe computers and later sold out to Sperry Rand. This caused problems for Hitachi which in May 1961 had been the first Japanese firm to conclude a computer technology agreement with an American firm, RCA. Similarly, Mitsubishi Electric was left in difficulties when TRW sold their computer interests.

Like the other Japanese companies, Fujitsu was also severely tested by the introduction of System 370 in 1970. It was only in 1968 that Fujitsu completed the FACOM 230-60 which it introduced in order to cope with IBM's 360 series which reached the market in 1964. With the FACOM 230-60 Fujitsu managed in 1968 to replace NEC and Hitachi as the Japanese firm holding the largest share of the domestic computer market. However, Fujitsu was making far less progress internationally. A major reason for this poor performance was the dominance of the world computer market by IBM and the fact that IBM software would not run on Fujitsu's computers. By 1968 Fujitsu had come to the realization that 'unless we could, without modifications, run the same software created for IBM systems on our computers built around the same architecture, we would never be able to compete in the international market'.[70]

Although Fujitsu had decided that IBM-compatibility was a longer-run necessity if progress were to be made in the international market, it was their liaison with Gene Amdahl that set the seal of approval on this decision. Amdahl was a major designer of IBM's 360 series and was an important figure in the design of System 370 at the time when Fujitsu first made contact with him. According to Taiyu Kobayashi, who became Chairman of Fujitsu's Board in 1981, Amdahl, who in 1969 was the director of an IBM research facility in Menlo Park, California, conflicted with the management of IBM over the question of the number of models that should be introduced as part of the 370 series. Amdahl argued that at least three were needed while management was unwilling to agree to more than one. As the conflict deepened IBM closed Amdahl's research facility. The decisive factor behind Amdahl's resignation from IBM in August 1970 was the company's opposition to his role as director with his younger brother in a consulting company. Informed about Amdahl's predicament by someone from the American firm Litton Industries,[71] Fujitsu sent a senior company representative to meet Amdahl in November 1969. As Kobayashi noted, 'Fujitsu saw tremendous potential in joining hands with Dr Amdahl, who knew so well the strengths, weaknesses, and overall situation of IBM.'[72] Apparently, Fujitsu also offered Hitachi the opportunity to join with Amdahl, but Hitachi declined.[73]

According to Kobayashi, Amdahl Corporation, set up by Gene Amdahl after he left IBM, had fulfilled two of the conditions necessary for entry into the world mainframe computer market:

In general, mainframe general purpose computer users are very conservative when it comes to replacing existing equipment. If, however, it were not necessary to make a new investment in software, that is, the replacement system were compatible with software presently in use, and it also represented a higher (sic) cost–performance level, there was ample leeway for the introduction of replacement systems. In other words, these were the two necessary conditions for new computers to be widely accepted in the mainframe computer market.[74]

However, Amdahl Corporation was unable to fulfil a third necessary condition for entry – raising adequate levels of finance – without losing its managerial autonomy. The capital market failed to provide the necessary support:

It was not easy to raise the huge sums required for [computer] development over an extended period. Depending on the speed of their development, it was estimated that from 33 to 44 million dollars in capital would be necessary. And despite Dr Amdahl's reputation, venture capital was not eager to come forth with such huge sums based solely on his 'confidence'.... RCA had already failed and start-up computer companies, such as MASCOR, had recently gone bankrupt.
(T. Kobayashi, 1986, p. 85)

It is also possible that Amdahl Corporation exhibited a number of internal weaknesses, which included their failure (perhaps derived from the constraints on external sources of capital) to realize important economies of vertical integration. This certainly was the conclusion reached by Fujitsu after its analysis of Amdahl's manufacturing facilities: '... after observing their manufacturing process, we did not think they could produce a machine that would operate well. They purchased IC's, printed circuit boards, literally everything from outside vendors. Only assembly was performed by Amdahl.'[75] This contrasted strongly with the situation in Fujitsu where vertical integration facilitated efficient flows of information between the semiconductor designers and producers and the computer designers and producers. Both these groups operated within the same corporation, under the same top managerial authority, and there was an important complementarity between their products. This facilitated significant information flows between them: 'Since all [Fujitsu's] components were produced internally, we had gathered comprehensive data on the reliability of each part. This is because a computer consists of an extraordinary number of individual parts and if the accuracy of this part or that part is off by just a little, the overall reliability of the whole system suffers dramatically.'[76] In other words, important information, of relevance to the designers and producers of computers since it has a bearing on the cost–performance of computers, is generated in the process of producing semiconductors. If semiconductor and computer production are undertaken in separate companies such information flows (a) may not be adequately generated or (b) may not be adequately used. From the point of view of the semiconductor company, these information flows may constitute an externality, the financial value of which cannot be realized as a result of the difficulties inherent in any attempt to charge computer producers for the use of the information.[77] Accordingly, market failure (the failure of an appropriate market transaction between the semiconductor and the computer companies to be concluded) might result in inefficiencies that can only be overcome through vertical integration.

Fujitsu felt that it was well placed to produce computers with a competitive cost–performance ratio and that the design skills of Amdahl Corporation would assist it to compete with IBM's System 370. Not only had Fujitsu, unlike some other computer producers, integrated the semiconductor division into the computer division, but it had also taken the decision to specialize almost entirely in the production of semiconductors for computer systems, ignoring the large market for semiconductors related to consumer goods:

A special characteristic of Fujitsu's semi-conductor development is that the whole effort is directed predominantly toward computers. Since semi-conductors (LSI and VLSI) are the 'lifeblood' of computers, this has had a decisive significance. Semi-conductor business at most other companies is based on production for consumer use – household appliances and the like. Semiconductor quality is not as high as it might be because their objective is to turn out large quantities and supply them cheaply to these primary markets. Fujitsu also did this at first. When a semi-conductor division is an independent entity concerned about their own bottom line, rather than produce a limited number of high performance devices for computers which require painstaking, time consuming design, they will tend to be more interested in selling large quantities of less complicated chips to consumer oriented markets. [78]

In large part this favourable form of organization had evolved in Fujitsu as a result of historical circumstance, rather than design. Unlike a company such as Hitachi which had a substantial consumer products division, Fuji Electric (the parent company of Fujitsu and itself a spin-off from the firm Furukawa) entered the home applicances market relatively late and had a weak consumer section. Accordingly, 'the decision was made [for Fujitsu] to become a manufacturer specializing in semiconductors for computers. This was accomplished by incorporating the semiconductor division into the computers division. By putting computer design teams together with semiconductor design groups, we were able to concentrate our engineers in such areas as integrated LSI memory and logic chips for computer use.'[79] This might have given Fujitsu an advantage over Hitachi.[80]

Mutual advantage therefore created the conditions for a marriage between Fujitsu and Amdahl. While the Amdahl Corporation possessed the necessary design ability, it lacked the needed finance since the American capital markets had failed to give it adequate funding. As a relatively small start-up company, the corporation also lacked the sophisticated manufacturing capabilities which play an important role in improving the cost–performance ratio, hence increasing competitiveness. Fujitsu possessed both the financial and the manufacturing 'assets' that would facilitate Amdahl's entry into the mainframe computer market. From Fujitsu's point of view the arrival of Gene Amdahl was a godsend in view of his intimate knowledge of the IBM architecture, which would give Fujitsu the IBM-compatibility it felt was a necessary condition for its own expansion into international markets. The result was that in 1972 Fujitsu was given access to some of Amdahl's technical information in exchange for the purchase of 24 per cent of Amdahl's equity. In 1974 the agreement was extended with Fujitsu agreeing to produce computers in Japan to be sold by Amdahl in the US. Gene Amdahl, however, as a result of the fundamental weakness which followed from his lack of access to an adequate supply of finance, was forced to pay a price – a loss of a significant degree of managerial control over Amdahl Corporation.[81]

From a social point of view, the significance of the Amdahl episode lay in the leakage of technological knowledge from IBM. IBM's ability to appropriate the returns from its investment in new technologies was to some extent limited by the outward mobility of some of its employees which resulted in a wider use of the technological knowledge and hence a greater degree of competition for IBM. As a consequence, additional social benefit was probably derived by computer users in the longer run in the form of a lower price, a greater choice with regard to computer functions and a more rapid rate of technical change. The failure of the American capital markets to support the Amdahl Corporation, however, meant that the knowledge leakage was not confined to the United States, and the spread of technological knowledge to Japan would increase international competition from that country. In 1979 Fujitsu overtook IBM to hold the largest share of the Japanese computer market. The Amdahl episode must have made some contribution to this achievement.

The twin occurrences in the first few years of the 1970s of an increasing probability and rate of liberalization of international trade and foreign investment in the Japanese computer market, and the introduction by IBM of System 370, highlighted the need for a strengthening of the Japanese computer producers. As already noted, the effect of the advent of System 370 on IBM's American competitors served also to destabilize those Japanese computer producers which had technology agreements with American partners. Furthermore, Fujitsu, the only Japanese computer company without a significant external technology agreement, had not yet consolidated its links with Amdahl. As always in the past, the issue for MITI officials was not whether the market alone, that is the Japanese companies themselves in the absence of government intervention, could pull the Japanese computer industry up by its own bootstraps, but rather in what ways MITI could provide relevant assistance. As early as June 1969 MITI had already drawn attention to the likely widespread future importance of what were labelled the 'knowledge-intensive industries'[82] and its commitment to fostering these industries had been made clear.

The overall MITI objective for the computer industry was relatively easily identified, namely to eliminate the technology gap with Western companies, and particularly with IBM, as soon as possible by increasing the technological capability of the Japanese computer producers. Three related means were chosen to achieve this objective: first, merger or a closer inter-firm coordination of general activities; secondly, research cooperation between the Japanese computer producers themselves and with MITI's Electrotechnical Laboratory; thirdly, an increased provision of subsidized finance.

These three means already had a relatively long and successful track record in MITI. Mergers, created under MITI's administrative guidance, had already been used in the postwar period in a number of successful attempts to reap the benefits of increased industrial concentration. For example, in June 1964 three companies which had been separated by the American authorities were reamalgamated to form Mitsubishi Heavy Industries. Similarly, in August 1966 the Nissan and Prince automobile companies were merged. The desire for merger or closer inter-firm coordination came not only from MITI but also from some parts of the private sector. In March 1966 the leaders of a number of the main industrial associations, including steel, electrical power, chemicals, machinery, textiles, trading, finance and securities, formed the Industrial Problems Research Association (or 'Sanken'). Under the intellectual leadership of Sohei Nakayama of the Industrial Bank of Japan, Sanken made a number of recommendations for restructuring Japanese industry in order to cope with problems such as excessive competition and the liberalization of trade and capital flows. In June 1967 the Nakayama Committee, which included representation from MITI and the Economic Planning Agency, recommended either merger or closer cooperation in the computer industry and six others (machine tools, steel, automobiles, petroleum refining, petrochemicals and synthetic textiles). This Committee also helped to shape the 1971 law discussed in more detail below which encouraged the emergence of mechatronics, the convergence of the mechanical engineering and electronics industries, for example in the case of numerically controlled machine tools.[83]

The second and third means, research cooperation and subsidized funding, had been used for a long time in the computer industry. As seen in the previous section, both the FONTAC project (1962–66) and the Very High Speed Computer Project (1966–72) involved research cooperation and subsidized funding. The encouraging of research cooperation was perhaps intended to facilitate a greater degree of specialization among Japanese computer companies, in this way overcoming some of the disadvantages of their small size relative to that of IBM.[84] On the other hand, the provision of subsidized funding would compensate for the tendency of Japanese companies to underinvest in research. This tendency results from the twin uncertainties regarding, firstly, the results of research and, secondly, the ability of firms to appropriate returns from the research when other firms gain access to, and use, the knowledge that emerges from that research.[85]

The three means were implemented in a number of policy measures that were introduced in the early 1970s. In 1971 the Temporary Measures Law for the Promotion of Specific Electronic Industries and Specific Machinery Industries (Law no. 17 of 1971) was passed. This enabling legislation required MITI to produce plans to improve technological and production capabilities and to rationalize the electronics and machinery industries concerned. At the same time, as noted earlier, the 1971 Law helped to promote the emergence of mechatronics in Japan.[86]

The Temporary Measures Law was enacted in April 1971. In November 1971 MITI announced two plans for the computer industry. The first plan concentrated on R & D and specified a number of well-defined objectives that were to be achieved. These included the development by Japanese firms of a new family of computers that would be able to rival the IBM 370 series. In order to achieve this objective funds were allocated for a new cooperative research project, the Mainframe Computer Project (or 3.5 Generation Project as it was often called) which lasted from 1972 to 1976 and made subsidies available to Japanese firms. [87] Further funds were allocated for research in the fields of logic circuits, memory devices, input/output devices, terminals and software. In addition, money was provided for the development of applications systems in eight fields including hospitals, education and pollution prevention. Extremely generous funding was provided for all these projects. The first plan was to be funded by MITI on a subsidy (*hojokin*) basis. It was estimated that a substantial amount of funding was required in order to cope with the twin threats of liberalization of the computer market and the great competitive leap taken by IBM with its introduction of System 370. The estimated funding requirements were:[88]

(1) 3.5 Generation Computer Programme
150 billion yen ($454.6 million)
(2) Developing and producing experimental machines and equipment for the 3.5 Generation Programme   30   billion yen ($90.9 million)
(3) Developing logic circuits, memory devices, input/output devices, terminal devices   75 billion yen ($227.3 million)
(4) Developing applications systems in eight fields
120 billion yen ($363.6 million)

The total estimated amount required from MITI subsidies for the first plan was, therefore, 375 billion yen ($1.14 billion).

In addition, it was estimated that a further 277 billion yen ($839.4 million) in the form of subsidized loans would be required for implementing the second plan, thus making a total of 852 billion yen ($1.98 billion).[89] This second plan dealt with the rationalization of the computer industry in order to assist in attaining the objective of equalling or improving upon the performance–cost ratio of foreign computers by the year 1977. The second plan was to be financed primarily in the form of subsidized loans from the Japan Development Bank.

While these estimated amounts represented extremely substantial funding levels, it is not completely clear how much was spent in the event by MITI and the Japan Development Bank for implementing these two plans. Peck and Tamura (1976, p. 571, emphasis added) state that 'The improvement plan for computers announced in November 1971 *represented a program of government support unmatched for any other Japanese industry*... The government [i.e. MITI] was to fund (about 100 million dollars) development of a high-performance computer, to be completed by 1978, as well as development of several smaller computers and peripheral equipment (another 100 million dollars) on a matching basis.' Figures provided in Anchordoguy (1988a) state that from 1970 to 1975 MITI gave subsidies of $178.5 million to the 3.5 Generation Programme (including subsidies for peripheral equipment and LSIs) (p. 540). This compared with total subsidies given by MITI to the computer industry during this period of $462.3 million. During the same period, total tax benefits given to this industry (in such form as special depreciation allowances) amounted to $174.3 million and total loans (primarily by the Japan Development Bank and the Japan Electronic Computer Company) to $1244.2 billion. This makes total loans, tax benefits and subsidies equal to $1.88 billion (pp. 541–2). During this period investment in plant and equipment by the *private* sector computer industry amounted to $392.1 million and total investment in R & D made by this industry came to $722.73 million (p. 543). *In other words, total government assistance to the computer industry in the form of subsidies, tax benefits and loans amounted to 1.68 times total private sector investment in plant and equipment and R & D during the period 1970–75.* Flamm (1987) provides somewhat different figures. As opposed to Anchordoguy's figure of $462.3 million for MITI subsidies given to the computer industry during this period, Flamm's figure is $272 million (p. 138). Flamm suggests that for the three years 1973 to 1975 the MITI subsidy amounted to 25, 27 and 21 per cent respectively of total information technology R & D in Japan (that is from both the public and private sectors) (p. 138).

Despite the discrepancies in these figures, there is agreement that MITI and the Japan Development Bank made substantial expenditures from 1970 to the late 1970s in the wake of trade and investment liberalization and IBM's System 370. In addition, further substantial sums came directly or indirectly, the latter in the form of procurement, from NTT. *In the light of these data, there are reasonable grounds for suggesting that in the absence of the government support given to the computer industry over this period, Japanese companies might have exited, like RCA and General Electric from the mainframe computer market.*

Although it has been suggested that MITI unsuccessfully attempted to encourage mergers in the Japanese computer industry,[90] in the event the Ministry's officials were forced to accept a degree of closer inter-firm coordination. Three groups were formed: Fujitsu–Hitachi who were to produce the M-series of IBM-compatible computers; NEC–Toshiba developing the ACOS-series based on the General Electric/Honeywell architecture; and Mitsubishi–Oki producing the COSMOS series of computers.

According to Taiyu Kobayashi, an executive of Fujitsu, 'in the fall of 1971, under the administrative guidance of MITI, the six principal domestic computer companies were encouraged to form groups for mutual assistance'.[91] Although Fujitsu was only to sign its first agreement with Amdahl in the following year, 'Fujitsu was paired with Hitachi because of Hitachi's connection with RCA. The RCA–Hitachi development of IBM-compatible systems accorded with Fujitsu's own compatibility strategy.'[92] While personal factors also influenced the coupling of Fujitsu and Hitachi,[93] there was some opposition, at least within Fujitsu, to the move. 'Initially, there was opposition within Fujitsu toward the plans for cooperative development with Hitachi. From a business standpoint, resistance was centered around the idea that Fujitsu had set out to become the top computer manufacturer in Japan with its independently developed FACOM technology.' However, the coming liberalization of the Japanese computer market, Fujitsu's desire to expand its operations internationally and last, but by no means least, the company's desire to take advantage of the generous funding made available by MITI, persuaded Fujitsu to become IBM-compatible and to collaborate more closely with Hitachi.

Several factors facilitated the pairing of NEC and Toshiba. The most obvious was their common link with General Electric and Honeywell, discussed earlier. Another facilitating factor was the degree of complementarity, as opposed to competitiveness, between the two companies arising from NEC's specialization in telecommunications equipment[94] and Toshiba's concentration on heavy electrical equipment and consumer electronics. Bringing up the rear in terms of relative computing capabilities were Mitsubishi and Oki. The latter was the weakest of the six computer-producing firms, although its position as one of the four Den Den family firms supplying NTT (the others being Fujitsu, Hitachi and NEC) gave Oki a degree of access to national cooperative research projects which it otherwise would probably not have enjoyed.[95]

The 3.5 Generation Project and the other projects which formed part of the package of measures for the computer industry announced by MITI in November 1971 had primarily short-term objectives, namely catching up with IBM's System 370 by 1977/8. However, MITI's 'vision' regarding the conditions necessary for the health of the Japanese computer industry also extended into the more distant future. In addition to short-term research it was also necessary to support longer-term research, to compensate for the tendency of private companies to underinvest in such research as a result of the uncertainties involved. For this reason MITI initiated the Pattern Information Processing System (PIPS) project which lasted from 1971 until 1980. The aim of the PIPS project was to develop computer technology for the recognition and processing of pattern information such as characters, pictures, objects and speech. The project also provided for the development of electronic devices to support these capabilities, such as a one-chip 16-bit microprocessor and a parallel image processor. MITI spent a sum of approximately 22 billion yen on the PIPS project, apart from the contribution made by the companies to the overall costs of the project.[96] Nine firms were involved in the PIPS project plus MITI's Electrotechnical Laboratory: Fujitsu, NEC, Hitachi, Toshiba, Mitsubishi, Oki, Matsushita, Sanyo and Hoya Glass.

What were the effects of the various government measures taken in the early 1970s? Although this question is inherently difficult to answer with precision, it is worth posing in an attempt to understand better the significance of government intervention in the Japanese computer industry. In order to begin answering this question, if only qualitatively, it is necessary to conduct a counter-factual thought experiment and ask what would have happened in the absence of these government measures. While such an experiment is unlikely to lead to incontrovertible conclusions, it is an exercise that is nonetheless worth undertaking in order to generate at the very least a number of hypotheses that can be further examined with more detailed information.

It seems reasonable to conclude, in the first place, that as a result of the government programmes referred to, a greater financial input was allocated to computer research than would have occurred in the absence of these programmes. This is strongly suggested by the substantial subsidies made available by MITI and documented above. Clearly, without these government funds a significant amount of computer research would still have been undertaken in Japanese companies. The computer market in Japan and worldwide was growing rapidly and the widespread applicability of computer-related technology had become apparent. Under these conditions it is likely that at least some of the Japanese computer-producing companies would have continued to devote substantial sums to computer research and development. However, in view of the significant subsidies provided by MITI, it is probable that more resources were made available in even those Japanese companies that would have in any event remained committed to the computer industry, than would have been allocated in the absence of these government programmes. Furthermore, other government measures, such as the continued protection of the Japanese computer market until 1976, must also have contributed to a feeling of confidence resulting from the knowledge that the government was making a strong commitment to the long-run development of the Japanese computer industry.

Promotional policies for the computer industry such as subsidies and protection served to decrease the uncertainties associated with the generation and commercialization of computer technology. It is likely that the uncertainty-reducing effect of government policy served to stimulate the Japanese computer industry to a significantly greater extent than would have occurred without these policies. At the same time, strong competition between the computer producers ensured that great pressure to innovate would be brought to bear on individual companies.

There are a number of indicators which suggest that by the middle to late 1970s the Japanese computer industry had succeeded in closing the technology gap with the world leaders.[97] Sobel (1986, p. 161), for example, notes that by '1974 Fujitsu introduced a clone of the extremely successful IBM 370 series, Fujitsu's 370 M, which was faster than IBM's machine. Hitachi followed and by the end of the decade IBM Japan's share of the Japanese market had shrunk to 27 per cent. In 1979 Fujitsu passed IBM as the nation's leading manufacturer of computers.' Although it is not possible to identify rigorously the extent to which government measures contributed to this outcome, it is likely for the reasons mentioned that they should be given credit for more than an insignificant proportion of the achievement.

A further source of information on the importance of government financing of computer research in Japan comes from an interesting table (Table 2.1) produced by Flamm (1985). A number of pertinent factors emerge from this table. The first is that in the period 1973 to 1976 MITI funding for computer research projects as a proportion of total information technology R & D in Japan increased substantially and remained at or above the 20 per cent level. Secondly, the proportion of research done inside the private companies on a self-funded basis fell sharply in 1974 and 1975 to 20 per cent and 29 per cent respectively of total information technology R & D. Thirdly, a substantial proportion of total R & D was undertaken under the auspices of MITI-initiated cooperative research programmes. Between 1972 and 1976 between 31 per cent and 51 per cent of total information technology R & D was undertaken under these programmes. (Flamm notes that, as a result of an official reclassification, research undertaken in these programmes was changed from 1973 from research done in 'public research institutions' to 'private research institutions'.)

The figures in the last paragraph suggest very dramatically that

Table 2.1. *Performance of information technology R & D in Japan, 1970–1981*

	1970	1971	1972	1973	1974	1975	1976	1977	1978	1979	1980	1981
Japanese R & D expenditure on information technology												
US $ million	83	118	168	300	314	348	397	437	627	725	725	976
% performed in:[a]												
industry	100	98	65	55	41	51	55	70	67	74	86	78
of which												
NTT[b]	33	34	34	22	21	22	19	25	24	22	23	19
remainder	67	63	31	33	20	29	36	45	44	53	63	60
central govt.	n.a.	1	4	3	3	3	2	2	3	4	2	1
private research institutions	n.a.	z	1	z	51	40	37	23	25	15	8	16
public research institutions	n.a.	z	31	41	z	z	z	z	z	z	z	z
universities and colleges	n.a.	n.a.	n.a.	n.a.	5	5	4	5	5	7	5	4
MITI research projects in information technology												
US $ million	7	7	24	76	84	74	79	58	75	67	53	60
% of information R & D	8	6	14	25	27	21	20	13	12	9	7	6

Key:
z positive, but less than 0.5 per cent.
Notes:
[a] No data available for universities and colleges 1970–3, government and research institutions 1970.
[b] NTT information R & D estimated as 50 per cent total NTT R & D budget.
Source: Flamm (1985).

government funding made a substantial difference to the progress of the Japanese computer industry. It is most unlikely that in the absence of such funding the private Japanese companies would have switched sufficient resources from other alternative uses to make up the shortfall and keep research expenditures at the same level that in the event occurred. Nevertheless, there are some reasons for suggesting that this conclusion may have to be modified. The first is that Flamm slides (in the table and in the text) between reference to 'information technology R & D' and 'computer R & D' with the result that some questions are raised about the strict comparability of the data. Most particularly, it may be that the method that he uses for calculating NTT's 'information technology R & D' leads to an understatement of the proportion of total R & D done in the private companies. (Flamm makes the assumption: 'NTT information R & D estimated as $\frac{1}{2}$ total NTT R & D budget.') Secondly, it is not clear whether the figures given for public and private research institutions include an estimate of the expenditure made inside the private companies for research undertaken as part of the MITI-initiated research projects. To the extent that the latter research expenditure is included under the public and private research institution headings, rather than under 'industry (remainder)', the proportional significance of private company information technology R & D will have been underestimated. Finally, on a related point, it is worth remembering that a good deal of innovative activity of relevance to the determination of international competitiveness is not captured by the R & D statistics. These include 'factory floor' innovation[98] which can result in significant incremental improvements. If non-R & D forms of innovation such as this are taken into account, the proportional significance of private companies in total innovation of all kinds increases greatly.

However, despite these qualifications, the figures in Flamm's table suggest that the Japanese government did make a significant contribution to the growth of the computer industry through the provision of funding. This is particularly the case in the area of longer-term or more basic research as will be shown below. If the contributions made by MITI is added to that of NTT (which became a semi-private company in 1985) this conclusion is strengthened.

It is less likely, however, that MITI contributed significantly to the Japanese computer industry by increasing the degree of sharing of technological knowledge between the competing private companies (that is, either actual or potential competitors). As noted earlier, MITI attempted to encourage inter-firm research cooperation by pairing the six Japanese computer-producing companies. In this way MITI was able to ensure that the *Japanese System as a whole* would be able to cover both the IBM-compatible option (Fujitsu and Hitachi) as well as the 'non-IBM-compatible' or independent strategic option (primarily NEC and

Toshiba). Whichever option turned out to be more successful in the longer run, the Japanese System as a whole would avoid being seriously weakened as a result of having backed the wrong horse. From this point of view there was a similarity with the earlier cases, documented above, of research on silicon and germanium transistors, and transistor- and parametron-based computers.[99]

Nevertheless, apart from some sharing of information on the broad outlines of computer architectures, there was very little genuine joint research between the paired companies. For the most part, the research undertaken with MITI subsidies was done inside the individual companies under the normal conditions of commercial secrecy. The reason for the lack of genuine joint research was the strong degree of competition that existed between the companies. Evidence of this comes from the change in company ranking in terms of Japanese computer market share. In 1968, for example, Fujitsu overtook NEC and Hitachi as the leading Japanese computer company. Furthermore, as we shall later see, three of the six Japanese companies exited from the mainframe computer market in the wake of the introduction of IBM's System 370 and the liberalization of international trade and capital flows. As a result of the degree of competition that existed between them, the Japanese computer companies were on the whole unwilling to blur the firm boundaries that separated them, and kept their stocks of technological knowledge private. This important conclusion emerged from interviews that the present author had with senior researchers from Fujitsu, Hitachi, NEC, and Toshiba.

The few exceptions prove the rule because they remained exceptions. For example, Nippon Peripherals Ltd, a company formed by Fujitsu and Hitachi, was a 'cooperative venture designed to help defray the tremendous expense of developing peripheral devices. NPL has been very profitable due to its successful development of high capacity magnetic disks and memory devices which automatically exchange magnetic cartridges. It has grown into an excellent company, expanded beyond the domestic market, and is now exporting in substantial volume to the United States and Europe.'[100] According to a Fujitsu executive, both Hitachi and Fujitsu agreed that they had derived important benefits from this example of joint research: 'Coming from different environments and holding different views, [the engineers from both companies] experienced a cross-fertilization of ideas that gave rise to new concepts and approaches to problems.' This cross-fertilization was particularly important in view of the constraints on such processes imposed by the Japanese practice of life-time employment: 'Because Japanese companies have a life-time employment system, once an employee joins a corporation, his chances of ever getting an inside view of another company are practically nil... Hitachi's way of thinking contributed greatly to

Fujitsu's management techniques.'[101] However, despite these convincing arguments in favour of joint research, it remains that the case of Nippon Peripherals Ltd demonstrated an exception rather than a rule. Two related reasons for the exception in this case are the relatively small market that existed for the specialized products that were developed and the high cost of development.[102] Neither was MITI able to encourage a substantial degree of inter-firm product specialization through its pairing of companies. As Flamm (1985) notes, 'Cooperation between Fujitsu and Hitachi did not last long, however. They were to jointly produce[103] an "M-series" of IBM-compatible computers, with Fujitsu producing the largest and smallest models, and Hitachi making two intermediate-sized machines. The first machines in this series were announced jointly in 1974, but by the following year, both had developed new models competitive with those that were supposed to be the exclusive province of the other.'[104]

It is likely, however, that MITI had a far greater degree of success from the early 1970s in facilitating longer-term or more basic research. As noted earlier, private companies tend to underinvest in such research as a result of the uncertainties involved. By taking on a substantial proportion of the costs of such research, MITI was undoubtedly able to ensure that a significantly greater amount of this research was undertaken than would have occurred in the absence of its programme. The obvious case in point in this period is the PIPS project 1971–80 outlined earlier. The PIPS project yielded a significantly larger number of patents than the earlier VHSCS project (1966–72) discussed above. While, according to one set of MITI statistics there were 365 patents from the PIPS project, the figure was 39 for the VHSCS project. However, very few of the PIPS patents were joint patents with the patent-holders coming from more than one company. Only 7, or 1.9 per cent, of the 365 patents were joint patents (with a maximum of 7 additional joint patents in those 7 cases where insufficient information was available to judge whether the patent was joint or not).[105] In all of the 7 confirmed joint patent cases the firms involved were non-competing companies.[106] To the extent that joint patents provide a reliable indication of joint research,[107] this suggests once again that there was very little joint generation and sharing of technological knowledge. The most likely explanation is the extent of competition, or potential competition, between the nine members of the PIPS project.

In contrast to the 3.5 Generation project, which was a MITI-subsidized project, the PIPS project like the VHSCS project was a contract project. This meant that formally MITI contracted the companies to do the research while it owned the resulting intellectual property rights. In principle this implied that MITI was in a position to encourage a greater diffusion of the resulting technology than would otherwise have occurred.[108] To the extent that this happened in practice, the intervention in this area by MITI would have resulted not only in the generation of additional technological knowledge in Japanese companies, but also in a greater diffusion of this knowledge than would have taken place, thus increasing the social benefit of the project.

Data are available which give some indication of the diffusion of the intellectual property rights owned by MITI and resulting from the PIPS project. These property rights fall into two categories: patents and know-how. (The latter refers to technological knowledge which has potential commercial value, is created as part of the MITI-funded contract research project, which can be made explicit in the form of writing, figures, drawings, etc., but which does not meet the criteria stipulated for patents.) At the end of March 1987 there were 454 patents emerging from the PIPS project which were available to be licensed from MITI. At the same date, 117, or 26 per cent, of these had been licensed. This is the highest of all the MITI projects for which information was obtained. Of the 643 'know-how' rights owned by MITI and available for purchase, 115, or 18 per cent, had been licensed by this date. A total of seven firms were involved in the licensing of patents and know-how. Unfortunately, it is not possible from the data to establish the extent to which the licensing involved companies purchasing from MITI technological knowledge which they themselves had generated under the MITI project. It is known, however, that the seven firms included Hitachi, Fujitsu, Toshiba and NEC, all of whom were amongst the nine firms participating in the PIPS project. Since these MITI-owned intellectual property rights are in principle available to any firm, including non-participating Japanese as well as foreign companies, the data suggest that the diffusion of PIPS-related knowledge through the sale of such property rights was limited largely to the participating firms. To the extent that this is correct, the social benefits of MITI's initiative in the case of the PIPS project do not include the diffusion through this mechanism of knowledge to other non-participating Japanese firms.[109]

The PIPS project also dramatically illustrates the importance of uncertainty in research aimed at long-term technical change. Until the early 1980s this project was widely regarded in MITI as a relative failure. Subsequently, however, this evaluation was substantially revised as a result of numerous successful technology applications which traced their origins to the PIPS project.[110] For example, Feigenbaum and McCorduck (1983, p. 129) note that 'PIPS was never exploited [in the MITI PIPS project] as a commercial product, and most Western computer scientists assumed that it had been a technical failure. It had not. Feigenbaum was to see some late PIPS models, for instance a PIPS for motion tracking, a difficult problem in computer vision... [It was] certainly on a par with any other pattern-information processing work going on in the world. PIPS was a marketing failure, but not a technological failure.' By 1986, however, even the qualification regarding the marketing success of PIPS technology had been revised. In that year a top-level delegation from the United States visited Japan and a year later produced the Japanese Technology Evaluation Program's (1987) panel report on advanced computing in Japan. Here it is noted that 'Japan's keen interest in man–machine interaction dates back to the earliest days of computing, motivated by the intractability of Kanji I/O [that is, Chinese characters used in the Japanese language] on teletype terminals... In the 1970s, MITI funded the... PIPS program. This program, a forerunner of ICOT [the institute for fifth generation computing], supported nearly 100 million dollars of vision and speech research. A number of commercial products appear to be direct descendents of PIPS projects, including the SPYDER image processing software system, the NEC-100 connected speech recognizer, and Toshiba's TROPIX image processing architecture' (p. 43). Toshiba also exploited PIPS technology in developing the first Japanese language word processor. With the benefit of hindsight, therefore, the MITI-initiated PIPS project facilitated longer-term research which, as a result of the uncertainties involved, would almost certainly not have received the same resources or attention at that time without the project.

It may be concluded, therefore, that in the various ways indicated in this section the implementation of government policy in the Japanese computer industry in the first half of the 1970s had a number of important positive consequences. However, as a result of the twin external shocks of IBM's System 370 and the liberalization of the Japanese economy, MITI's policies were insufficient to ensure the survival of all six Japanese computer producers in the mainframe computer market. While Fujitsu, NEC and Hitachi remained in this market, Toshiba, Mitsubishi and Oki exited. Although the latter three companies continued to derive substantial benefit from the policies and programmes initiated by MITI up to the mid-1970s, and went on doing so through the late 1970s and the 1980s, they decided to opt out of the mainframe market. Somewhat ironically, therefore, MITI achieved the aim it had articulated in 1971 of increasing the degree of concentration in the computer industry, but as a result of market processes (influenced by government policy) rather than direct attempts to encourage either merger or a significantly greater degree of inter-firm coordination.

Finally, it is worth noting that the survival and growth of Fujitsu, Hitachi and NEC in the mainframe computer market were also to a significant extent results of the special position that these three companies enjoyed in the telecommunications market. As members of NTT's so-called Den Den Family of supplying firms, Hitachi, Fujitsu and NEC were closely involved with NTT in the development of large mainframe computers that also had application outside the telecommunications field. As is discussed in detail in the present author's forthcoming research on telecommunications in Japan, the three companies benefited greatly from their relationship with NTT's Electrical Communications Laboratories. Furthermore, NTT was the largest single customer in Japan for mainframe computers, a market which the three companies shared, with the result that sales to NTT constituted a significant proportion of these companies' total sales for this type of computer.[111] (Oki, also a member of the Den Den Family, was excluded by NTT from computer production as a result of its relative weakness in this field.) An important more general implication of the present discussion is that it is essential to look beyond MITI and its policies and programmes in order to gain an understanding of the importance of government policy in the computer and electronics industry. This is one of the points that emerges, for example, from the statistics in Table 2.1 on NTT's contribution to information technology R & D. A conceptualization of the Japanese Technology-Creating System, such as that developed later in this book, must therefore also give a prominent place to the special role played by NTT.

3
The VLSI Research Project, 1976–1980

Background

By 1976, as was shown in the preceding chapter, the Japanese had made substantial progress in considerably narrowing the technology gap between local producers and the world leaders in the area of computing and electronic devices. In part this was attributable to the government policies and measures which were analysed. In 1975, however, an event occurred that was to be the proximate cause of the establishment of a new MITI-initiated research project with some fundamentally novel features. A senior member of NTT visited IBM in the United States and was shown what he thought to be a one-megabit VLSI chip which allegedly would form the basis of IBM's next series of computers, codenamed 'Future System'. On his return to Japan news of this event spread rapidly. Eventually MITI's Machinery and Information Industries Bureau (which was established in 1973, partly with the purpose of bringing together machinery and information technologies) took the initiative in setting up a special committee under the auspices of the Japan Electronic Industries Development Association (JEIDA). This committee examined the state and expected future importance of VLSI technology and recommended the establishment of the VLSI Research Project, 1976–80.

Foreigners' conventional wisdom regarding the VLSI project

The conventional wisdom held by foreigners regarding both the VLSI project and the other MITI-initiated research projects is well summarized in the conclusions drawn from hearings held by United States congressional subcommittees into the question of Japanese cooperative research. The 'hearings were prompted by repeated accounts in the Nation's newspapers and trade journals regarding recent Japanese technical successes, particularly in microelectronics where collective research supported by the government is said to have greatly aided the Japanese efforts'.[1] On the basis of these hearings, which were held in 1983, D. Walgren, Chairman of the Subcommittee on Science, Research and Technology, and A. Gore, Chairman of the Subcommittee on Investigations and Oversight of the US

House of Representatives, summarized the conclusions that had been reached in a report to D. Fuqua, Chairman of the House Committee on Science and Technology. The hearings were concerned with two specific questions: did Japanese companies benefit from the MITI-initiated cooperative research projects?; were US companies inhibited from enjoying similar benefits as a result of the US anti-trust legislation? While the second question will not be discussed further here, both the first question and the answer given to it are pertinent as an indication of a common non-Japanese conception of the way in which research is undertaken in the cooperative research projects and of the consequences of these projects.

Regarding the reasons for the Japanese performance in the world market, the report noted that 'the Subcommittees have concluded that the Japanese successes in technology development and international competition are the result of many factors, including government policies, the workforce, management styles, and Japanese national goals' (p. 3). With regard to government policy in Japan it was argued that 'MITI has been successful in organizing large-scale R & D efforts. During the 1970s, the most successful of these was MITI's VLSI circuit program . . . MITI funding for the research effort amounted to better than 41 per cent of the total cost of the venture. The success of the effort is evidenced [by the fact that] by the end of 1982, Japanese firms held 66 per cent of the world market for the then state-of-the-art 64K RAM microchip' (p. 7). Elsewhere, the report was even more explicit regarding the cause of the Japanese success in this area: 'In the semiconductor industry, *coordinated research* (partially underwritten by the Japanese government) has given Japanese companies a major share of the world market in 64K RAM microchips' (p. 1, emphasis added).

There are two implicit assumptions behind statements such as these. The first is that through the MITI-initiated research projects competing Japanese firms were able to cooperate to a significant extent. The second is that this cooperation resulted in a more favourable state of affairs for the Japanese electronics industry than would have occurred in the absence of these projects. Both these assumptions must be subjected to closer scrutiny since it was shown earlier in the preceding chapter that the major MITI-initiated projects in the computer and electronic devices areas from 1962 to 1976 (including the FONTAC, VHSCS, 3.5 Generation, and PIPS projects) involved very little *research* cooperation between the participating Japanese companies, *at least insofar as this refers to the joint generation and sharing of technological knowledge.* Was this also the case in the VLSI Project?

The establishment of the VLSI Project

It is clear that the 'IBM-factor', that is the perceived threat from IBM as the dominant player in the international computer industry, helped to galvanize a significant degree of solidarity and cooperation in Japan. It was obvious that Japanese computer producers were under far greater competitive pressure from IBM than they were from each other. The dominance of IBM therefore helped to create the conditions for a closer degree of cooperation between the Japanese companies. At the same time, both MITI officials and the companies were not willing to see all their hard efforts at catching-up undermined.

Although VLSI technology represented the latest technical advance in an approach to microelectronics that went back to the development of the integrated circuit, it constituted an important breakthrough which had to be mastered by Japanese companies involved in electronics. As Rosenberg and Steinmüller (1982, p. 180) note: 'It is our contention that, while VLSI represents a dramatic step forward in chip complexity, it is fundamentally a step within the parameters of the existing IC (integrated-circuit) industry; this new technology is governed by a similar set of parameters and cost factors. In the IC industry both the cost of devices and their performance have changed dramatically over the life cycle of individual products and with the advent of new product types. The primary factor responsible for these changes in cost and performance has been the process technology underlying IC production.' Not only was it necessary for Japanese companies to master VLSI technology, including process technology, but also there was a need for speed in achieving this. A significantly widening gap with IBM might result in hysteresis, a loss in market share which could not easily be regained once the gap was later eliminated. This need for speed was a further factor promoting a substantial degree of inter-firm cooperation.

The economies of joint research

Although unprecedented in Japan, a number of people on the JEIDA VLSI committee argued that if the twin objectives of mastering VLSI technology, and of doing so within a short period of time, were to be achieved, it was desirable to establish joint research facilities with researchers drawn from the participating companies and from MITI's Electrotechnical Laboratory. In theory, four alternative options, or a combination of them, existed: first, government could adopt a hands-off policy, leaving the companies to choose and finance their own responses to the VLSI revolution; secondly, MITI could opt for the isolated in-house research alternative whereby it subsidized VLSI research undertaken in the companies without any attempt to define or coordinate the research activities; thirdly, MITI could choose the coordinated in-house research option involving the subsidization and coordination of research undertaken in the companies (such as was done in all the previous MITI-initiated research projects in the computing and devices areas from FONTAC to the 3.5 Generation and PIPS projects);

finally, MITI could insist on the establishment of joint research in joint research facilities as a *quid pro quo* for subsidies being granted. The proponents of the fourth option included Professor Shoji Tanaka of the Applied Physics Department of Tokyo University, an influential, if at that time not widely known, member of the committee.

Those supporting the fourth option argued that it was the most efficient way of achieving the objectives. Although there is no evidence that they put it this way, the reasoning behind their preference may be analysed in terms of the *economies of joint research*. These economies, *which are realizable only under the fourth option*, include the following:

(a) *Avoidance of duplication in research* MITI (and possibly also the Ministry of Finance) had long been concerned to avoid the duplication of research effort. As Suzumura and Okuno-Fujiwara (1987, p. 63) note: 'The Law on Research Association of Mining and Manufacturing Technology was passed in 1961, which was meant to avoid unnecessary duplication of funds and researchers, which would occur unless research activities were coordinated by government intermediation, and promoted cooperative research in frontier technologies by giving tax benefits.' It is likely that the motivation behind this law was the same as that which led to the choice of the third option mentioned above, namely coordinated in-house research, as the basis for the MITI-initiated research projects in the field of computing and electronic devices from the FONTAC project in 1962 until 1976 when the VLSI Project began.

However, a number of points should be noted in connection with attempts to avoid research duplication. The first is that it is highly probable that such attempts will be more successful in the case of joint research in joint research facilities than in that of coordinated in-house research. The reason is that in the former case there is a more efficient flow of information between researchers as a result of physical proximity and significantly reduced company-imposed restrictions on inter-researcher communication. Accordingly, it is to be expected that greater economies resulting from the avoidance of research duplication will be realized where there is joint research undertaken in joint research facilities. The second point to note is that there are important factors constraining the extent of such economies. These follow from strategic decisions made by the participating firms to safeguard their competitive position by ensuring that they have the necessary in-house capabilities in areas which they judge to be of central importance. Firms will accordingly undertake their own research in these areas, even where the research theme has been allocated to another firm participating in the government-initiated project. This will increase the extent of effective duplication.

(b) *Blending of firm-specific distinctive competences* Although actually or potentially competing firms, such as those which participated in the VLSI project, operate in similar environments structured by the product and factor markets in which they operate, they are characterized by an important degree of idiosyncrasy as a result of the unique technologies and forms of organization which they generate in response to their internal and external circumstances. Accordingly, such firms exhibit distinctive competences which may provide the basis for important economies at the same time, ironically, as they constrain the possibilities for joint research. An example of economies realized through the blending of distinctive competences comes from the cooperation referred to above between Fujitsu and Hitachi in Nippon Peripherals Ltd set up in the early 1970s under MITI's administrative guidance. Although as was noted earlier the activities of this company related to a relatively small and specialized area, the joint research which it carried out was judged to have produced important benefits. As Taiyu Kobayashi, Chairman of the Board of Fujitsu from 1981, later reflected: 'I think there were definite benefits obtained from having engineers and technical people from different companies working side by side. Coming from different environments and holding different views, they experienced a cross-fertilization of ideas that gave rise to new concepts and approaches to problems.' The benefits resulting from the blending of distinctive competences were felt to be particularly important in Japan where the institution of lifetime employment limits inter-firm labour mobility and therefore the ability of companies to learn from the experiences of other companies. 'Because Japanese companies have a lifetime employment system, once an employee joins a corporation, his chances of ever getting an inside view of another company are practically nil. In Hitachi, because they are involved in a wide range of enterprises from heavy electrical equipment to semiconductors, employees have greater opportunity than we [in Fujitsu] to move to different divisions and be stimulated by a new perspective. They do not ordinarily, however, have an opportunity to see how things work outside the Hitachi Group' (T. Kobayashi, 1986, pp. 97–8).

However, while the existence of distinctive competences provides a source of potential benefit from joint research cooperation, it also limits the possibilities of such cooperation. As Michiyuki Uenohara (1985, p. 140), an Executive Vice President of NEC, has noted: 'Even in Japan, cooperation among competing companies is almost impossible as technical development moves closer to product levels. This is not only due to business competition, but also due to differences in fine details of process technology, which has been accumulated for many years and integrated into [the individual company's] major automation systems.'

(c) *Pooling of information about VLSI technology* Not only may competing firms benefit from blending their distinctive competences in the case of joint research, but they may also gain from sharing their information relating to VLSI technologies. In a world of imperfect information, where knowledge is not evenly distributed among firms, important benefits may derive from a pooling of information. Furthermore, the international stock of knowledge may be more efficiently searched.

(d) *Creating 'industrial system coherence' in a more rigorous way* As will be shown later in an evaluation of the VLSI project, there is some evidence to suggest that the joint research option may be more efficient than the other three options in developing effective information flows between the complementary user and supplier firms that are part of the industrial system. This evidence is based partly on the role that firms such as Nikon and Canon came to play as suppliers of VLSI equipment following their participation as subcontractors, rather than member firms, in the VLSI Project.

(e) *Enhancing research competition between the member firms* Particularly in Japan, where company researchers do not entirely lose their corporate identity even when they are doing joint research with members of other companies in joint research facilities, it may be that the closer proximity afforded by joint research encourages a greater degree of research competition than would occur under the other three options. As will be seen later, this is likely to have been the case in the first three of the joint laboratories in the VLSI Project, each of which was dominated by one of three competing companies. Competition between the laboratories was enhanced by the fact that the three laboratories had the same research objectives.

(f) *Sharing of expensive, non-divisible, equipment* Although, in theory, it is possible for either competing or non-competing firms to reach agreement over the sharing of such equipment in the absence of joint research between them, it is likely that the costs of reaching a sharing agreement will be lower and the efficiency in sharing greater in the case of joint research in joint research facilities. A case in point is the use by some of the VLSI Project researchers of synchrotron orbital radiation equipment in the University of Tokyo.

The above economies of joint research have two important further implications. First, they imply that there will be an increase in the 'socialization' of technological knowledge over and above what would exist in the case of the first three options (that is, the hands-off, isolated in-house research, and coordinated in-house research options). In other words, a greater proportion of the total stock of technological knowledge will be in the semi-public sphere. This knowledge, however, remains semi-public, rather than public, because it will be shared by the members of the joint research project, while non-members will have only relatively restricted access. In theory, as noted earlier, particularly in *itakuhi* projects, where formally the firms undertake contract research with MITI retaining the intellectual property rights, government should be able to make use of the greater socialization of knowledge by diffusing more widely the project-generated patents and know-how that it owns. Our earlier analyses of the diffusion of MITI-owned patents and know-how, however, suggest that in practice this way of spreading socialized knowledge tends to be limited. An important factor constraining the diffusion of this knowledge is the extent of tacit knowledge which cannot readily and at reasonable cost be made explicit and which therefore limits MITI's ability to effectively appropriate the knowledge which it legally owns. Such tacit knowledge therefore increases the firm's effective control over the knowledge which it has created and consequently limits the spread of this knowledge to other firms.

The second implication is that, to the extent that economies of joint research are realized, there will be an increase in the rate of technical change. In some cases this additional speed may provide important further benefits. In the case of VLSI technology in the mid 1970s, for example, it was suggested earlier that the Japanese computer companies had a need for speed in order to avoid losing market share to IBM, which might for numerous reasons be difficult to regain even when the technology gap had once again been closed.

The preference expressed by Shoji Tanaka and some of his colleagues on the JEIDA VLSI committee for the fourth option, joint research in joint research facilities, may therefore be justified in terms of the social benefits derived from the economies of joint research. From the point of view of the Japanese companies, however, more concerned with private than with social costs and benefits, the joint research option was unattractive and they expressed their strong opposition to this unprecedented form of research organization.

Company opposition to joint research

It is clear that at the outset the companies were strongly opposed to the undertaking of joint research in joint research facilities. The view of the majority of companies[2] was expressed in a detailed interview held by the present author with a director of one of the VLSI Project's joint research laboratories. The following extracts make this view clear: 'Before the VLSI Project there was MITI support for "next generation" computers, but there was no joint laboratory established. Companies never liked joint laboratories – they were forced.'; 'The companies did not want to have joint laboratories. We were forced'; 'The companies wanted as little money as possible to go to the joint laboratories [arguing that the greatest possible proportion of VLSI Project funds should be allocated to in-house research in the companies]'; 'We were all forced by government to cooperate and had no other alternative.'

While a deeper analysis of the sharing of technological knowledge by companies is postponed to the concluding chapter, the reasons behind their opposition to joint research in joint research facilities may be briefly mentioned here. First and most importantly, the companies were both actual and potential competitors in many product areas influenced by VLSI technology. Secondly, and related to the first point, private firms have a tendency to attempt to privatize those parts of their stock of knowledge which are expected to have a direct effect on their competitiveness, market share and, ultimately, profit. It was felt that the undertaking of joint research in joint research facilities would increase the chances of leakage of this portion of their knowledge stock. Thirdly, the participating companies had never before experienced such joint research activities and were still wary of the consequences. For these reasons the companies opposed joint research. MITI officials, however, were adamant that some degree of joint research was a *sine qua non*; accordingly, the companies were 'forced' to comply, that is if they wanted to enjoy the financial and other benefits of participation, they were required to accept a degree of joint research in joint research facilities.

The structuring of the joint laboratories

Structuring laboratories 1, 2 and 3

In view of the opposition to joint research, it would not have been possible for a joint research agreement to be concluded by the companies themselves acting alone. For a joint research agreement to evolve, mediation was necessary by an agency that was neutral with respect to the interests of the competing participating firms, an agency that would also effectively limit leakages of knowledge undesired by the company possessing the knowledge. It was MITI, with its long history of involvement in the computer and electronic devices industry, which played this role. The task of negotiating the establishment of the VLSI Technology Research Association was allocated to Yasuo Tarui of ETL and Masato Nebashi of MITI.

From the outset, a difficult problem confronted Tarui and Nebashi. As a director of one of the joint laboratories, himself a member of one of the participating companies, later recalled in an interview with the present author: 'The most difficult situation . . . was at the time of the start-up of the joint laboratories . . . I was a member of the committee planning joint research a year before start-up. There were many serious, bad [i.e. rivalrous] and good discussions. But, with the support of MITI, Mr Tarui and Mr Nebashi, both very experienced people, tried to have joint laboratories, even against the companies' wishes . . . We didn't like to open up our firm's technologies . . . The discussions were very complicated.'

Tarui's problem was to establish viable criteria that would enable him to distinguish between research that the companies could, with persuasion and the incentive of subsidized financing, agree to do jointly, and that which they could not. As Tarui later noted in an interview with the present author, one way of establishing joint research 'is to undertake new areas of research, largely unrelated to research already being done in the companies. They then feel freer to join.' The difficulty that he faced, however, was that the participating companies were already undertaking VLSI-related research and were keen to keep private the resulting knowledge. Eventually, Tarui 'made a slogan to distinguish between research that could be done jointly and that which could not – [in order to be done jointly, the research had to be both] "common and basic".' By 'common' Tarui meant that the technology had to be 'useful for every participant'. The reasoning behind this criterion is straightforward – only if companies have a common interest in the technology will they be willing to consider developing it jointly. The requirement that the research be 'basic' is, however, more complicated. In several parts of the interview, Tarui attempted to clarify what he meant by 'basic' research which could be undertaken jointly in joint research facilities: 'Basic research does not depend on existing technical know-how. The most basic form of research is mathematics – there is no need for know-how'; 'It is not possible to have joint research aimed at developing a particular [commercializable] electronic device. Research on an actual device is not basic'; 'An analogy for "basic" is the basement of a house ... For example, microfabrication is important for VLSI. So we developed microfabrication equipment [in some of the joint laboratories]'; the 'common and basic' criteria were for Tarui 'a slogan for persuasion which helped me to organize the joint laboratories'.

In passing it is worth comparing Tarui's two criteria, generated as a pragmatic response to a MITI-imposed need to identify areas for joint research, with criteria that have been developed elsewhere in order to define fields for government-sponsored research. Reflecting on the successful US experience in the areas of aviation and agriculture, for example, Eads and Nelson (1986, p. 243) argue that 'the governmental R & D support in these fields had focused on the development (and, in the agricultural case, the dissemination) of generic technologies – that is, technologies not associated with particular proprietary product designs. The commercialization decisions involving specific products were left to private industry.' In Britain a similar search for criteria to identify a field where private companies, assisted by state funding, could join in the quest to exploit scientific knowledge occurred in the establishment of the new Centre for Exploitation of Science and Technology (announced in November 1987). The centre was set up as a result of a report written by a working party established by the Advisory Council for Applied Research and Development (subsequently renamed the Advisory Council for Science and Technology). As Williams (1988) notes, the report defined an 'exploitable area of science' as one 'in which the body of scientific understanding supports a generic (or enabling) area of technological knowledge; a body of knowledge from which many specific products and processes may emerge.' The common basis which emerges from these three pragmatic attempts made in Japan, the United States and Britain to establish grounds for joint science and technology research is obvious.

Far less obvious, however, is the way in which the common definition should be applied in any particular case. The problem, of course, arises from the difficulty in establishing when a generic technology ceases to be that and becomes associated with particular proprietary product and process designs and commercialization decisions. As the Director of one of the joint laboratories in the VLSI Project observed, 'there are numerous process technologies [in the case of VLSI] – it is very difficult to define what is common and basic, and what is practical.' Furthermore, it is by no means obvious that firms always have an interest in sharing generic technological knowledge. The decision to share will be based on corporate calculations of the costs and benefits of sharing as compared to the alternative of in-house development of that knowledge, including amongst the possible costs the consequences for company competitiveness, market share and profits of the sharing of generic technologies. In some cases firms may well decide not to share such generic knowledge.

The difficulties quickly became apparent in the attempt to organize joint research in the VLSI Project. For example, while Tarui defined microfabrication equipment as a 'basic' or 'generic' technology, with this area therefore suitable for joint research, several of the participating companies were unwilling to undertake joint research in this field. In particular, Hitachi, Fujitsu and Toshiba, which had already embarked on research on microfabrication equipment, were reluctant to mix their researchers with those from the other two compaines. As a senior researcher from one of the firms put it: 'MITI wanted every one of the five participating companies to participate equally in all the joint laboratories. But this was difficult for Hitachi, Fujitsu and Toshiba to agree to in the case of lithographic systems. These companies wanted their laboratories to be staffed entirely by researchers from their own company. But that was impossible because MITI insisted on joint research.' Tarui acknowledged the difficulty that he confronted: 'Even in Japan it is very difficult to make a cooperative laboratory. So I had to think carefully about how to structure the joint laboratories. Too much mixing makes the companies very secretive.' The solution was to modify the extent of joint research in the first three of the six laboratories by placing each of them under the control of one of the companies (Hitachi, Fujitsu and Toshiba) and denying membership of the laboratory to researchers from the other two companies. In explaining the separation of the researchers from these three companies Tarui pointed out that they 'were already doing research on microfabrication and equipment in their laboratories. And some of this research was continued in each laboratory.' Accordingly, the first three laboratories competed with one another, concentrating largely on the design and prototype development of microfabrication equipment, such as electron beam pattern delineators, for VLSI production. However, researchers from the two remaining companies, NEC and Mitsubishi, were included in the first three laboratories although the bulk of researchers in these laboratories came from one of the three companies (Hitachi, Fujitsu and Toshiba). As a senior researcher in one of the laboratories explained, from the point of view of Hitachi, Fujitsu and Toshiba, 'Mitsubishi and NEC were not competing companies in this technical field. Even if Mitsubishi and NEC scientists took the information acquired in the joint laboratory back to their companies, this would not pose a problem [for Hitachi, Fujitsu and Toshiba] because [the former companies] did not have significant business in this field.' Furthermore, there is an important degree of tacit knowledge involved in laboratory research. This means that only a smaller subset of the total stock of knowledge generated in the research is embodied in the reports, papers, patents, prototypes, etc. which emerge from the research. In turn this implies that the knowledge acquired by a company from joint laboratory research is directly related to the number of researchers it has in that laboratory. Since the greatest number of researchers in the first three joint laboratories were from the companies that directed these laboratories, this meant that these companies were able to effectively appropriate the bulk of the research carried out in 'their' laboratory.[3]

It is clear from the present account that the composition of the first three laboratories was significantly influenced by the underlying competitive relationship in this technology field between Hitachi, Fujitsu and Toshiba. The composition of these laboratories implied consequently a significant limitation on the joint generation and sharing of technological knowledge between the researchers from these three companies. In turn this limited the realization of some of the economies of joint research. These conclusions emerge clearly from an interview between the author and the Director of one of the joint research laboratories:

Director: Scientists from the joint laboratories were free to visit any of the laboratories and attend their meetings. But in the first two years of the four-year project researchers [in the first three joint laboratories] were very nervous about sharing information because we brought our own company technology. After two years the information flow increased because the advance of technology was so rapid; almost all the technology was new after two years.
Fransman: How did firms know that they were getting a fair exchange of information from the other firms represented in the joint laboratory, given that each firm had an incentive to minimize information outflow and maximize information inflow?
Director: This evaluation is always difficult, but we are scientists and engineers

and to some extent we can judge when they are being open with their information – but not quantitatively.

Fransman: Was there complete sharing of information between the first three of the joint laboratories?

Director: It's hard to answer that. In the last two years of the project, researchers in each of the laboratories were rushing to complete their own versions of the electron beam machine. People were interested in information from the other competing laboratories, but this was not that important for their own work, since their work was to produce their own kind of machine. Each of the laboratories produced a different kind of electron beam machine. The design concept of the machines was different but they were all used for the same purpose in the microfabrication process. The three laboratories competed, but they did not have the time to be interested about what was going on in the other laboratories – they were preoccupied with their own research.

Therefore, to summarize, the composition and functioning of the first three laboratories were influenced by the competitive relationship between the three main competing firms in the field of VLSI microfabrication equipment. In turn this limited the realization of some of the economies of joint research. The main economy which probably was realized in these laboratories was enhanced research competition since, as noted, each laboratory developed a different design and prototype electron beam machine. It is possible that the close proximity of the three laboratories increased the sense of competition between them, thus increasing the rate of technical change compared to what would have occurred had the research been done in-house. However, the separation of researchers from three of the main companies which had already embarked on substantial research into microfabrication technology must have restricted the realization of some of the other economies of joint research. Thus it is possible that there was more duplication than would have resulted if the first three laboratories had been merged. Conversely, however, it might be possible to argue that the separation of the first three laboratories that actually occurred, together with competition between them, resulted in a greater degree of diversity in the design of the electron beam machines, therefore increasing the chances of innovative breakthroughs. Nevertheless, it seems clear that greater advantages from the blending of firm-specific distinctive competences would probably have resulted from closer interaction between the researchers of Hitachi, Fujitsu and Toshiba. This follows from the fact that these researchers had done most work on microfabrication equipment. Although there must have been some gain from the sharing of distinctive competences with researchers from NEC and Mitsubishi, it is likely that the gain would have been greater if members of the five firms had interacted. Similarly, it is probable that economies from the pooling of information would also have been greater. It is also possible that there would have been greater industrial system coherence, a point that is taken up again later in the evaluation of the VLSI Project.

Lithography research in laboratories 1, 2 and 3

As Tarui and Takeishi (1981) point out in a summary of the technical achievements of the VLSI Project, five research areas were selected for examination within the joint laboratories. These were '(1) fine-line lithography systems, (2) crystal technology, (3) dry etching and processing technologies, (4) diagnostic techniques and (5) basic device structures.' The interrelationships between these areas is shown in Fig. 3.1 taken from their paper.

Tarui and Takeishi note that 'Most importantly, much effort was made on lithography, in particular *electron-beam technology*, because it *was recognized to be a key for VLSI fabrication*' (p. 6, emphasis added). At the time of the VLSI Project three competing lithographic technologies were in existence: photolithography, electron-beam lithography and X-ray lithography.[4] While photolithography was most widely used and was being improved in numerous ways such as the replacement of contact lithography by projection lithography, its effectiveness was felt to be constrained by an inherent limitation. Since the wavelength of light is greater than the wavelength of electron beams and X-rays, it was felt that the latter two technologies would ultimately be preferable for the production of integrated circuits at sub-micron levels. It was for this reason that the MITI officials involved in the VLSI Project wanted to concentrate on these two technologies, with particular emphasis on electron beam technology. As Oldham (1980), writing at around the time of the VLSI Project, explained: 'Electron-beam lithography is an older and maturer technology, having its basis in electron microscopy. Actually a system for electron-beam lithography is much like a scanning electron microscope. A fine beam of electrons scans the wafer to expose an electron-sensitive resist in the desired areas.' At the time, however, there were a number of drawbacks with electron-beam lithography resulting in its cost-ineffectiveness. 'Although impressive results have been demonstrated, the application of electron-beam lithography is limited by its present high cost. The machines are expensive (roughly 1 million dollars per machine), and because the electron beam must scan the wafer rather than exposing it all at once the time needed to put the pattern on the wafer is quite long.' Nevertheless, although at that stage electron-beam lithography was not used for direct writing in the wafer-fabrication process as a result of the high cost, it was routinely used for the production of photolithographic masks. 'With the aid of the electron-beam method it is possible to eliminate two photographic-reduction steps and write the pattern directly on the mask from the information stored in the computer memory. Masks can thereby be created in a few hours after the design is finished.' It was therefore concluded that 'The advantages of higher resolution, simplicity of manufacture and shorter production time may well result in the complete conversion of the industry to electron-beam mask-making.' (See Fig. 3.1 for the role of these

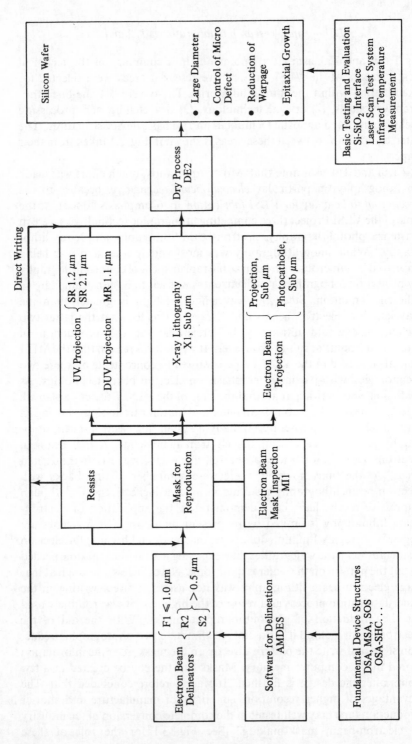

Fig. 3.1 Research areas in the VLSI Project's joint laboratories (*Source:* Tarui and Takeishi, 1981).

technologies in the VLSI production process.) According to Oldham, writing in 1980, in the field of electron-beam lithography the 'rate of progress... is rapid... and more practical systems are clearly on the way... Gradually, as the cost decreases, electron-beam lithography will be introduced directly into the fabrication of wafers, and a new generation of even more complex microelectronic circuits will be born' (p. 61).

As a result of the expected future improvements in electron-beam lithography,[5] both absolutely and relative, in particular, to photolithography, MITI officials involved in the VLSI Project decided to prioritize electron-beam technology. However, this did not mean that photolithography was ignored. One example is research that was done in the third joint laboratory by researchers from Toshiba and Nikon (Nippon Kogaku K. K.) on an optical step-and-repeat machine. Although Nikon was not a member of the VLSI Research Association, it acted as a subcontractor for the joint research on this machine. Interestingly, in this particular case discussions between Toshiba and Nikon predated the VLSI Project. However, the research was not undertaken earlier as a result of the uncertainty surrounding the future of photolithographic systems. It would appear, therefore, that in this case availability of MITI funding plus, perhaps, the existence of a large national research project in which alternative technologies could be explored, resulted in additional benefits in the form of an optical step-and-repeat machine that would not otherwise at this time have been produced in Japan.[6]

Sigurdson (1986, p. 85) makes the point that while the companies that were members of the VLSI Research Association were self-sufficient in the skills necessary for electron-beam lithography, this was not the case in photolithography:

[It is important to realize that photolithography] is a very special technological field for the major electrical companies. Optical engineers are needed but they are not available from the universities. Optical engineers in Japan are in fact only found in optical companies. Consequently, the integrated circuit-makers do not have easy access to optical engineers and have been and still are dependent on optical companies. This situation should be compared with the situation for electrical equipment like testers and electron beam lithography equipment, where the integrated circuit-makers have enough technical skills in their own divisions. This is particularly true for Toshiba and Hitachi and on this basis the companies are likely to become technologically very strong in electron lithography in the future.

In view of the lack of optical engineering capabilities in the major Japanese electronics companies and the significant degree of uncertainty which surrounded the future of photolighography technology, it is possible that the VLSI Project played an important role in facilitating the blending of distinctive competences between firms such as Toshiba, Hitachi and Fujitsu on the one hand and Nikon and Canon which possessed the optical expertise on the other. By providing the conditions that at this time were necessary for research into optical projection systems, including subsidized finance and an efficient flow of information between the would-be users of these systems, namely the integrated circuit-making companies, and the optical companies that produced them, it may be that the VLSI Project significantly accelerated the domestic production of photolithographic equipment. At the same time, as Sigurdson suggests, the VLSI Project might have contributed to the creation of a more effective inter-firm industrial system linking the users and suppliers of integrated circuit equipment.[7]

Structuring laboratories 4, 5 and 6

Although research on electron-beam lithography, photolithography and X-ray lithography systems was undertaken in the first three joint laboratories, and therefore fell under Tarui's classification of common and basic technologies, we saw earlier that, at least in the first two years of the four-year VLSI Project, Hitachi, Fujitsu and Toshiba were reluctant to share fully their technological knowledge in this area. As a result, their researchers were separated in the first three laboratories although they did undertake joint research with a significantly smaller number of researchers from the remaining two companies, NEC and Mitsubishi, which were not strongly competitive in this research area. While there was a measure of research cooperation *within* each of these three laboratories, there was strong competition *between* them to produce lithography equipment on the basis of different designs. This competition was a manifestation of the underlying competitive relationship in this field between Hitachi, Fujitsu and Toshiba.

In view of these limitations on a complete sharing of knowledge between researchers in the first three laboratories, and the degree of competition between them, it is important to note that there was a significantly greater sharing between researchers in the fourth, fifth and sixth laboratories. As the Director of one of the project's joint laboratories put it, harking back to Tarui's twin criteria for joint research: 'In the case, for example, of crystallography all the companies had an interest in this field, and the research was basic; therefore they shared. In three of the laboratories, therefore, there was an equal sharing – crystal technology, processing technologies (oxidation, diffusion, etching, etc), device technology – that is, in the fourth, fifth and sixth laboratories.' Further evidence in support of this conclusion will be derived from an analysis of joint patents as an indicator of joint research and knowledge sharing.

It may therefore be concluded that the 'propensity to share technological knowledge' was unequal over the five research topics selected for the joint research laboratories: (a) fine-line lithography systems (laboratories 1, 2 and 3); (b) crystal technology (laboratory 4), (c) dry-etching and processing technologies (laboratory 5); (d) diagnostic techniques (laboratory 5); and (e) basic device structures (laboratory 6). This conclusion is examined further in the following section with the aid of joint patents.

Joint generation and sharing of knowledge in the VLSI joint laboratories: a patent-based analysis

The number of joint patents, that is patents held by the member of more than one company, emanating from the VLSI Project has been widely used to evaluate some of the benefits of this project. This is partly as a result of the prominence given to this statistic in Tarui's (1982) widely read book on the VLSI Project. Tarui's graph on patents is reproduced in Fig. 3.2. As can be seen from Fig. 3.2, in 59 per cent of the patents there was only one patent-holder; in 25 per cent of cases there was more than one researcher from the same company; while in 16 per cent of the patent, the patent-holders were from different companies, that is the patents were joint in the sense used in the present book. According to Tarui the 16 per cent figure is significant. As he explained in an interview with the present author: 'A patent does not usually result from cooperation. It is usually the result of the brain of a single person . . . Therefore 16 per cent is significant.'

A careful disaggregated analysis of joint patents provides an important indication of the extent of the joint generation and sharing of knowledge in

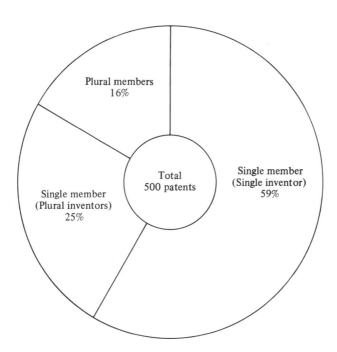

Fig. 3.2   Joint patents in the VLSI Project (*Source:* Tarui, 1982).

the VLSI joint laboratories, where these activities took place, and between whom. It is, however, necessary to be cautious about the use of this indicator. Joint patents provide a measure only of the kind of research activity that leads to the creation of patentable knowledge. The patent data obviously do not capture the extent of joint research which did not result in knowledge for which patents could be applied. However, it is reasonable to assume that joint patent data provide an indication of the extent of joint research between researchers from different companies.[8] More significantly, however, it is important to note that joint patent data do not adequately reflect the extent of other forms of joint research which do not usually result in patents, for example a more casual and shorter-term sharing of ideas, such as results from *sake*-time conversation, may be a cumulatively important source of cross-fertilization of ideas and represent a significant benefit from joint research in joint research facilities. It must therefore be kept in mind in using joint patent data that the whole story of joint research is not being told.

Despite these reservations, the joint patent data do reveal important features of the research undertaken in the VLSI joint research laboratories. This emerges from an analysis of joint patents in Table 3.1, produced for the first time here.[9] In Table 3.1 information is provided on 71 out of the total of 75 joint patents that have emerged from the VLSI Project.

Laboratories 1, 2 and 3: fine-line lithography systems

It was seen earlier that researchers from Hitachi, Fujitsu and Toshiba were separated in the first three laboratories. In these laboratories the majority of researchers came from one of these companies as did the director of the laboratory. This was taken to be a manifestation of the underlying competitive relationship between these three companies.

Further evidence in support of this conclusion comes from Table 3.1. A number of relevant points emerge from this table. First, there were a total of twenty-four joint patents from laboratories 1, 2 and 3. Of these only one was a joint patent between two of the main competing firms' – a joint patent between researchers from Hitachi and Toshiba in laboratory 3 under the control of Toshiba. (Although this contradicts the statement that the researchers from the three companies were separated, it appears to be the only exception.) In other words, twenty-three out of the total of twenty-four joint patents from the first three joint laboratories involved in research on fine-line lithography systems, or 96 per cent, were between firms that were not strongly competing in this particular field. This supports the earlier conclusion that the realization of economies of joint research was constrained by the structuring of the first three laboratories, which itself reflected the underlying competitive relations between the three major firms in this field.

Table 3.1. *Joint patents in the VLSI joint laboratories*

	Laboratories						Total Labs. 1–3	Total Labs. 1–6
	1	2	3	4	5	6		
Firms								
F–H	0	0	0	0	0	0	0	0
F–M	0	0	0	0	0	0	0	0
F–T	0	0	0	0	2	0	0	0
F–ETL	0	0	0	0	0	0	0	0
F–N	0	0	0	1	0	1	0	2
H–M	5	0	0	1	0	0	5	6
H–T	0	0	1	3	2	0	1	6
H–ETL	0	0	0	0	2	0	0	2
H–N	2	0	0	0	0	0	2	2
M–T	0	0	14	0	0	0	14	14
M–ETL	0	0	0	0	1	0	0	1
M–N	0	1	0	0	6	4	1	11
T–ETL	0	0	0	0	0	1	0	1
T–N	0	0	1	1	0	2^a	1	4
ETL–N	0	0	0	0	0	6	0	6
Total	7	1	16	12	13	14	24	57
H–N–T	0	0	0	2	0	0	0	2
H–F–T	0	0	0	2	0	0	0	2
H–F–T–N	0	0	0	2	0	0	0	2

Key:

F	Fujitsu	N	NEC
H	Hitachi	T	Toshiba
M	Mitsubishi	ETL	Electrotechnical Laboratory (MITI)

Note:
[a] Joint patents also held by ETL.

Secondly, the twenty-four patents from laboratories 1, 2 and 3 appeared in three main clusters: fourteen between Toshiba and Mitsubishi researchers in laboratory 3, five between Hitachi and Mitsubishi in laboratory 1, and two between Hitachi and NEC again in laboratory 1. Outside these clusters there were only three other joint patents: one (mentioned above) between Hitachi and Toshiba in laboratory 3, one between Toshiba and NEC also in laboratory 3, and one between NEC and Mitsubishi in laboratory 2. This tends to support the conclusion that in the first three laboratories most of the joint research was undertaken by researchers from companies that were not competing strongly in this particular technology field. (It will be recalled here that at this time research on fine-line lithography systems was least developed in NEC and Mitsubishi.) Further

Table 3.2. *Ranking of firms in terms of number of joint patents held with one other firm in the first three laboratories of the VLSI joint laboratories*

Firm	Number of joint patents
Mitsubishi + 1	20
Toshiba + 1	16
Hitachi + 1	8
NEC + 1	4
Fujitsu + 1	0
ETL + 1	0

evidence in support of this conclusion comes from Table 3.2 which ranks the firms in terms of the number of joint patents they held with one other company in the first three laboratories.

From Table 3.2 it can be seen that Mitsubishi had the largest number of joint patents, namely twenty. Although Toshiba ranked second with sixteen joint patents, fourteen of these were with Mitsubishi, which is in line with the general conclusion being drawn here. Similarly, Hitachi which ranked third with eight joint patents, had five of these with Mitsubishi and two with NEC, another relatively non-competing company. From these data it would appear that Mitsubishi, which, it will be recalled, was originally excluded from plans for the VLSI Project on the grounds of its relative weakness in this area, was in the best position for something of a 'free ride' by taking advantage of joint research with the stronger companies. The benefits from Mitsubishi's private point of view are obvious and must have vindicated the company's decision to use the political muscle of the Mitsubishi group in order to gain access to the VLSI Project. Conversely, the 'free rider' problem may have been viewed as a cost of participating in the VLSI Project by the stronger companies, to the extent that the access that Mitsubishi obtained to VLSI technology was used by it to the competitive detriment of the former companies. From a social point of view, however, this data provides some evidence of a beneficial diffusion of technological knowledge from the stronger Japanese companies in this field of technology to the weaker ones *within* the confines of the VLSI Project, with the possible important consequences of a strengthening of the Japanese industrial electronics sector as a whole.

Furthermore, from Table 3.3, which is presented and discussed further below, it can be seen that while there were eight joint patents involving researchers from different laboratories, there were no cases of inter-laboratory joint patents for the first three laboratories. This reinforces the earlier conclusion that competition, rather than cooperation, characterized the dominant mode of interaction between laboratories 1, 2 and 3. On the

Table 3.3. *Inter-laboratory joint patents in the VLSI joint laboratories*

Organizations holding joint patents	Laboratories involved	Number of joint patents
NEC + ETL	planning office	3
Hitachi + ETL	1 and 6	2
Toshiba + Hitachi + Fujitsu	4 and 5	1
Mitsubishi + ETL	4 and planning office	1
Mitsubishi + NEC + ETL	5 and planning office	1
Total:		8

one hand, therefore, the joint generation and sharing of knowledge between researchers from the five participating companies was limited by the composition of each of the first three laboratories which restricted such interactions between members of the three strongest competing companies. On the other hand, the joint generation and sharing of knowledge as a result of interactions across these three laboratories was significantly constrained by the requirement that each laboratory work on different designs of lithographic equipment that would perform essentially the same functions. While the joint patent data analysed here provide strong evidence for these limitations on sharing – evidence which further supports the quotations given earlier – it should nevertheless be reiterated that this does not rule out the existence of more casual and shorter-term forms of joint research which may have constituted an important input into some of the research.

Laboratories 4, 5 and 6

A number of illuminating observations may be made on the basis of the analysis of joint patents in the fourth, fifth and sixth laboratories contained in Table 3.1. The first observation is that there was a significantly greater degree of joint generation and sharing of knowledge in these laboratories than in the first three laboratories. While in the first three laboratories there were twenty-four joint patents, the figure was thirty-three for the second three. Furthermore, the holding of joint patents is more widespread, involving research cooperation between a greater number of combinations of companies. Thus while only six of the cells are filled in the case of the first three laboratories, the number is fourteen for the second three. There is also less of a clustering of joint patents in the second three laboratories. From this it may be concluded that the 'propensity to share technological knowledge' was greater for the research topics covered in the second three laboratories than in the first three.

Secondly, in terms of individual laboratories it was laboratory 4, which did research on crystal technology, where the propensity to share technological knowledge was greatest. This emerges neither from the total number of joint patents in this laboratory (which totalled twelve compared to sixteen for laboratory 3, fourteen for laboratory 6, and thirteen for laboratory 5), nor from the number of cells filled in the column for laboratory 4 (four as opposed to five each for laboratories 5 and 6). Rather, the conclusion that the propensity to share technological knowledge was greatest in the case of crystal technology emerges from the significant number of patents involving researchers from three or four companies. (There were no joint patents involving researchers from all five participating companies.) In total there were six intra-laboratory joint patents (that is, with the researchers coming from the same laboratory) where the patent was held by researchers from three or four companies. All these six cases came from laboratory 4 which did research on crystal technology. In Table 3.3 information is given on inter-laboratory joint patents. From this table it can be seen that of the three joint patents that excluded ETL researchers, one involved laboratory 4. Furthermore, this was the only inter-laboratory joint patent involving researchers from more than two companies.

The propensity to share technological knowledge

Based on the above analysis of joint patent data it is possible to derive for the VLSI Project a tentative estimate of the propensity to share technological knowledge both by technology area and by firm. The propensity to share technological knowledge by technology area refers to the apparent ease with which firms are able to engage in joint research in the area, as measured by the joint patent data.

The information on joint patents from the VLSI Project suggests that the propensity to share technological knowledge by technology area must be expressed along a continuum ranging from a low to a high propensity as reflected in Fig. 3.3. This figure measures in relative terms the propensity to share technological knowledge in four technology areas relating to VLSI technology: commercializable devices; lithography equipment; dry etching and processing technologies/diagnostic techniques/basic device structures;

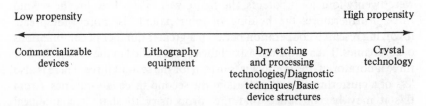

Fig. 3.3   The propensity to share technological knowledge in four technology areas relating to VLSI technology.

and crystal technology. The propensity to share knowledge in commercializable devices was very low as is evident from the fact that none of the joint research in the VLSI Project involved the production of such devices. Furthermore, as will emerge later in this chapter, none of the cooperative research projects undertaken in Japan has related to the development of commercializable devices.

There was a greater propensity to share knowledge in the area of lithography equipment compared to that of commercializable devices. However, as our earlier discussion concluded, there was a significant degree of reluctance on the part of the main competing firms to share knowledge in lithography equipment. In view of this reluctance, a compromise was necessary which resulted in an effective limitation on the joint generation and sharing of knowledge among the five participating companies within and between the first three laboratories.

On the other hand, there is evidence of a greater propensity to share knowledge in the research areas allocated to laboratories 5 and 6 (dry etching and processing technologies/diagnostic techniques/basic device structures) than in those undertaken in the first three laboratories. This evidence comes in the form of the corporate participation in the fifth and sixth laboratories and the number of cells filled in these laboratories in Table 3.1. Finally, as analysed in detail above, the propensity to share was greater in the field of crystal technology.

Working backwards, as it were, from the assumption that a firm's reluctance to share knowledge increases the greater the expected direct impact of that knowledge on the firm's competitiveness, market share and profits, it may be inferred that crystal technology has the smallest such direct impact.[10] Conversely, at the other end of the spectrum, the knowledge embodied in commercializable devices will, by definition, have an immediate effect on the firm's sales and therefore its competitiveness, etc.

In Table 3.4 information is presented on the propensity to share

Table 3.4. *Propensity to share knowledge by firms participating in the VLSI Project*

	Number of joint patents	Percentage of total two firm joint patents
Joint patents between two of the following firms: Hitachi/Fujitsu/Toshiba	8	14
Joint patents between one of the firms Hitachi/ Fujitsu/Toshiba and either NEC or Mitsubishi	28	49

Note: Total number of joint patents between two firms = 57.

knowledge by firm. As known in this table, there were eight joint patents, or 14 per cent of the total of fifty-seven patents, held by researchers from two of the three firms, Hitachi, Fujitsu and Toshiba. On the other hand, there were twenty-eight patents, or 49 per cent of the total, involving one of these three firms and either NEC or Mitsubishi. This provides strong evidence to support the conclusion that the propensity to share knowledge is greater the lower the degree of competition between the firms involved in the relationship.[11] While this is what one would expect in normal market-based relationships, this conclusion is more surprising, particularly in view of the arguments given in the United States Congressional subcommittee hearings quoted earlier, in the context of the MITI-sponsored VLSI Project. This conclusion is further supported by the fact that, as shown in Table 3.1, the firm with the largest number of joint patents with one other firm in all of the joint laboratorties was Mitsubishi with thirty-two such joint patents.

Funding the VLSI Project and the in-house laboratories NTIS and CDL

The total cost of the VLSI Project was 73.7 billion yen of which 40 per cent, or 29.1 billion, was subsidized by the government.[12] *It is extremely important to emphasize, however, that only between 15 and 20 per cent of this amount is allocated to the joint laboratories* which employed about 100 researchers from the five participating companies and MITI's Electrotechnical Laboratory.[13] *The remaining 80 to 85 per cent of the funds was allocated to research done primarily inside the individual participating companies.* Formally, the funds were allocated to two research associations, NEC–Toshiba Information Systems (NTIS), consisting of NEC and Toshiba, and Computer Development Laboratory (CDL), which included Fujitsu, Hitachi and Mitsubishi. These two groupings went back to the attempt made by MITI in the early 1970s (and analysed in detail above) to encourage closer inter-firm coordination through the formation of three pairs of companies. After Oki pulled out of mainframe computers, Mitsubishi joined Fujitsu and Hitachi in the area of IBM-compatible computers, while NEC and Toshiba concentrated on non-IBM-compatible models.

Practically all the funding that went to NTIS and CDL was allocated to research done inside the member companies under the normal conditions of commercial secrecy. There was, however, a small amount of research that was done jointly. For example, CDL bought an electron beam pattern generating machine imported from the United States. As was pointed out by a senior researcher involved in the VLSI Project in an interview with the author:

> Informant: It was better for the three companies to check jointly the capability of this machine; otherwise they would have had to buy the machine separately at high costs.

Fransman: Was there any flow of information between CDL and NTIS?
Informant: ... they had open conferences and produced thick reports. But of
course the reports did not contain all the relevant information about know-
how.

*It may therefore be concluded that the VLSI Project consisted of a combination
of what has been referred to in this book as coordinated in-house research and
joint research in joint research facilities. Although the VLSI Project has
achieved a large part of its fame as a result of its status as the first Japanese
research in joint research facilities, only a small proportion of the total
resources spent on this project was allocated to such joint research.*

An evaluation of the VLSI project

What is to be evaluated?

With regard to the evaluation exercise, the first point that must be clarified
is whether it is the effects of the VLSI Project as a whole that are to be
evaluated, or rather whether we are concerned with the feature of the
project that until 1976 was unique, namely the joint research undertaken in
joint research facilities. The failure to clarify this issue has led to a certain
amount of confusion. Thus, for example, the US Congressional hearings
referred to earlier were implicitly concerned with the latter kind of
evaluation. This conclusion follows from the concern of the Congressional
subcommittees with the implicit infringement of antitrust provisions. For
these subcommittees the problem was not simply one of subsidies being
given by the Japanese government to support R & D. Rather the issue was
the 'coordination' and research cooperation of companies that were
supposed to be competing. From this perspective it would be necessary to
evaluate the effects of research coordination/cooperation. It would be
difficult to see how research done inside the companies under normal
conditions of commercial secrecy, even though different areas of research
were allocated to each company by MITI through a process of negotiation,
would violate antitrust provisions. Accordingly, in order to address the
antitrust issue it is necessary to evaluate the costs and benefits of the joint
research done in the VLSI joint research laboratories which, as we have
seen, constituted only a relatively small proportion of the total research
done under the VLSI Project. However, this distinction was not made by
the Congressional subcommittees, nor by most other analyses of the VLSI
Project.

A critical appraisal of some attempts at an evaluation of the VLSI Project

Patents and papers as a measure of research output

A number of studies have used patents (and perhaps also research papers) as
a measure of research output. The following quotation from Suzumura and

Okuno-Fujiwara (1987, pp. 63–4) is fairly typical: 'The most visible and successful [cooperative research] association was the [VLSI] Research Association... Judging from the research output of this association as measured, for example, by the number of patents obtained, the promotion of the VLSI Research Association was a great success.'

The assumption that the success of the project may be measured by the output of patents raises a number of questions. How many patents must be produced for the project to be a success rather than a failure? What is meant by 'success' and why is number of patents an adequate indicator of success or failure? If it is the quality of the patents or their commercial effects rather than simply their quantity that is important, how are these other magnitudes to be measured? If patents are to be taken as the indicator of project benefits then surely they must somehow be compared with project costs in order to ascertain the net benefit or benefit–cost ratio? Finally, how many patents would have resulted in the absence of the VLSI Project, bearing in mind, as documented earlier, that in a number of important cases *pre-existing* research being done in the companies was taken into the VLSI joint laboratories? This last point also raises the question of whether it is the joint research in the joint laboratories that is to be evaluated, or the project as a whole. At the same time the last point poses the issue of *additionality* which is taken up in more detail below.

Market share as an indicator both of 'revealed competitiveness' and VLSI Project success

It will be recalled that the US Congressional hearings concluded, with reference to the VLSI Project, that the 'success of the effort is evidenced [by the fact that] by the end of 1982, Japanese firms held 66 per cent of the world market for the then state-of-the-art 64K RAM microchip'. This measure of success, based on market share, at least has the merit, unlike patents, of attempting to restrict attention to only that research output which has a positive effect on international competitiveness. There are, however, major problems with the way in which market share is used in this instance as an indicator of project success.

To begin with, in addition to some of the problems discussed in the last section, there is the difficulty of clarifying the connection in terms of the cause and effect between the VLSI Project and the market share achieved by Japanese companies. Without going here into the requirements for a rigorous explanation in terms of cause and effect,[14] it is worth noting that the Japanese share of the world RAM (random access memory) market began increasing significantly before the end of the VLSI project. This emerges clearly from Fig. 3.4 where it is shown that the Japanese share of the world market for RAMs increased from 5 per cent in 1970–74 to 15 per cent in 1974–78 and to 40 per cent in 1978–81. The VLSI Project only began in 1976 and it took a number of years before its results began feeding into the

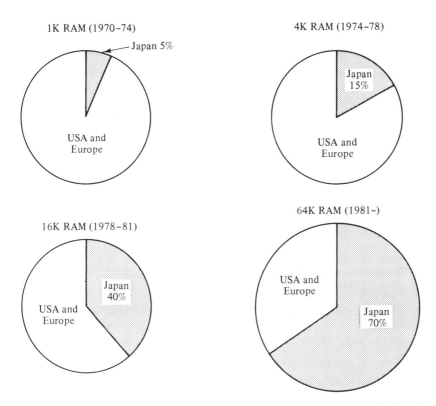

Fig. 3.4 Japanese market share of memory LSI (*Source:* Quoted in National Institute for Research Advancement, 1985).

companies which were members of the VLSI Project. Clearly, it is necessary for an alleged cause to precede the effect in time if it is to qualify as a possible cause. In view of the rapid rate of increase in Japanese market share *before* the VLSI Project began producing results, there is reason for caution before attributing great causal significance to this project. Furthermore, there were a number of other relevant events that occurred at the same time as the VLSI Project, such as the NTT research project on VLSI which is considered in more detail below. The effects of other simultaneous events such as this would have to be disentangled in any attempt to attribute causal significance to the MITI-initiated VLSI Project. As we shall see, in practice this is extremely difficult to do.

Direct evaluation of commercializable products emerging from the VLSI Project

One way of overcoming some of the inadequacies of patents and market share as appropriate indicators of project benefits is to conduct a direct

Table 3.5. *Commercializable products which have emerged from the VLSI Project*

1. A method of evaluating circuit design by computer
2. Test-pattern generation of combination circuit blocks by statistical method
3. Electron beam lithography machine using field emission cathode
4. Variable-beam type electron lithography machine
5. Electrical-mechanical, hybrid-type electron beam lithography machine
6. Software system for electron beam lithography
7. Mask pattern tester
8. Eight-inch-diameter silicon wafer technology
9. Defect-free, uniformly thin epitaxial layer growth technology
10. Optical pattern projection machines
11. Submicron pattern projection machines
12. Dry etching machines
13. Dry etching technologies for submicron patterns
14. VLSI material evaluation technology
15. Evaluation technology for oxide and nitride layers by liquid crystal
16. Device evaluation and measurement system
17. VLSI device computer-aided design (CAD) and simulation technology
18. New VLSI memory element design
19. Eighteen-bit Register Arithmetic Logic Unit of 400 ps
20. High-speed bipolar memory – 4-kilobit CML random access memory (RAM)
21. 256-Kilobit MOS RAM
22. 512-kilobit read only memory (ROM) using direct electron beam lithography

Source: Okimoto *et al.* (1984)

evaluation of the commercializable products which emerge from the project. This is done, for example, in Okimoto *et al.* (1984) and a list of the products is presented in Table 3.5. As Okimoto *et al.* report, 'How significant are these results, in light of the work that has already been done in the United States? Asked to evaluate this list of Japanese accomplishments, a leading American expert on VLSI technology expressed the opinion that, except for the work using liquid crystal (no. 15), the Japanese did not appear to have made any major breakthroughs. In most areas, he felt that the Japanese had simply extended their technology in ways comparable to developments that had already occurred in the United States' (pp. 38–9).

As with market share, the advantage of a direct evaluation of the project's commercializable products is that attention is restricted to those outputs which are internationally competitive. Furthermore, the cause-and-effect problems that arise in the use of market share data are overcome to the extent that it is possible to identify those products which have resulted from the project itself and would not have otherwise been produced. There are, however, a number of problems that arise with the use of this measure of project benefit (quite apart from the difficulty of establishing the criteria that are to be used in the evaluation of the commercializable products and applying these criteria). To begin with, the focus on products results in a failure to capture process innovations and know-how that may also be important components of the project's output and therefore its stream of benefits. Related to this, the evaluation of products fails to capture other project 'outputs', such as the strengthening of inter-firm linkages and information flows which Sigurdson (1986) strongly argues constituted one of the major benefits of the VLSI Project. It is worth quoting Sigurdson at length in view of the importance of this point:

specifications based on the experience of the five companies [which participated in the VLSI Project] and also on research in the joint laboratories were channelled to Nikon and Canon together with development contracts for specific machines. These contracts and linkages in fact triggered an almost completely new development at Nikon – wafer-stepper printers – and served as a stimulus for Canon for its proximity aligner. A further effect of the development contracts given to the optical companies was that they in their turn gave a substantial development contract to Ushio Denki to develop the very special lamps needed in the IC-printers. The Ushio company, which already had a strong base in plain copier lamps where it maintains a healthy 70 per cent share of the world market, has rapidly captured 40 per cent of the global market for lamps used in IC-printing equipment. Canon is today the leading producer of proximity printers and Nikon is well on its way to establish a similar position for wafer-steppers.

Similar linkages were also created between the crystal laboratory and the crystal vendors with a frequent exchange of information. However, the producers of silicon wafers were at the time already fairly well established which is also true for the major maker of photo-resist and other chemicals needed in the manufacturing process. The printing companies Dainippon Printing and Toppan Printing also benefitted from close contacts with the joint laboratories which in a way served as a clearing house for the various groups within the IC-manufacture system . . .

Thus, it is possible to see a number of ripple effects flowing from the VLSI Project. First, the material suppliers who were already fairly well established were further strengthened. Second, the equipment makers who were already strong in back-end equipment established an almost equally strong position in front-end equipment – exemplified by IC printers. Third, the sub-suppliers of which there are likely to be more examples than Ushio Denki climbed into a new very strong position. (pp. 119, 121)

In other words, the benefits of the VLSI Project extended beyond those enjoyed by the participating firms to include a number of other supplier firms which undertook subcontracted work from the project. In this way the VLSI Project assisted in creating an *industrial system* in which both competing and complementary firms were linked.

However, a number of further problems must be confronted if it is to be argued that one of the important benefits of the VLSI Project (if not the most important benefit) was the creation of such an industrial system. The general problem here is that it is necessary, if this argument is to be made, to establish what kinds of linkages would have been forged between these competing and complementary firms in the *absence* of the VLSI Project. It is then necessary to ascertain the *additional* linkages that were realized as a result of the project and the benefits of these linkages.

A number of more specific problems arise, such as the following. First, as noted earlier, a number of linkages existed between complementary companies *before* the VLSI Project was established. These included the investigation by researchers in Toshiba and Nikon in the area of optical step-and-repeat machines. It is necessary, in evaluating the benefits of the VLSI Project, to ask whether there were constraints on the strengthening and extending of those linkages which proved to be advantageous in the longer run (bearing in mind that this is not necessarily true of all linkages), which the project helped to reduce. Clearly, in some cases a market-mediated relationship between the firms, without any government intervention, will suffice to establish the link which is of longer-run benefit. However, in other cases 'market failure', that is the failure of the firms to conclude the necessary agreements, may prevent or limit the establishment of an appropriate industrial system. One example of such market failure emerges in the following extract from an interview between the author and a senior researcher from Toshiba:

> Fransman: Could the cooperation between Toshiba and Nikon on the optical stepper not have been achieved without the MITI programme?
> Informant: Before the joint laboratory started I had many discussions with Nikon people. But the companies had no intention of working together on optical lithography because no-one was convinced about the future of lithographic systems.

In this case it is possible that the uncertainty (as opposed to risk, for which a probability distribution can be derived) surrounding the future of lithography systems would have led to the failure to conclude a contract, based on their complementary distinctive competences, between the two companies. Under these circumstances it is quite possible that the funding provided through the VLSI Project was enough to cement the link that otherwise would have dissolved. But here a further problem arises. In order to cope with this market failure could MITI not have simply responded to the firms' initiatives and provided subsidized funding in this and similar cases without intervening directly to establish the VLSI Project and its joint research element? In dealing with this question it is necessary to ask whether there were *additional* benefits that resulted from the VLSI Project, including the joint research, compared to what would have happened had MITI adopted the more 'passive' mode of supporting Japanese companies. It would also be necessary on the cost side to take account of the costs of these two alternative modes of intervention. While these issues will not be examined further here, it is noted that it seems reasonable to hypothesize that the VLSI Project made an important *additional* contribution in the area of collecting information in the fields selected for study, to some extent sharing this information among the participating companies, and using the information to more effectively develop the linkages between the user and supplier companies. To give a more concrete example, it is likely that Nikon received better information, in terms both of quantity and quality, regarding user requirements for optical steppers from the third laboratory in the VLSI Project, in which researchers from Toshiba, Mitsubishi, NEC and Hitachi participated, than it would have received had it been left to establish a market-mediated relationship with Toshiba, or a relationship supported by subsidized government funding.

Some further problems in estimating additional effects of the VLSI Project

It has already been seen that the fact that ongoing research in Hitachi, Fujitsu and Toshiba in the area of lithography was transferred to the joint laboratories creates difficulties for the estimation of the additional effects of the VLSI Project. Another example is noted by Sigurdson (1986, p. 53):

An interviewee notes that the VLSI Project ran into 'trouble' when one of the non-participating VLSI-manufacturers, Matsushita, announced that it had already developed a 64K bit static RAM chip which in terms of integration was basically identical to the target of the VLSI Project. It was then suggested by MITI that the project should be able to do still better and the integration target was temporarily set at 512K bit and was subsequently revised to 1M bit.

A further example of the problems posed by the issue of additionality in evaluating the benefits of the VLSI Project comes from the establishment at around the same time by NTT of a distinct research project also in the area of VLSI technology. This latter project involved NTT and three members of its so-called Den Den group of supplying firms, Fujitsu, Hitachi and NEC. As Okimoto *et al.* (1984, p. 18) describe:

The communications-oriented project began in 1975 under the management of the Electrical Communication Laboratories of Nippon Telegraph and Telephone Public Corporation (NTT), which falls under the administrative guidance of the Ministry of Post and Telecommunication. NEC, Hitachi and Fujitsu cooperated in this project, and government support was provided in the form of procurement. NTT did not give direct financial support, and the three cooperating companies invested their own R & D money on the supposition that the investment would be recovered through future procurement. In the first phase of the project, which ended in the 1977 fiscal year, the major objectives were to investigate the practical limit of photolithography and to study basic micron and submicron device technologies. The second phase, lasting for another three years, applied the results of the first phase to develop special purpose VLSI for communications and to carry on the development of other new technologies for communications.

The possibilities for a cross-fertilization of research ideas and results between the researchers working on the MITI and the NTT VLSI Projects in the laboratories of the participating companies are suggested by the

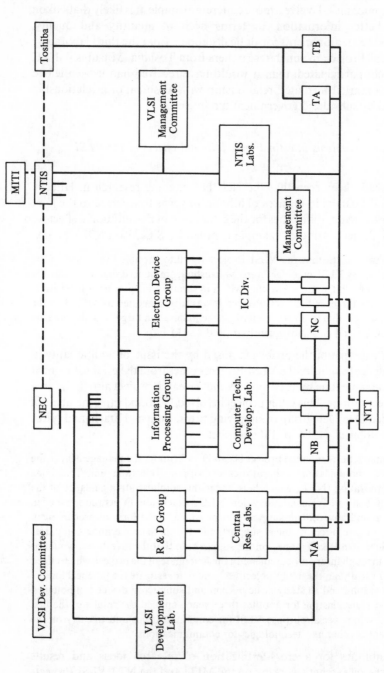

NA, NB and NC   NEC units involved in the VLSI Project organized by MITI.
TA and TB   Toshiba Laboratories A and B.
NTT   Units involved in NTT's VLSI Project.

Fig. 3.5   NEC's management system for VLSI development (*Source:* Uenohara, 1982).

information presented in Fig. 3.5. This figure, from Uenohara (1982), shows the way in which NEC integrated researchers involved in these two projects into its research laboratories and operating divisions. While this integration probably had the effect of yielding synergies from the research undertaken in these projects, from an analytical point of view it makes more difficult the task of disentangling the additional consequences of MITI's VLSI Project.

Towards an evaluation of the VLSI project

Some general considerations

From what has been said so far it is clear that a definitive evaluation of the VLSI Project (or for that matter other similar projects) is extremely difficult, if not impossible. Nevertheless, it is possible to go some way towards an evaluation by clarifying the main factors that must be taken into account and applying them to the VLSI Project.

An outline on the approach to be followed is given in Fig. 3.6. In this figure, four different states of affairs are distinguished:

(I) *No government support (NGS)* This is where intra-firm research is

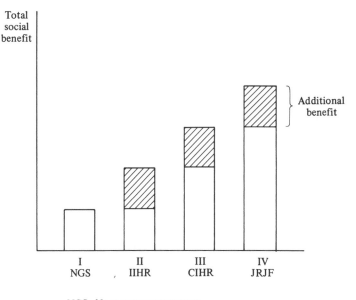

NGS No government support
IIHR Isolated in-house research
CIHR Coordinated in-house research
JRJF Joint research in joint research facilities

Fig. 3.6 The benefits of alternative forms of government research support.

privately funded and inter-firm research is market mediated without any government intervention. At the end of the period, these forms of research will yield an amount of benefit as shown on the vertical axis.

(II) *Isolated in-house research (IIHR)*   Here government adopts a relatively passive mode of intervention, responding to initiatives taken by the companies and perhaps even identifying priority areas for research, but making no attempt either to coordinate inter-firm research or to encourage joint research. Policy under this option will be carried out with the use of instruments such as subsidies, tax incentives and trade protection.

(III) *Coordinated in-house research (CIHR)*   In this case government adopts a more active mode of intervention, perhaps using many of the same instruments as in the IIHR option, but supplementing them by measures aimed at coordinating the research undertaken by the firms. The research itself, however, is undertaken inside the firms and the extent of joint generation and sharing of knowledge is limited.

(IV) *Joint research in joint research facilities (JRJF)*   Here government follows an even more active mode of intervention, again using many of the same instruments as in the cases of IIHR and CIHR, but insisting as a *quid pro quo* for the support that it gives that the participating firms engage in the joint generation and sharing of knowledge through the establishment of joint research facilities.

As can be seen from Fig. 3.6, the total social benefits increase from I to IV. This requires an explanation. In the NGS case, the social benefits from innovation will be positive as the firms, in the absence of government intervention, generate technical change both inside the firms as well as through inter-firm interactions. However, in this case there are a number of factors which will limit the total social benefit derived. These include the following. First, as a result of the uncertainty (as opposed to risk) inherent in technical change, for-profit firms are likely to underinvest in innovation because they will be unsure about the effects of this investment. In general, the greater the degree of uncertainty which attaches to the area of innovation invested in, all other things being equal, the lower the level of investment in this area. Secondly, firms will also be uncertain about their ability to appropriate the rent from innovation. This uncertainty follows from the fact that technology often has the characteristics of a public good, that is technological knowledge can often be acquired by others at a cost considerably below that which the original creator of that knowledge must bear. To the extent that this happens, the original creator of the knowledge will not be able to appropriate the full benefits that are realized by that knowledge. While in all capitalist societies attempts are made to legally secure the creator's property rights over that knowledge, this does not always guarantee adequate appropriation of the fruits of that knowledge by the creator. In general, the greater the uncertainty regarding the ability to appropriate the benefits of the knowledge created, all other things being equal, the lower the level of investment in that area. For these two reasons it is likely that firms will underinvest in innovation. Thirdly, firms may fail to coordinate their research efforts adequately, thereby duplicating research and failing to realize sufficiently economies of specialization. Fourthly, firms may fail to engage in joint research to the extent that they might, thus failing to realize the economies of joint research which were analysed earlier. The third and fourth points are examples of 'market failure', that is where firms interacting through the market fail to realize potential social benefits. Reasons for such failure include the fear of knowledge leaking to rival firms, and the concern that cooperating firms may opportunistically take advantage of the interactions that are established. Difficulties such as these increase the transactions costs of establishing cooperative agreements and in some cases may mean that firms locate research activities within their companies, rather than undertaking research through a process of negotiation with other firms. Accordingly, the social benefits referred to may fail to be realized.

In the case of IIHR, the use by government of policy instruments such as subsidies, taxes and protection may to some extent overcome the difficulties referred to in the first and second points mentioned in the last paragraph. To the extent that this happens, the total social benefits derived from innovation will increase. However, since, under the IIHR option, government makes no attempt either to coordinate inter-firm research or to encourage joint research, preferring a relatively passive mode of intervention, the difficulties of market failure discussed in the third and fourth points remain. It may therefore be concluded that in the IIHR case *additional* social benefits from innovation might be realized relative to the NGS case as a result of government measures to alleviate the negative effects of uncertainty on investment in innovation (as discussed in the first and second points in the last paragraph). Against this additional social benefit will have to be weighed the additional social cost involved in the use of the IIHR option.

In the CIHR case, government, in addition to the use of instruments such as subsidies, tax incentives and trade protection, plays a more actively interventionist role by coordinating the research undertaken by the firms. In this case *additional* social benefits are realized compared to the IIHR option as a result of factors such as economies of specialization, the avoidance of duplication, the sharing of expensive equipment, etc. However, since the research is done inside the companies, the joint generation and sharing of knowledge is limited (although project regulations might require the divulgence of some information given in the form of reports on research progress, etc.). In other words, the socialization of knowledge, as opposed to its privatization, is significantly limited. In assessing the net social benefits of CIHR, the additional social benefits will have to be weighed against the additional social costs involved in organizing and financing this option.

Finally, in the case of JRJF, *additional* benefits, over and above those of CIHR, are realized as a result of the joint generation and sharing of knowledge through the joint research activities undertaken in joint research facilities. Although several of the advantages of JRJF will to some extent also be realized under the CIHR option, for example the creation of greater industrial system coherence, it is likely that the former option will yield additional benefits. The reason, as pointed out earlier in the section dealing with the economies of joint research, is that under the JRJF option there is a greater socialization of knowledge compared to the other three options and this will often result in a larger amount of social benefit under this option. It is, however, necessary in evaluating the net benefits of this option to weigh the additional social benefits against the additional social costs.

The outlines of an evaluation of the VLSI Project

The following points must be taken into account in an evaluation of the VLSI project:

(1)   To begin with, it must be stressed that attention is focused in this section on the joint laboratories, omitting the other research done under the VLSI Project in CDL and NTIS. As noted above, about 11.1 billion yen, or about 15 per cent of the total of 73.7 billion yen, was spent in the joint laboratories. In effect the joint laboratories will be considered as a separate project and evaluated accordingly. This is done for two reasons. The first is that, as seen earlier, joint research in joint research facilities was at this time a novel form of organization in the Japanese electronics industry. Therefore, it is worth enquiring further into the additional benefits that this form of organization provided. The second reason is that, as was shown above, concern has been expressed outside Japan about the extent to which Japanese companies have benefited from MITI-coordinated inter-firm research cooperation. Since the degree of cooperation was greatest in the joint laboratories, it is worth examining the social benefits that resulted from the research undertaken in these laboratories.

(2)   It is clear from Fig. 3.6 and from our earlier discussion that to the extent to which firms can be persuaded to engage in JRJF, there are potential *additional* social benefits that may be derived compared to the other three alternative forms of research organization (that is NGS, IIHR and CIHR). For the joint laboratories in the VLSI Project these social benefits included the following:

   a. Increased national industrial system coherence, that is over and above what might have been achieved by the other three alternative forms of organization, as a result of the greater socialization of knowledge and improved information flows between both competing and complementary firms. The most visible form of this benefit is the VLSI equipment produced by the companies that were members of the VLSI Project and their subcontractors. This point has been strongly emphasized by Sigurdson (1986).

b. Greater blending of the distinctive competences located in the participating firms (including the subcontractors), although as was seen, the blending process was to some extent limited by the underlying competitive relations between Hitachi, Fujitsu and Toshiba.

c. The limitations on blending, however, were to some extent offset by the competition in research between the first three laboratories and the diversity of lithography equipment design that this led to.

d. An increased pooling of information was achieved as a result of the greater proximity of the researchers. It is also likely that there was a more efficient search of the international stock of knowledge in the VLSI area, partly as a result of the size of the joint laboratories and the diverse backgrounds of their researchers which allowed a more effective division of labour in the search process.

e. A greater avoidance of duplication as a result of the joint generation and sharing of knowledge, although, as noted earlier, it is likely that in areas judged to be of strategic importance the companies will have ensured that they possessed the necessary in-house capabilities even where the research tasks had been allocated to other companies in the VLSI Project.

f. Economies resulting from the sharing of expensive equipment, examples including synchrotron orbital radiation equipment and an electron beam pattern-generating machine.

These social benefits followed from the realization of economies of joint research. They are, however, extremely difficult to quantify in the absence of a significantly greater amount of information than is currently available, which would be costly to collect. A further important benefit of the VLSI Project's joint laboratories was the *learning effect* which was generated, which included the establishment of a routine and form of organization for joint research in joint research facilities (which would be followed closely in some of the later MITI-initiated projects such as the Optical Measurement and Control Project to be discussed in some detail in the following chapter).

(3) One of the important implications of the present study, however, is that to some extent JRJF and CIHR are not alternatives. The reason is that firms are not willing to share equally all parts of their stock of knowledge. The propensity to share knowledge is inversely related to the direct impact of

that knowledge on the firm's competitiveness, market share and profit. Accordingly, the lower the propensity to share knowledge in a particular area, the higher will be the amount of compensation, incentive or coercion necessary to establish JRJF. Rather than attempting to make a clear-cut dual distinction between research areas where there is a relatively high propensity to share knowledge (referred to by the Japanese as 'basic' research and by some others as 'generic' research) and other areas where there is a relatively low propensity, the present study suggests that it is preferable to conceptualize a continuum. The present study has shown that although there is a strong tendency for firms to resist attempts made to get them to share knowledge, they can be persuaded to share in some areas when the combination of compensation, incentive and coercion is right. *The experience of the VLSI joint laboratories also suggests that the concept of pre-competitive research is misconceived* (although it may serve the politically expedient purpose of persuading pro-market governments to fund research towards the 'basic' end of the spectrum). To the extent that firms are actual, or potential, competitors, considerations regarding competitiveness and the possible consequences of knowledge leakage are *always* present. This does not deny, however, that there are differences in the propensity with which firms will share various parts of their stock of knowledge. As has been shown, the smaller the direct impact of this knowledge on the firm's competitiveness, etc., the more willing will the firm be to share this knowledge and the lower will be the compensation, etc. necessary to persuade it to agree to share. It is on this basis that it is possible to identify areas for joint research, rather than on the misguided attempt to identify pre-competitive fields for such research.

(4) In an evaluation, account must also be taken of the costs of JRJF. These costs may usefully be broken down into (a) the negotiation costs involved in the establishment of the project and (b) the direct and indirect costs of running the project. As always in an economic evaluation the cost should be measured in terms of the opportunity cost of the resources involved, although once again this is difficult to do in practice. With regard to (a), the costs are probably significantly higher for JRJF than the other options because of the greater threat to the firms from knowledge leakage. In general, the stronger a firm is in a technology area relative to other competing firms, the less willing it will be to enter into JRJF and the greater the compensation, etc. that it will require. The converse will hold too. While the costs of JRJF will therefore be higher than CIHR, the latter costs will be higher than those for IIHR as a result of having to negotiate the coordinated research among the firms. Similarly, IIHR costs will exceed those of NGS as a result of the administrative and other costs involved in the use of policy instruments such as subsidies, tax incentives, etc. The cost differences for these four options are shown in Fig. 3.7. In order to calculate the net social benefits from the project it is necessary to deduct the costs

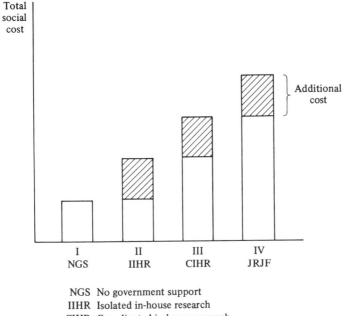

Fig. 3.7 The costs of alternative forms of government research support.

associated with the policy option from the corresponding benefits shown in Fig. 3.6.

Although, for the reasons mentioned, the costs of JRJF will exceed those of the other three options,[15] *government intervention will result in an economizing of the negotiation costs.* The reason is that, as a neutral arbitrator, although with a vested interest in the attainment of national goals, government officials are able to reduce the possibilities for opportunistic behaviour on the part of the participating firms and *limit* undesirable leakages of knowledge. In the VLSI joint laboratories this role was played by MITI and Tarui and Nebashi who were seconded to the laboratories.

(5) There is no evidence from this study either that MITI was in absolute command of the situation, or that the Japanese companies which participated in the project behaved with regard to their willingness to share knowledge any differently from their Western counterparts. The statement quoted earlier that 'we were forced by MITI to agree to joint laboratories' must be interpreted to mean that in view of the national benefits resulting from the economies of joint research, MITI insisted on joint research as a *quid pro quo* for its funding. From a private point of view the firms would

have preferred to be given this funding without having to increase their sharing of knowledge. As the Director of one of the joint laboratories put it: 'Every company unofficially said that it would have been preferable for MITI to have given money *directly* to the individual companies.' However, JRJF, for the reasons given in this section, increased the social benefits derived from the research of the joint laboratories. In view of the divergence between the priorities of MITI and those of the firms, compromise was necessary. The extent of MITI's compromise is evident from (a) the small proportion of the project's resources that went to the funding of the joint laboratories and (b) the structuring of laboratories 1, 2 and 3.

(6) There is no evidence that the joint research generated significant costs in terms of reduced competition between the participating firms. Its effect was rather to increase the socialization of knowledge, that is the generation of a common pool from which the firms could draw in developing their commercializable products. It will be recalled that no commercializable device was produced in the joint laboratories. In fact the joint research undertaken in the VLSI laboratories may have increased longer-run competition, both in Japan and worldwide by (a) helping the firms to remain in the computer and electronic devices area in the face of strong international competition and (b) strengthening the two firms, NEC and Mitsubishi, that were relatively weak in some of the related technology areas.

(7) In view of the above, it is likely that there has been an exaggerated reaction in some Western circles to the Japanese VLSI Project, as is evident, in the light of the findings of the present study, from the quotations given above from the US Congressional hearings. If there has been a uniquely Japanese element in this area, it is the decisiveness with which MITI, mindful of the national interest and the needs of the Japanese system as a whole, coaxed the firms into JRJF. In this, MITI's hand was strengthened by its control over public funds and its determination to allocate them as far as possible in the national interest. However, as we have seen, MITI's intervention was constrained by the at times conflicting interests of the firms.

Conclusion

It is apparent from the present study that the issues raised by the VLSI Project, both conceptual as well as theoretical, are far more complex than is usually acknowledged. In view of the ambiguities that this complexity inserts into the conclusions that are to be derived regarding the benefits of the VLSI Project it is perhaps appropriate that the Director of one of the joint laboratories be given the last word:

> Fransman: Was it good that MITI forced firms to come together in the VLSI project?

Director: This is now a common conclusion [*laughter*].

Fransman: And do you agree with this?

Director: No, not always. But now this conclusion is already history, a myth [*laughter*]. I don't deny that.

Fransman: Do you think the history is written correctly?

Director: Any history is written by someone [*laughter*]. But many people agree with this – that should be history [*laughter*].

Fransman: But in your view was the role of MITI essential for the success of the project? If MITI played a passive role and left it to the firms to arrange to cooperate privately do you think the project would not have been as successful?

Director: [*Long silence*] Yes, I agree. The role of MITI was important. Also, much more money went to NTIS and CDL than to the joint research laboratories. That money was very helpful for the individual five companies, I think, to develop practical technologies.

4

The Optical Measurement and Control System Project, 1979–1985

Introduction: from frontier-follower to frontier-leader

The late 1970s marked a watershed in the evolution of the Japanese computing, electronic devices and optoelectronics industry. In many technology areas in this industry Japanese companies had caught up with the international leaders by this time and had begun to pull ahead in some of them.

This had extremely important implications for technology policy in companies and in government. The main reason was that it was now far more difficult to learn by following the international leaders. Where Japanese companies were leaders or joint leaders with companies from other countries, they were unable to take their cue from more advanced companies and had to make their own decisions about the technological directions they wished to pursue. Furthermore, since they had become an increasing competitive threat, moves were made by Western companies and their governments to limit the outflow of technological knowledge to Japanese companies. This further reinforced the need for Japanese companies to increase their own longer-term research activities. An additional pressure, with similar effects, came from Western governments who argued that Japan must increase its contribution to the international stock of technological knowledge from which it had derived so much benefit. Finally, as a result of their attempts to compete through innovation, Japanese companies, having developed considerable strengths in 'downstream' areas such as manufacturing and processing, now tended to move increasingly 'upstream', into areas that in the final chapter of this book are referred to as oriented-basic research.

A major implication of the move, for the reasons just analysed, into longer-term oriented-basic research was that *uncertainty regarding the commercial viability of the technologies themselves now became a major problem for policy-making in both companies and government.* As a follower attempting to catch up with the international leaders, uncertainty resulted more from questions about the ability to catch up while earning reasonable returns on the investments in innovation required to do so, than from uncertainty regarding the technologies themselves. Now, however, it was necessary to make complex decisions regarding which technologies should be developed for 'the day after tomorrow' and how they should be developed. Furthermore, this was a task which companies were constrained in undertaking. The reason was that even if the decision-making horizons of Japanese companies were somewhat longer than their Western counterparts as a result of their different relationship with banks and the Stock Exchange, they were still required to generate a reasonable profit in the short to medium term in order to satisfy creditors and shareholders. The need to develop technologies for 'the day after tomorrow', with profits accruing only in the longer term, therefore posed a challenge. It was in confronting this challenge that the Japanese government played a very constructive role, selecting, in close consultation with the companies, technology areas for longer-term development. Furthermore, the Japanese government also acted as a go-between, economizing on the costs of negotiating cooperative research between competing companies and establishing cooperative research projects in order to develop these future technologies.

In this and subsequent chapters the national cooperative research projects in the areas of optoelectronics, supercomputers, future electronic devices and fifth generation computers are anlaysed in turn.

The origins of the Optical Measurement Project, 1979–1985

One of the main aims of the Optical Measurement Project was the development of optoelectronic integrated circuits. There were a number of reasons for interest in this kind of device. Already in the 1960s firms such as NEC had begun to do research on, and produce, gallium arsenide-based light-emitting diodes. Furthermore, from around 1970 optical fibre technology had become important in communications systems. Advances in this technology in turn further stimulated the need for devices capable of transforming optical signals into electrical signals and vice versa. This was one reason for the increasing interest in the material gallium arsenide. This material, under appropriate conditions, emits light and, as discussed in the chapter on the Supercomputer Project, electrons move significantly faster through gallium arsenide than through silicon, the most widely used material for electronic devices.

As a device based on III-V compound materials, gallium arsenide semiconductors were therefore of interest largely because of their potential speed and their use in optoelectronic systems. In proportional terms, however, III-V compound semiconductor devices remained fairly insignificant compared to silicon devices. This emerges clearly from Table 4.1[1] which shows a breakdown of semiconductor sales in Japan in 1985. As shown in this table, sales of III-V semiconductors in 1985 were about 6 per cent of sales of silicon semiconductors. Of the total sales of III-V

Table 4.1. *Japanese semiconductor sales, 1985*

	(US dollars)	
	III-V	Si
Substrates	50 million	1.0 billion
Devices		
Discrete	616 million[a]	2.4 billion
ICs	—	7.6 billion
Total Devices	616 million	10.0 billion

Note:
[a] Optical 546 million; electronic 70 million.
Source: Merz, 1987, p. 2.

discrete devices amounting to 616 million dollars, 546 million, or 89 per cent, were of optical devices while the remainder were of electronic devices. A breakdown of III-V compound devices according to number of units sold is given in Table 4.2. Here it is shown that among the optical devices, light-emitting diodes (LEDs) were by far the most important in terms of quantity of units sold. Following far behind, laser diodes (LDs) were the second most important category. In the case of the III-V compound electronic devices, Hall elements, used in video cassette recorders, were quantitatively the most important. Table 4.1 also shows that by 1985 integrated circuits using III-V compound materials had not

Table 4.2. *III-V compound devices sold in Japan*

	(millions of units)	
	1985	1990 (est.)
Optical		
LEDs	3800	11700
LDs: visible (CDs)	2.8[a]	11.4
LDs: IR (opt. comm.)	0.03	0.2
Detectors	0.03	n.a.
Solar cells	2.0	n.a.
Electronic		
μwave diodes	0.7	n.a.
FETs	7.5	11.7
Hall elements	243	370

Note:
[a] US estimates are $\frac{1}{3}$ higher.
Source: Merz, 1987, p. 4.

yet been developed. In the late 1970s when the Optical Measurement Project was first conceived the concept of an optoelectronic integrated circuit was extremely imprecise. A high degree of uncertainty therefore attached to proposed research in this area since it was by no means clear how optical signals and electronic signals could be integrated on the same device.

In the light of this uncertainty the origins of the Optical Measurement Project are of importance. The original ideal to establish a national optoelectronic project came, not from the Japanese companies, but from a researcher from MITI's Electrotechnical Laboratory (ETL). As a senior MITI official who was closely involved in the establishment of the Optical Measurement Project stated in an interview with the present author: 'Dr Sakurai in ETL (who died several years ago) was the actual initiator of the optoelectronics project [i.e. the Optical Measurement Project]. He had for some time been insisting on the importance of optotechnology. At that time we [in MITI and in the Japanese companies] were more interested in silicon and VLSI devices and such technology. But Sakurai was strongly insistent. He assured us that in the long term optoelectronic technology would replace current technology.'

The fact that the Optical Measurement Project originated in ETL requires further comment. As was shown earlier, ETL had played a particularly important role in the development of the first transistors and computers in Japan. However, as the Japanese companies, which were originally based in telecommunications and heavy electrical equipment, successfully diversified into electronics, the role of ETL changed. Before this diversification had been achieved, ETL tended to give a lead to the companies by doing research on, and even developing, new electronics-based products which were then transferred to the companies. One example is the ETL transistorized computer which was discussed in detail above. In this way ETL facilitated the diversification process by reducing the uncertainties associated with the introduction of new products based on new technologies. At the same time ETL in effect subsidized the cost of the development of these new products. But as the companies successfully entered the electronics field, and as their technological capabilities in this area began to grow, so their reliance on ETL for assistance with the commercialization of currently available technologies diminished. By the late 1970s, with the completion of the catch-up phase in the field of computers and electronic devices, the role of ETL began to be transformed. There was, however, a continuity in ETL's function insofar as the organization still concentrated its activities in areas expected to be of longer-run benefit to Japanese companies and therefore the Japanese economy as a whole, areas where the companies themselves were not devoting sufficient attention or resources. It was these areas that began to change by the late 1970s. Whereas previously the firms required assistance with the commercialization of currently available technologies, *now ETL's role was increasingly to help with the longer-run development of future technologies. For a number of reasons firms tend to underinvest in the development of such technologies.*

Several reasons for this underinvestment may be briefly mentioned here (and are considered in more detail in the concluding chapter). First, the longer the term of research and the greater the divergence from current knowledge that is anticipated, the greater the amount of uncertainty that attaches to the prospects for a successful outcome to the research. Secondly, as a result of the public-good nature of much technology (the fact that others can often acquire the knowledge at a cost significantly below that incurred by the inventor), uncertainty also attaches to the ability of the firm to appropriate adequate returns from its investment in longer-term technical change. Thirdly, as analysed in detail in the concluding chapter, the 'vision' of firms is largely constrained by (a) their current activities and (b) their need for an adequate financial pay-off. This implies that fields of research, which may in the longer run prove to be important to the firm, might in the shorter term lie outside the firm's 'bounded vision' and therefore be neglected by it. These three reasons together suggest that in some areas of longer-term, more basic, research, firms acting in the absence of government corrective measures might fail to invest a socially appropriate amount.

It was this kind of reasoning that helped to define a new role for ETL from the late 1970s. While the Japanese firms were able to commercialize currently available technologies, and while on the basis of their growing size, international competitiveness and financial strength they were increasingly willing to venture into new areas of longer-term and more basic research, they remained vulnerable to failures of the kinds mentioned in the last paragraph. It was here that ETL could help by playing a positive leading role in the identification and development of technologies for the longer-run future. ETL's structural conditions equipped it well to play such a role. To begin with, ETL research was government funded and this meant that the research was not constrained by the need to earn a financial return within a fairly short period of time as was the case in the firms. Furthermore, ETL's position as part of MITI's Agency for Industrial Science and Technology (AIST) implied that much of its research would be directed towards the national goal of longer term Japanese international competitiveness. In this respect ETL research tended to differ from that done in the Japanese universities where the link with Japanese competitiveness was far less well defined. However, despite for these reasons being well placed to play this role, ETL suffered from an important disability. As a result of overall constraints on government expenditure, ETL's size in terms of research staff and real budget increased significantly more slowly than that of the Japanese electronics companies. Accordingly, although ETL was often able to identify and do research in important new technology areas in advance of the Japanese companies (as is documented in the present book in the cases of the Optical Measurement, Fifth Generation and Supercomputer Projects), it at times lacked the human and financial resources to undertake the amount of research that was necessary. Partly as a result of these limitations, ETL attempted in a number of cases to establish national research projects involving cooperation between company and ETL researchers. As a senior MITI official explained, MITI's 'major role at this moment [in the area of technology research] is to proceed with basic research... The ideal way is for us to do this by ourselves, that is ETL alone, without the cooperation of the companies... But this is impossible because of limited resources, equipment and experience. So we have to ask industry people to join. It also means benefit to the companies.'

In the light of the present discussion of the changing role of ETL from the late 1970s it is hardly surprising that the idea of a national project in the area of optoelectronics originated in ETL and was sponsored by MITI. As already pointed out, while optical communication systems were expanding, the concept of optoelectronic integrated circuits remained highly uncertain despite their possible longer-run importance. This was therefore the kind of field that it was ETL's job to promote.

In proposing a national research project in the area of optoelectronics, Dr Sakurai had to persuade other MITI officials and company represen-tatives of the wisdom of research on optoelectronic integrated circuits. This he apparently managed to do without great difficulty. Many of the companies were already undertaking research on III-V compound semiconductor devices and their activities on optical communication systems were expanding. Furthermore, research had already been done under the PIPS project on semiconductor lasers and there was therefore some history of cooperative research in this area. While little or no research was being done in the companies on optoelectronic integrated circuits as a result of the uncertainties involved, with significant MITI funding and support it was fairly easy to get agreement that this was a desirable area to investigate.

Far more controversial, however, was the form of organization that should be adopted in order to pursue research on optoelectronics. As in the case of the VLSI Project, MITI officials were very keen to have joint research in joint research facilities as a result of economies of joint research which existed.[2] As a senior MITI official closely involved in the establishment of the Optical Measurement Project put it: 'MITI always wants a joint laboratory because we believe it is more efficient to proceed this way – budget, equipment, researchers are used more efficiently this way. But we cannot force firms to come to a joint laboratory. The decision finally is theirs.'

However, the firms that were strongest in the area of optoelectronics were initially most reluctant to agree to joint research in joint research facilities. As a senior executive of one of the major companies later recalled:

Informant: ... in the beginning the strong companies were very reluctant especially to form joint laboratories.
Fransman: Which were the strong companies?
Informant: NEC, Fujitsu and Hitachi. Before [the Optical Measurement Project] we had a joint project with NTT [in the area of optoelectronics].
Fransman: How was agreement achieved with the stronger companies?
Informant: There Dr Sakurai played a very important role. He convinced us [in the stronger companies] and also government officials in the Ministry of Post and Telecommunications. Dr Sakurai came from a very influential family in the telecommunications area.
Fransman: So he could persuade the Ministry of Post and Telecommunications to agree to MITI doing a project in this area [where the responsibility of the two ministries overlapped]. But how did he persuade the three leading companies to take part?
Informant: I was a very good friend of his [*laughter*]. And he had very good friends in [the other two companies]. So we said if he took the key role in this project, we would go along. We would not do it if others were involved... We stressed that the research target [for the joint laboratories] must be very basic. No member companies were willing to invest their own money in the Optoelectronic Joint Laboratories – this was very risky.

Further light was thrown on the reluctance of the firms to establish joint research by a senior MITI official involved in the establishment of the Optical Measurement Project: 'Frankly speaking, the industrial people were not so eager to establish a joint research laboratory because their first priority is to do research in their own company. That is the best way for them. Then they can control the knowledge and information and everything.' However, 'in some cases it is very difficult for them to do [the research entirely in-house]. One factor is money... it was difficult for them to get the budget for this kind of project – risky, basic research with uncertain prospects for commercialization. Secondly, at the initial stages the companies could not afford to allocate many researchers to such areas. Thirdly, equipment: to get data and information, experimentation is required. The equipment is expensive and highly specific – it is not used for general purposes.' Finally, if the aim of 'the project is to check on technical feasibility, a trial and error process [is required. This] makes it easier to do joint research.'

Several comments may be made on the basis of the above quotations. The first is that although Japanese companies were already doing research in the area of optoelectronics, the stimulus for a research project on optoelectronic integrated circuits came in the first instance from ETL and then from MITI more generally. In view of the uncertainty regarding financial pay-off, the companies were not inclined at this stage to take the initiative and establish research in this area. On the other hand, as a result of the structural factors which conditioned its activities and which were analysed above, ETL was in a favourable position to make the first moves in establishing national research in this field. In evaluating the Optical Measurement Project the effect of the ETL/MITI initiative on the allocation of company research resources to the area of optoelectronics will later be examined. Secondly, it was argued by the MITI official that while it would have been preferable for ETL to do its own research on optoelectronics (including optoelectronic integrated circuits) and then transfer the results to the companies, this was not possible as a result of the resource constraints on ETL's activities. The point of interest here is the recognition that although ETL is structurally well-placed to do uncertain longer-term research, in some instances better placed than the companies, the constraints on government expenditure have meant that over time ETL *in resource terms* has become weaker relative to the companies. It must be stressed, however, that this does not imply that the role of ETL is becoming obsolete. For despite the growth of the Japanese electronics companies and their increasing international competitiveness, they are still vulnerable to the three kinds of failure analysed above.[3] While ETL suffers other disabilities such as constraints of human and financial resources, its research is not subjected to the same possibilities of failure as that of the companies. In this sense, therefore, the roles played by ETL and the companies in the Japanese system are complementary. This point is examined in detail in the concluding chapter. An additional point emerging from the MITI official's statement is that it is by no means obvious that it would have been preferable for ETL to do the optoelectronics research entirely in-house and then transfer the results to the companies. As will emerge from the evaluation of the Optical Measurement Project, the national research project which brings together researchers from the companies and ETL in addition to some university-based researchers provides an extremely efficient mode for the generation and diffusion of new technologies.

The third comment relates to the reluctance of the stronger firms to agree to the establishment of joint research in joint research facilities. This reluctance may be attributable to two distinguishable kinds of concern. The first, mentioned by the MITI official, is a concern about the leakage of knowledge. As he observed, research done inside a company (including that done under the auspices of what was referred to earlier as coordinated in-house research projects or isolated in-house research projects[4]) remains under the control of the company. This is particularly so in Japan where the practice of lifetime employment minimizes knowledge leakages due to the turnover of research staff. On the other hand, if company staff mix with researchers from other companies in joint laboratories the company has less control over outflows of knowledge. The second concern related to the special problem posed by the participation of weaker companies. This problem arose from the possibility of free-riding by the latter companies on the knowledge generated and financed by the stronger firms. In the case of the stronger companies, attempts could be made (for example, by ensuring that they all sent researchers of an equally strong calibre to the joint laboratories) to guarantee that there was a fair exchange of knowledge in the laboratories. However, the participation of weaker firms meant that, all other things equal, the stronger firms would have to be compensated in other ways, or coerced, in order to be encouraged to share their knowledge in joint laboratories.

One solution to the problem of compensation for knowledge leakage was hinted at by the MITI official. He pointed to the constraints on the company doing the research entirely in-house on a self-financed basis. A national project, partly government financed, would alleviate these constraints and increase the amount of research done in the uncertain area, thus compensating the firm for any knowledge leakage which it suffers. But there is another dimension to the problem of knowledge leakage and knowledge sharing which was discussed in detail in connection with the VLSI Project and which is relevant here. This is that a firm's propensity to share knowledge differs for different parts of its stock of knowledge. In general, the greater the direct effect of that knowledge on the firm's profitability, market share, etc., the less willing will the firm be to share that knowledge. It is for this reason that the executive of one of the stronger companies quoted above stated that 'We [that is, the stronger companies] stressed that the research target [for the joint laboratories] must be very basic.' In other words, the propensity to share basic knowledge, defined here as that knowledge which does not have a significant direct effect on the firm's profitability, etc., was sufficiently great that the firms could agree to do joint research in this area. Given this propensity, the compensation which they received in the form of government funding of the joint laboratories and of a portion of the Optical Measurement Project research that they did in-house, and in the form of access to knowledge created by researchers from the other companies, was sufficient to make them willing to join the project. It is, however, significant that the stronger companies nevertheless insisted that only 'if [Dr Sakurai] took the key role in this project, would we go along. We would not do it if others were involved.' Dr Sakurai was known personally to the key decision-makers in the stronger companies and was trusted by them. As a neutral party he could be relied upon to ensure that knowledge leakages and knowledge sharing would by and large be mutually beneficial.

As a first step in establishing the Optical Measurement Project Dr

Sakurai set up an informal study group which he chaired and which met over 1978–9 when the project formally began. The membership of the study group included the following firms: Fujitsu, Hitachi, NEC, Toshiba, Mitsubishi Electric, Oki, Matsushita, Sumitomo Electric, Furukawa, Fujikura and Nippon Sheet Glass. In addition NTT, MITI and ETL were represented in the study group. The inclusion of NTT at this stage, but the exclusion of NTT and its Electrical Communications Laboratories (ECL) from ultimate participation in the Optical Measurement Project, is noteworthy.

As noted earlier, Dr Sakurai, with his good connections in the telecommunications area, had to smooth the way for a MITI-initiated project in the area of optical communications. This area also fell under the responsibility of the Ministry of Post and Telecommunications and NTT and, as pointed out, the three strongest companies, Fujitsu, Hitachi and NEC, had already taken part in an NTT-initiated optoelectronics project. Furthermore, six of the eleven firms which participated in the informal study group were members of NTT's so-called Den Den Family of supplying firms. This was a closed group of firms which until April 1985, when NTT was partially privatized, had exclusive rights to supply NTT. Since, as will shortly be seen, the Optical Measurement Project was applied within an industrial context and did not link in with the Japanese telecommunications system, it was probably felt that MITI's involvement was justifiable. At the same time, the input from ETL, which unlike ECL was not wholly pre-occupied with telecommunications research, might have added different dimensions to the development of optoelectronic technology thus increasing the diversity of experience and capability in the companies. Finally, the inclusion of Sumitomo Electric, Furukawa and Fujikura in the informal study group is of interest. These three firms were the major suppliers of copper and optical fibre cable to NTT, and Sumitomo furthermore was a major producer of gallium arsenide. Their participation in the study group from the beginning is an indication of the intention from the outset to strengthen an optoelectronics communications-creating *industrial system*, consisting of both competing and complementary firms. This point will be further discussed later.

The research design of the Optical Measurement Project

The rationale behind the research design

The design of the research undertaken under the Optical Measurement Project is of particular interest. *In general terms, the research was structured in such a way as to ensure that both 'use-pull' and 'generic research-push' determinants shaped the evolution of the component technologies.* More concretely, this was achieved by not only undertaking research on the generic or enabling technologies, but by simultaneously creating a specific technological system embodying these technologies in such a way as to serve the needs of a given user. Thus the immediate aim of the project was the creation of an optical measurement and control system for the Mizushima oil refinery which belonged to Nippon Mining Co. Ltd.[5] A central part of the research for the optical measurement and control system involved the development of optoelectronic integrated circuits and optical sensors. These components of the system were not developed in isolation, but as part of the total system. The blending of 'use-pull' and 'generic research-push' determinants in the Optical Measurement Project mirrored a similar practice in Japanese electronics companies whereby a significant proportion of the research done in the central research and development laboratories is financed by the operating divisions which are thereby able to exercise a 'use-pull' influence on the research done in the laboratories.

Outline of the research design

An outline of the research design for the Optical Measurement Project is given in Fig. 4.1. As this shows, there were three broad research tasks that the Optical Measurement Project set out to accomplish. The first was generic research on III-V compound materials, material growth and fabrication technology. For the most part gallium arsenide (GaAs) was the material chosen for this research as well as related, lattice-matched compounds such as aluminium gallium arsenide (AlGaAs). The second task was the development of specific optoelectronic integrated circuits and optical sensor devices. The third was the development of a broader

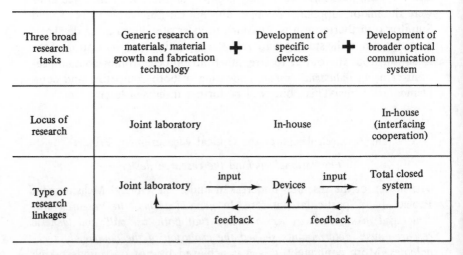

Fig. 4.1   The research design for the Optical Measurement Project.

optical measurement and control system for use in the Mizushima oil refinery.

Figure 4.1 also shows the locus of research for each of these three research tasks. While the first task was to be undertaken in the Opto-electronics Joint Research Laboratory (OJL), located on a Fujitsu site, the second and third tasks were to be done inside the participating companies with cooperative work to resolve the interfacing problems necessary for the development of the optical measurement and control system as a whole. Of the fourteen companies which became members of the Engineering Research Association for Optoelectronics Applied System, nine participated in the Joint Laboratory, namely, Fujitsu, Furukawa, Hitachi, Matsushita, Mitsubishi, NEC, Oki, Sumitomo and Toshiba. The remaining members were Fuji Electric, Fujikura, Nippon Sheet Glass, Shimadzu Seisakusho and Yokogawa Electric. In terms of the terminology of the present book, the accomplishment of the first task involved joint research in joint research facilities (JRJF), while the second and third tasks were achieved through coordinated in-house research (CIHR). The choice of different types of research cooperation for these tasks is important and requires further comment.

It has already been noted that the strongest firms insisted that only 'very basic' research be undertaken in joint laboratories. This point is elaborated upon by James L. Merz, Director of the Compound Semiconductor Research Center at the University of California, Santa Barbara, who was Visiting Research Scientist in the Optoelectronics Joint Research Laboratory of the Optical Measurement Project in the autumn of 1985. Merz (1987, p. 12) notes that the Joint Laboratory had the responsibility of

working on generic materials technology that would be of use to all of the companies in developing III-V devices. Thus, [the Joint Laboratory] did not work on devices themselves, but worked on a broader range of basic materials research which the member companies needed for device development. This approach had a number of advantages: for example, the companies did not have to give away any of their processing and fabrication secrets that are so important in device development and manufacturing, and at relatively low cost, they could participate in materials research that might be considered too expensive for any one company.

Elsewhere in the same paper Merz states that joint research on generic technology 'allows participation of the companies without compromise of privileged information regarding processing and fabrication techniques and device design concepts' (p. 18).

As they stand, these quotations beg two questions of fundamental importance. The first relates to the *ability* of firms to share particular kinds of knowledge, that is how easy is it for them to share these types of knowledge if they want to do so? The second deals with the *willingness* of firms to share different kinds of knowledge. The quotations imply that the firms are in general more willing to share 'generic', or as the Japanese put it 'basic', knowledge than they are to share knowledge about processing, fabrication and device design concepts. But if this is correct, what is the explanation?

To take these questions in order, it must first be noted that there is a high-degree of firm-specificity or idiosyncrasy in knowledge relating to processing, fabrication and device design concepts. Thus for example Scace (1981, p. 17) of the US National Bureau of Standards observes that

the particular characteristics of the [semiconductor production] processes in use by each manufacturer are different. These properties lead to requirements, called design rules, which apply in the preparation of the photo-masks, and which are different for different manufacturers – even for different process sequences within the same manufacturer's house. In general, processes in use by different firms, even to produce devices with essentially identical properties, are sufficiently different that the masks used by manufacturer A will not work in manufacturer B's environment.

For present purposes, one of the main implications of this idiosyncrasy is that the *ability* of firms to share knowledge in the areas of processing, fabrication and device design concepts is constrained. Although some of this knowledge could be made explicit and conveyed to the other firms participating in the cooperative research project, much of it would not be relevant in view of the firm-specificity referred to. Accordingly, the ability to cooperate is constrained. This important point is emphasized by Uenohara (1985, p. 140): ' Even in Japan, cooperation among competing companies is almost impossible as technological development moves closer to product levels. This is not only due to business competition, but also due to differences in fine details of process technology, which has been accumulated for many years and integrated into major automation systems [in the individual companies].'

Quite apart from the ability of firms to share knowledge in various areas, however, is their *willingness* to do so. More specifically, are firms more willing to share knowledge in generic or basic areas, and if so why? Further light is thrown on this question in an important interview between the author and a senior executive of one of the leading electronics companies which participated in the Optical Measurement Project:

Fransman: In the Epitaxial Growth Joint Laboratory... NEC had two members, Mitsubishi and Sumitomo had three each, while Matsushita, Oki and Toshiba had one each. The researchers who go there obviously interact with researchers from the other companies. Isn't there a danger that the knowledge they bring with them will leak to the other companies?
Informant: There is a danger, but there we have to compromise. That is why we limit the research activities in the joint laboratories to very basic

research. Otherwise no company will be willing to send very capable members.

Fransman: What is meant by 'basic' in this context?

Informant: It is basic to the industrial technologies. *Such technologies cannot be immediately applied to the production of the product. There is a certain period of further development necessary for the product to be produced by the company. There is a further time span required.* After the joint research has ended, people go back to their companies and it will still take several years for products to be developed. *This time period gives the firm the opportunity to influence its competitive position through its own activities.*

Fransman: In the case of the electron beam machine in the VLSI Project, was this also basic research?

Informant: This machine is used for only a *part* of the process [of VLSI production]. The electron beam machine is only used for the mask-making – this is only a fraction of the total process. At the time we did not know whether electron beam, optical or X-ray lithography would become the main technology for VLSI. In the VLSI joint laboratories we evaluated these alternative technologies. The information was very useful for the member companies. [*emphasis added*]

The last quotation suggests a more precise conceptualization of those parts of a firm's stock of knowledge where there is a relatively high willingness to share. Attempts in the literature to define these areas have relied to a large extent on conventional definitions of the terms generic and basic. According to the *Concise Oxford Dictionary* the term generic refers to the 'characteristic of a genus or class; applied to (any individual of) a large group or class; general, not specific or special.' The two elaborations on generic technology discussed above in connection with the VLSI Project[6] followed this definition closely. The first defined 'generic technologies' as 'technologies not associated with particular proprietary product designs' while the second defined 'a generic (or enabling) area of technological knowledge' as 'a body of knowledge from which many specific products and processes may emerge'. *The last quotation from the senior executive, however, suggests that it is not the property of 'generality' or wide applicability which is responsible for the relatively high willingness to share, but rather the fact that additional time, knowledge, effort and resources are required to transform this 'generic knowledge' into profitability, competitiveness, market share, etc.* In other words (words used elsewhere in this book), generic knowledge for which there is a high willingness to share is knowledge with widespread application which does not have a significant *direct* impact on profitability, etc. One of the implications of this definition is that a distinction can be made between that generic knowledge which does not have a significant direct effect on profitability, etc., and where there is, accordingly, a relatively high willingness to share, and other areas of generic knowledge where there is an important direct effect and where the willingness to share is therefore lower.

Finally, it is useful to develop a new concept, the *propensity to share knowledge,* by amalgamating the ability to share knowledge with the willingness to share knowledge. The propensity to share knowledge will be capable of dealing with those cases where there is a high willingness to share but where effective sharing is limited by a low ability to share as a result of factors such as firm-specific idiosyncratic knowledge. Applying this concept to the research design for the Optical Measurement Project, it was necessary to have different types of research cooperation for the first research task on the one hand, and the second and third tasks on the other (as shown in Fig. 4.1), because while there was a relatively high propensity to share in the research required for the first task, the propensity was substantially lower in that needed for the latter two tasks. Accordingly, the commercializable devices (such as the optoelectronic integrated circuits and optical sensors) and subsystems of the total optical measurement and control system were developed *inside the member companies* with the minimum cooperation necessary for interfacing, an example of coordinated in-house research.

The final feature of the research design which requires comment is the linkages which were established between the three research tasks.

As shown in Fig. 4.1, in principle the joint laboratories were to do the generic research on materials, materials growth and fabrication technology. The output from this research would constitute an input into the second research task, namely the development of specific optoelectronic integrated circuits and optical sensors. In turn, the output from the second research area would feed into the third area, the subsystems and ultimately the total closed optical measurement and control system. At the same time, and again in principle, feedback loops would operate to ensure that the research done 'upstream' was relevant for the 'downstream' users. In this way a synthesis between 'use-pull' and 'generic research-push' would be achieved. At the same time the research design ensured that a potentially commercially useful system would emerge from the research.

The total optical measurement system and its subsystems

The total optical measurement and control system and its various subsystems are shown in Fig. 4.2. Further information is provided in Table 4.3 on each of the five subsystems according to the firm in overall charge of the subsystem, the components (OEICs, sensors, etc.) produced for each subsystem, and the firms given responsibility for the production of these components. As mentioned, cooperation was required between the firms in order to achieve the interfacing necessary for the configuration of the system as a whole.

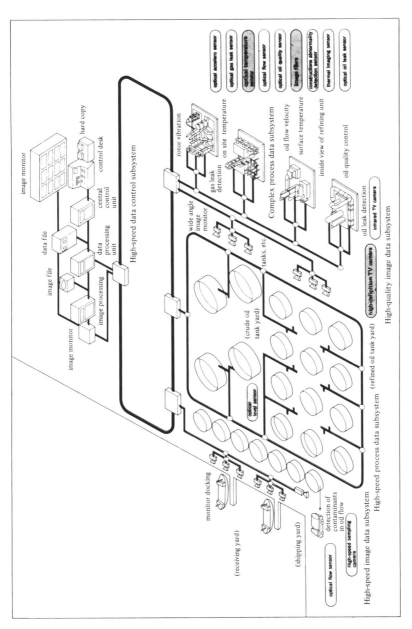

Fig. 4.2 The total Optical Measurement System and its subsystems (*Source:* Engineering Research Association for Optoelectronics Applied System).

Table 4.3. *The subsystems and components and the firms involved in the Optical Measurement Project*

Subsystem	Firm in overall charge	OEICs, optical sensors and elements	Firm in charge of OEICs, etc.
High-quality image data subsystem	Fujitsu	Multichannel OEIC switch	Fujitsu
		Image fibre	Sumitomo
High-speed process data subsystem			
	Mitsubishi	High-power semiconductor laser array	Mitsubishi
		Optical flow sensor	Shimadzu
		Optical temperature sensor	Fuji Electric
		Optical accelerosensor	Mitsubishi
		Optical level (pressure) sensor	Shimadzu
High-speed image data subsystem	NEC	Visible semiconductor laser	NEC
High-speed data control subsystem	Hitachi	Transmitter OEIC high-speed modulation semiconductor laser	Hitachi
		Receiver OEIC	Hitachi
Complex process data subsystem	Toshiba	Wavelength-controlled laser diode	Toshiba

The Optoelectronics Joint Research Laboratory

Funding of the Joint Laboratory

The funding of the Joint Laboratory is shown in Fig. 4.3. The Optical Measurement Project lasted officially from 1979 to 1985 although in practice the research in the Joint Laboratory was only concluded in March 1987. Research in the Joint Laboratory began in 1981. As is shown in Fig. 4.3, during the period MITI allocated a total of 16 billion yen to the Optical Measurement Project. In addition, some of the total costs of the project were borne by the participating companies. The Joint Laboratory had a total budget of 9 billion yen during the period of its operation. 6 billion of this was contributed by MITI, while the remaining 3 billion came from the companies. In other words, *6 billion out of a total of 16 billion spent by MITI on the Optical Measurement Project, or 38 per cent of the total, went to the Joint Laboratory. This means that while 38 per cent of the funds went to joint research to joint research facilities, the bulk of the money, 62 per cent, went to the coordinated in-house portion of the research.*

Professor James Merz, who was a Visiting Research Scientist in the Joint Laboratory (OJL) during the autumn of 1985, notes that about 60 per cent of the MITI funds allocated to OJL was spent on capital equipment Accordingly, he observes,

the effect of MITI's sponsorship of this project was that OJL was a very capital-intensive laboratory; the management of OJL assembled the most impressive collection of high-technology, materials-oriented, state-of-the-art equipment that I have ever seen. The rather small space rented from Fujitsu in their Kawasaki facility was literally crammed with machines for sophisticated crystal growth, such as molecular beam epitaxy (MBE) and metalorganic chemical vapor deposition (MOCVD), and the finest characterization and analysis equipment available.   (Merz, 1987, p. 12)

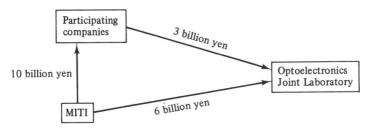

Fig. 4.3   The funding of the Optoelectronics Joint Laboratory.

Membership of the Joint Laboratory

As Merz (1987, p. 18) notes,

OJL's long-range materials research [focused] on the concept of optoelectronic integrated circuits (OEICs); that is, the integration of optical devices with high-speed electronic integrated circuits. Since the technology for high-speed electronic devices is expected to be dominated by GaAs [gallium arsenide] for some time in the future (GaAs MESFETs now, high-mobility devices utilizing 2-D electron gases in the future), it was felt by the organizers of OJL that a focus on GaAs would be appropriate.

In the event six joint groups were established:

(1) Bulk crystal growth
(2) Maskless ion implantation (FIBI)
(3) Epitaxial growth
(4) Applied surface physics
(5) Fabrication technology
(6) Materials analysis and characterization

Through a process of negotiation between the individual companies and the leaders of the Joint Laboratory, mainly seconded from ETL, decisions were made about (a) the research topics to be covered, (b) the firms that would take the lead in the major research areas, and (c) the allocation of each firm's researchers among the six groups. The companies had a fair degree of autonomy in selecting the research areas in which they wanted to specialize. For example, Fujitsu decided in consultation to head the second group dealing with maskless ion implantation because this was felt to be a central technology and Fujitsu wanted to increase its expertise in this area.[7] Ultimately, Fujitsu supplied the manager for the second group in addition to three other researchers while Matsushita and Sumitomo each supplied one researcher. Similarly, Toshiba agreed to take the lead in group 1, the group dealing with research on bulk crystal growth. Toshiba decided to concentrate on this area (a) because bulk growth of gallium arsenide crystals is an extremely important technology, (b) at that time the research was at the 'pre-competitive stage' which meant that the company did not mind sharing knowledge with researchers from other firms, and (c) expensive equipment was required which would have been difficult for the company to finance.[8] While Toshiba eventually had three researchers in group 1, Mitsubishi and NEC had two each, with Fujitsu, Furukawa and Hitachi one each.

However, the process whereby decisions are made regarding research topic, leadership of each group and company membership of the group is complex. As a senior executive of one of the companies which participated in the Optical Measurement Project put it: 'There are many strategies employed by the companies. Before we finally formulate the form of the organization and its membership there are a lot of games played [*laughter*].'

To begin with, having taken the decision to participate in the joint laboratory, each company attempts to steer the research done in a direction consistent with its own priorities. 'When discussions take place about setting the priorities for the joint laboratories each company wants to influence the kind of research that is to be done in line with its own objectives.' However, one of the costs from the company's point of view of the attempt to influence the research agenda arises where information of a possibly strategically important kind is given to competing companies. 'In attempting to influence the decision [regarding the research agenda], the companies give and receive information about each other's objectives, strengths and weaknesses, which they would not get from research conferences. This is a give-and-take relationship.'

Further difficulties arise where there is a sigificant gap between the technological levels of the participating companies. Under these circumstances the stronger companies may be expected to be unhappy about the possibilities for free-riding. This was a problem in the formation of the Joint Laboratory of the Optical Measurement Project as emerges from the following quotation:

> Fransman: In the process of give and take, aren't companies worried that other companies will be taking more and giving less?
> Informant: Oh yes! When the project discussions begin there is a big difference between the companies in terms of their technological level. It is therefore necessary to select the member companies so that the gap is as narrow as possible. That is why it is very difficult for small companies to join.
> Fransman: I believe that when Oki entered the Optical Measurement Project their technology was weaker than that of the strongest companies.
> Informant: Right. At the beginning we were reluctant [to participate in the project with weaker companies], but finally we compromised.
> Fransman: Why did you compromise?
> Informant: If there were only weak companies and one strong company the project would never materialize. But there were other strong companies [from whom we could learn].[9]

In addition to access to the knowledge provided by other strong firms as a factor compensating a stronger firm for the possibility of free-riding, mention must also be made of the subsidized finance provided by MITI and referred to above. All of these factors taken together were responsible for the ultimate willingness of the stronger companies to compromise.

Once the final decisions have been made regarding the areas of research and the research groups, the companies will make further strategic decisions about the quality of their participation. These too are complex decisions. In general, the more competitive a company is relative to the other companies in a particular research area and the more important it expects this area will be, the more the company will tend to allocate weaker or less experienced research staff to this research group. On the other hand, the weaker a company is in an area and the more important it expects the area to be, the more it will tend to allocate stronger, more experienced researchers. However, there are other influences which may counteract these tendencies as is evident from the following quotation:

> Fransman: Is it true to say that if a company is particularly strong in an area they will aim to send younger, less experienced researchers? But if they are weak in that area they will try and send stronger researchers? Informant: Yes. That is generaly true. But we cannot be too obvious about this because there is a social evaluation, particularly of the strong companies. It makes a very bad impression.

As these quotations imply, there is the possibility of a conflict of interest (a) between MITI and the stronger firms and (b) between the firms themselves participating in the national research project. While each firm has an interest in maximizing its information inflow and minimizing its information outflow, MITI, with the brief of improving Japan's longer-run international competitiveness, has an interest in ensuring the widest possible diffusion of technological knowledge amongst Japanese electronics companies. Although the free-rider problem as just discussed might limit the participation of smaller and weaker companies, MITI is likely to want a wider diffusion of technological knowledge than the stronger firms. This underlying tension will mean that MITI will have in a number of ways to bring pressure to bear on the companies in order to ensure the high quality of their participation and the wide diffusion of the knowledge resulting from the joint research.

The potential for conflict between the stronger and the weaker firms is obvious. The stronger firms, as noted above, will tend to send weaker researchers in those areas where they already have a competitive advantage in order to minimize free-riding. On the other hand, the weaker firms will tend to maximize their inflow of knowledge from the joint research by sending strong researchers to the joint laboratory.

In resolving conflicts such as these, ETL plays a particularly important role: 'ETL plays a crucial role in the cooperative projects. ETL staff know the key members of each company. When companies don't agree ETL can mediate. Sometimes MITI officials put pressures on the president of that company. ETL is neutral.'

The membership of the Joint Laboratory in autumn 1985 is shown in Table 4.4. Several comments may be made on the basis of this table. The first is that in all cases, with the exception of the last group, dealing with materials analysis and characterization, the company with the largest number of researchers in the group also supplied the manager of the

Table 4.4. *Membership of the Optoelectronics Joint Laboratory*

	Director-General:		T. Iizuka		
	Technical Director:		I. Havashi		
	Research Planning:		M. Hirano		
	Administration:		A. Okamura		

Group

	Bulk Growth	FIBI	Epitaxial Growth	Surface Physics	Fabr. Tech.	Characterization
Manager: & Company:	Fukuda Toshiba	Hashimoto Fujitsu	Ishii Mitsub.	Naka-shima Hitachi	Asakawa NEC	Ishida NEC
ETL						1
Fujitsu	1	4				1
Furukawa	1				1	1
Hitachi	1			3		
Matsushita		1	1	2		1
Mitsubishi	2		3			2
NEC	2		2		2	1
Oki			1	2		
Sumitomo		1	3	1		
Toshiba	3		1			1
Totals:	10	6	11	8	3	8

Note: Information from autumn 1985. Some researchers subsequently returned to their member companies because of the limited remaining lifetime of the laboratory. *Source*: Merz, 1987, p. 19.

group. In other words, and again with the exception of the last group, *there was a clear single firm dominance in each of the groups.* Secondly, there appears to be some relationship between the dominant firms which supplied managers for the groups and the number of researchers which these dominant firms sent to the Joint Laboratory as a whole. Thus, with the exception of Hitachi, the dominant firms sent the largest number of researchers. However, while Toshiba supplied the manager for the bulk growth group and sent five researchers to the Joint Laboratory, Matsushita and Sumitomo also sent five researchers although they did not manage any of the groups.

The presence of dominant firms in each group and the difference in the number of researchers from each of the firms represented in the group raises the important question of the differential benefit that these firms derive from the joint research in terms of the eventual inflow of knowledge to the company. More specifically, do each of the firms represented in the group have equal access to the knowledge jointly generated in the group irrespective of the number of researchers they have sent, or is the benefit directly proportional to the number of researchers sent? This question is extremely important because the answer to it will determine factors such as the benefit which the firms derive from their participation, the extent to which free-riding is likely to take place, and the implicit strategies that the firms have followed as revealed by their decision to specialize in particular areas of the joint research.

This question was posed in interviews held with several of the firms which participated in the Optical Measurement Project's Joint Laboratory. The consensus which emerged from these interviews was that there is an important degree of *tacitness* in the knowledge generated in the joint research group. This implies that not all the knowledge generated in the group can be made explicit and transferred to others who have not participated in the research of the group. To the extent that the knowledge generated is tacit, it will remain in the effective possession of these who have created it. This means that the participating firms will derive benefit from the joint research (in terms of the knowledge that eventually flows into the firm) in proportion to the number of researchers that they have in the research group. Accordingly, the dominant firm as previously defined will be the major beneficiary from the joint research. Thus, to take an example, in group 1, dealing with bulk crystal growth, Toshiba with the largest number of researchers in the group will derive more benefit from the joint research in this group than any other single company.

A number of important implications follow from this conclusion. The first, and perhaps the most important, is that the degree of tacitness in the research increases the incentive to take part in joint research. *Rather than being involved in the joint creation of knowledge which is entirely in the public domain, the participating companies in the joint research groups are generating knowledge which may to a significant extent in the future be privately appropriated by themselves.* This may occur as the effective possessors of the tacit knowledge, the researchers who have created the knowledge, return to their company where the knowledge is transformed, together with other knowledge, into profitability, etc. The second implication is that the possibilities for free-riding are limited and therefore that the obstacle to joint research posed by such free-rides may turn out to be not very substantial. To the extent that the knowledge created is tacit, weaker firms will not be able to effectively possess all this knowledge. Where weaker firms have a smaller number of researchers in the group than the dominant firm, which we have seen was the typical case in the Joint Laboratory of the Optical Measurement Project, they will enjoy smaller inflows of knowledge than the dominant firm. These two implications taken together mean that the existence of tacitness in joint research works to increase the possibility of joint research in joint research facilities by increasing the private nature of such research.[10]

A further mechanism used to limit free-riding and increase the incentive to participate in joint research is to increase the benefit derived by the dominant firm by raising the relative quality of its researchers. As the senior executive of the participating company observed, the benefits derived by a company 'depends upon the ability of the researchers. The company with the majority of members will send some key researchers. If there is a minority company represented in the joint laboratory, their researcher is most likely to be younger and more of an assistant. We cannot organise when all in the laboratory are experts. We need assistants. If the assistant is very capable, he will acquire a lot of new knowledge. But at the same time he will give research support.'

Evaluation of the Optical Measurement Project

As emerged from the evaluation exercise undertaken in the case of the VLSI Project, the evaluation of a national project such as the Optical Measurement Project is an extremely complex business. In this section the evaluation of the Optical Measurement Project will be approached from a number of different perspectives. First, an evaluation will be undertaken of parts of the output of the Joint Laboratory. In this subsection an examination will also be undertaken of the extent to which a synthesis of 'use-pull' and 'generic research-push', which as was shown above constituted an inherent part of the research design for the Optical Measurement Project, was realized in the project. Secondly, the project will be evaluated according to the extent that it helped to consolidate and strengthen an industrial system consisting of both competing and complementary firms together capable of developing optical communications systems. A third perspective will involve an appraisal of the project according to its influence on the allocation of research resources within the participating firms and the extent to which it served to focus national attention on the constituent technologies thereby enhancing their development. Fourthly, as in the case of the VLSI Project, the Optical Measurement Project will be evaluated according to the additional benefits it yielded over and above the benefits that would have been produced under the alternative form of organization, namely coordinated in-house research. A fifth approach to evaluation will deal with the degree to which the project facilitated a greater diffusion of technological knowledge than would otherwise have occurred. Finally, account will be taken of some of the main costs of joint research which must be offset against the benefits produced.

An evaluation of the output of the Joint Laboratory

The Optical Measurement Project began in 1979 and the research of the Joint Laboratory in 1981. By 1986 *Fortune* concluded that 'Everyone concedes that the Japanese lead the world hands-down in one important new technology originally developed in the US. It is optoelectronics, a marriage of electronics and optics that is already yielding important commercial products such as optical fiber communications systems' (*Fortune*, 13 October 1986). In 1987 the United States Science Board Task Force on Defense Semiconductor Dependency concluded not only that in the area of optoelectronic semiconductors Japan led the United States, but also that the latter's position was declining.[11]

However, it would be incorrect to conclude that this state of affairs is a result of the Optical Measurement Project. To begin with, from the mid-1970s the Japanese were developing optical fibres with world-leading transmission loss rates. Not only was research being done in the Japanese electronics companies in the area of optoelectronics before the Optical Measurement Project, but other national research projects, such as that involving NTT and its supplier companies, had previously been established in this area. Furthermore, the research done in the Joint Laboratory was of a basic or generic kind and given the time that must elapse before such research is commercialized, it is likely that the full impact of this research had not been felt by the mid 1980s. Similarly, the demonstration optical control and mesurement system was only installed in the Mizushima oil refinery in 1986 making it likewise unlikely that the technology developed for this system was having a significant commercial effect by the mid 1980s.

Nevertheless, there is evidence to suggest that the Joint Laboratory has been extremely successful in terms of the quality of much of its research output. As is well known, there are substantial difficulties involved in any attempt to measure the quality of research output. In the light of these difficulties, one method that is frequently resorted to is that of peer group review. In the case of the Joint Laboratory of the Optical Measurement Project, as in the case of some of the other national projects examined in the present book, use will be made of the evaluations of a special peer group, namely foreign specialists involved in research in the same technology areas. Based on visits to Japan and on close observation of research being done there, these specialists have made judgements on the quality of Japanese research. These observations are used in the present book as the basis for an evaluation of the quality of Japanese research output. This is not to pretend that these judgements consistute an objective evaluation of the quality of research. There are many reasons why caution should be exercised in the use of such judgements. In some cases, as will later be seen, the judgements of foreign specialists are inconsistent so that, without any way of evaluating the evaluators, a final conclusion on the quality of the research is difficult to reach. Furthermore, it is possible to think of reasons why some foreign specialists might be biased in their judgements. For example, the desire to see more resources made available in the specialist's research area in his or her own country might motivate, if only unconsciously, an exaggeration of Japanese research achievements and their strategic and competitive implications. Nevertheless, despite drawbacks such as these, the judgements of recognized foreign specialists do provide one potentially important indicator of the quality of Japanese research output. To begin with, they have an intimate knowledge of at least part of the research area being evaluated and, based on their own experience of similar research undertaken in the same area in their own country, are often able to make a reasonable comparative evaluation of the international quality of the research. Furthermore, since their long-term research interests usually lie outside Japan, they do not have the same vested interest in judging the research output positively as might some of their Japanese colleagues. Finally, and somewhat more defensively, there are few preferable alternative ways of evaluating research output.

In the case of the Optical Measurement Project we are particularly fortunate to be able to use the detailed appraisal of Professor James Merz.[12] Merz, Director of the Compound Semiconductor Research Center at the University of California, Santa Barbara, spent the autumn of 1985 as Visiting Research Scientist in the Optoelectronics Joint Research Laboratory of the Optical Measurement Project. During 1986 he visited the Joint Laboratory and many of the participating firms twice more.

Merz's (1987, p. 26) overall conclusion is that 'truly innovative materials and processing research is underway at the Optoelectronics Joint Research Laboratory (OJL), and that progress has been significant during the limited lifetime of this laboratory. As was the case with the VLSI Project, it appears that Japan will go from a position behind the United States to virtual domination of the Optoelectronic device market during a time span only a little longer than the lifetime of this cooperative project.' However, he goes on to caution that in 'neither [the VLSI nor the Optical Measurement] case can the cooperative research laboratory be the direct cause of [Japan's] leadership, since it takes many years for research results to impact the marketplace, and the cooperative projects represented only a small percent of the resource commitments made' (p. 35).

More specifically, Merz describes

a very high level of basic research competence at ... OJL in a carefully-chosen agenda of research topics on basic and generic materials problems which need to be solved if GaAs optoelectronic integrated circuits are to become an economic reality. Considerable (I'm tempted to say astonishing) progress has been made, both within OJL and within the individual laboratories of the member companies themselves. Particularly impressive have been OJL's advances in crystal growth (both bulk and epitaxial), advanced processing such as maskless implantation and dry etching, the fabrication and processing of superlattice structures for novel device applications, and the characterization of defects in bulk, semi-insulating GaAs. In parallel with this, the member companies have carried out equally impressive research activities in their own laboratories on compound semi-conductors, and have moved the simpler GaAs devices into the market place, virtually dominating the III-V compound device market.   (p. 34)

Merz reports that research of an internationally high quality was under-taken in some of the groups working in the Joint Laboratory. For example, group 1, dealing with bulk crystal growth, 'is one of the best in the world at developing advanced techniques for bulk growth using the liquid-encapsulated Czochralski (LEC) technique... OJL currently has the best control over defect introduction, and compositional control and uniformity of any laboratory in the world, and hence is in a strong position to carry out a systematic investigation of the principal defects in this material... These improvements in GaAs bulk growth are critical to the development of GaAs integrated circuits as well as [to] the optoelec-tronics industry' (p. 20).

In the case of group 2, researching on maskless ion implantation, a group dominated by Fujitsu, Merz states that 'Fujitsu will clearly have a large lead in what could amount to a very important technology in Japan. Maskless ion implantation features a focussed ion beam implanter (FIBI) coupled through a common ultra-high vacuum (UHV) system with a molecular beam epitaxy (MBE) crystal-growth system...The potential of this coupled FIBI/MBE system is extremely great, and the investiga-tion of its capabilities represents one of the major contributions of OJL' (p. 21).

Group 3, researching on epitaxial growth, was under the leadership of Mitsubishi although Sumitomo was also strongly represented in this group. Regarding the latter company, Merz comments that 'It is interest-ing that Sumitomo, long the world leader in bulk GaAs substrates, considers epitaxial growth so important. That leadership is currently threatened by [a] large number of Japanese companies' (p. 22). Clearly, Sumitomo appears to have made the strategic decision to use the opportunity of research in the Joint Laboratory to strengthen its com-petitive position in this technology which is of possible significance for one of its most important products. In group 3 'Both MBE and low-pressure Metal Organic Chemical Vapor Deposition (MOCVD) are investigated. Two themes that run through much of this work are the investigation of growth over patterned wafers for new active device configurations (particularly those that will lead to a planar technology), and the use of novel configurations of quantum wells and superlattices to tailor the properties of devices.' Merz notes that in undertaking this research OJL enjoys the advantages of an abundant endowment of state-of-the-art capital equipment as well as synergies between many of the areas being researched by the groups in the Joint Laboratory: neither of the two themes just mentioned were ideas 'originated by the Japanese, but their capital equipment advantages allow them to pursue these ideas in conjunction with other, unusual capabilities, such as FIBI' (p. 22).

In group 5, which does research on fabrication technology and which has only three members, 'The emphasis...has been on Reactive Ion Beam Etching (RIBE) for the microfabrication of a variety of device structures necessary for the formation of optoelectronic integrated circuits. Although some of the earliest research using RIBE techniques was reported by researchers at Bell Laboratories...the OJL work has made some of the more recent advances in perfecting this technique, with important applications to device fabrication' (p. 24).

Merz observes that 'Unlike most of the other groups, which tend to be dominated by one or two of the member companies, the characterization group has eight members from seven different companies. Everyone wants to be able to determine the quality of their material...Because of the strong concentration of characterization expertise...in the same laboratory having so strong an effort in bulk growth of GaAs, I believe that OJL stands at the threshold of making a major contribution to the understanding of the principal defects in this material...This is probably the only laboratory in the world currently capable of mounting a systematic study of bulk GaAs with carefully controlled changes in stoichiometry' (p. 23).

According to Merz, in the last few months of the existence of OJL an important experiment was carried out with possibly important consequences in this field of technology. This experiment involved the realization of important synergies between the different areas of research carried out in the Joint Laboratory:

During the final months of the laboratory...OJL is attempting a daring and truly synergistic experiment which will combine much of the expertise described [in Merz's paper]. During my last month at the laboratory a huge UHV system was assembled that incorporated not only the focussed ion beam implanter, MBE, and the analysis chamber described above, but also a new focussed ion beam *etching* (FIBE) system, a radical gun for defect-free surface cleaning, and an electron-beam annealing system designed to eliminate the damage resulting from FIBI...This massive vacuum system should be able to 'do it all', complete in-situ crystal growth, maskless implantation and/or etching, implant-damage anneal, surface cleaning, and analysis of the results at any stage of processing, all within a UHV environment! *Nothing like this has been (or could be) attempted anywhere else in the world!*...should they succeed, the implications are enormous for the future of optoelectronic integrated circuits – all the growth, fabrication, and processing steps could be done in-situ, in one system, in a completely maskless way, without the need for photolithography, wet chemical processing, or exposure to any other hostile environment! A truly remarkable achievement. Even if success is not realized during the limited remaining lifetime of this laboratory, there will certainly be follow-through within industry.

(pp. 26–7, emphasis added).

Accordingly, Merz concludes that 'in the case of optoelectronics...the

Japanese have made a massive, long-range commitment to III-V compounds that far outstrips the effort made by industry in the United States and Europe. Not only is this commitment evident at OJL itself, but at each of the basic research laboratories of the member companies. For example, the semiconductor research at Fujitsu is approximately one-third HEMT (GaAs) [high electron mobility transistor, discussed in more detail below in connection with the Supercomputer Project], one-third optoelectronics (GaAs), and one third silicon (fine-line lithography, processing, etc.)' (p. 35). This situation contrasts starkly with that in the United States. 'The majority of III-V research in the United States is military, with relatively little basic research carried out in the industrial environment, except for a handful of the largest industrial labs.' (p. 37).

To the extent that Merz's observations provide an accurate portrayal, it would appear that the Joint Laboratory of the Optical Measurement Project has produced significant research output. It is, however, not possible to provide a quantitative estimate of this output in terms that would facilitate a calculation of the social cost–benefit ratio. For one thing, the research output of the Joint Laboratory feeds into the research and development activities of the participating companies, and only with its combination with other forms of knowledge is it transformed into a commercializable output. Furthermore, as was noted earlier in connection with the Pattern Information Processing System (PIPS) project, a substantial time period is required in order to assess the commercial impact of generic or basic research. In addition, a point that will be taken up again later, it is difficult to estimate the extent to which the research output is the result of the activities of the Joint Laboratory itself, as opposed to output that would in any event have emerged had the research been done inside the companies with their financing. For these reasons it is not possible to quantitatively measure the benefit of the research output of the Joint Laboratory. Merz's comments are nevertheless valuable in that they provide an indication of the international comparative quality of the research output.

Still on the question of the quality of research output, it was shown above that the design of the research undertaken under the Optical Measurement Project was intended to synthesize 'use-pull' and 'generic research-push' determinants shaping the research. This meant, for example, that the role of the Joint Laboratory was not simply to do 'enabling' generic or basic research in the area of gallium arsenide materials. Its role was more specifically tailored to the production of knowledge which would be drawn on by individual participating firms in their production of specific optoelectronic integrated circuits and sensors. These circuits and sensors, in turn, would be integrated into the broader optical measurement and control system developed for the oil refinery. In this way the research design was intended to ensure that the research of the Joint Laboratory was constrained and 'pulled' by the requirements of the total system. In evaluating this aspect of the project it is necessary to examine not only the quality of the research of the Joint Laboratory but also the kind of research that was done and the way in which the research contributed to the overall functioning of the optical measurement and control system. While it is accepted that some of the research generated by the Joint Laboratory will provide benefit even if it is not relevant for the total system, it is also important to ask how successful the research design was in bringing about the synthesis of 'use-pull' and 'generic research-push'.

Once again, it is extremely difficult to provide an evaluation of this aspect of the project. Nevertheless, through interviews with one of the major participating companies involved in all three research tasks (managing one of the research groups in the Joint Laboratory, developing optoelectronic integrated circuits, and developing one of the subsystems for the optical measurement and control system), it is possible to draw some conclusions.

The role of the subsystem developed by this company was to collect data (for example, from a microscope or on a particular production process), to transmit this data via optical fibre cables to a switching system, and from there again via optical fibre cables to a data processing system. An important part of the research involved the development of an optoelectronic integrated circuit which would be used in several parts of the subsystem. The original aim was to integrate all the electronic and optical components on a single chip and to draw on the research of the Joint Laboratory for the materials work required in designing and producing the device. In practice, however, things turned out rather differently. Since somewhat different materials were used for the optoelectronic integrated circuit developed inside the company compared to those researched in the Joint Laboratory, in practice the company device research moved in parallel to that of the Joint Laboratory rather than sequentially. Interviews with one of the other major participants revealed the same parallel research process. In the latter case the semiconductor laser that was developed in the company used aluminium gallium indium phosphide, which differed from the gallium arsenide used in the Joint Laboratory. The first firm eventually failed to integrate the electronic and optical components on the same chip and had to combine separate devices.

This suggests that the 'use-pull' determinant in practice operated more from the total system and its subsystems to the specific devices, both of which were developed in-house, than from the specific devices to the generic materials research done in the Joint Laboratory (see Fig. 4.1). Similarly, the 'generic research-push' from the Joint Laboratory to the design and manufacture of specific devices and sensors inside the firms appears to be not as strong as intended by the reserch design. This is not to suggest, however, that 'use-pull' and 'generic research-push' determinants were absent from the project; rather that they were probably not as pervasive as originally intended.

In evaluating the research output of the Joint Laboratory there is one important further indicator of significant benefit derived by the participating companies. This is the decision taken by the main companies to undertake a further optoelectronic project after the ending of the Optical Measurement Project in March 1987. This project, which is to concentrate on indium phosphide,[13] is smaller than the previous one and is located in Tsukuba. It is financed by the Japan Key Technology Center. The proof of the pudding is in the eating; clearly, on the basis of the benefits which they derived from the Optical Measurement Project the main participating firms were willing to do some more joint baking.

Creation of an industrial system as one of the Optical Measurement Project's benefits

It may be argued, as Sigurdson (1986) suggested in the case of the VLSI Project, that one of the 'outputs' created by the Optical Measurement Project was the development of an industrial system consisting of both competing and complementary firms which together have the capability to generate optical communications systems. Although there is undoubtedly some truth in this argument, care must be taken in its proposal.

There are several reasons for the need for care. To begin with, the possibility that such an industrial system could have evolved through market relationships, that is interactions between firms unmediated by government, must be allowed for. To the extent that the market would have generated this industrial system in the absence of the Optical Measurement Project, the benefit of such a system obviously cannot be attributed to the project. Furthermore, there already were close linkages between many of the companies which participated in the project. For example, Sumitomo Electric and Nippon Sheet Glass are closely linked to NEC through the Sumitomo group of companies. Furukawa has close connections with Fujitsu and both are members of the Furukawa and Dai-Ichi Kangyo Bank groups. Fujikura works closely with Toshiba with both of these companies being linked to the Mitsui group. In general, these inter-firm linkages are a reflection (a) of the vertical disintegration that has always existed in Japan between the electronics companies and the telecommunications cable manufacturers, and (b) the pattern of industrial organization prevalent in Japan whereby many *complementary* companies are linked through industrial groupings.

A further consideration is that most of these companies were already linked to each other through NTT's so-called Den Den family of supplying firms. Until April 1985 when NTT was partly privatized, this closed group of firms included NEC, Fujitsu, Hitachi, Oki, Sumitomo Electric, Furukawa and Fujikura. This group cooperated closely with NTT in the development of materials and equipment for the telecommunications network. In other words, NTT had already created an industrial system around its activities.

Nevertheless, despite these considerations, it is likely that the Optical Measurement Project facilitated the extension and strengthening of an industrial system in the area of optoelectronics-based communications. In the first place, the Optical Measurement Project incorporated companies that were excluded from NTT's Den Den Family. Notably these included Toshiba, Matsushita and Mitsubishi. As was shown earlier, Toshiba and Mitsubishi in particular played important roles both in the Joint Laboratory and in the development of subsystems for the optical measurement and control system for the oil refinery. Secondly, the Optical Measurement Project extended the application of optoelectronics technology beyond the area in which NTT and the Den Den firms did most of their research. While the latter's research related primarily to the NTT-run telecommunications network, the Optical Measurement Project involved in effect the development of a specific kind of local area network (LAN). LANs generally lie outside the bounds of the Japanese telecommunications network. Thirdly, it is likely that the activities of the Joint Laboratory significantly strengthened the generic or basic research base of the optoelectronics-creating industrial system in Japan. While there must have been some overlap between the research of the Joint Laboratory and that done in NTT's Electrical Communications Laboratories (ECL), it is nevertheless likely that the work in the Joint Laboratory contributed to a widening and deepening of the generic research base. The optoelectronics area therefore provides yet another example of the complementary roles played by the MITI-initiated projects and those organized by NTT. Fourthly, it is possible that the Optical Measurement Project also contributed to the strength of the optoelectronics-creating system by encouraging a process of specialization between the participating companies. As was shown, the companies specialized in the project, both in the Joint Laboratory and in the development of subsystems for the total system installed in the oil refinery. While it is likely that for strategic reasons many of the technologies developed by specializing firms under the auspices of the Optical Measurement Project were reproduced inside some of the other participating companies , thus leading to a certain degree of overlap, it is also probable that in some areas a degree of specialization was encouraged within the optoelectronics-creating system as a whole. To the extent that this actually occurred, the overall efficiency of the system may have been enhanced. Finally, as a result of the substantial degree of uncertainty inherent in many of the optoelectronics technologies, it is likely that the Optical Measurement Project also contributed to the overcoming of market failures which, in the absence of government direction and subsidization, would have resulted in the delayed development of many of these technologies.

However, having stressed the benefits that have flowed from the strengthening of the optoelectronics-creating system, it is important not to exaggerate the extent and the quality of the linkages between the firms that comprise this system. Interviews held with a number of the firms which participated in the Optical Measurement Project revealed that there were important restrictions on the sharing of knowledge resulting from those parts of the project done in-house (see Fig. 4.1). For example, the three main optical fibre and cable makers which participated in the Optical Measurement Project specialized in different areas. While Fujikura produced radiation and heat resistant optical fibre, and Sumitomo made image fibre for use in video, etc., Furukawa produced fluoride fibre. Although the *results* of this research were published in the conferences and meetings that were held as part of the project, there was no additional exchange of information between these companies. Accordingly, information relating to factors such as process technology remained private. The same pattern existed in the case of the main companies which developed the subsystems for the optical measurement and control system for the oil refinery. The main reason for the restriction on information flow was the competitive relationship that existed between several of the member firms. These underlying competitive relationships therefore determined the research tasks that would be done in-house while at the same time limiting the flows of information between the competing firms in the industrial system.

MITI also helped to define and strengthen the optoelectronics-creating system in another important way, namely by facilitating the creation of the Optoelectronic Industry and Technology Development Association which was established in July 1980. This Association had the following founders: Fujikura, Fujitsu, Furukawa, Hitachi, Matsushita, Mitsubishi, NEC, Nippon Sheet Glass, Oki, Sumitomo Electric and Toshiba. The Association serves to define and articulate the general interests of the approximately 250 firms that are members and acts as a useful policy-making bridge between MITI and these firms. MITI officials are seconded for the management of the Association. Amongst the Association's functions are standardization (an area where the market often fails to generate standardization necessary for overall efficiency), feasibility studies, research on optoelectronic industrial trends, and public information. Significantly, the Association is also involved in the transfer of optical measurement and control systems, similar to that developed for the Mizushima oil refinery, to other Asian countries, including China, Korea and Thailand.

Influence of the project on the allocation of corporate research resources and on the focus of national research attention

One of the main effects of the Optical Measurement Project has been on the allocation of research resources to the area of optoelectronics. In a number of ways the project resulted in the allocation of a greater amount of such resources than would have occurred in the absence of the project. Furthermore, these resources were allocated sooner than would otherwise have happened.

To begin with, as a result of the substantial uncertainty that surrounded the concept of optoelectronic integrated circuits at the time when the Optical Measurement Project was initiated in 1977–8, it is highly probable that there would have been significantly less research investment in this area had the decision been left entirely up to the private companies without any initiative from MITI. In other words, the market would have failed to produce as much investment in research in this field as in the event was made. Support for this conclusion comes from the following extract of an interview with a senior researcher from one of the three strongest companies in the optoelectronics area:

We would certainly have made less progress in the optoelectronics area in [our company] without the Optical Measurement Project. When we started, the idea of optoelectronic integrated circuits was considered too uncertain. People had no idea of what an optoelectronic integrated circuit was. Therefore, our division would have found it difficult to attract sufficient funding in this area. However, with a national research project, with the other major firms working in this area, and with an agreed schedule for the research, we have been able to make substantial progress. Government acted as a trigger for this.

In analysing the resource allocation effect of the Optical Measurement Project, two different resource flows must be distinguished. The first is the flow of government resources into the selected technology area. The second flow is that which is allocated to the area by the private companies. The first flow took the form of government funds allocated to the Joint Laboratory and to the research done in-house by the participating companies. As was shown earlier, about 38 per cent of the 16 billion yen spent by MITI on the Optical Measurement Project went to the Joint Laboratory, while 62 per cent went to in-house research. The latter funds had a substantial effect on research in the chosen technology area in the participating firms. This emerges, for example, from figures obtained by the author from one of the three strongest firms in the field of optoelectronics (a different firm from that referred to in the last quotation). *This firm received a total of 1 billion yen from MITI for research done in-house under the Optical Measurement Project. This sum represents 10.1 per cent of the total amount allocated under this project by MITI for the purposes of in-house research. According to the manager of the laboratory in the firm which had responsibility for the firm's total contribution to the Optical Measurement Project, the 1 billion yen (or 5.56 million US dollars at the exchange rate of 180 yen = 1 US dollar used in this book) received from MITI represented about 25 per cent of the company's total R&D in the optoelectronics area.*

It is necessary, however, to examine the two resource flows referred to in the last paragraph together since they are interrelated. From interviews held with the participating firms it seems clear that the MITI funds did not simply substitute for additional company resources that would have been allocated to research in optoelectronics in the absence of the Optical Measurement Project, which would have resulted in no additional resource allocation to this area. Rather, *the MITI funds acted as a magnet attracting additional corporate investment in research in optoelectronics.* One reason for this additional corporate investment was suggested by a senior MITI official closely involved in the establishment of the Optical Measurement Project. According to this official, one factor affecting the decision of companies to participate and to allocate corporate funds to the selected area

is risk insurance. This is my personal opinion. A research association like [the Optical Measurement Association] is in the public domain. The members of the association are acknowledged as leading companies in that field. So [the member firms] were afraid not to participate in that kind of project. Also competing companies were joining and if the project succeeded the non-participating company would lose out.

From interviews in several of the participating firms it seems clear that the company's initial decision to participate in a prestigious, high-profile national project such as the Optical Measurement Project considerably strengthens the bargaining hand within the firm of the researchers involved in the selected research area. Since the company's performance in the national project is to some extent public, a certain amount of honour, not to mention the opportunity for publicizing the research prowess of the company, is at stake. In this way the researchers in the chosen area inside the company are given an extra strong card in their intra-firm competition for research resources. Accordingly, at the margin more resources tend to be allocated to the research areas covered by the national project. It is widely acknowledged that the participating companies end up allocating a substantial (but difficult to quantify) amount of corporate resources to complement the funds made available by MITI for the national project. In cases such as that of optoelectronics where extremely expensive equipment is involved, the purchase of equipment with MITI funds tends to make it easier to attract additional but smaller sums for complementary research. In these ways, therefore, *additional* resources are attracted into the selected technology area as an indirect effect of the MITI-initiated project.

From the above it is clear that the Optical Measurement Project has served to focus national attention on a set of interrelated technologies in the area of optoelectronics. These technologies were selected through a process of bargaining and consensus-formation involving MITI officials and the representatives of the participating companies. Their selection gives the signal to all concerned that it is the collective view of MITI and the most powerful companies in the area in Japan that these technologies are expected to be of central importance in the longer run. In turn, this influences the allocation of research resources, not only within the companies that participate in the national project, but also, through a demonstration effect, on other companies.

An evaluation of the benefits of joint research

It was pointed out earlier that 38 per cent of the 16 billion yen spent by MITI on the Optical Measurement Project, or 6.08 billion yen, was allocated to the Joint Laboratory. As a MITI official who was closely involved in the establishment of the Optical Measurement Project explained, 'MITI always wants a joint laboratory because we believe it is more efficient to proceed this way – budget, equipment, researchers are used more efficiently this way.'

It is, however, important to acknowledge that the 6.08 billion yen could have been allocated in alternative ways through different forms of organization. For example, rather than allocating this sum to the Joint Laboratory, an example of joint research in joint research facilities (JRJF), the funds could have been allocated to coordinated in-house research (CIHR) as happened to the remaining 62 per cent of the total MITI budget for the project. Instead of working in joint laboratories, the researchers might have tackled a similar research agenda in a coordinated way in the laboratories of their own companies.

In order to evaluate the benefits of the joint research *per se*, it is necessary to estimate the *additional* benefits realized from this research (JRJF) over and above the benefits that would have resulted from the next-best way of allocating these research resources. As in the case of the VLSI Project analysed earlier, it is assumed that coordinated in-house research (CIHR) represents the next-best alternative. Such an evaluation procedure is sensible because CIHR is an alternative to JRJF.[14] If JRJF is chosen in preference, it should be expected to yield greater net social benefit than the alternative of CIHR.[15] The present evaluation procedure requires a more rigorous analysis of these two alternatives.

The additional benefits yielded under JRJF as compared to the next-best alternative of CIHR are summarized by the *economies of joint research*. These economies include the following:

Blending of distinctive competences

To some extent each company develops its own idiosyncratic technologies in any particular technology field. Furthermore, each company will have its own specific strengths and weaknesses. By combining researchers from different companies in a joint research laboratory it may sometimes be possible to produce a fruitful synthesis based on differences such as these, a synthesis that would not be achieved were the researchers to do their work inside their own companies. It is possible that such a synthesis has been behind some of the achievements of the Joint Laboratory in the Optical Measurement Project, although more detailed research would be required to be more precise about this. For example, in the case of group 6 of the Joint Laboratory dealing with materials analysis and characterization, Merz (1987, p. 23) notes that 'the characterization group has eight members from seven different companies... Because of the strong concentration of characterization expertise... in the same laboratory having so strong an effort in bulk growth of GaAs, I believe that OJL stands at the threshold of making a major contribution to the understanding of the principal defects in this material...' (p. 23). It is likely that in addition to the number of researchers working on characterization, importance in terms of research results also attaches to the varying background and experience of the researchers acquired in the idiosyncratic environments of their companies. Similarly, although the other groups did not have representation from as many participating companies, it is likely that they also benefited from the diversity of their researchers.

Advantages of large size

It is possible in some cases that the concentration of a fairly large number of researchers in one location will achieve better research results than if the same number of researchers were scattered in different locations.[16] This point is made in an issue of *Fortune* which examines the relative strength of the United States in a number of technology areas including optoelectronics and quotes Professor Merz in this connection. Although many of the fundamental breakthroughs in the area of optoelectronics were made in the United States in laboratories such as Bell Labs., *Fortune* concludes that the Japanese now dominate this field. The United States lead

slipped away not because the US lacks theoretical knowledge in physics and optics. In fact, while the Japanese are now beginning to make first-rate theoretical contributions, the US still shines in those fields. It is far ahead in fundamental optics...What's missing in the US are size, direction and sustained effort. In optoelectronics, only Bell Labs mounts an effort that matches what a single Japanese company like Hitachi is doing. 'The trouble is that the Japanese have ten Bell Labs' Merz says...All told, the US may have more researchers in optoelectronics than Japan does, but for the most part they are scattered in tiny groups doing defense-related work, with only secondary fallout for civilian industry. None of the teams is as production-oriented as the Japanese.

(*Fortune*, 13 October 1986)

A number of important points are made in this quotation, including the contrast between the defence orientation of much American research and the production orientation of Japanese research. However, it is the issue of laboratory size that will be taken up here.

There are several advantages that may follow from larger-sized laboratories. (The Joint Laboratory in the Optical Measurement Project had a total of forty-six researchers as shown above.) To begin with, it is possible to develop a division of labour, with different research groups specializing in various areas of the research field. The proximity of the researchers, and the frequency of their contact, facilitates an efficient flow of information between the different specialist areas. (The Joint Laboratory was located in one part of one large building and this meant that there was frequent contact between the specialist researchers.) Secondly, and following from the first point, it is possible to generate synergies between the various complementary research areas. Merz (1987) repeatedly stresses that important advantages were derived from the synergies generated in the Joint Laboratories. For example,

During the final months of the laboratory ... [the Joint Laboratory] is attempting a daring and truly synergistic experiment ... a huge UHV system was assembled that incorporated not only the focussed ion beam implanter, MBE, and the analysis chamber ... but also a new focussed ion beam etching (FIBE) system, a radical gun for defect-free surface cleaning, and an electron-beam annealing system designed to eliminate the damage from FIBI...This massive vacuum system should be able to 'do it all'... Nothing like this has been (or could be) attempted anywhere else in the world.   (p. 27)

Thirdly, relating closely to the previous two points, extremely expensive equipment can be afforded and utilized more efficiently in a larger laboratory. Furthermore, the generation of synergies may be facilitated by the availability of such equipment within the same laboratory. Fourthly, a large-sized laboratory, and particularly one which is at the centre of a prestigious, high-profile national research project, is likely to attract more international attention than a number of smaller, scattered laboratories commanding the same total resources. In turn this attention might facilitate a more efficient search of, and drawing on, the international stock of knowledge in this technology area. Professor Merz's presence at the Joint Laboratory, and his replacement by a French researcher on his departure, tends to support this fourth point.

For these four reasons, joint research might result in greater benefits than would be achieved under coordinated in-house research.

Other economies

Two other economies that were realized through the joint research in the Optical Measurement Project were the avoidance of overlap and the pooling of information.

It is likely that there is less overlapping research in the case of JRJF than CIHR. In the former case there is a superior flow of information between the participating companies as a result of the proximity of, and communication between, their researchers. With CIHR, on the other hand, the research is done inside the companies, and although research results are exchanged at regular meetings and conferences, there is in general significantly less opportunity for inter-firm flows of information. As a result of the superior information flow it is likely that there is less research overlap with JRJF. This is not to suggest, however, that overlap will be eliminated since for strategic reasons competing firms will want to ensure their own research presence in areas judged to be of competitive significance. Nevertheless, to the extent that a reduction in overlapping research is realized through JRJF, this may be regarded as an additional benefit of this form of organization.

Through JRJF the participating companies may also be able to improve their collective efficiency in the collection and use of information relating to the selected technology field. By pooling those parts of their information stock which they are willing and able to share, the firms may reduce their collective cost of acquiring and using technological information. Furthermore, through their negotiations and the interactions of their researchers and other staff, firms engaged in JRJF also exchange a greater amount of information about their research activities, strengths and weaknesses than would be exchanged under CIHR. With this superior information at their disposal, firms are likely to make more efficient strategic decisions regarding matters such as specialization and choice of areas in which to compete. As a vivid example of such superior information, the author was particularly struck by the degree of consensus among research managers in the companies participating in the Joint Laboratory of the Optical Measurement Project regarding the 'pecking order' of these companies in the area of optoelectronics. Thus there was general agreement that NEC was the most advanced in this area followed closely by both Fujitsu and Hitachi. (It may be no coincidence that NEC has identified three technology areas – microelectronics, optoelectronics and bioelectronics – as underlying its activities in communications, computers and software, which together make up its specialization in C & C, computers and communications.) Firms were often well informed regarding the quality of research being done in competing companies. For example, NEC officials said that Toshiba was a strong competitor in the field of visible semiconductor lasers, although the latter was a little way behind. Particularly in view of the practice of lifetime employment which virtually eliminates the inter-firm transfer of researchers, it is likely that JRJF has contributed significantly to an increase in the quality of information which the participating companies have regarding the research done in competing firms.

Additional diffusion of knowledge as a project benefit

One further feature of the design of the Optical Measurement Project and the other national projects like it which has not been mentioned until now is state ownership of the intellectual property rights created with the use of state resources. Although this aspect of state ownership has been watered down in the more recent national projects financed by the Japan Key Technology Center, it has been central in the national projects launched by MITI in the late 1970s and early 1980s.

There are two justifications for state ownership of such property rights. The first, of lesser social importance, is that since the research was financed with the use of public funds, the public should benefit from the fruits of this research through ownership of the intellectual property rights that result from this research. This is achieved through legal ownership by MITI of both the patents and the know-how that have resulted from the cooperative research project. The second justification, of potentially greater social importance, is that through state ownership of the intellectual property rights which are produced by the national project the state is able to diffuse the resulting technological knowledge more widely than would otherwise occur. In other words, through this means *the state is able to bring about a greater socialization of technological knowledge.* In the absence of such state ownership the knowledge will be privatized to a greater extent, controlled by the private participating companies and released by them only when it is in their private interest to do so. With state ownership the state is in principle able to ensure that the knowledge is spread to the other companies which have participated in the project through the sale of patent and know-how rights to them, and even to other non-participating companies. In general, the wider the diffusion of useful technological knowledge, the greater the social benefit.

However, while this may be true in principle, the effective realization of social benefit is reduced by the divergence between private and social benefit. This divergence comes about because the private firms have a vested interest in privatizing the knowledge that they have created with the use of public funds, rather than passing ownership of this knowledge to MITI. And since it is they who have created the knowledge, they remain in effective control over the knowledge. This is true for both CIHR and JRJF. In the latter case it was shown earlier that the importance of tacit knowledge gives particularly the dominant firm a measure of control over the knowledge generated in the joint research laboratory. Clearly, however, the firm will retain less control in the case of JRJF as compared to that of CIHR, and it is precisely for this reason that the firms tend to resist MITI attempts to impose joint research.

In view of this divergence between private and social benefit, and the firms' degree of effective control over the knowledge generated with public funds, how does MITI come to possess the knowledge that legally belongs to it? The answer to this question was given in an interview with a senior MITI official:

> Informant: We [in MITI] always fear that the companies may be reluctant to open their information and are hiding their results. So we always monitor the members' activities. In the large-scale projects we have adopted a 'seal procedure'. Before starting the project we ask the participating firms to report their own patents and know-how related to the project, that is before the project begins. We permit their ownership of their own technology and know-how. We put in a box the information given by the company. The company trusts that MITI will keep this information confidential. The information is sealed in the box. We [in MITI] are not familiar with the contents themselves. Of course, we know the titles and the rough contents, but not the details. If some troubles take place [that is, if there are later disputes over the ownership of technological knowledge], we can open the box and check on who has the right to ownership. The contents of the paper in the box belong to the firm. This is a conflict resolution procedure. The documents [in the box] contain information on patents as well as other know-how possessed by the firm.
>
> Fransman: Patents are relatively easy to find out about. But what about the prior know-how that the company had? [How is this know-how distinguished from the know-how generated under the national project which belongs to MITI?]
>
> Informant: The firm is free to describe this know-how or not. But if there are disputes later their hand will be strengthened if they have reported the know-how or research. But MITI owns the knowledge that is created by the project.
>
> Fransman: Do the firms oppose this and want to keep the intellectual property rights [created under the national project] themselves?
>
> Informant: I think so.

In numerous interviews with both MITI officials and company representatives it was confirmed that MITI has never had to open the 'black box' in order to resolve a dispute over property rights between MITI and participating companies.

However, it would be incorrect to suggest that MITI's regulations regarding intellectual property rights work in such a way as to give MITI effective ownership and control over the technological knowledge which it has financed, and to allow MITI to diffuse this knowledge widely. A flavour of the way the system works in practice was given in a remarkably frank interview with a senior executive from one of the major Japanese industrial electronics companies. In practice he points out, 'most of the government patents have not been used. Because MITI does not know how to sell them. They don't have manpower to do the promotion. Only when users make a request do they act. Even if companies infringe government patents, there is no way of knowing [because MITI does not have the staff to police their patents].' In general, as pointed out, the firms have an interest in retaining effective control over the knowledge they have generated, even if this is on the basis of the use of public funds. And this, as the executive candidly acknowledged, is the way they tend to behave, at least as far as they can get away with it: 'It is very important for us to acquire the patents ourselves, outside the bounds of the project. This is common, human behaviour [*laughter*] – for any company [*laughter*]. This is information outside this interview [*laughter*] – this is *honne* [that is, underlying reality, as opposed to *tatemai* or surface appearances].'[17]

It may accordingly be concluded that while MITI does come to effectively possess some of the technological knowledge which it has financed, other parts of this stock of knowledge will remain in the effective control of the participating firms and will therefore be privatized by them. But how widely does MITI diffuse the patents over which it has ownership? Some light may be thrown on this question by an analysis of patent data relating to the Optical Measurement Project.

On the basis of figures supplied by MITI to the author, on 31 March 1987 MITI held 472 patents that emerged from the Optical Measurement Project. At the same date, 28 patents, or 5.9 per cent of the number of patents available, had been licensed out. In addition, at the same time MITI held 593 pieces of know-how. 23 of these, or 3.9 per cent of the total, had been sold to users. In all a total of 7 firms had purchased the 28 patents and 23 items of know-how. Unfortunately, for reasons of confidentiality, the names of the purchasing companies were not made available. It is therefore not possible to state how many of these firms had not participated in the Optical Measurement Project and therefore to give an indication of the extent of knowledge diffusion beyond the bounds of this project.[18]

A separate list of patents arising from the Optical Measurement Project and supplied to the author by MITI was analysed in order to estimate the extent of *joint research outside the Joint Laboratory*. The total of 315 patents contained in this list for the Optical Measurement Project were analysed in order to establish the existence of joint patents, that is patents held by inventors from more than one private company. This exercise revealed that while there were no definite joint patents, there were only eight questionable cases where there was insufficient information on which to judge whether there was, or was not, a joint patent. To the extent that joint patents serve as an adequate indicator of joint research, that is the joint creation and sharing of knowledge,[19] it may be concluded from this analysis of joint patents that there was very little joint research outside the Joint Laboratory.

Still on the question of diffusion of knowledge, and relating once more to the issue of 'free-riding', there is evidence to suggest that some of the companies which in the initial stages were relatively weak in the area of optoelectronics benefited significantly from their membership of the Joint Laboratory. Thus, for example, Merz (1987, p. 35) concludes that 'It does appear that participation in a cooperative laboratory has a very positive effect on newcomers to the technology. For example, Oki Electric has catapulted into the mainstream of III-V compound materials and devices during the short period of its participation in OJL.' More concretely, Merz gives an example of Oki's achievements in this area. One important current field of research involves transmission electron microscopy of gallium arsenide grown on silicon. Merz points out that the 'importance of being able to grow high-quality galium arsenide on silicon substrates is obvious – such a technology makes possible combining the best of both worlds, high-speed optoelectronic devices in gallium arsenide with the current sophisticated VLSI technology of silicon.' He notes that many 'groups in Japan, Europe and the United States are working on this problem. One such group, at Oki Electric, has succeeded in making device-quality gallium arsenide by first growing an amorphous layer of gallium arsenide on silicon at a very low temperature (too low for single-crystal growth), and then increasing the growth temperature to grow the final (device-quality) layers. Excellent results have been obtained by Oki using this approach' (p. 26). This example is particularly interesting since, although research in this area has been done in group 6 of the Joint Laboratory, working on materials analysis and characterization, Oki is not represented in this group.

Finally, although there were some spin-offs from the Optical Measurement Project in terms of *collaborative university research*, these do not appear to have been substantial. To quote Professor Merz once more:

Joint Laboratory researchers are also involved in a number of collaborations with university professors... In addition, a number of professors serve on [the Joint Laboratory's] advisory board. All of these collaborations are established on the basis of mutual interest; some were initiated by Joint Laboratory researchers, and some by the faculty members. However, the Joint Laboratory (as well as any other program funded by MITI) cannot provide research funds to the university for such collaborative research; that is the function of a totally separate ministry within the Japanese government, the Ministry of Education, Science and Culture (MESC). Most Japanese researchers believe that considerable friction exists between this ministry and MITI, although this may be a well-orchestrated plan on the part of the government to provide parallel and competing paths for government seed money to university and industry research. MITI has little … to do with university research. (p. 31)

Merz accordingly concludes that 'whereas cooperative research works extremely well between government and industry in Japan (far better than in the United States,) it works badly between university and industry' (p. 32).

The costs of the Optical Measurement Project

The benefits of the Optical Measurement Project examined in this section must be weighed against the costs of the project. For an economic evaluation these costs must be measured in terms of the opportunities forgone as a result of using the resources for the Optical Measurement Project. While such a calculation will not be attempted here, comment will be confined to some of the *additional* costs involved in the setting up of JRJF as opposed to the alternative of CIHR. These additional costs are important to bear in mind since they must be offset against the additional benefits of JRJF analysed in detail above.

The main reason for additional costs in establishing JRJF stems from the greater flow of information between the firms which participate in the joint laboratory. In view of the greater flow, the participating firms, and in particular the stronger firms, took steps to protect themselves from potentially harmful leakages of information. These steps included ensuring that the joint research was confined to those areas where there was a high propensity to share knowledge, namely in areas of generic or basic research; making sure that possibilities for free-riding by weaker firms were limited, or that the stronger firms were compensated in other ways for the existence of free-riding; and insisting that overall responsibility for the project lay in the hands of neutral MITI officials who would guarantee that unjustifiable leakages were minimized. From the point of view of project costs, however, *the taking of such precautionary steps implies relatively high negotiation costs in establishing the project.* These negotiation costs are significantly higher than what would arise in the case of CIHR where the opportunities for knowledge leakage are much less.

It is important for an understanding of the feasibility of JRJF to realize that *the negotiation costs tend to be higher in the absence of government intervention than in its presence.* The reason is that some of the firms that would potentially stand to benefit from JRJF will be competing firms. These firms possess knowledge that might have an impact on the performance of their rivals. This knowledge relates not only to their technologies, but also, as we have seen, to matters such as their strategies, strengths and weaknesses. In negotiating, competing firms therefore tend to conceal knowledge and information which they judge would, in the hands of competitors, put them at a disadvantage. This concealment can increase negotiation costs and can perhaps lead to the choice of joint research projects which are not as beneficial as they might be. *The high negotiation costs in the absence of government intervention explain the extreme scarcity in Japan of joint research projects involving competing firms in the industrial electronics sector negotiated privately without any government intermediation.* Interviews with most of the major Japanese industrial electronics companies confirmed that there are no such projects in post-war Japan which are on a par, in terms of scale and significance, with those projects which have been organized by MITI and NTT. With national rather than sectional objectives, and being neutral with regard to the rival interests of the competing firms, both MITI and NTT have been in a position to organize a degree of joint research among these firms. The structurally determined position of MITI and NTT has enabled these bodies to overcome many of the disadvantages arising from the tendency of the private competing firms to conceal knowledge and information. In other words, *intervention by government or semi-government bodies like MITI and NTT has enabled an economizing on negotiation costs which has resulted, in turn, in a higher degree of joint creation and sharing of knowledge than would otherwise have occurred.*

From the point of view of an evaluation exercise, however, it must be kept in mind that the costs of negotiating joint research, part of which are borne by the private companies and part by government, may be substantial. For example, the different interests of stronger and weaker firms and the possibilities for free-riding will require delicate handling as was seen in the cases of both the Optical Measurement and VLSI Projects. These costs must be offset against the benefits, analysed earlier, which the project yields.

Conclusion

Of the many conclusions that may be drawn from the Optical Measurement Project several will be highlighted here and will be elaborated upon in the concluding chapter of this book.

The first conclusion deals with the relationship between uncertainty and the long-run development of technologies. In general, the longer the period of time required for the development of a new technology, the greater the degree of uncertainty relating to the successful development of that technology. Furthermore, the greater the degree of uncertainty, the more difficult it will be for private companies to bear the costs of investing in the creation of the association technologies. Two issues, both involving uncertainty, may be distinguished here. The first is uncertainty regarding the technical and economic feasibility of the technology that is to be created. The second is uncertainty regarding the ability of the company investing in the creation of the technology to appropriate the returns from the technology. In view of these two factors, the private decisions of private firms, uninfluenced by government intervention, are unlikely to result in as much investment as would be socially desirable. This situation is a form of market failure which justifies government intervention.

The Optical Measurement Project is a case in point. Uncertainty was an important consideration at various points in the project. Furthermore, uncertainty was increased by the fact that the Japanese had reached the international technology frontier and were not able in this area to learn from the experience of leaders. For example, in many areas relating to III-V compound materials, generic or basic research remained to be done. The concept of optoelectronic integrated circuits, involving the integration of optical and electronic functions in the same device, was novel and when the Optical Measurement Project was first considered few had any concrete idea of how such a device might be developed. There were also numerous other uncertainties involved in the construction of the optical measurement and control system as a whole.

It is likely that in the absence of government intervention there would have been significantly less research in the field of optoelectronics. Accordingly, the MITI-initiated Optical Measurement Project produced additional benefits that would not otherwise have been realized. However, the point is not simply that in the face of uncertainty MITI facilitated additional optoelectronics research. This result could also have been achieved through the sponsoring of isolated in-house research or coordinated in-house research, even if less research benefit may have occurred than resulted from the Optical Measurement Project. Rather, MITI took steps to ensure that there was a substantial degree of joint research in joint research facilities, this absorbing about 38 per cent of the funds which MITI invested in the project. This, as we saw in the evaluation section, resulted in the realization of additional benefits compared to what would have been achieved under either isolated in-house or coordinated in-house research.

The attempt to organize joint research in joint research facilities, however, in the process of breaking down some of the barriers which impede the flow of knowledge and information between firms and, in particular, competing firms, raises the tensions which emerge from the uneasy relationship of cooperation and competition between firms. While cooperation *per se* may yield important benefits for private companies, there may be a trade-off in terms of a company's competitive position. It is for this reason that firms generally find it difficult to organize cooperative research with competing companies. As mentioned earlier, there are no significant examples of substantial cooperative research being organized by competing Japanese industrial electronic companies in the post-war period without government intervention. However, in view of its national perspective and objectives which transcend the sectional interests of individual companies, and in view of the resources which it is able to command independently of the shorter-term yield of these resources, government is in a position to economize on the negotiating costs necessary for the establishment of cooperative research. As a result, government is able to resolve some of the tensions that arise from the ambivalences of cooperation and competition and realize some of the additional benefits that follow from cooperative research and, when the circumstances permit, joint research in joint research facilities. The various actions and interventions of government which have facilitated the achievement of this result have been documented in detail in this chapter in the case of the Optical Measurement Project. These government activities, which lie beyond the market, have been responsible for an important part of the benefits yielded by this project.

5

The High-Speed Computing System for Scientific and Technological Uses Project (The Supercomputer Project), 1981–1989

Background to the Supercomputer Project

A number of factors converged in the late 1970s to produce the Super-computer Project. Not necessarily in this order of significance, the first was the reaching of the limits of some of the core computer technologies and the desire to develop newer, potentially efficient, yet still highly uncertain, technologies. More specifically, increasing processing speeds had begun to be limited by the sequential structure of the conventional von Neumann computer architecture thus aiding the search for alternative parallel processing architectures. Although VLSI technology had considerably increased the performance of silicon memory and logic devices, new materials such as gallium arsenide held out the hope of substantially faster electron mobility and therefore processing speed. Devices operating at cryogenic temperatures, such as Josephson junctions, if they could be developed in a cost-effective way, similarly appeared to offer a potentially viable way of greatly increasing electron mobility. However, as will be documented in more detail shortly, research on these technologies was impeded by the significant degree of uncertainty that existed regarding longer-run outcomes. A government-funded project in this area appeared to offer a solution to the problem of uncertainty and underinvestment in Japan in these technologies and provide a way of further developing Japanese technological capabilities in the fields of computing and electronic devices.

The second factor influencing the establishment of the Supercomputer Project, as in the case of the earlier national computer projects analysed in this book, was the 'IBM factor'. As was seen above, by the mid 1970s the performance of the computers produced by the Japanese mainframe producers had equalled that of IBM. However, IBM's international dominance hinged not only on technical excellence, but also on its effective control of marketing networks reinforced by its domination of the current international stock of computers and software. IBM's market power, as opposed to its technical superiority, constituted a formidable entry barrier to the would-be Japanese entrants, who, although they had managed to compete effectively with IBM in the Japanese market, still failed to make substantial headway in the international market.

In the late 1970s MITI initiated discussions with the major Japanese industrial electronics companies regarding appropriate longer-term strategies for the Japanese computer industry. The detailed alternatives that were considered are discussed later. Here we simply note that a two-pronged strategy emerged. The first was to press on with the attempt to develop the next generation of computer and device technologies which it was hoped would in the longer run substantially improve computer performance. As just noted, these technologies, such as parallel processing and new devices, still exhibited substantial uncertainty, which in turn led to a strong tendency for Japanese companies to underinvest in these areas. MITI, however, through its consultations with the companies and with its long history of involvement in, and guidance of the development of, the Japanese computing and devices industry, saw the need for more work in this area and took the initiative in organizing a national cooperative research project which would address these technologies. The project itself focused on the development of a high-speed computing system that was intended for scientific and technological applications. Although IBM had not entered this area of supercomputers, leaving the relatively small market to other American firms such as Cray and CDC, the core technologies that were to be developed in the Supercomputer Project, such as new devices and parallel processing, had both technical and economic relevance beyond the narrow field of supercomputers.[1] Parallel processing techniques could also be used in other computing areas as could the new devices which, in addition, had other possible applications in fields such as telecommunications. Therefore, although the immediate objective of the Supercomputer Project was the development of a high-speed computing system, it would be incorrect to see this project as limited to the field of supercomputers. Further evidence in support of this proposition comes from the participation in the Supercomputer Project of Toshiba, Mitsubishi Electric and Oki which as we saw earlier had already abandoned the mainframe computer market, let alone the more specialized supercomputer market.

The first prong of the Japanese strategy, therefore, involved moving on, with the coordination, guidance and financial support of MITI, to tackle the next generation of computer-related technologies. The current generation of technologies, it should be noted, including silicon-related technologies, was left to the individual firms to deal with. The second prong of the strategy was a far more bold attempt to develop fundamentally new kinds of computers, the so-called fifth generation computer. Whereas the first prong of the strategy involved an attempt to improve the performance of numerical processing, the second would use developments in the field of artificial intelligence to create novel computers for the purposes of knowledge information processing. This second line implied an attempt not merely to beat IBM at its own game, as was the objective of the first, but rather to redefine the game itself by developing fundamentally new types of computers that would serve new purposes. The Fifth Generation Computer Project which resulted from this second line is analysed in chapter 7, while in this chapter attention is confined to the Supercomputer Project.

The importance of new electronic devices

The performance of electronic devices can have a significant influence on the overall performance of a computer. This is also true in the case of supercomputers where the benefits of substantially improved architectures may be undermined in terms of competitiveness by relatively poorly performing electronic devices. One example of this is the 'Hep' super-computer, produced by the American firm Denelcor, which was a pioneering machine. The following account of the fate of the Hep is given in the US National Science Foundation-sponsored JTECH (1987, p. 59) Panel Report on Advanced Computing in Japan:

The Denelcor 'Hep' was one of the earliest-implemented and still one of the most innovative designs of a multiple instruction stream/multiple data stream (MIMD) parallel computer. It had an instruction execution pipeline that allowed a significant degree of parallelism within a single processor. It had multiple sets of registers that, in essence, allowed a context switch in a single instruction cycle. It had a symmetric locking–unlocking synchronization method usable on any word in memory. What this marvelously innovative computer design did not have was the best available device technology. The chips available to the Denelcor designers were inferior to those being used to implement the contemporary Japanese supercomputers. Because of a simple lack of raw speed, the Denelcor Hep could not compete in terms of cost/performance, and the company declared bankrupt in 1985.

As this example rather dramatically illustrates, the performance of electronic devices can have a significant influence on the overall perfor-mance of a supercomputer. It was for this reason that the improvement of device technology was made a central objective of the Supercomputer Project. However, it was decided that the project should not concentrate on current device technologies which were based on silicon. The VLSI Project, analysed earlier, had already helped to facilitate the mastery of silicon technology by Japanese companies and it was felt that these companies were sufficiently well equipped to make improvements in this technology. Attention was rather focused on new devices which used materials and principles that were not as well understood as those associated with silicon. While the possible future performance of these devices made them attractive candidates for further research and development, a significant degree of uncertainty attached to the outcome of such work. The Japanese companies accordingly tended to underinvest in research on these devices as a result, firstly, of uncertainty regarding the results of this research and, secondly, uncertainty regarding their individual ability to appropriate adequate returns from the research.

The devices that were ultimately chosen for research and development under the Supercomputer Project included two devices that were based on gallium arsenide. These were the gallium arsenide field effect transistor (or MESFET, metal–semiconductor field-effect transistor) and the gallium arsenide high electron mobility transistor (or HEMT or MODFET, modulation-doped field-effect transistor). The reason for interest in gallium arsenide devices for supercomputing was obvious. As Meindl (1987, p. 55) notes: 'The principal reason that chip designers resort to gallium arsenide is speed. Under a low applied electric field, conduction-band electrons in gallium arsenide drift six times as fast as they do in silicon.' However, electron-drift mobility may not present an accurate picture of the advantages of gallium arsenide over silicon. To quote Meindl again: 'A more accurate comparison is provided by a different material limit, namely the time required for a carrier under the influence of an electric field near the breakdown value to undergo a drop in electric potential of, say, one volt. (The breakdown electric field is one that shakes so many valence electrons loose from the lattice that a self-ionizing avalanche begins.) By this measure gallium arsenide is about 2.5 times faster than silicon' (pp. 55–7). A further disadvantage of gallium arsenide compared to silicon is that it has lower thermal conductivity. 'A transistor can be made to switch faster by applying more power to it, but so doing increases the build-up of heat in the device. For extremely small devices the speed of switching may be limited by the capacity of the substrate to conduct heat away from the device. Because silicon has three times the thermal conductivity of gallium arsenide, very small silicon devices may be able to switch just as fast as those made of the ostensibly "faster" material' (p. 57).

As the above quotations make clear, there is an important degree of uncertainty in the competition between silicon and gallium arsenide as materials for electronic devices. Despite the potential advantages of gallium arsenide as a result of some of its properties, this material has other disadvantages and, furthermore, the enormous progress that has been made with silicon, the dominant technology, further undermines the relative attractiveness of gallium arsenide. Nevertheless, in spite of the uncertainty, the potential of gallium arsenide-based devices is recognized, making these devices justifiable candidates for inclusion in a government-sponsored research project which aims at the development of technologies which otherwise might not get the attention they deserve. As Meindl (1987, p. 61) notes: 'Silicon will undoubtedly remain the dominant material. The focus of scientific interest and economic growth, however, will shift to other materials. Among them are cryogenic superconductive integrated circuits; thin films of semiconductors on insulator materials; and substrates formed from several materials by means of molecular-beam deposition' (p. 61). It is acknowledged that several important innovations, involving the development of gallium arsenide devices, could have a significant influence on integrated circuit technology:

There are several innovations that could have such a dramatic effect on integrated circuit technology, and they are best understood in terms of the scales of length on which they will have their effects. One scale is provided by the distance an electron or a hole can travel in silicon before colliding with a vibrating silicon atom or a dopant atom. That distance is called the mean free path; the longer it is, the faster the carriers travel. The mean free path can be increased merely by substituting gallium arsenide for silicon, as in the MESFET (metal–semiconductor field-effect transistor). A more radical departure is the MODFET (modulation-doped field-effect transistor), in which a thin layer of aluminum-gallium-arsenide is deposited on a gallium arsenide substrate containing no dopant. The absence of impurity atoms increases the mean free path, rendering MODFETs faster than MESFETs, which in turn are faster than MOSFETs [metal oxide–silicon field-effect transistors].

(Meindl, 1987, p. 61)

In view of the potential performance of these gallium arsenide-based devices, it was decided that the Supercomputer Project should concentrate on MESFETs and MODFETs, the latter referred to in the project as HEMTs, or high electron mobility transistors. While the MESFETs would be developed for use at room temperature, HEMTs would be produced to function at room temperature and at liquid nitrogen temperature ($-196\,°$C), the latter temperature facilitating even greater electron mobility. In addition, another cryogenic device would be developed, namely Josephson junctions operating at liquid helium temperature ($-296\,°$C).

Josephson junctions (JJs) get their name from Brian Josephson, the British physicist from Cambridge. They make use of the property of superconductivity that some materials possess when cooled to temperatures close to absolute zero ($-273\,°$C). When cooled to the temperature of liquid helium, these materials, including silicon, lose almost all resistence to the free flow of electrons. If an electric current is applied to these materials, the electrons will continue to flow even after the current has been turned off. However, the application of a magnetic field across the path of the electrons will cause the flow to stop. This effect can be used as the basis for an on/off switch as is done in the Josephson junction. At liquid helium temperature, circuit switching speeds of 13-trillionths of a second can be achieved. In the mid 1960s IBM began to do research on JJs and this probably contributed to the Japanese interest in this device. Significantly, it was proposed that JJs be included as one of the research topics in the VLSI Project, although this idea was eventually dropped.[2] Many difficulties, however, remained to be resolved before JJs became a high-performance and cost-effective device. For example, problems were posed by the differential contraction of circuit parts made at room temperature, when the device is cooled to liquid helium temperature. In other words, substantial uncertainty was confronted regarding the longer-term technical and economic viability of JJs. This uncertainty was compounded by the dramatic improvement in the performance of silicon devices operating at room temperature. As we shall later see, the uncertainty posed a number of difficult problems for the planning of long-term research in the computer industry. Furthermore, as will also be examined, the development of high-temperature superconducting materials in the mid 1980s added a new unexpected twist to the fortune of the JJ.

Initiating the Supercomputer Project

In the late 1970s it was the opinion of Japanese researchers in the companies and MITI's Electrotechnical Laboratory (ETL) that supercomputing would become extremely important in scientific research and that Japan ought to be producing its own supercomputers, an area that until then was dominated by American firms such as Cray. This proposal was fed into the policy-making process in MITI and this led to discussions with university researchers and the representatives of the major Japanese electronics companies involved in the production of computers. Two other alternatives were apparently simultaneously considered. These were the development of an advanced office automation system and a large knowledge-based system. The former alternative was eventually dropped on the grounds that incremental technical changes, rather than more substantial breakthroughs, were required and these could viably be done in the companies without state assistance. The knowledge-based system eventually became part of the proposal for a fifth generation computer sponsored by MITI (and discussed in detail in chapter 7).

In pursuing the supercomputer option the electronics companies were asked three questions. Was it technically feasible to produce a supercomputer that would operate at least an order of magnitude faster than the fastest current supercomputers? How large was the prospective market for such a supercomputer? Was the company willing to second researchers to a supercomputer project?

Response of the companies

The general view of the companies in answer to the first question was that it was indeed technically feasible to attempt to develop a substantially faster supercomputer. However, in response to the second question it was felt that there was substantial uncertainty regarding the profitability of supercomputers. This conclusion seemed to be supported by IBM's decision not to enter the market for supercomputers.

According to a senior MITI official closely involved in the establishment of the Supercomputer Project, MITI policy-makers were keen to increase the capabilities of the Japanese companies in the related technology areas since they felt that their existing weakness in these areas was a source of potential vulnerability.

So we began the persuasion of some companies such as Fujitsu, Hitachi and NEC. And we succeeded initially in the persuasion of one or two of the companies. The others then agreed to participate. It was not so easy to persuade the companies. But it was easier than in the case of the fifth generation computer because, although the market [for supercomputers] was limited, the timing of the realization of the market was more certain than in the case of the market for artificial intelligence-related computers [like the fifth generation computer]–perhaps the twenty-first century in the case of the latter.

Why was MITI able to persuade the companies to join the Supercomputer Project despite the uncertain profitability in the supercomputer market? In answering this question it is necessary to distinguish the mainframe producers, Fujitsu, Hitachi and NEC, from the other companies that participated. Although these three companies had already decided to enter the supercomputer market and were to bring out their first supercomputers in the early 1980s, they were keen to get government financial assistance for the development of next-generation computer technologies that remained too uncertain to attract substantial corporate funding. According to a leader of the Fifth Generation Computer Project, there was, for example, significant enthusiasm on the part of the three companies from the outset for the development of Josephson junctions as part of the Supercomputer Project. As mentioned earlier, JJs had been under research in IBM since the mid 1960s and serious consideration had been given to their inclusion in the VLSI Project, although this proposal was subsequently dropped. Furthermore, some of the companies were interested in the further development of gallium arsenide-based MESFETs and HEMTs. Therefore, although there may have been some initial reluctance on the part of these three companies to enter the Supercomputer Project as a result of the uncertain prospects of profitability, they were not unwilling to engage in government-subsidized research on next generation electronic devices. A major factor that must have had a bearing on their decision was the possible applicability of these high electron mobility devices to areas of computing other than supercomputing. In the case of IBM, research on JJs went together with a decision to remain out of the supercomputer market. Accordingly, the three companies did not have strong reasons for opposing the Supercomputer Project since the package of technologies to be developed as part of the high-speed computing system included technologies which in any event were of interest to them.

Although having been out of the mainframe computer market for some time, the other companies which eventually joined the Supercomputer

Project, Toshiba, Mitsubishi Electric and Oki, also had reasons for participating. Most importantly, they were all heavily involved in the field of electronic devices and had an interest similar to that of Fujitsu, Hitachi and NEC in receiving government support for research on uncertain technologies. Furthermore, participating in the Supercomputer Project meant that they would receive fuller information than they would otherwise get on the progress being made in the related technology areas. It is this desire for fuller information that MITI officials often see as an anxiety about being excluded from a national project. Japanese firms, they argue, do not want to be left out of a national research project which in some ways may be looked at as insurance against the risk of competing companies developing new technologies without providing related information. Although, as will shortly be seen, information flows may be relatively restricted between the participants in a national research project, each member will have a fuller information set about the research activities and results of the other members than would occur if the research were done outside the bounds of such a project. This provides a further incentive for firms to join a national research project. From MITI's point of view, on the other hand, concerned as they are with national objectives, the spread of information to the major industrial electronics companies strengthens the national electronics system as a whole.

The question of a joint laboratory

In the case of the Supercomputer Project MITI officials originally supported the idea of a joint laboratory. As a senior MITI official put it: 'MITI always wants a joint laboratory because we believe it is more efficient to proceed this way – budget, equipment, researchers are used more efficiently ... [In the case of the Supercomputer Project] I remember that we studied the feasibility of a joint laboratory.'

At first sight there would appear to have been a *prima facie* case for a joint laboratory in the Supercomputer Project. To begin with, as shown earlier in the VLSI and Optoelectronics Projects, a joint laboratory would have facilitated the realization of important economies of joint research. Furthermore, there were some reasons for thinking that, as in the case of the latter two projects, the participating companies might be persuaded to agree to joint research in joint research facilities. In the first place, it must have seemed possible to identify a cluster of generic or basic technologies as had been done for the VLSI and Optoelectronics Projects. For example, generic research on materials such as gallium arsenide or niobium (the latter was later used in the Supercomputer Project for JJs) could have been undertaken in a joint laboratory. Similarly, joint research could have been done on parallel processing architectures and software. It could have been argued in the late 1970s when the project was being established that these and other similar technologies were at a 'pre-competitive' stage of development. Silicon formed the basis of current device technology, and von Neumann architectures and corresponding software, which were based on sequential rather than parallel processing, were at that time dominant. Hence it may have seemed that a good case could be made for a joint laboratory.

In the event, however, there was strong opposition from Fujitsu, Hitachi and NEC to the idea of a joint laboratory. A senior academic, who has been closely involved in the establishment and evaluation of the Supercomputer Project, explained this opposition: 'It is very difficult for the firms to share in the Supercomputer Project because the research is much closer to commercialization. Each company already has its own supercomputer technology and the companies are not prepared to share this knowledge. The companies do not like to dispatch researchers to a joint laboratory.' A senior research manager from one of the three companies corroborated this explanation saying that he had personally opposed the suggestion for a joint laboratory on the grounds of the commercial sensitivity of the technologies.

Several comments are needed in order to arrive at a more rigorous explanation of the absence of a joint laboratory in the Supercomputer Project. To begin with, as already pointed out, there were several factors which at first sight favoured the establishment of a joint laboratory. It was possible to identify generic or (in the Japanese sense) 'basic' technologies which could be jointly researched with commercializable applications being developed inside the individual companies. Furthermore, some of the technologies were still far from the commercialization stage. This was particularly true in the case of Josephson junctions where commercialization was not expected before the mid or late 1990s. Although some HEMTs were commercialized by Fujitsu in the early to mid 1980s and Hitachi and NEC later adopted this technology, it was only in 1988 that Fujitsu was due to deliver its HEMT for use in the supercomputer developed under the Supercomputer Project. MESFETs, on the other hand, were available sooner. The time to commercialization of the technologies from 1981 when the project began was a further factor in favour of joint research. The uncertainty implied by this time period meant that participating firms could benefit from the joint search activities undertaken through joint research.

There was, however, an overriding consideration which prevented these factors which favoured joint research from resulting in the establishment of a joint laboratory. This was the commercial sensitivity of the technologies chosen for development under the Supercomputer Project. As noted, Fujitsu, Hitachi and NEC had already made the decision to move into the supercomputer market, and shortly after the start of the Supercomputer Project were producing and selling their own supercomputers. Although these supercomputers were based on silicon bipolar devices and operated at speeds about one-tenth of those aimed at by the Supercomputer Project, the successful development of MESFETs, HEMTs, and JJs could clearly have important implications for these companies' success in the supercomputer market. Therefore, although a significant degree of uncertainty attached to the successful development of these electronic devices and their ability to compete effectively with silicon devices, the commercial implications of possible success in these technologies made the major computer-producing firms unwilling to agree to joint research in joint research facilities. Furthermore, these new electronic devices together with the parallel processing architectures and software also developed under the Supercomputer Project could be applied to other areas of computing apart from supercomputing. This possibility further increased the commercial sensitivity of the technologies selected for the Supercomputer Project and reinforced the reluctance to establish joint research laboratories.

Design of the Supercomputer Project

The basic organizational principle chosen for the Supercomputer Project was that of coordinated in-house research. According to this principle, the research activities of the participating companies would be coordinated in order to avoid overlap, but the research itself would be undertaken inside the companies. In the case of Fujitsu, Hitachi and NEC it was understood that while, under the Supercomputer Project, they would specialize in different designated research areas, they would simultaneously do their own privately funded research in areas allocated to the other companies. In this way it was hoped that each of the three companies would eventually produce their own supercomputer meeting the performance objectives of the Supercomputer Project and based on a mix of technologies, some of which were developed under the Project and some through the company's own activities. This would result in the development of three non-identical supercomputers. The other companies which participated in the Supercomputer Project, namely Mitsubishi Electric, Toshiba and Oki, would be involved on a more selective basis and would not necessarily end up producing entire supercomputers with the same perfomance objectives.

Further information on the allocation of research tasks is given in Table 5.1. As shown in this table, three distinct research tasks can be identified: first, the development of three types of high electron mobility devices, namely MESFETs, HEMTs, and Josephson junctions; second, the production of the three main subsystems for the supercomputer, namely the high-speed parallel processing system, the large-capacity high-speed memory system and the dedicated parallel processing system (which, together with the other subsystems are shown in Fig. 5.1); and finally the development of the software, including the overall systems control software and the parallel processing software. One firm, Fujitsu, was allocated responsibility for the integration of the whole system. As Table 5.1 shows, there is little overlap

Table 5.1. *Supercomputer Project: allocation of research tasks to the participating companies*

| | Company | | | | | |
	Fuj	Hit	NEC	Mits	Tosh	Oki
Research Task						
MESFETs		x	x	x	x	
HEMTs	x					x
JJs	x	x	x			
Subsystem A	x					
Subsystem B			x			
Subsystem C				x	x	
Software (overall systems control software; parallel processing software)		x				
Configuration of total system	x					

Key:
Fuj   Fujitsu
Hit   Hitachi
Mits   Mitsubishi
Tosh   Toshiba

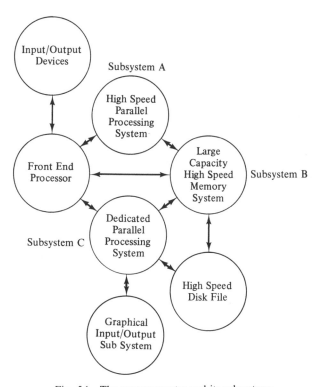

Fig. 5.1   The supercomputer and its subsystems.

between the research of the participating companies. Where the companies worked in a similar area, for example in the case of the electronic devices, they were allocated non-overlapping research tasks.

As in the Optical Measurement Project, the design of the Supercomputer Project attempted to ensure a synthesis of 'use-pull' and 'generic research-push' determinants in shaping the evolution of the supercomputer and its component technologies. Rather than simply encouraging research on the enabling technologies *per se*, the shape of the final high-speed computing system and its performance characteristics were made explicit. For example, a system performance goal of 10 gigaflops (floating-point operations per second) was specified. Furthermore, specific applications areas were identified such as image processing, the analysis of nonlinearity problems, VLSI design and the analysis of nuclear fusion. As will be seen, some of the research tasks involved the development of subsystems specifically designed for the carrying out of some of these applications. In this way it was intended that user requirements would, together with the development of superior technologies such as high electron mobility devices and parallel processing, have an important influence on the ultimate characteristics of the high-speed computing system.

Examples of coordinated in-house research

In this section, two examples of coordinated in-house research under the Supercomputer Project are briefly discussed in order to present a more tangible picture of the research cooperation that has taken place. The first involves cooperation on the HEMT between Fujitsu and Oki. While in the next section the development of the HEMT in Fujitsu is analysed in detail, here attention is confined to the pattern of cooperation between this company and Oki.

Through negotiations involving the MITI officials organizing the Supercomputer Project and the participating companies it was decided that Fujitsu and Oki would specialize in the development of HEMTs. Fujitsu had already in 1975 made a commitment to some of the basic technologies underlying HEMTs when the decision was taken to purchase very expensive molecular beam epitaxy equipment (T. Kobayashi, 1986, p. 126). Although, as is discussed later, the basic ideas underlying the HEMT had originated in the United States, Fujitsu chose to devote resources to the development of practical HEMT devices and in 1980 made an important breakthrough in this area with the production of a new device. The Supercomputer Project began one year later in 1981 and Oki was also selected to do research on HEMTs. Although MITI apparently wanted at least two companies working on each of the devices (see Table 5.1), the bulk of the funding for research on HEMTs under the Supercomputer Project went to Fujitsu rather than Oki, thus acknowledging the superiority of the former company in this area.

Fujitsu's research on HEMTs involved the development of two kinds of devices. The first operates at room temperature and at this temperature has a higher performance than gallium arsenide MESFETs. The second operates at the temperature of liquid nitrogen ($-196\,°C$). In the Fujitsu device the first layer is made of gallium arsenide while the second consists of aluminium gallium arsenide. This is the usual structure for HEMTs or MODFETs. The device produced under the project by Oki, however, inverts these two layers. According to a senior research manager in one of these firms, there is some sharing of knowledge and research results between the two companies. Asked to be more specific, he mentioned research results on molecular beam epitaxy for crystal growth and also measurement and evaluation technology for high-speed performance. Despite some degree of sharing, however, he noted that 'in comparatively few fields are we sharing technologies. Basically we are competing companies.' As a result of the constraints on the sharing of knowledge imposed by the underlying competitive relationship between the two companies, it is perhaps justifiable to characterize their pattern of research cooperation as one of *constrained joint search*. In other words, the firms are involved in a process of search in a similar area, in this case HEMTs, while exchanging some, but by no means all, of the knowledge thereby acquired.

The second example of coordinated in-house research involves the development of the dedicated parallel processing subsystem (see Fig. 5.1). The main purpose of this subsystem is to provide a facility that will assist in natural resource exploration with the use of satellite imaging. Two firms are involved in the coordinated research, namely Mitsubishi Electric and Toshiba. Mitsubishi is developing a cellular array processor (CAP) for the subsystem which will allow the processing of image-based data to be done in parallel. The CAPs are arranged so that they share a memory with other CAPs. Each CAP can consist of up to 64 processing elements arranged in an 8×8 array with local memory. The CAPs also share a variable processor pipeline (VPP) developed by Toshiba. The VPP is a MIMD (multiple instruction, multiple data-stream device) which can deal with several instructions at one time with data being obtained from more than one location. Although the local memory was originally based on silicon, the plan was to introduce gallium arsenide memory devices in order to increase the operating speed. The overall subsystem was demonstrated using data taken from a LANDSAT satellite over Osaka Bay. While the bulk of the research for the components of the subsystem was undertaken inside Mitsubishi Electric and Toshiba, cooperation was necessary for the interfacing of these components.

In addition to the constrained exchange of knowledge and information of the kind referred to in these two examples of coordinated in-house research, further flows of information occur between the participating companies at regular meetings and conferences convened to report on and discuss research progress under the project. In this way, although the research is done primarily in-house and the exchange of knowledge and information is constrained, a significantly greater quantity is exchanged than would occur under isolated in-house research. In the latter form of organization, while government influences the quantity and kind of research through the provision of subsidies, no attempt is made to coordinate the research activities of the firms, which are not required to exchange information as a condition for receiving funding.

An evaluation of the Supercomputer Project

Several factors must be taken into account in any evaluation of the Supercomputer Project. To begin with, it was stressed earlier in this section that a significant degree of uncertainty attached to the technologies that were chosen for development under the Supercomputer Project. In evaluating the project it is important to ask, in the light of this uncertainty, what effect it had on the development of these technologies in Japan. This question will be examined with particular reference to the case of HEMTs and Josephson junctions.

Secondly, it has already been stressed in this section that the sharing of knowledge and information was constrained in the Supercomputer Project. This was decidedly the case compared to the sharing in the VLSI and Optical Measurement Projects. In view of these constraints, it is necessary to enquire further into the benefits that were derived from the constrained sharing of knowledge and information in the project.

Thirdly, the other benefits and costs of coordinated in-house research must be analysed. While for reasons that have already been explained joint research in joint research facilities was not a viable alternative form of organization for the Supercomputer Project, there remained in principle a policy choice between coordinated in-house research and isolated in-house research. This theoretical choice will be used in an analysis of the benefits and costs of coordinated in-house research.

Fourthly, an attempt will be made, as in the case of the VLSI and Optical Measurement Projects analysed earlier, to evaluate the output of the Supercomputer Project. Account will also be taken here of the extent to which the attempt to synthesize use-pull and generic research-push determinants of the evolution of technologies developed under the Supercomputer Project was successful. Finally, a brief comment will be made on the role of university research and researchers in the Supercomputer Project.

Overcoming the effects of uncertainty

The following is an extract from an interview with a senior Japanese academic who was closely involved in the establishment and evaluation of the Supercomputer Project:

> Informant: The supercomputer has been identified [by MITI] as an essential tool for next-generation industries. So the supercomputer is very important.
> Fransman: If there were no government projects in the area of supercomputers, do you think there would be much less research done in this field in Japan?
> Informant: Yes, I think so. It is very difficult to achieve the supercomputer goal for a processing capability in excess of 10 gigaflops. Without the national project maybe 2 or 3 gigaflops would be achieved by the end of the decade.

While it remains to be seen whether the goals of the Supercomputer Project will be achieved within the allotted time and whether competing firms in other Western countries will be able to keep up with the performance levels achieved, there are reasons for hypothesizing that government intervention in Japan in the area of supercomputing will speed the development of the association technologies and therefore the performance realized. One such reason stems from the negative effects of uncertainty on the development of technology. As stressed in this chapter, the technologies chosen for the Supercomputer Project in the late 1970s were associated with significant degrees of uncertainty. From the point of view of the for-profit companies potentially interested in these technologies, there are two areas of uncertainty which are important. First, there is uncertainty regarding the chances of developing efficient technologies capable of competing with other alternative technologies. Secondly, there is uncertainty regarding the extent to which the company investing in the creation of the technology will be able to appropriate adequate returns from the investment. Potentially problematical here is the 'public good' characteristic of technological knowledge which may allow competing companies to obtain and use the knowledge without paying the full costs of its development, thus reducing the return to the company originally investing in the creation of that technology. As a result of these two areas of uncertainty there will be a tendency for for-profit companies to underinvest in the creation of technologies that are uncertain. Government support for these technologies may counteract the tendency to underinvest, resulting in their faster and fuller development.

There is some evidence to suggest that support by MITI for the technologies included in the Supercomputer Project did indeed lead to their faster and fuller development. This evidence is examined now in more detail in the case of the HEMT and Josephson Junction devices.

The HEMT story

Early fundamental research on HEMTs was done in 1969 in IBM's Yorktown Heights Research Laboratory by Leo Esaki and Raphael Tsu and in ATT's Bell Laboratories (Gregory, 1985, p. 252; Kobayashi, 1986, p. 120). Fujitsu became committed to research in this area when the decision was made in 1975 to purchase extremely expensive molecular beam epitaxy equipment. 'In 1980, Fujitsu Laboratories announced the successful development of . . . the High Electron Mobility Transistor (HEMT). A great variety of possible applications from computer memory and logic circuits to microwave transmission and optical transmission systems are being studied [in Fujitsu] for this versatile device' (T. Kobayashi, 1986, p. 75). Taiyu Kobayashi, who was Chairman of the Board of Fujitsu, explains the company's interest in the device:

The HEMT . . . compared to the gallium arsenide transistor [or MESFET], the fastest of the devices now in practical use . . . is ten times as fast. When compared with the Josephson junction device upon which attention has been focused in recent years and which is still under development in our research laboratory, the HEMT operates nearly as fast and has the advantage of being much easier to test. The Josephson junction device can only operate at temperatures approaching absolute zero (minus 269 degrees) and testing must also be conducted at this low temperature. The HEMT can be tested at room temperature and its performance evaluated. At a low temperature (minus 196 degrees), it approaches the speed of the Josephson device. Thus, HEMT devices are much easier to produce, and research can proceed that much faster. With the Josephson device, which only works at very low temperatures, there are distinct disadvantages, because it is impossible to evaluate the performance until the project is completed. If the development of the Josephson device takes ten years, the HEMT will only require five, and we will have been able to create something with the same level of performance in half the time. *This is why we expect the HEMT to be the most appropriate device for the next generation of powerful computers.*   (ibid., p. 119, emphasis added)

According to a senior research manager at Fujitsu, although large scale integration is not yet possible with HEMTs, the company expects that in the future HEMTs will replace silicon bipolar devices in areas where high speed is necessary.

However, this chronicle of Fujitsu's rationale underlying its interest in HEMTs should not lead one to conclude that the company invested all the resources that were necessary for the development of the HEMT. The following information, given to the author by a senior research manager from Fujitsu, has important public policy implications. Fujitsu began to receive financial support from MITI for the development of the HEMT in 1981, a year after the company made its first major breakthrough in developing a prototype HEMT device. However, despite the development of this prototype, substantial uncertainties confronted the attempt to improve the cost–performance of the device so that it would be able to compete effectively with the other alternative device technologies. *From 1981 to 1986 Fujitsu received a total of 2 billion yen from MITI for its research on HEMTs. This compares with a total estimated expenditure by MITI of 23 billion yen for the whole Supercomputer Project from 1981 to*

1989.[3] *The 2 billion yen received by Fujitsu from MITI represented between 20 and 25 per cent of the company's total expenditure on HEMT R & D from 1981 to 1986.*

In assessing the significance of the 20 to 25 per cent figure, account must be taken of the so-called additionality problem. In other words, in the absence of MITI funding it is possible that the money allocated to HEMT research in Fujitsu would have declined by significantly less than 20 to 25 per cent. MITI funding might have served to free for other uses Fujitsu resources which otherwise would have been allocated to HEMT research. To the extent that this would have happened in practice, the net effect of MITI funding was less than an additional 20 to 25 per cent allocated to HEMT research in Fujitsu.

It is impossible to estimate the additional effects of MITI's funding of HEMT research in Fujitsu under the Supercomputer Project. Even interviewing company officials on the research funding decisions that they would have made in the absence of this MITI-initiated project would not necessarily yield the same results as would have occurred had these decisions been made in practice. Nevertheless, it is likely that the funding received under the Supercomputer Project did have a positive additional effect on HEMT research. A number of factors are likely to have limited the willingness of Fujitsu to allocate further resources to research on HEMTs. To begin with, as already noted, there remained considerable uncertainty regarding the extent to which significant improvements could be brought about in the cost–performance of HEMTs. Secondly, the enormous improvements in silicon technology would have acted as a further deterrent. Finally, there was also uncertainty regarding Fujitsu's ability to appropriate adequate returns from its investment in this technology. In the event, Fujitsu's successes with HEMTs led Hitachi and NEC, previously sceptical regarding the prospects of this device, to enter the field. By 1984–5 the latter companies were producing their own HEMTs for microwave amplifiers.

For all these reasons it seems unlikely that Fujitsu would have allocated an additional 20 to 25 per cent to research on HEMTs in the absence of the MITI funding. To the extent that this is correct, the MITI Supercomputer Project had a positive additional effect on HEMT research. Furthermore, in assessing the global effect on HEMT research, account must also be taken of the research also done under the Project by Oki on HEMTs. Although this company received only a small proportion of the resources given to Fujitsu, Oki also made a positive contribution by exploring research avenues, drawing on a different stock of distinctive corporate competences, that may not have been examined in the same way by Fujitsu. Through the encouragement of joint search and pluralism in research the Supercomputer Project must have contributed further to the advancement of knowledge in the area of HEMTs.

The Josephson junction story

The inclusion of Josephson junctions as devices to be developed under the Supercomputer Project probably owed a good deal to IBM's highly publicized research in this area from the mid 1960s. As mentioned earlier, attempts were made to include JJs in the VLSI Project, although this idea was subsequently dropped. Although the JJ was still far from the commecialization stage and research on the device was bedevilled by the problems of testing at a temperature of $-269\,°C$, there remained the hope that the JJ would facilitate substantially increased processing speeds. To coincide with the establishment of the Supercomputer Project, a special section was set up in July 1981 in MITI's Electrotechnical Laboratory for the purpose of undertaking systematic research on the basic technologies required for the Josephson computer.

In IBM a major technology used in JJ research was lead alloy technology involving an alloy made of lead, tin and gold. There were, however, difficulties in using lead alloy technology for the production of integrated circuits. The Electrotechnical Laboratory (ETL) group therefore developed an alternative technology based on niobium. This technology was transferred without charge to the three companies involved in research on JJs under the Supercomputer Project, Fujitsu, Hitachi and NEC. To facilitate the technology transfer process, engineers were sent from the three companies to ETL to learn the niobium technology. Interestingly, these companies, working in isolation and with very little sharing of knowledge and information, had tried but failed to develop niobium technology. ETL's success may in part have been related to the fact that it devoted more resources than any one of the companies to JJ research.

At about the same time as ETL was transferring its niobium technology to the three firms, IBM made the dramatic decision to substantially reduce its research on JJs. The reasoning behind the decision to all but abandon JJ research was discussed by John Armstrong, Research Director at IBM and then a newly-elected Vice-President of the company, in an interview with David Fishlock of the *Financial Times*. Summarizing the reasoning involved, Fishlock noted that IBM's

research management would take a collective decision to stop a research project. Armstrong himself was part of the management team which decided in 1983 to abandon a major project on the superconducting computer. Despite a world-class research effort, it was agreed that technology based on the superconducting Josephson junction was simply not going to make it in competition with the still fast-developing silicon chip. (Other companies appeared, then and since, to take the same view.)[4]

Fishlock goes on to observe that 'IBM abandoned its main project in superconduction in 1983, and redeployed a large team in the research division, mainly in studying very high performance silicon.'[5]

Further information on the decision to de-emphasize research on Josephson junctions was supplied to the present author by the IBM Thomas J. Watson Research Centre, Yorktown Heights, New York.[6] Technical assessments of Josephson junction devices for high-speed computer logic and memory were carried out in IBM in 1980 and in 1983.[7] A summary of the 1983 study was later published; see Pugh (1985). According to an IBM official, the 1983 study 'was an important input to the decision to "de-emphasize"...IBM's Josephson computer effort...but it was not the only input'.[8]

The same methodology was used in the 1980 and 1983 technical assessments in IBM of Josephson junction devices. This methodology involved comparing three alternative devices that could be used in high-speed computers. The devices were bipolar semiconductor devices, used as the base technology against which the other alternatives, HEMT gallium arsenide devices and Josephson junction devices, were compared. The method involved creating 'equivalently optimistic paper designs ... for devices and packaging for two different lighographic capabilities [i.e. linewidth] for each technology' (p. 1760).[9] Using simple extrapolation on the basis of historical data, the linewidths obtainable from the lithographic technologies were projected to 1988 and 1994. The technical assessment which was completed in 1980 'indicated a factor-of-four or more performance advantage for Josephson circuits' (p. 1761). However, the 1980 study also identified 'numerous unknowns and risks'. One 'particularly difficult problem' that had arisen in the 1980 study was how to treat the devices in an 'equivalent way' in the light of their somewhat different processing requirements. In the 1980 study, projected performances were calculated on the basis of circuit linewidth. However, Josephson devices required much tighter linewidth control than the other two devices. Accordingly, in the 1983 study the projections were made on the basis of linewidth control, rather than linewidth. 'This made Josephson logic paths 50 per cent longer than they would have been if the same [linewidth] rather than [linewidth control] had been used. A plot of logic path delays versus [linewidth control] indicated that Josephson logic would be only about two times faster than silicon bipolar logic if the primary factors limiting progress in each technology were lithography and structure-making' (p. 1761).

However, since it was recognized that there were many other factors which also influenced progress, particularly in the case of 'new technologies [such as Josephson junctions] where problems must be solved with smaller resources than are available for established technologies', it was felt that the projected improvement in Josephson devices 'should be regarded as an optimistic estimate' (p. 1761). One of the other factors influencing progress was limitations on the ability to reduce linewidth. This presented further problems because the 'best understood Josephson family (CIL) was already in difficulty for linewidths under about 1.0 micron' (p. 1761). Accordingly, these 'limits to scaling would force a shift to the less well-understood DCL Josephson devices even before CIL devices could be brought to market' (p. 1761). The 1983 study concluded that at 'the projected density limits for both technologies, the performance advantage of DCL Josephson circuit paths might be as much as four to five times that of silicon bipolars. However, even assuming no abatement in the historical rate of improvement in [linewidth] and [linewidth control], these limits were not projected to occur until after the year 2000' (p. 1761).

With regard to the decision to substantially deemphasize research on Josephson junctions, Pugh concludes that the 'major Josephson effort at IBM was terminated in 1983 because neither the short-term nor long-term advantages appeared to warrant continuation of such a high level of technical effort compared to the efforts being applied to other alternatives. Only a small research activity in cryogenics was retained. Greater emphasis was placed on [gallium arsenide] devices because they offered almost as much potential with less risk, and silicon devices were reaffirmed as the primary route to high-performance computers in the foreseeable future' (p. 1761).

Having stated this general conclusion, however, Pugh goes on to mention the pitfalls confronting the present assessment. One major difficulty arises from the fact that technical assessments are not always independent of the values and biases of the experts making them: 'Because individuals with in-depth knowledge of a given technology normally have strong biases – not fully supported by the facts – the study should be led by someone with no strong commitment to any one technology' (p. 1762).

There were, however, a number of other difficulties bedevilling the assessment. The first of these was that 'the available data may not have been treated correctly' (p. 1761). The second was that new 'device inventions will invalidate specific assumptions and conclusions' (p. 1762). The third related to the methodology itself. 'Were the features selected as the primary basis of comparison equally fundamental to both technologies? Will new knowledge show our methods to have been faulty?' (p. 1762). Prophetically, Pugh concluded that there 'are no general answers to these questions – no way to guarantee that advances in technology can be 'achieved without surprise' (p. 1762). Accordingly, the 'correctness of a technology assessment, like the value of a stock market purchase, is best determined long after the fact. Thus it is too early to judge the correctness of the Josephson technology assessment' (p. 1761).

IBM's decision to significantly decrease research on JJs highlights the complexity of resource allocation choices in large companies with substantial internal science bases. On the one hand, IBM has achieved an outstanding reputation for the quality of its scientific research, winning four Nobel prizes in physics in just one year. On the other hand, the company remains a commercially driven entity with the result that commercial priorities ultimately override purely scientific ones. This order of priorities is clearly reflected in IBM's allocation of research resources. In 1987, for example, the company's science budget accounted for about one-tenth of the total R & D budget of 3.97 billion dollars. The remaining nine-tenths is mainly spent in IBM's twenty-five product development laboratories around the world, although joint research programmes are also organized between these laboratories and the company's three research centres: Yorktown Heights, New York; Amalden, California; and Zurich, Switzerland. As Fishlock points out, the IBM 'science budget goes into quests it has selected carefully, not on the offchance they may advance knowledge and earn a Nobel prize, but because there is a very good chance they may become important to IBM in the next 10–15 years, says John Armstrong.'[10] As we shall shortly see, however, there is a considerable margin of error in making predictions about research areas that have a 'very good chance' of providing adequate commercial pay-offs 10 to 15 years in the future. The existence of significant uncertainty over this kind of time period makes calculations based on optimization impossible.

How did the Japanese, who had been tracking IBM in their choice to include JJ research in the Supercomputer Project, react to the latter's decision to virtually abandon this area in 1983? A brief insight into the Japanese response is given in the following extract from an interview with a senior Japanese academic who was closely involved with the Supercomputer Project:

> Fransman: The Japanese companies must have said in 1983 when IBM pulled out of JJ research, 'Let us carry on with this research, but we cannot give it very high priority. IBM's pulling out is a good signal that this technology is not very promising.' But maybe ETL could continue because they are not a commercial organization. Would you agree with this?
>
> Informant: Let's see. [*pause*] I should confess the management of the Japanese companies thought, as you say, 'we would like to give up the Josephson project'. But 1983 was the period of the Supercomputer Project and [a significant amount of the] JJ research was to be completed by the end of 1987. So Government [that is, MITI] did not allow the research [in the companies and ETL] to stop. Fortunately, ETL then established niobium technology and this technology was transferred to the companies.

As this quotation makes clear, it was a decision made by MITI, possibly with the support of ETL and based on non-commercial criteria, which was responsible for the continuation of the Japanese research on JJs. Had the decision been left up to the Japanese companies, it seems likely that research in this area would have been downgraded the way it was in IBM.

In 1986, however, an ironic twist was introduced into the JJ story. This occurred when K. Alex Mueller and Georg Bednorz, researchers from the IBM Zurich Research Laboratory, published their famous paper[11] which launched an international race to develop high critical temperature superconducting materials and on 14 October 1987 won them the Nobel Prize for physics. This paper, and the related research that it catalysed, added a new dimension to research on JJs because it raised the possibility of producing the Josephson effect in devices operating at temperatures considerably higher than the −269 °C at which JJ research had hitherto taken place. As the Japanese academic referred to in the previous quotation noted in a interview in 1987:

> Informant: We are now at a critical point in JJ research because high temperature superconductors have become available. So far we have been working on niobium technology, up to last year. We are now discussing various possibilities. One possibility is to make a high critical temperature JJ. However, we are not sure whether high critical temperature JJs can compete with semiconductors. So we are now discussing. JJs still need more than 10 years for practical commercializability.

IBM was also forced to invest in superconductivity research as a result of the possible competitive implications of the Bednorz and Mueller work. As Rippeteau notes, 'IBM must invest because of superconductors' potential to transform the computer business. Worldwide, research is fragmented, and IBM runs the risk a rival will acquire proprietary technology first.'[12] Accordingly, a 'group of researchers at IBM's Yorktown Heights Research Centre under Alan Kleinsasser is following up on any possible connections between the new superconducting materials and Josephson junction technology... IBM several years ago abandoned efforts to build a Josephson computer, but a small part of the team kept an eye out for the other applications of the technology. "Now high-temperature superconductors have come along", says Kleinsasser. "All of a sudden I'm handed this extra rationale for transistor-like devices."[13] Although IBM has now rediscovered the possible importance of the Josephson junction in the light of the research on high-temperature superconductors, Fishlock's interviews at IBM revealed that the company's scientists in the two major US research centres at Yorktown Heights and Amalden 'admit, somewhat shamefacedly, that they were slow to catch on to the superconducting ceramics discovery of their European colleagues, Georg Bednorz and Professor Alex Mueller'.[14]

Meanwhile, with their research capabilities substantially boosted by the focus and resources provided under the Supercomputer Project, Japanese companies were well positioned to take advantage of the new superconducting materials in their attempt to develop new types of Josephson junction. While it is still too soon to predict how these companies will perform in this technology area relative to their international competitors, there is evidence that some of the Japanese companies have rapidly been able to apply the new superconducting research to the field of Josephson junctions. For example, in April 1987 NEC announced that it had developed a Josephson device made of single-phase yttrium barium copper oxide which demonstrated the Josephson effect at nearly −183 °C (90 °K). This, it was claimed, was the first time that the Josephson effect had been observed at above liquid nitrogen temperature.[15] Shortly thereafter, it was announced in June 1987 that a research group working under an assistant professor at Tokyo University, Yoichi Okabe, had produced a similar device consisting of two superconductors – made of yttrium-barium-copper ceramic and niobium – that sandwich a 0.005-micron aluminium oxide insulator film.[16]

Postscript: In December 1989 it was announced that ETL had successfully developed the world's first complete Josephson junction computer. (In February 1989, Fujitsu and Hitachi developed a Josephson junction microprocessor which lacked some logic and memory circuits and therefore could not be used as a comprehensive computer chip.) The ETL computer, ETL-JC1, uses four large-scale integrated Josephson junction circuits. It contains all the basic computer functions and can run common programs. The computer operates at a temperature of −269°C. (*Japan Economic Journal*, 23 December 1989, p. 14).

Some conclusions

The case studies concerning the development of HEMTs and JJs clearly illustrate the difficulties raised by uncertainty for decisions regarding the allocation of resources to research. There were a number of sources of uncertainty. To begin with, there were a number of potentially competing technologies. Apart from silicon-related technology, currently the dominant technology in terms both of usage and cost–performance, there was potential competition from gallium arsenide-based devices such as MES-FETs and HEMTs, and from Josephson junctions. While with a short time horizon, silicon was clearly the dominant technology, an extension of the horizon to 10 to 15 years injected significant uncertainty into the decision-making situation. Secondly, there remained the possibility of the occurrence of unexpected exogenous events which might have an influence on the relative merits of the current competing technologies, or lead to the introduction of new alternative technologies. The discovery of superconducting materials at high critical temperatures is a case in point. Finally, uncertainty existed regarding the ability of the individual firm to appropriate adequate returns from its investment in research in the uncertain technology.

All of these sources of uncertainty pose difficulties for commercially oriented companies. This is illustrated by IBM's decision to pull out of scientifically relevant research on Josephson junctions, because of the expected commercial implications of the rapid progress being made with silicon technology. This example also illustrates the futility of attempts to use rational optimizing models to analyse decision-making under these conditions of uncertainty (as opposed to risk where probability distributions can be derived and used). From the vantage point of 1983, with the information then at its disposal, was IBM 'rational' in its decision of opt out of JJ research? At the same time, was MITI 'rational' in deciding to continue its JJ research under the Supercomputer Project and in ETL? A qualitatively different light is thrown on these questions, with hindsight, as a result of the breakthroughs in 1986 in high temperature superconductors. The meaninglessness of these questions becomes apparent.

The irreducible existence of uncertainty poses further questions regarding the responses of different types of organization and the appropriate role of government. In the case of JJ research in Japan, for example, a crucial determinant of continued work in this area was the *non-commercial* decision by MITI, probably with the support of ETL, to carry on with this research. (An alternative way of expressing this is that the decision of MITI and its research arm ETL was uninfluenced by considerations of shorter-term commercializability, unlike that of IBM and the Japanese companies.)[17] Similarly, in the case of HEMT research, government involvement, as argued earlier, probably had the effect of significantly increasing work in this area in Japan. The important implications of the points raised in this paragraph are analysed in greater detail in the concluding chapter of this book.

The benefits of knowledge sharing

Amongst the large number of MITI officials, senior company research managers, and academics who were closely involved in the Supercomputer Project and who were interviewed, there was a consensus that there was minimal sharing of knowledge and information in this project. For example, a senior research manager form one of the three major mainframe producing companies stated that although the participating firms are required by MITI to produce regular reports on the research they are undertaking under the Supercomputer Project, these reports are not passed on to the other member companies. He had never seen a report from one of the other companies. This was corroborated by a senior research manager from another one of the three companies. The same point was made by a senior academic intimately involved in the evaluation of the Supercomputer Project:

> Fransman: Is there very little research cooperation in the Supercomputer Project?
> Informant: Yes, in this project the companies are working independently, except for the transfer of niobium Josephson junction technology from ETL to ... Fujitsu, Hitachi and NEC.
> Fransman: Why do they not share technological knowledge?
> Informant: Because they are strongly competitive. At the time of the VLSI Project the companies were not so strong and therefore were more willing to share. Now each company can support its own research projects.

As noted earlier, there was minimal sharing of knowledge between Fujitsu and Oki, both of whom were involved in research on HEMTs. There was even less sharing between Fujitsu, Hitachi and NEC in the area of JJs, although each of the companies had important interactions with ETL in connection with the initial transfer of niobium technology.

Independent evidence of the minimal sharing of the information in the Supercomputer Project comes from an analysis of the patents that have emerged from this project. Information on Supercomputer Project patents was provided in two sets of data supplied to the author by MITI officials. The first list, providing information to the end of 1986, recorded a total of ninety-eight patents under the Supercomputer Project. Further details on all of these patents were examined in order to ascertain the number of joint patents, defined as patents held by inventors from more than one company. Joint patents may be used in this context as an indicator of the sharing of knowledge of the kind that might result in patent applications. The examination revealed no joint patents, supporting the conclusion that there was minimal knowledge sharing in the project. Furthermore, the second list revealed that no diffusion of knowledge had occurred through the sale by MITI of the patents and know-how which it owned under the Supercomputer Project. In contrast to the other MITI-initiated projects analysed earlier in this book where some of the MITI-owned patents and know-how were sold, none were similarly sold in the case of the Super-computer Project. The data up to 31 March 1987 showed that MITI owned a total of 263 patents and 141 'know-hows' under this project. The rights to none of these, however, had been sold by the same date. As a senior MITI official, who was closely involved in the establishment of the Supercomputer Project, explained, 'the patent does not describe all of the knowledge required to reproduce the related technology; the patent is only a juristic form of description of the technology.' Since the knowledge to which the patents refer was created inside the companies, these companies retained effective private control over the knowledge. The fact that none of the rights to the patents or know-how was sold is no doubt a reflection of the commercial sensitivity of the knowledge.

Nevertheless, while strong evidence has been given suggesting that the sharing of knowledge under the Supercomputer Project was highly constrained, this does not mean that there were no social benefits derived from knowledge sharing. To begin with, and despite the constraints determined by the competitive relationship between the participating companies and the possible importance for their competitive position of the technologies developed under the project, there was some sharing of knowledge. One example was the sharing of some research results on molecular beam epitaxy for crystal growth and measurement and evalua-tion technology for high-speed performance between Fujitsu and Oki in the case of HEMTs. Furthermore, the regular conferences and meetings held between the researchers from the participating companies and ETL at which research results were reported (if not the more commercially sensitive knowledge of the ways in which these results could be achieved), improved the flow of information between the companies. In some instances the information acquired in this way must have assisted the companies to make better informed decisions regarding issues such as research specialization and research directions to be explored. It is undoubtedly the case that information flows under the Supercomputer Project were significantly superior compared to what would have been achieved had the research been organized in an isolated in-house way. For instance, it is likely that the entry of Hitachi and NEC into the HEMT area was facilitated by their membership of the Supercomputer Project.

The economies of coordinated in-house research

As was pointed out in the earlier analyses of the VLSI and Optical Measurement Projects, government has in principle four alternatives in the area of technology development. First, it can opt for non-intervention, leaving the development of technology to the private decisions of corporations. Secondly, it can choose what has been referred to in this book as the isolated in-house research option, IIHR, where the creation of technology inside private companies is subsidized by government, but where no attempt is made to coordinate the research activities of the firms so subsidized. Thirdly, government can establish coordinated in-house research, CIHR, where attempts are made to coordinate the subsidized research undertaken inside the participating companies. Finally, government can opt for joint research in joint research facilities, JRJF, in order to achieve the greatest possible degree of joint creation and sharing of knowledge.

Both the VLSI and Optical Measurement Projects involved a mix of CIHR and JRJF. In other words, in these projects CIHR and JRJF were alternative modes of organizing cooperative research. Since, therefore, a choice existed between CIHR and JRJF in these projects, their evaluation included an analysis of the *additional* benefits provided by JRJF over and above what could have been achieved through CIHR.

In the case of the Supercomputer Project, however, for reasons that have been exhaustively discussed in this section, an effective choice did not exist between JRJF and CIHR. The technologies that were chosen for development under the project were judged by the participating companies, particularly Fujitsu, Hitachi, and NEC, to be too commercially sensitive to allow for JRJF. Nevertheless, MITI did have a choice between CIHR and IIHR in attempting to promote the capabilities of Japanese companies in the field of supercomputing. MITI could simply have decided to subsidize research areas which either it, or the companies, or both, had selected, but without making any effort to coordinate the research done inside the companies. In view of this choice, one way of evaluating the Supercomputer Project is to examine the *additional* net benefit that was obtained as a result of opting for CIHR rather than IIHR. In undertaking this examination, account must be taken of the fact that the costs of negotiating the research project and coordinating it are significantly higher under CIHR as compared to IIHR. Are there additional benefits under CIHR that compensate, or more than compensate, for these extra costs? In order to answer this question it is necessary to examine the economies of coordinated in-house research.

A number of economies of coordinated in-house research were achieved in the Supercomputer Project which would not have resulted under isolated in-house research. To begin with, as was shown for example in the case of the HEMT research, a degree of joint search for improved technologies took place, even though the extent of sharing the fruits of this research was constrained. Under IIHR it is reasonable to assume that the amount of joint research would have been considerably less. Secondly, through the Supercomputer Project there was a greater flow of information between the participating companies regarding their respective areas of research and the strengths and weaknesses of this research. This flow must have improved the information at the disposal of the companies and facilitated their strategic decision-making in areas such as product and technology specialization. However, in view of the commercially sensitive nature of the technologies developed under the project, there was relatively little international exchange of information under the auspices of the Supercomputer Project, unlike the cases of the VLSI, Optical Measurement and Fifth Generation Projects discussed elsewhere in this book. Under IIHR it is unlikely that there would have occurred the same quantity and quality of information flow as was realized under the Supercomputer Project.

Thirdly, and relating closely to the last point, there was, as was shown earlier, a degree of diffusion of technological knowledge through the activities undertaken under the Supercomputer Project, athough diffusion was not aided by the sale by MITI of patent and know-how rights. The main example of diffusion given in the present study is the entry of Hitachi and NEC into the field of HEMTs which probably was facilitated by their participation in the project. Again it is likely that less diffusion would have occurred under IIHR.

Finally, economies of specialization were achieved by coordinating the research of the participating companies in such a way as to avoid research duplication. Although for strategic reasons the companies would have duplicated privately some of the research allocated under the Supercomputer Project to other companies, it is likely that coordination resulted in a greater degree of specialization than would have taken place under IIHR. For example, under the project NEC, the largest producer of semiconductor memories in the world, was allocated the development of the large-capacity high-speed memory subsystem (see Fig. 5.1). NEC's specialization and relative competitive strength in memories can be traced back at least to 1966 when the company concentrated on memories under the MITI-initiated Very High Speed Computer System Project (VHSCS).[18]

Although a quantitative calculation is not feasible, the additional benefits derived from these four economies of coordinated in-house research must be weighed against the additional costs associated with this form of organization. These additional costs compared to IIHR arise from the costs of negotiation and coordination. In view of the commercial sensitivity of the technologies concerned, the underlying competitive relationship of the participating companies, and the threat of possible knowledge leakage, these costs, which would have been significantly less under IIHR, must have been considerable.

Evaluation of the project's direct output

A further way of evaluating the Supercomputer Project is to attempt to evaluate the direct output of the project. There are, however, a number of difficulties that confront such an attempt. The first is that many of the technologies developed under the project have not yet been commercialized. It is therefore not yet possible to evaluate the performance of the technologies. Secondly, even where the technology has begun to be commercialized, the additionality criterion requires that only the additional effects which have resulted from the project, and which would not otherwise have been realized, be taken into account. For example, in 1986 Fujitsu announced that it 'began sales of its low-noise, high-gain HEMT for use in K-band (18 GHz band) ground stations'.[19] In 1987 the company reported that 'a 3.4 ns access time was achieved with a 16 kbit/s SRAM' and declared that this 'represents a big step toward putting HEMT ICs into practical use'.[20] As was shown earlier, government contributed at most 20 to 25 per cent additional resources to HEMT research in Fujitsu between 1981 and 1986. It is clearly not possible to estimate the extent to which these company achievements can be attributed to government support.

One possible way round the difficulty posed by the additionality criterion is to use the data on patents and know-how that have resulted from the Supercomputer Project itself. As noted, MITI is the owner of the technological knowledge created under the project. To the extent that (a) MITI has been able in practice to acquire the ownership of the technology to which it has legal right, and (b) this ownership is accurately reflected in the data on patents and know-how, such data could be used as an indicator of project output. As noted above, there were about 98 or about 263 patents, depending on which MITI information is used, and about 141 know-how rights that had resulted from the Supercomputer Project by the beginning of 1987. Significant further problems, however, arise in attempting to use this data. Since it is difficult to measure the commercial significance or the quality of the patents and know-how rights, the data are limited in their usefulness as output indicators. Not much meaning can be attributed to the number of patents or know-how rights *per se*. For instance, it does not make much sense, in the absence of an adjustment for quality and/or commercial significance, to compare the number of patents generated by the Super-computer Project per unit of resource allocated with that produced under another project. The same would hold for other possible indicators of output such as technical papers.

Another possible source of evaluation is the judgements made by outside observers, subject to the qualifications noted earlier in the evaluation of the Optical Measurement Project. For example, a science adviser working in one of the Western embassies in Tokyo arrived at the following conclusion in a report on the progress of the Supercomputer Project in 1986: 'Clearly, both Hitachi and Oki are making steady progress in their representative fields and we can be confident that the technologies of both companies, and the overall Supercomputer Project, will emerge on time.'

The observations of more specialized teams consisting of researchers who themselves are closely involved in the areas being examined may be even more helpful from an evaluation point of view. One example is the Japanese Technology Evaluation Program's panel report on advanced computing in Japan (Japanese Technology Evaluation Program, 1987) sponsored by the United States National Science Foundation. Some of the conclusions arrived at by this panel are relevant for an evaluation of supercomputing capabilities in Japan. For instance, the panel noted that:

supercomputers are the locus of many technological frontiers: solid-state physics, VLSI design, ALU design, component packaging, optimizing compilers, etc. The Japanese achievements in these areas should be regarded as a central measure of the state of computer science in Japan, indeed as a more representative measure than the somewhat inconclusive results of the research sponsored by ICOT [the institute of fifth generation computing]. We can say with confidence that in the area of supercomputers the Japanese have achieved parity with the United States, and are moving in whatever direction the US might go ... there are no areas of conventional hardware design in which the Japanese lag significantly behind the US. If the US still dominates overwhelmingly the mainframe market, this is among other things because of economic and historic realities (installed hardware, visibility, distribu-tion networks, etc.) and to a lesser extent because of scientific leadership... Economic dominance does not come from technical wizardry alone (p. 49).

Furthermore, it was judged that Japanese performance in the area of software, often held to be a field of comparative weakness in Japan, was as strong as in the area of hardware:

The best way to summarize our findings is to contrast them with the conclusions of the 1984 Japanese Technology Evaluation Program Panel Report on Computer Science in Japan ... The 1984 Report found that basic research in software in Japan was behind the US and losing ground, and that advanced development was also behind. This has changed substantially in the course of two years. In this short period, the Japanese have mobilized substantial resources, through ICOT and FGCS [the Fifth Generation Computer System], *through the Supercomputer project*, and throughout the Japanese industry. As a result, there is now active research, both pure and applied, in most areas of software. In our view, when the relative sizes of the research establishments of both countries is taken into account, there is no sizable technological gap between the United States and Japan in these areas (p. 48, emphasis added).

The report, however, also suggested that while there was a keen research interest in both the hardware and software aspects of parallel processing, a major focus of the Supercomputer Project, there was less immediate commercial interest in these areas in Japan. 'While at least keeping pace with America in the development of conventional supercomputers, the Japanese are clearly behind the U.S. in the design of large-scale multi-processors or parallel machines' (p. 5). Elsewhere in the report it is stated that

Our hosts at Fujitsu, NEC, NTT and Hitachi were well aware and interested in the progress of the connection machine and the ultracomputer, to mention two visible American efforts in this area. But we heard explicit scepticism on the part of several top designers, as to the practicality of large-scale parallelism for general computing. There seemed to be a consensus that FORTRAN and vector machines would remain the computing environment for large-scale scientific computing and that only small-scale parallelism (4–16 processors) would present any commercial interest (p. 49).

The last quotation raises questions about the importance attached to parallel processing in the Supercomputer Project. Further questions are raised about the synthesis of generic research-push and user-pull determin-ants of the technology developed under the project. What in practice was the relative significance of these two determinants? The opinion of a senior MITI official on the Supercomputer Project may throw some light on these issues:

Regarding the Supercomputer Project, I am dubious about the ultimate develop-ment of one integrated system. Each company already has its own in-house technology. They are already selling supercomputers. I do not think it is possible to integrate the components [into a supercomputing system under the project]. Originally MITI people were wanting to do basic research on JJs, gallium arsenide devices, HEMTs, and highly parallel algorithms and software and finally to review the functioning of the experimental system. It is true that they had such a plan. But later each company succeeded in producing their own supercomputer [that is, Fujitsu, Hitachi and NEC]. These use silicon devices, not gallium arsenide. The research of the Supercomputer Project is more involved in future devices [than anything else].

This suggests that in the event the Supercomputer Project has become largely a 'future device-push' project.

However, while the panel report just quoted does provide a useful source for the evaluation of supercomputing capabilities in Japan, it does not take us any further in resolving the additionality problem in evaluating the Supercomputer Project. The supercomputer capabilities which the panel members observed were the combined result of research and experience accumulated privately within the companies, as well as their participation in national research and development projects such as the Supercomputer and Fifth Generation Computer Projects. More detailed analysis of the evolution of the technologies developed under these projects would be needed in order to analyse more convincingly their additional effects.

A note on the role of universities in supercomputing in Japan

According to a senior MITI official closely involved in the establishment of the Supercomputer Project, 'the university role in this project is very limited'. More specifically, the major role played by university academics was to act as commentators in the initial stages when MITI officials were canvassing opinion and forming a consensus on the shape that the project should take, and to take a leading role in the evaluation committee. This evaluation committee meets several times a year to review the progress being made on the project and to make suggestions regarding future directions and priorities. Its role is primarily to provide feedback from a relatively neutral body of informed specialists, rather than to attempt an evaluation of the project in the sense in which that term is used in this book.

Some of the comments made by the Japanese Technology Evaluation Program's (1987) panel report on advanced computing in Japan on the role of the universities in supercomputing are relevant here:

Japanese universities and their computer science departments have not yet attained the reputation and scientific standing of American ones, and the best Japanese computer scientists are still trained abroad, chiefly in the US but also in Western Europe. Most computer science students leave after obtaining an MS degree. We heard repeatedly that industrial enterprises find that students with only the MS are generalists that are easily trainable (in-house) in any subspeciality, while students with PhD's are likely to be prematurely specialized.

Universities depend directly on the Ministry of Education, and academic research projects are less lavishly funded than those that are sponsored by MITI. The Ministry of Education is in any case as interested as MITI in fostering the development of computer science, and it has created seven supercomputer centres in seven prominent universities through the country (p. 55).

The practice of taking into company research departments students with master's rather than doctor's degrees, a practice heavily influenced by the institution of lifetime employment which gives firms a strong incentive to invest in the training of their employees, has a number of important consequences for the Japanese System. First, it tends to weaken university research since it deprives universities of potentially good researchers who otherwise might stay for a further three or four years. Research done for the purposes of a master's degree clearly lacks the depth and sophistication of PhD research. Secondly, and conversely, it serves to strengthen the companies which are able to ensure that the work of their researchers relates more closely to the needs of the company and less to more academic or professional interests. Finally,

Since the universities generally produce students only to the masters level, who go on to industry or government laboratories to pursue their more advanced training, the more advanced research projects that we saw were generally found in industry much closer to the market. This contrasts with the United States, in that the more advanced research tends to take place in the larger university research centres and slowly transfers to industry research centres. While the overall research pursued in Japan may not be viewed by some to be as advanced as that being pursued in the United States, advanced research in Japan is pursued much closer to the marketplace (p.C-3).

Conclusion

One of the main themes that has run through this chapter on the Supercomputer Project has been the importance of uncertainty and the difficulties that its existence has posed. Uncertainty is inherent in long-run technical change and can never be eliminated. Beyond the promise of the Josephson computer lies the possibility of the optical computer. But, as Hecht (1987, p. 48) notes:

past predictions that have come to naught have taught some veterans to be cautious. The trend in computing does seem to point to optics, or 'photonics' as some call it. Optical technology is young; electronics may be approaching some plateaus. But neither the promise of light nor the limitations of semiconductor electronics are certain. A decade ago, Josephson junctions were the supercomputing technology of tomorrow. However, conventional electronics made better progress than expected, while Josephson junctions ran into technical roadblocks severe enough to cause IBM to abandon the technology. Now, though, room-temperature superconductors may revive the Josephson junction. Electronics has a headstart on optics in experience, resources and basic technology. Optics has much promise but will not find it easy to catch up, especially as the threat of optical devices will spur on those who have dedicated their lives to conventional electronics.

For reasons that have been elaborated upon here, under such conditions of uncertainty, for-profit corporations face a number of constraints in their efforts to allocate resources to long-term technology development. As a result, government has a potentially important role to play. Seen in this light, the final comment from a senior MITI official who was closely involved in the establishment of the Supercomputer Project has a degree of relevance, whether or not his judgement is entirely correct: 'I do not believe that the firms could have organized [such] a supercomputer project themselves because business people did not believe in the feasibility and profitability of this kind of supercomputer in the near future. Our pressure or promotion was needed.'

6
The Future Electronic Devices Project, 1981–1990

Introduction

From the late 1970s the undertaking of basic or generic research in Japan received high priority. In the area of electronic devices the decision was made to sponsor research in several areas which were highly uncertain, indeed, according to the Director of a VLSI laboratory in one of the large Japanese industrial electronics companies, even academic and speculative. Under the Future Electronic Devices (FED) Project three kinds of devices were chosen for development, namely superlattices, three-dimensional devices and fortified devices for extreme conditions. In 1986 biochips were added to the FED Project.

Background to the FED Project

The background to FED has been discussed by Dore (1983). The following is a summary of the main points of interest here.

FED formed part of a larger programme which, together with new materials and biotechnology, aimed at the development of technologies for the future. The programme was called the Next Generation Base Technologies Development Programme, or Jisedai.

The Jisedai Programme emerged from MITI's increasing commitment from the late 1970s to the development of new industrial technologies for the future. In 1977 an *ad hoc* advisory council was established, called the Working Party for the Formulation of a Long-Term Plan for the Development of Industrial Technology, which reported to the Director-General of MITI's Agency for Industrial Science and Technology. The Chairman of the Working Party 'was the head of the Engineering Futures Laboratory at the Tokyo University of Technology and its members were ten university professors (one economist, one management and one social engineering expert; the rest scientists and engineers); two members of research institutes; one newspaper leader-writer and eight from private industry (two each from electronics, chemicals and engineering; one from steel, one from textiles)' (Dore, 1983, p. 8).

Dore strongly implies that in practice the Working Party was significantly influenced by the priorities and directions identified by MITI
officials and that it played a supportive role in establishing a social-
political consensus or legitimation around these MITI-determined objectives:

The MITI officials who 'serviced' this working party are more apt to talk as if the
working party serviced them, though they readily acknowledged that they learned
a great deal... The working party also acted as a useful sounding board on which
they could try out their opinions and plans; it provided a budget out of which it
could be persuaded to commission surveys, and, when it was summoned for its
seventh two-hour meeting (the first in ten months) in August, 1980, it provided
useful applause and legitimation for MITI's Next Generation Base Technologies
programme just as it was about to be presented to the Ministry of Finance for
approval (p. 8).

A good deal of research of a technology forecasting kind was done in-house
in the Research Department of MITI's Agency for Industrial Science and
Technology under the auspices of the Working Party. According to Dore,
however, the 'body which played the major role in creating the consensus'
for a substantial R & D programme focusing on future industrial technologies 'was not the Working Party, but the Industrial Structure
Council' of MITI (p. 11). The Industrial Structure Council was established in 1964 and is referred to by Johnson (1982, p. 102) as 'MITI's
number one official channel to the business community'.
    Apparently, 'a group of MITI officials' had been 'constituted as a
"working party for trade and industry policy of the 1980s"' (Dore, 1983,
p. 12). Dore does not make clear the relationship, if any, of this latter
group to the MITI personnel who worked with the Working Party which
reported to the Director-General of the Agency for Industrial Science and
Technology. Nevertheless, the group of MITI officials prepared a highly
influential draft report which was first circulated in August 1979. This
draft report, known internally as 80V, served as the first draft prepared
within MITI of the document 'Vision for the Eighties'. (One of the main
roles of the Industrial Structure Council was to prepare 'visions' and its
vision for the 1970s, emphasizing the growing importance of knowledge-
intensive industries, had been influential.)
    In August 1979 the Industrial Structure Council set up a Drafting
Committee to work on the new Vision document. This Drafting Committee was given the draft report 80V, prepared by the group of MITI
officials, as a basis for its deliberations. The Drafting Committee had a
Tokyo University economist as its Chairman, seven other professors,
eleven businessmen, three economists from research organizations, four
newspapermen, one novelist, six representatives of organizations such as
the National Chamber of Commerce and the Association of Prefectural
Governors, two trade unionists, and two representatives of women's

associations (p. 11). According to Dore, 'it is an open question how far the Drafting Committee served to legitimate the report [of the Working Party reporting to the Director-General of the Agency for Industrial Science and Technology], how far to make substantive contributions' (p. 12). Nevertheless, Dore concludes that

The basic criteria and purpose of what was to become the Next Generation Base Technologies programme were thus already well formulated and widely accepted within MITI by the autumn of 1979, and within the wider 'economic policy community' as the contents of 80V became generally known over the winter and spring and were widely discussed in the press after its formal publications in April 1980 (p. 13).

Once the basic criteria and purpose of the Jisedai Programme had been agreed, it remained to decide on the specific technologies that would be chosen for development. Although the Machinery and Information Industries Bureau of MITI had already decided to sponsor the Fifth Generation and the Supercomputer Projects, the latter, as was seen earlier, involving a significant electronic devices component, it was eventually agreed that the Bureau would also participate in the Jisedai Programme. Dore recounts that

When it was decided that the Bureau should come in, a very junior member of the Electronic Devices Department [in the Machinery and Information Industries Bureau] had the task of devising an outline programme in the space of a week. He rapidly took advice from the directors of the research laboratories of one or two private firms. From these discussions emerged three front-runners: three-dimensional integrated circuits, superlattices, and bio-sensors. To these he added a fourth which was suggested to him by (or rather, which he was asked to include by) the Space Industries Office in the same bureau – environmentally resistant chips; specifically chips with resistance to cosmic rays, heat and impact...

The next step was to send the preliminary outline to the Agency For Industrial Science And Technology's Electrotechnical Laboratory [ETL] and to the research directors of seven companies for comment: Hitachi, Toshiba, NEC, Mitsubishi Electric, Oki, Fujitsu and Sumitomo Electric. The head of the leading semi-conductor technology laboratory at Tohoku University was also consulted. The replies from firms were nearly all in terms of feasibilities and levels of interest in the results (p. 20).

The choice of devices

Superlattices and three-dimensional devices

Anderson (1984, p. 237) notes that the

idea of a superlattice semiconductor stems from research carried out by Japan's Nobel Laureate Leo Esaki, (now employed by IBM) and his collaborator Raphael

Tsu. They proposed that a superlattice – a semiconductor built layer by layer of different materials – could show ultra high-speed operation at room temperature and thus be superior to other high-speed devices, such as Josephson junctions, that operate at cryogenic temperatures. Superlattices can be built by molecular beam epitaxy, in which a beam of evaporating molecules in an ultra high vacuum is controlled by computer-timed shutters.

In a survey of the state-of-the-art in the area of electronic devices published in October 1987, Meindl (1987) points out that both super-lattices and 3-D devices are quantum-well devices. For example, in a superlattice consisting of two layers, one of gallium arsenide and the other of aluminium gallium arsenide, the

physical properties of one material (gallium arsenide) are such that it acts as a 'quantum well', capturing many electrons from the other material (aluminium gallium arsenide). By means of superlattice technology it may be possible to construct quantum wells vertically and horizontally in a crystal whose cross section would resemble a checker-board. Electrons that 'tunnel' between squares might be exploited to perform digital operations. Quantum-well devices could be more than 10 times as fast as the most optimistically imagined MOSFET's [metal oxide silicon field-effect transistors] of the year 2000 (p. 62).

However, although the 'most rudimentary quantum-well device – the MODFET [modulation-doped field-effect transistor] – has already been formulated', what remains 'is to extend that concept to three-dimensional structures, provide connections among them and put such devices in the context of new computer architectures. If those things can be done,' Meindl adds concluding his survey, 'it may be possible to transcend all the limits currently in view on chip design and fabrication.' However, alluding to the significant degree of uncertainty that still overhangs this area of research, Meindl notes that 'no three-dimensional quantum-well devices have yet been constructed, but their construction remains an intriguing prospect just over the technological horizon...Indeed, the current situation could be compared to the one prevailing in the 1950s between the invention of the transistor and that of the integrated circuit' (p. 62).

As was shown, although MITI officials had decided on a programme that would support research on future electronic devices, the proposals for specific devices were worked out in close consultation with several of the industrial electronics companies. What factors motivated the suggestion that 3-D devices be included, given the substantial degree of uncertainty surrounding the commercial viability of this kind of device? NEC was one of the main proponents of 3-D devices under the FED Project. In an interview with the author, a senior manager of one of NEC's research laboratories stated that at the time the FED Project began the company had not done any research on 3-D devices. There were two related factors that accounted for the absence of such research.

The first was the cost of doing the research, in terms of both equipment and staff. The second factor was the uncertainty regarding pay-off in this particular field. While NEC applied to do research on both 3-D devices and superlattices under the FED Project, MITI officials put the company in the 3-D group only, possibly because NEC was such a strong proponent of research on this device.

ICs for extreme conditions and biochips

Dore (1983) provides further information on the choice of ICs for extreme conditions.

The environment-proofing project was of interest to only three firms – NEC, Toshiba and Mitsubishi Electric – the only ones supplying chips for Japan's space programme. But (although it was not really a good candidate under [Jisedai] criteria, the development path being already well charted) there was such strong support from the Space Industries Office [in MITI] that the project survived when one of the four had to be cut out in the final budgeting-stage (p. 20).

Although biosensors had also been proposed by some of the companies, 'Biosensors went instead. To those in the electronics industry it seemed the most droppable because it had evoked the least support of the three from industry contacts' (p. 20). In the event, however, research on ICs for extreme conditions was terminated in 1985, the objectives having been achieved, and a new project on biochips began in 1986. Dr Isao Karube (1986), of the Tokyo Institute of Technology, argues that 'bio-molecules are thought to hold the key to successful development of biochips' which he defines as 'molecular devices possessing self-assembly and self-organizing functions'. He notes that the 'biochips which are presently using natural protein molecules do not satisfy electric properties and stabilities. This means that protein engineering must be used to design and synthesize proteins for biochips at the molecular level. Without this technology, it will be impossible to manufacture practical electronic devices using proteins' (p. 34).

The question of a joint laboratory

According to the leader of one of the other MITI-initiated cooperative research and development projects, it 'was Shoji Tanaka [a Tokyo University professor] who informally proposed a joint laboratory for the Jisedai Project' on future electronic devices. The reasoning underlying this proposal was presumably based on the potential economies of joint research analysed earlier in this book. In the event, however, the proposal was rejected and the FED Project became a coordinated in-house research project.

Interviews held with both government officials and company representatives who had been closely involved with the FED Project confirmed that in principle it was possible for this project to have been organized on the basis of joint research in joint research facilities. The research that was to be undertaken had a significant conceptual dimension, thus meeting the generic or 'basic' research requirement often necessary for joint research. Furthermore (with the exception of the environmentally resistant devices) there was a relatively long time-lag before the commercialization of superlattices, 3-D devices and biochips and the outcome of the research as noted was highly uncertain. For all these reasons, joint research in joint research facilities was possible.

A number of reasons were suggested by these informants for the absence of joint research in the FED Project. The project leader just quoted argued in the case of the VLSI Project that

Because people believed that VLSI technology was very important it was possible to get agreement for the establishment of a joint laboratory. But in the case of the FED Project the technologies are not as important. From my point of view, VLSI, optoelectronics and fifth generation computer technologies are more important. The companies don't want to lose researchers to the joint laboratories so they agree on some projects [for example, the VLSI, Optoelectronic and Fifth Generation Projects] but resist in the case of others [such as the FED Project].

It should be noted that the 'importance' of the FED technologies referred to by this informant must be taken to indicate expected commercial importance within the planning horizon of the participating companies. As already indicated in the survey by Meindl (1987), from a scientific point of view the technologies associated with the FED Project are of great interest.

Further evidence testifying to the relative lack of interest in the FED technologies comes from the resources allocated by MITI to the FED Project compared to the other device-oriented projects. Over the first six years 7.6 billion yen were spent on the FED Project. This compares with 73.7 billion yen for the VLSI Project, 1976–80, 16 billion yen for the Optical Measurement Project, 1979-85, and 23 billion yen for the Supercomputer Project, 1981–89 (all in current prices). As noted earlier, significant proportions of the latter projects were concerned with devices. Most of the company representatives interviewed felt that the relatively small amount of resources committed to the FED Project was probably an important reason accounting for the absence of a joint laboratory.

Organization of the research

The same factors that provided the possibility of joint research in the FED Project also created the conditions for a relatively unconstrained sharing of knowledge generated under the project. This sharing may be seen as a process of *joint search* whereby the participating companies

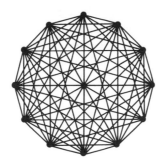

Fully interconnected

Fig. 6.1 A model of joint search.

explore different research areas and applications and share much, though not all, of the knowledge resulting from the research. Drawing on the analogy of a fully interconnected architecture in the case of parallel processing where every processor is connected to every other processor, a model of joint search is presented in Fig. 6.1. This model depicts a case of coordinated in-house research with relatively unconstrained joint search. Information flows between the participating companies through two main channels. The first is regular monthly meetings attended by the researchers of the participating companies where research results are reported while the second is the circulation of research papers and informal discussions between the researchers. In addition, an annual conference is held which is also attended by outsiders and where main results are presented.

While the model captures some of the essential features of the FED Project, it must be supplemented by a discussion of the research relationship between the participating companies. The case of 3-D devices will serve as the main example.

In all, seven firms are participating in the FED Project: Matsushita, Mitsubishi, Sanyo and Sharp from the Kansai region and NEC, Oki and Toshiba from the Kanto region. The four Kansai firms, with Mitsubishi as the strongest in this particular technology area, worked particularly closely together in order to jointly develop a research programme. In contrast, the three Kanto firms proposed more independently the research areas in which they wanted to work. The MITI officials in charge of the FED Project provided the function of over-all coordination, ensuring that priority areas were covered while avoiding unwanted overlap.

The research areas allocated to each of the Kansai companies are shown in Table 6.1. In a number of the cases, two or more companies are working in the same technology area. In these cases, however, each

Table 6.1. *FED Project: areas of research specialization by the Kansai companies involved in research on three-dimensional devices*

	Mats	Mits	Sanyo	Sharp
Stucked SOI (silicon-on-insulator) technology				
Recrystalline technology	x	x		x
Epitaxial silicon technology			x	
Stucked process technology				
Wiring technology		x		
Planarization technology				x
Through-hole technology	x	x		
Design and evaluation technology				
Design technology	x	x		x
Device technology	x	x	x	x

Key:
Mats   Matsushita
Mits   Mitsubishi
Source: Information supplied to the author by the Research and Development Association for Future Electron Devices.

company pursues different research directions. The choice of the research directions to be pursued is made through a process of close consultation between the four companies, with additional input and final approval from the MITI officials running the FED Project. The unifying research theme for the Kansai group stems from their objective to develop High Capacity Multifunction Three-Dimensional Devices for use in areas such as signal processing. Both NEC and Oki, choosing their research areas independently, though in consultation with the FED Project leaders from MITI, are doing research on High Density Integrated Three-Dimensional Devices. In the case of NEC this device has potential use in the area of memories, a field as noted earlier in which NEC has tended to specialize in MITI-initiated projects, and microprocessors. In both these areas three-dimensionality offers the hope of miniaturization, greater circuit density and greater speed. Toshiba, also operating relatively independently, has specialized in the area of High Speed Multifunction Three-Dimensional Devices with potential application in the field of logic devices.

The specification of applications areas and the orientation of in-house research not only to generic issues but also to the development of specific devices is an important feature of the organization of the FED Project. As in the case of the other MITI-initiated cooperative research projects examined in this book, this means that both generic research-push and user research-pull determinants of technical change are an inherent part of the design of the FED research.

The model illustrated in Fig. 6.1 needs further modification to take account of the flows of information between the participating companies. While some information on research results, methods and processes used flows to all the member companies, information flows are particularly dense between the Kansai group of firms as a result of their closer inter-firm coordination. This, however, does not mean that all technological knowledge generated under the FED Project is shared even between the members of the Kansai group. To begin with, for strategic reasons the firms may not wish to share all the knowledge they have created and the fact that this knowledge has been generated in-house gives them an important degree of control. Furthermore, some of the knowledge will inevitably remain tacit even where there is a willingness in principle to share. For these reasons, less information will be shared than would be in the case of joint research in joint research facilities.

Four companies are involved in the superlattice research under the FED Project, namely Fujitsu, Hitachi, Sumitomo Electric and Sony. The research interaction between these companies is similar to that of NEC, Oki and Toshiba in the case of the 3-D research. The areas of specialization of the four companies is shown in Table 6.2.

Eight companies and two government research laboratories are involved in the research on biochips which began in 1986. The research on

Table 6.2. *FED Project: areas of research specialization by the companies involved in research on superlattices*

Company	Material	Target
Superlattice devices		
Fujitsu	molecular-beam epitaxy for aluminium gallium arsenide/gallium arsenide	resonant hot electron transistor (RHET)
Sumitomo Electric	molecular-beam epitaxy for indium gallium arsenide/ indium phosphide	permeable base transistor (PBT)
Superstructure devices		
Hitachi	molecular-beam epitaxy for silicon	permeable base transistor (PBT)
Sony	metal organic chemical vapour deposition for aluminium gallium arsenide/ gallium arsenide	hot electron transistor (HET)

Source: Information supplied to the author by the Research and Development Association for Future Electron Devices.

biochips is divided into two areas: analysis of biological information processing involving Fujitsu, NEC, the Electrotechnical Laboratory and the National Chemical Laboratory; and the development of molecular assembly technology incorporating Hitachi, Matsushita, Mitsubishi Electric, Mitsubishi Chemical, Sanyo, Sharp and the Electrotechnical Laboratory. Mitsubishi Chemical is the only biotechnology company to be involved. Its Institute of Life Sciences does basic research in related areas of the life sciences.

An Evaluation of the FED Project

The FED Project is an example of coordinated in-house research (CIHR). As noted elsewhere in this book, in principle the Japanese government had four options with regard to future technologies. The first was not to intervene, leaving the decisions regarding the development of future technologies entirely to the private and university sectors. The second option was to subsidize research in selected technology areas but without attempting to coordinate the activities of the companies involved, that is to introduce isolated in-house research (IIHR). Thirdly, the government could introduce CIHR by coordinating at the same time as subsidizing the research activities of the participating companies. The fourth option was for the government to institute joint research in joint research facilities (JRJF).

Although CIHR was ultimately chosen as the form of organization for the FED Project, it is important to stress that, as noted earlier, there was a wide consensus amongst those interviewed who were closely involved in this project that in practice a choice existed between CIHR and JRJF. Since the research was (a) of a generic nature, not involving the development of directly commercializable devices (b) highly uncertain and (c) probably not of great commercial importance within the planning horizon of the participating companies, there was a willingness amongst these firms to entertain the possibility of JRJF. Despite this willingness, however, probably as a result of the relatively low funding allocated to the FED project, the decision was made to opt for CIHR rather than JRJF.

Clearly, there was also a choice between CIHR and IIHR. It was possible for MITI to announce that it would support research proposed by Japanese companies in the area of specified devices but without making any attempt to coordinate the research or influence the pattern of communication between the firms regarding the outcome of this research.

From an evaluation point of view, it is neccessary to take this choice into account in examining the benefits and costs of CIHR compared to the other alternatives of JRJF and IIHR. This will be done in the rest of the discussion in this section.

Five major points will be covered in evaluating the FED Project. First, the benefits from knowledge-sharing will be examined. Secondly, the other economies of CIHR will be analysed. Thirdly, the benefits from overcoming the effects of uncertainty will be discussed. Fourthly, the implications of MITI ownership of the knowledge generated under the project will be examined from the point of view of the degree of diffusion of knowledge that resulted. Finally, a brief comment will be made on the role of universities in the project.

The benefits of knowledge-sharing under CIHR as compared to JRJF and IIHR

The same conditions that underlay the willingness of the companies to engage in JRJF led them to agree to a relatively unconstrained process of joint search. This was particularly the case amongst the Kansai companies doing research on 3-D devices where, as was seen, there was a close interaction between the companies.

There was also a process of relatively unconstrained joint search in the case of other companies doing research on the other devices. For example, both Fujitsu and Sumitomo Electric were involved in the super-lattice group. Both these companies were doing research on molecular beam epitaxy. In Fujitsu's case this involved work with an aluminium gallium arsenide (AlGaAs) layer and a gallium arsenide (GaAs) layer while Sumitomo did research on an indium gallium arsenide (InGaAs) layer and an indium phosphide (InP) layer. The target of the Fujitsu research was the production of a resonant hot electron transistor (RHET) while that of Sumitomo was a high electron mobility transistor (HEMT). According to a manager of one of Fujitsu's research laboratories, since the companies are involved in different areas working with different materials 'there is not much need to share information'. However, 'when the need arises, it is easy to share information – much easier than in the case of the Supercomputer Project'.

The last quotation requires further comment. In our earlier discussion of the Supercomputer Project it was shown that the commercial sensitivity of the technologies under development was responsible for the refusal of the participating companies to accept a MITI proposal for JRJF and for the highly constrained nature of inter-company information flows in that project. In contrast the FED Project involved technology areas where the companies were more willing to share knowledge, as the quotation makes clear.

It is fairly safe to assume, however, that despite the relatively unconstrained nature of the information sharing under the FED Project, less information was shared than would have occurred had JRJF been chosen as the appropriate form of organization for the project. As mentioned earlier, in some instances the firms would have wanted for strategic reasons not to share knowledge, while in other cases the degree of tacitness in the knowledge would have limited the amount of sharing that could have taken even if there were a willingness to share. Under JRJF, on the other hand, the fact that the research was done jointly in the same location would have tended to increase the amount of *de facto* sharing. To the extent that this assumption is correct, and to the extent that economies of information sharing would have been realized, the benefits achieved under the FED Project would have been somewhat less than what could have been achieved under JRJF. Against this, however, must be weighed the additional negotiation costs that are likely to have arisen in organizing JRJF.

It is also fairly safe to assume that more sharing of knowledge occurred in the FED Project than would have occurred had MITI opted for IIHR. As has been seen earlier in this book, underlying competitive relations can substantially increase the negotiation costs of inter-firm research cooperation. This is a major explanation for the relative absence in Japan of privately negotiated research cooperation between large competing firms in the area of industrial electronics. To the extent that this assumption is correct, it is likely that the benefits from knowledge sharing in the FED Project exceeded what would have been achieved under IIHR. However, it is also possible that the costs of setting up an IIHR project would have been less than what occurred under the FED Project. Since MITI coordination would not have taken place and since the participating firms would not have been required to share knowledge as a condition for entry into the project, it is possible that the negotiation costs of setting up the project would have been lower.

The benefits of joint search under CIHR

The participating companies have benefited in numerous ways from the process of joint search facilitated by the sharing of knowledge. To begin with, the companies taken as a whole, rather than as individual entities, are more able to effectively allocate the resources at their disposal in their search for cost-effective and high performance new electronic devices. Rather than each company pursuing similar lines of enquiry while privatizing the results of their individual research, it is possible for the group to jointly agree on the research directions to be followed and to allocate research tasks to each member. In this way a process of specialization is possible, although for strategic reasons the companies are all likely to insist on capabilities in areas judged to be of importance for reasons of competition. By sharing the results, all the members will be alerted to areas of promise revealed by research undertaken somewhere in the group. As the coordinating authority, with its decision-making power supported by the resources which it has allocated in the group,

MITI is in a good position to overcome inter-member conflicts based on self-interest and ensure that the project as a whole covers those areas that seem to offer most promise. Similarly, MITI is well placed to prevent opportunistic behaviour on the part of the member companies. Furthermore, by jointly searching, the group as a whole is able to draw on the distinctive competences, based on past experience and specialization, of its members. In these ways joint search is likely to lead to a more favourable social outcome than individual search.

Overcoming the effects of uncertainty

It would seem that a major benefit of the FED Project has arisen from overcoming some of the effects of uncertainty. As noted in the survey by Meindl (1987), no 3-D device has yet been constructed and a significant amount of uncertainty surrounds the future of this type of device. But at least Japanese companies have made a significant start in exploring the possibilities and difficulties in this area of research, a start that must have been made sooner and been undertaken with a greater amount of resources than would have been the case without MITI's initiative in this field. Even if the 3-D project does not yield cost and efficiency-effective 3-D devices, it is still likely that the project will have produced commercially and technologically important knowledge. Knowing why something does not work and the difficulties that would have to be resolved for it to work can still represent a major advance.

In interviews with representatives from most of the major members of the FED Project respondents were asked to name Western companies where significant research was being undertaken on 3-D devices. None of them could think of important cases, although some Western university-based research was named. While this answer might reflect the respondents' lack of information, it is also possible that there is significantly less research in this area in Western companies. To the extent that this is correct, and in the event that breakthroughs are made in the field of 3-D devices with important commercial implications, it may be confidently predicted that the Japanese companies with their stock of technological capabilities built up largely as a result of this MITI-initiated project will make a rapid and successful entry into this device niche.

The diffusion of knowledge from the FED Project: a patent-based analysis

Between the start of the project in 1981 and May 1987, 63 patents had been applied for in the area of superlattices and 355 in 3-D devices. However, there were no examples of joint patents emerging from this project. A joint patent is defined as one involving the members of two or more of the companies participating in the FED Project. *This is an indication that although the member companies engaged in joint search, they were not involved in joint research.* In general, they worked in different areas, sharing some of the knowledge which they generated in the process.

In law, the ownership of the patents emanating from the FED Project belongs to MITI rather than the firms. Accordingly, MITI is in principle in a favourable position to ensure that the knowledge embodied in the patents is diffused more widely. Unfortunately, we were unable to get information on the extent of sale of MITI-owned patents and know-how from this project.

Information, however, is available for the Next Generation (Jisedai) Programme as a whole. This information is presented in Table 6.3. According to this table, a total of 4 patents were licensed out of the 495 patents emanating from the Jisedai Programme and applied for or granted by 31 March 1986 in Japan. This amounts to a mere 0.8 per cent of these patents. A total of 4 companies were involved in the licensing of the 4 patents. A further 25 patents were applied for or granted in foreign countries.

Since these patents are for the Jisedai Programme as a whole, it may be safely concluded that minimal diffusion of knowledge has occurred through the mechanism of licensing of MITI-owned patents generated under the auspices of this programme. While no information is given on the identity of the companies which were licensed for the four patents, it is possible that at least some of the licenses were taken out by companies which had undertaken the research on which these patents were based. Since it was MITI that retained ownership of the intellectual property rights produced under the programme, the participating company generating the intellectual property and wishing to use it was required to obtain a licence on the technology from MITI.

Table 6.3. *Diffusion of patents from the Next Generation (Jisedai) Programme*

(1)	Number of Jisedai patents available for licensing in Japan	495
(2)	Number of Jisedai patents available for licensing in foreign countries	25
(3)	Number of other Jisedai property rights available for use in Japan	0
(4)	Number of Jisedai patents licensed in Japan	4
(5)	Number of firms obtaining licences on the patents referred to under (4)	4
(6)	Number of Jisedai patents available for licensing in Japan and licensed to foreigners	0

Source: Agency for Industrial Science and Technology, 1986b, p. 490

To the extent that this possibility is correct, minimal diffusion would have occurred as a result of the licensing of government-owned patents.

The role of universities in the FED Project

As noted earlier, university academics were involved in the FED Project primarily in an advisory capacity. This, however, involved only a small number of academics. According to Dore (1983, p. 25) this represents 'one large gap in ... [MITI's] consensus-tapping procedures'. A major reason for this gap

is the 'vertical society' bureaucratic rivalry between MITI and the Ministry of Education, somewhat tinged by jealousy of the latter for the superior prestige (and power, consequently, to attract brighter recruits) of the former. The crucial expression of this is the rule of non-additionality. Any national university department or research institute which receives a grant under a MITI scheme automatically suffers an equal reduction of its Ministry of Education grant. In practice the issue has hitherto arisen primarily in relation to subvention from the Science and Technology Agency which, like the universities, is concerned with basic research. But now that MITI's research concern is moving towards the 'basic' end of the spectrum the problem is acquiring importance for MITI too. The theory is that 'the state' has only one purse, and consequently can have only one expression of expenditure intentions, which expression the Ministry of Education alone is authorized to make where universities are concerned (p. 26).

Dore notes, however, that 'national universities can accept contracts from private firms ... (and some of the Next Generation money is in fact reaching universities via private firms)' (p. 26).

Conclusion

The Future Electronic Devices Project has a number of unique features when compared to the other projects analysed in this book. It is an example of coordinated in-house research (CIHR) but, unlike the Supercomputer Project which is also a case of CIHR, relatively unconstrained joint search takes place in the Future Electronic Devices Project. The unconstrained nature of the joint search is such that it was concluded that this project could have been organized as a project involving joint research in joint research facilities (JRJF). The main reason for the unconstrained nature of the joint search is the absence of expected significant *direct* effects of the technologies being developed in this project on the competitiveness of the participating companies. It may therefore be concluded that, although there are no joint research facilities in the Future Electronic Devices Project, this project occupies an intermediate position in terms of the extent of joint creation and sharing of knowledge between the other 'pure' CIHR project analysed in this book, namely the Supercomputer Project, and the JRJF projects, the VLSI Project, the Optical Measurement Project, both of which had elements of CIHR *and* JRJF, and the Fifth Generation Project, which is the nearest to a 'pure' JRJF case. The Fifth Generation Project is analysed in more detail in the following chapter.

7
The Fifth Generation Computer Project, 1982–1991

Introduction

The present chapter deals with the Fifth Generation Computer Project initiated by the Ministry of International Trade and Industry. In the following section the background to the project is analysed in order to understand the antecedents that influenced the form that the project took. Next, the objectives of the project are discussed while in the following section attention is paid to the discussions and negotiations that took place as part of the process of establishing the Institute for New Generation Computer Technology (ICOT). The initial opposition of the electronics firms to this particular project is examined as is the conflict over the choice of Prolog as the kernel language for the project.

In the following section, which constitutes the main contribution of the present chapter, the role of ICOT is analysed as a form of organization for the acquisition, assimilation, generation and diffusion of technological knowledge in the field of knowledge processing. It is shown that a firm division of labour exists between ICOT, which undertakes generic research, and the private companies which take responsibility for the commercialization of the generic technologies. The important implications of this division of labour are examined. In analysing the role of ICOT it is shown that this organization is particularly well adapted for the purposes of drawing on the international stock of knowledge in this area. The contribution of Japanese universities and companies to ICOT research is also examined. The importance of the complementary development of hardware and software in ICOT is stressed. Attention is then shifted to the benefits that the member firms are deriving from the project. Particular attention is paid to the tensions that arise from the underlying competitive relationship between the firms that are jointly involved in this cooperative research project and to the ways in which these tensions are resolved. Furthermore, the importance of the Prolog culture is examined. An illuminating case study is then considered which gives a more detailed picture of the impact of ICOT on one company's research in the artificial intelligence area. The role of ICOT in the diffusion of technological knowledge is then analysed and special attention is paid to the implications of the tacitness that is inherent in the creation of such knowledge. Finally, attention is paid to the research environment within ICOT and its relative strengths compared to that of the companies in generating generic technological knowledge.

In the following section the funding of ICOT is examined and the question posed and answered about the significance of MITI funding for company research in this area.

In the concluding section a qualitative evaluation of the Fifth Generation Project is undertaken. Here the evaluation method employed by the MITI evaluation committee is contrasted with an economic evaluation stressing the importance of opportunity costs. Following an economic evaluation, the major advantages of a joint research project undertaken in joint research facilities, such as in the case of the Fifth Generation Project, are compared with two other ways in which government might stimulate research in an uncertain area such as knowledge processing. These two alternatives are coordinated in-house research, involving a process of coordination of research essentially conducted in the member companies, and isolated in-house research where there is no government-initiated coordination or cooperation in research.

Background to the Fifth Generation Project

Before analysing the Fifth Generation Project in greater detail it is necessary to examine the background against which the project emerged.

There were a number of factors that together encouraged the Ministry of International Trade and Industry (MITI) and most of the major electronics companies to establish a cooperative research project in the area of advanced computing. One of these factors was their previous successful experience with such projects as analysed earlier in this book. Against this background the Fifth Generation Project represented the latest in a series of cooperative research projects aimed at strengthening the Japanese computing industry. At the same time the fifth generation project aimed at contributing to the general body of knowledge in the fields of artificial intelligence and concurrent computing by developing a prototype fifth generation computer.

One overriding consideration which influenced all of these cooperative research projects was the international dominance of American computer producers, particularly IBM. Although by 1987 IBM Japan occupied third place in the Japanese data processing market, with revenue of $3.82 billion compared to Fujitsu's $5.46 billion, NEC's $5.12 billion and Hitachi's $3.81 billion, IBM continued to dominate the world market. Japanese computer producers were particularly vulnerable – not only were Hitachi and Fujitsu IBM-compatible, but NEC, while not IBM-compatible, was also heavily influenced by the IBM architectures and designs which dominated the world computing industry. Although it is widely agreed that by the late 1970s the Japanese mainframe producers had eliminated the technology gap with IBM in hardware (though for a number of complex reasons they still lagged behind in some areas of software), their vulnerability to IBM's strategic moves remained. This was an important consideration motivating the search for new kinds of computers that would process knowledge on the basis of non-von Neumann architectures.

A further set of factors that influenced both the establishment of the Fifth Generation Project and the form that it eventually took related to a number of scientific advances that had occurred which made it possible to begin the search for fundamentally different kinds of computers. These included breakthroughs in the area of very large scale integration (VLSI) technology which held out the promise of substantial improvements in processing speeds. In addition, important progress had been made in parallel processing technology. These included the earlier advances in pipeline control and array processor technology, the later development of multiple instruction stream/multiple data stream (MIMD) technology, and improvements in programming languages for parallel processing. (See Moto-oka and Kitsuregawa (1985) for a readable account of the importance of these technologies for the Fifth Generation Project.)

Furthermore, important advances had taken place in the field of artificial intelligence which had begun to make knowledge processing (as opposed to numerical processing) a viable possibility. For example, a number of the firms involved in the Fifth Generation Project were by the late 1970s doing research using the artificial intelligence language Lisp which was developed in the United States in the 1950s. Fujitsu, for instance, in 1978 began the development of a machine translation system and in 1980 started research on a Lisp machine, both of which are now being marketed. But it was the development of Prolog (*programming in logic*) that was to have a particular significance for the Fifth Generation Project.

The early papers on Prolog were written around 1971 and 1972 by Colmeraur in France and Kowalski at Imperial College, London University. Around 1974 Kazuhiro Fuchi, then Director of the Pattern Information Section of ETL, and later to become Director of ICOT, was introduced to Prolog and was immediately impressed by the potential of this language. Fuchi's belief in Prolog, the weight he carried in ETL (he was one of the designers of the famous ETL Mark IV computer), and his ability to persuade a number of his colleagues of the importance of Prolog, were significant influences shaping the form that the Fifth Generation Project eventually assumed. Referring to the choice of Prolog Professor Moto-oka from the Faculty of Electrical Engineering at the University of Tokyo, who played a leading role in the establishment of the Fifth Generation Project, observed that early on 'We had many discussions – in particular with Colmeraur in France, who has played such an important part in the practical implementation of the programming language Prolog' (Moto-oka and Kitsuregawa, 1985, p. 6). As will be seen later, the development of Prolog and its practical demonstration constituted an important input into the Fifth Generation Project. For one thing, the use of a logical language like Prolog promised to lighten the burden of software production:

Using logical languages such as Prolog very often enables programmers to describe human ideas quite naturally. Basically, this means they can simply write down the specification of the problem and then leave the processing entirely up to the hardware. When the programmer writing a Prolog program knows in advance about what rules will apply to finding solutions to queries, then he can list the rules and facts in the order that they will be applied, thus creating a program that can be executed in a short time and run very efficiently (p. 92).

To conclude, therefore, a number of factors conditioned the development of the Fifth Generation Project. These included the history of cooperative research projects in Japan, particularly in the area of computing; the continuing international dominance of IBM; and the emergence of a number of scientific advances such as VLSI, parallel processing technology, and Prolog which made it possible to begin to think about, and to try to develop, fundamentally different kinds of computers based on knowledge, rather than numerical processing.

The objectives of the Fifth Generation Project

While conventional computers are used for numerical processing, the fifth generation computer is intended for use in knowledge and information processing. Knowledge pertaining to a particular area will be stored in such a computer using a knowledge representation procedure.[1] This knowledge base must be managed in such a way as to minimize the amount of processing that is required in generating deductions. Another part of the computer is in charge of working out a suitable line of reasoning which will lead to a solution to problems that are posed, drawing on the knowledge contained in the knowledge base. The line of reasoning is based on an inference procedure which in turn depends on the problem-solving strategies that are chosen. It is intended that people will be able to interact with the fifth generation computer using natural language as an interface.

There are essentially three subsystems that make up the fifth generation computer system. These are the knowledge base and knowledge-base management subsystem, the problem-solving and inference subsystem, and the man–machine interface. In the Fifth Generation Project each of these subsystems has a corresponding software and hardware dimension.

Prolog was originally chosen as the kernel language for the entire system, although, as will be seen, related languages such as Flat Guarded Horn Clause were subsequently developed. Since it is envisaged that the fifth generation computer will be capable of handling a large knowledge base and since a substantial amount of computing power is required in order to carry out the inference procedures, the development of parallel processing hardware and software systems is an essential part of the project. In this connection VLSI is an important enabling technology since it has created the possibility of providing devices that are appropriate in terms both of speed and cost.

Only the briefest account of the fifth generation computer has been necessary in this section in order to facilitate the rest of the analysis in this chapter. More detailed descriptions of the fifth generation computer and project are to be found in Feigenbaum and McCorduck (1983), Moto-oka and Kitsuregawa (1985) and ICOT (1986).

The establishment of ICOT

Preliminary discussion on the setting up of a new advanced computer project began in MITI in 1978. The Electronics Policy Division of the Machinery and Information Industries Bureau, at that time under the directorship of Mr Norihiko Maeda, played an important role in the initial deliberations. Mr Masataka Nakano, Deputy-Director of the Electronics Policy Division, was centrally involved in the negotiation. Representation in these discussions was broadened by the transfer to the Electronics Policy Division of Mr Kiyonori Konishi, a computer software researcher with Nippon Telegraph and Telephone's (NTT) Electrical Communications Laboratories (ECL).

In April 1979 the Electronics Policy Division requested the Japan Information Processing Development Centre (JIPDEC), an extra-governmental organization under the control of MITI with representation from universities and electronics companies, to undertake a survey relating to the prospects for developing a fifth generation computer in Japan. Professor Moto-oka of the Department of Electrical Engineering at the University of Tokyo was asked to chair the committee that was accordingly set up under the auspices of JIPDEC. Three working groups were set up under the guidance of the Fifth Generation Computer Survey Committee. The first was the Basic Theory Group under the chairmanship of Kazuhiro Fuchi, while the second group, the Architecture Group, was chaired by Professor Hideo Aiso of the Department of Electrical Engineering at Keio University. The third working group was to consider the 'social environment' for the fifth generation computer and a year later its title was changed to the Systems Technology Group. This group was led by Hajime Karatsu, who at that time was a member of the Matsushita company. As the leadership of the working groups indicates, a special effort was made to ensure important representation from ETL and the universities so that the longer-term future of computer technology would be examined. Some of the MITI organizers of the project felt that the firms tended to take a shorter-term, more commercially-oriented, view of the priorities for advanced computer research and that the need for a longer-term vision therefore necessitated strong representation from the universities and ETL.[2] Furthermore, it was also felt that since criticism from the United States would be likely if MITI made an attempt to assist Japanese firms directly in their competitive rivalry with IBM and the other American computer producers, a more basic research project was desirable.

Two-and-a-half years elapsed between the time of the setting up of the JIPDEC committee and the working groups and the holding of the International Fifth Generation Computer Conference in October 1981 when the form of the Fifth Generation Project was finally sealed. Before a consensus could be reached, a number of critical conflicts had to be resolved. The most important conflict related to the desirability of an advanced computer project in the area of artificial intelligence or, more specifically, knowledge information processing. On this question there was sharp disagreement. On the one hand, the Basic Theory Group under Fuchi felt that the time was ripe for a project on knowledge information processing based on a non-von Neumann architecture. On the other hand, others on the committee and working groups felt that artificial intelligence in general, and knowledge information processing in particular, was not sufficiently developed to form the basis of a realistic project. Instead many supported what they felt was a more realistic proposal to do research on advanced von Neumann computers. The latter view was held by *all* of the electronics firms and by a number of the engineers in MITI and ETL. In short, there was a distinct difference in *expectations* regarding the future of computer-related technologies with only Fuchi and his group believing at this stage that knowledge information processing had a viable future. The belief in knowledge information processing, however, did not emerge automatically, but had to be actively sold. Here Fuchi played an important role.

A further important question related to the choice of the kernel computer language if the knowledge information processing project were to be chosen. Fuchi was the first person in ETL (and probably in Japan) to become convinced of the importance of Prolog as a computer language. As mentioned earlier, it was in 1974 that Fuchi began to develop an expertise in Prolog. Some time after this a Prolog working group was set up in ETL on Fuchi's initiative in order to make other researchers aware of the potential of Prolog and to further develop ETL research in this area. Later, discussions on Prolog were held under the auspices of JIPDEC. These initiatives helped to introduce Prolog to a wider audience including a number of company researchers who attended some of the meetings in ETL and JIPDEC.

At around this time researchers at Edinburgh University sent Fuchi a Prolog program that demonstrated to Fuchi's satisfaction the viability of Prolog as a computing language and its suitability as the kernel language for knowledge information processing. The receipt of this program was to significantly strengthen Fuchi's hand in the delicate negotiations over the form of the Fifth Generation Computer Project. A working version of the Edinburgh program was established at ETL and this was used to demonstrate the importance of Prolog. As a senior researcher recalled in an interview with the author: 'I think Edinburgh's Prolog program played a very important role in the Fifth Generation Project because it could be used to show that Prolog is a very good programming language.'

There were therefore two related battles that had to be fought. The first was to ensure that knowledge information processing systems were chosen as the theme for the Fifth Generation Computer Project. The second was to establish that Prolog would be accepted as the kernel programming language. The latter battle was as difficult to win as the former. By 1979–80 the firms had had no experience with Prolog, although some of them had just commenced their first research in the area of artificial intelligence using Lisp as the computer language. Lisp was already relatively widely accepted in the United States, unlike Prolog, and it seemed by no means obvious that Prolog was the preferable language.

In the event, however, Fuchi was able to win over the support, first of a number of his colleagues in ETL, and then of a few key bureaucrats in MITI's Machinery and Information Industries Bureau. (One of the author's informants believed that it was significant that the latter bureaucrats had law rather than engineering backgrounds and therefore, being less constrained by current technologies, were more open to the future potential of knowledge information processing and Prolog.) Be this as it may, the international conference held in October 1981, and the positive world interest that was shown in the Fifth Generation Project that was proposed, set the final seal. With strong support from the Machinery and Information Industries Bureau, knowledge information processing and Prolog would become the key initial features of the Fifth Generation Project.[3] This is not, however, to suggest that at this stage Fuchi's opponents had been convinced. In their book, Feigenbaum and McCorduck (1983, p. 101) state that the researchers sent by the eight member firms to ICOT 'come from firms that sent them grudgingly, firms that think the Fifth Generation Project is going to be an international embarassment for the Japanese, firms that contributed their workers only under duress from MITI'. Three or four years after the project's start in 1982, however, the firms, as will later be seen, had changed their views and become more positive about the prospects.

ICOT as a form of organization for the acquisition, assimilation, generation and diffusion of technological knowledge

In order to evaluate the Fifth Generation Project it is helpful to see ICOT as a form of organization designed (through a process of discussion, negotiation and compromise) for the purpose of acquiring, assimilating, generating and diffusing technological knowledge in the area of knowledge information processing.

The central feature of the ICOT form of organization is that it brings together, for the purposes of research cooperation, firms, universities, and government research laboratories. (The latter comprise both MITI's Electrotechnical Laboratory and NTT's Electrical Communications Laboratories. In April 1985 NTT was partially privatized but its participation in ICOT remained essentially unchanged.)

A crucial question regarding the ICOT form of organization relates to the role played in its research by the firms. This question is crucial for the simple reason that the firms are actual, *or potential*, competitors in the field of knowledge information processing. In general, competing firms can be expected to try to protect those parts of their knowledge base which have a significant direct effect on their present, or expected future, competitiveness. Since both the firms and MITI now expect that knowledge information processing will become increasingly important in the area of computing, and since the firm's *relative* competence in this knowledge area (i.e. relative to the other competing firms) is therefore expected to be a significant determinant of its competitiveness and hence profitability, the question is raised of why the firms agreed to cooperate in the joint creation of technological knowledge in this area. The pertinence of this question is all the more obvious when it is noted, as was shown in an earlier chapter, that the form of organization of the Supercomputer Project, begun at around the same time as the Fifth Generation Project, is significantly different from the latter in that there is no joint laboratory. In the case of the Fifth Generation Project joint research is done in a joint research laboratory, namely ICOT. In fact there are only two other examples of such joint research done in joint facilities in MITI-organized R&D projects in the electronics and computing areas. These are the joint laboratory in the VLSI Project (1976–79) and the joint laboratory in the Optical Measurement Project (1981–87), which were both examined in earlier chapters. However, while in the latter two cases only 20 and 36 per cent respectively of total expenditure on the projects went to the joint laboratory, the figure was 100 per cent for the Fifth Generation Project.

It is necessary to take a number of considerations into account in answering this important question. Perhaps the most important consideration is that the research done in ICOT is *basic* (or *generic*) in the sense that it does not involve immediately commercializable technological knowledge. Indeed, the very uncertainty referred to earlier regarding the future of knowledge information processing and Prolog, which resulted in the divergent expectations of the protagonists in the debate on the form that the Fifth Generation Project should take, also created the conditions for the possibility of a joint research project. Not only were the prospects for commercial returns from the project uncertain, it was also clear that if such returns were to accrue this would only happen after a fairly long period of time, perhaps as long as ten years or more. Under such conditions each firm had an incentive to take part in the joint research project. Generic technological knowledge in the field of knowledge information processing and Prolog could be jointly produced and the firms could then draw to the best of their ability on the joint product for the purpose of producing commercializable products. Since competitiveness is more strongly a function of technological knowledge relating *directly* to the production of commercializable output than of basic or generic knowledge *per se*, the firms could cooperate to jointly create the latter kind of knowledge while preparing themselves to compete at the commercialization stage. Furthermore, by jointly creating such generic knowledge, important *economies of cooperative research* could be realized resulting in a more productive use of research resources than if the research were done in isolation.[4] For these reasons, therefore, the eight competing, or potentially competing firms, that took part in the Fifth Generation Project were able to cooperate in setting up a joint research laboratory.

A further consideration is that the firms retain a degree of *de facto* control over the technological knowledge which they generate in-house for ICOT. Perhaps the best example of this is the case of the hardware which is jointly designed in the ICOT laboratory but developed and produced in specific firms that are contracted by ICOT for the task. In these cases, while MITI retains *de jure* ownership of the technological knowledge that is created, in reality the firms maintain a degree of control over the knowledge that they have created. A major reason for this is the impossibility of specifying and transferring to MITI all of the knowledge that is created with the use of government resources. This follows from the *tacitness* that is inherent in technological knowledge. To put the matter more concretely, the firm that develops and produces the hardware (in the present case, for example, a parallel inference machine) will, through the development and production processes, generate a larger knowledge set than it will be able to convey to outsiders, for instance

MITI or the other cooperating firms. Through the experience of its members the firm will know more about the hardware than it will be able to relate to outsiders (even if it wishes to transfer as much knowledge as possible to them). For present purposes a major implication of this is that the incentive to cooperate with other firms in research is increased since even in joint research in joint laboratories such as ICOT the firms manage to retain a degree of control over the technological knowledge that they contribute to the research programme through their in-house research. A number of other important implications that follow from this point about the tacitness of technological knowledge will be taken up later.[5]

The considerations discussed in this section *explain* the form of organization chosen for the Fifth Generation Project. The aim of the joint research undertaken in ICOT is to generate the basic concepts, to design and perhaps ultimately develop a prototype of the 'intelligent' fifth generation computer. This research may be referred to as *oriented-basic research*. The research activity is sharply focused by the detailed specification of the goal to be eventually achieved. As is clear from ICOT (1986) these specifications involve a detailed account of the software and hardware that will be required, as well as a timetable for the achievement of the various subgoals in the initial, intermediate and final stages of the project. The detailed specification of these goals provided an integrating theme for the different kinds of research being done on both the hardware and software sides and therefore functions as an important attention-focusing device. In this way the 'science push' provided by the earlier developments in fields such as VLSI, parallel processing and logic programming is united with the expected future demands for computers which will perform different functions and have different capabilities. Or, as the Japanese prefer to think of it, 'seeds' are integrated with 'needs'.

The generation of the basic concepts and most of the design work is done within ICOT. In performing these tasks ICOT draws on the stock of accumulated knowledge, experience and skills of the firms, government research laboratories and universities. The bulk of ICOT's almost 100 researchers come from the eight member electronics companies which in this way contribute their technological knowledge in the fields of software and hardware. The firms are Fujitsu, Hitachi, NEC, Toshiba, Mitsubishi, Oki, Matsushita and Sharp. However, the firms also contribute by doing in-house research on contract from ICOT. In this way ICOT is able to draw on the experience and skills of the firms, particularly in the hardware area. Such research done in-house is a significant part of the overall project. For example, one particular firm has roughly three researchers working full-time in the company on ICOT work for every one researcher they send to ICOT. The funding received from ICOT for this in-house research is a significant boost to the firm's research on artificial intelligence and logic programming and, as was mentioned earlier, the firm retains a degree of control over the technological knowledge that this research yields.

The acquisition, assimilation and generation of oriented-basic technological knowledge by ICOT

Drawing on the international stock of basic knowledge

One of the major advantages of a high profile national research institute like ICOT is that it provides the channels for efficiently drawing on the international stock of basic knowledge. While all scientific and technological knowledge has *public-good characteristics* in the sense that the knowledge can often under the right circumstances be acquired at a cost below the development cost of that knowledge, this is particularly so in the case of basic knowledge. The fruits of basic knowledge are made available through publication, conferences, lectures, visits and other similar forms of communication and in this way they become part of the public, as opposed to the private, proprietary, domain. An ability to draw efficiently on the international stock of basic knowledge is an important determinant of competitiveness particularly in the science-based industries. ICOT is particularly well adapted to this task.

Reference has already been made to the way in which individuals in ETL first became aware of, and later developed an expertise in, logic programming. In this connection it is of interest that the first case in Japan of the acquisition and assimilation of internationally available knowledge in the field of logic programming came from a government research institution (namely ETL) specifically set up with the brief to do industrially oriented research, including that without immediate commercial promise. It was in such an institution, rather than in the firms, that Japanese expertise in logic programming first began. In this connection there are some obvious parallels with the ETL Mark IV examined in chapter 2 which was the first commercially successful transistorized computer developed in Japan and the production of which was later transferred to a few of the electronics companies.

Although research in artificial intelligence and logic programming continues in ETL, the main locus of activity in this area has now shifted to ICOT. In drawing on the international stock of basic knowledge ICOT has a number of important advantages. To some extent ICOT has been able to ride on the growing reputation enjoyed by Japanese electronics firms and MITI, underpinned from the mid 1970s by increasing Japanese success in world markets for electronic goods. Evidence of this comes from the great international interest shown in the 1981 conference which launched the Fifth Generation Project and which greatly surprised the conference organizers. Similarly, the attempts made by other Western governments and firms to establish their own programmes in the same area also supports this point. Clearly, this reputation has also imposed costs on ICOT, in some cases making the task of drawing on the stock of international basic knowledge – particularly that part which is transmitted through more discretionary means – more difficult. There is no doubt that there is a good deal of paranoia in many Western quarters which serves to distort perceptions of how Japanese institutions work. Nevertheless, the growing Japanese reputation has resulted in a heightened Western interest in projects such as the Fifth Generation. And the obtaining of further information inevitably involves a two-way flow.

As a result of this reputation ICOT researchers have at times been given privileged access to international knowledge. This emerges clearly from some of the comments of ICOT researchers. For example, Hajime Kitakami from the Artificial Intelligence Laboratory of Fujitsu made the following comment:

When we make an overseas trip on company orders, the facilities we visit are far more limited than in the case of a trip organised by ICOT. On that score it was highly stimulating for me to meet and talk with world-class researchers while I was with ICOT.[6]

A similar point is made by Nobuyoshi Miyazaki of the Knowledge Base Section in Oki's Computer Systems R & D Department:

If I made an overseas business trip in the capacity of a company employee, I would receive basically the same [open] treatment from universities I visited. But that would not be the case with visits to other companies or rather closed research institutes. They would not easily accept our request to visit them. As ICOT members, by contrast, we would be readily received by them partly because they were interested in the fifth generation computer project. I consider myself very fortunate to have been able to visit various establishments.[7]

Another ICOT researcher summarized the situation: 'ICOT is the crossroad for information from all over Japan and all over the world.'[8]

In addition to being able to send ICOT researchers to Western research institutions, ICOT receives a steady stream of visitors who are specialized in the related disciplines. Technical information is exchanged with numerous foreign researchers through the attendance of conferences both in Japan and abroad and through the exchange of papers such as the ICOT Technical Reports and Memoranda. An important advantage of an institution like ICOT with its almost 100 researchers is that there are probably significant *economies of scale in research* in this as in many other research areas (although the nature and extent of such economies remains to be documented). For example, with this number of researchers it is possible for a division of labour to emerge, not only in terms of research tasks, but also in the case of information gathering. Since the research and information gathering are being done in the same institution where the researchers are in close proximity to one another, the institute as a whole is likely to gain from the numerous interrelationships that exist between the different specialized research areas. These gains might be thought of as externalities arising from research in sub-specialities which may be efficiently captured by an institution of ICOT's size. In addition to such economies of scale in research, further dynamic gains are achieved by the raised profile of research into fifth generation technologies as a result of their selection by MITI and the firms as a priority for future-oriented research. With a greater 'national consciousness' of the importance of this research more resources are devoted to this area than would probably be the case if the research were done in a piecemeal fashion in a number of different institutions. Furthermore, it is possible in an institution of this size to encourage a diversity of approaches which might increase the chances of breakthroughs.

However, it is necessary to stress that ICOT is not only drawing on the international stock of knowledge, but is also contributing to the increase of this stock. This has become increasingly the case as expertise has developed in ICOT in the fifth generation technologies. In the absence of quantitative studies such as bibliometric and citation examination (despite the inherent limitations of such work), it is not possible to begin to speculate about whether there is a net inflow to, or outflow from, Japan in these areas of research. Nevertheless, although possibly presenting only a partial and perhaps misleading picture, anecdotes such as the earlier one about the importance of Edinburgh University's Prolog program in the run-up to the establishment of ICOT do provide some additional information. In this connection it is of interest that a Prolog program with a number of novel features recently developed at the Tokyo Institute of Technology in a project closely related to ICOT research has been sent to a number of researchers at British universities in much the same spirit that the Edinburgh program was given.

The role of Japanese universities

Since the Japanese universities make an important contribution to the work of ICOT it is necessary to examine their role more closely.

In general it is probably accurate to conclude that the boundary between universities and the other functionally specialized organizations which make up the Japanese science and technology system is more firmly drawn in Japan than in most other Western countries. University teachers and researchers are paid by their institution for the full-time teaching and researching which they do. They are therefore not expected to be able to do paid research for other organizations such as private firms or government research institutions. This is true for both the state-financed national universities and the private universities. Certainly the practice of the Massachusetts Institute of Technology (MIT), for example, which is to allow university professors 20 per cent of their time for the purpose of private consulting, is totally alien in Japan.

However, as in the case of other Japanese rules and formalities, the rigidities which are implied retain a significant degree of flexibility. For instance, while university staff cannot work on a paid basis for companies, they can work on company-financed research that takes place in the university and addresses company needs. The leading university-based researchers in the field of artificial intelligence do research in this way for a number of companies. The company does not pay the professor directly, but through the university (with the Ministry of Education, Culture and Science (MECS) taking a share in compensation for the university resources, both human and material, used by the company which the Ministry has financed). The payment does not supplement the professor's personal income, at least officially,[9] but is intended to cover the costs of the research. The practice is the same in both the national and private universities. Furthermore, as one senior university researcher, closely connected with ICOT research, pointed out, 'It is sometimes very easy to get money from companies for travelling abroad and for the associated expenses, and there are no obligations to the company. The company donates the money to the university which then pays the researcher.'[10]

While similar restrictions on the receipt of personal payment apply in the case of government research institutes (such as MITI's Electro-technical Laboratory (ETL) or the Institute of Physical and Chemical Research (RIKEN)), it is possible for university researchers to be seconded to work in these institutes. Although some university researchers are closely involved with ICOT research through the working groups that have been established by ICOT, it is very difficult for university researchers to work in ICOT.

It may therefore be concluded that while the boundary dividing the university from other functionally specialized institutions like firms and government research laboratories is relatively firmly drawn, this does not prevent the establishment and development of important inter-institutional research linkages. These linkages are further cemented by the university's training function. Close ties usually exist and continue to exist both between former students from the same university (and particularly between those who were in the same year), and between them and their former professor. Frequently these ties remain after the graduates have left to joint other institutions (including in some instances competing companies). In this way the degree of inter-institutional linkage is enhanced, as well as its flexibility.

However, the restrictions on personal payment (even though as suggested these might not be absolute) probably result in a generally greater degree of autonomy of university research in Japan than is the case in many other Western countries where, recently, closer ties between universities and industry have been facilitated by the introduction of numerous material incentives.

The effectiveness of university–industry linkages is also a function of the internal organization of universities. Here there are further differences between Japan and other Western countries. In most Japanese universities, particularly the national universities, the *kōza* constitutes the unit of research at the micro level. The *kōza* is led by a full professor (*kyōju*) who typically has one or two associate and assistant professors under him. In addition there are usually several postgraduate students. In this research group the *kyōju* wields a significant degree of influence. He has an important say over the direction of the group's research. Although there are some important exceptions, promotion within the university is largely on the basis of seniority with the result that full professors are usually from an older age group than their juniors. While full professors routinely get a small amount of funding for research purposes, the bulk of research funds come from grants which are competitively applied for. In some of the private universities, however, a few of the newer departments have abolished the *kōza* system.

A number of criticisms have been levelled at the Japanese university system from the point of view of its ability to generate research in the area of artificial intelligence. For example, it has been argued that the *kōza* system at times constrains entry into new research areas. This follows from the influence of the *kyōju* over the research direction of the group. Younger researchers, who in some instances may be quicker to adapt to new areas of research, have correspondingly less influence. According to a senior MITI official interviewed by the author, an example comes from the case of a doctoral student at the University of Tokyo who developed an important modified version of one of the artificial intelligence languages. On receiving his doctorate, however, he was unable to find a position in one of the university's research groups. He later became an ICOT researcher.

Furthermore, it is argued that the vertical organization of the *kōza* in some instances makes difficult inter-*kōza* interaction of the kind that would be necessary if larger scale cooperative research projects were to be undertaken. It is suggested that this limits the ability of the universities to undertake larger scale research. It was acknowledged by both the MITI and ICOT officials interviewed by the author that Japanese universities in general are not making as important a contribution to the development of artificial intelligence in Japan as their colleagues are in countries such as the United Kingdom, the United States and France.

One of the reasons for the establishment of ICOT was to compensate for these weaknesses in the universities in the area of artificial intelligence.

Although university staff cannot be employed by ICOT (which ICOT officials feel to be a problem), university artificial intelligence researchers are incorporated into the ICOT structure through the numerous *working groups* that have been established around ICOT. Of the approximately 200 members of these working groups about 125 are from the universities. 'University people spend a lot of time on the working groups. They meet once a month in general, but once each two weeks in some cases, and sometimes they have workshops for two or three days at a time. They also do ICOT-related research in their own laboratories.'[11] Through this arrangement university researchers get access to funding and equipment, link into the ICOT network, which as noted serves as a clearing house for information in the area of applied artificial intelligence, and take part in larger mission-oriented cooperative research. On the other hand, ICOT research benefits from university expertise in more fundamental or specialized areas. In addition, many ICOT-related ideas and applications receive further research in university laboratories where professors and postgraduate students are involved in the experimentation and testing processes. (University researchers who are involved in ICOT working groups are paid a small fee, but this barely covers their associated expenses.)

In total there are about fifteen working groups associated with ICOT. The activities of each group are a function of the group's membership, and in particular its chairman. However, all the groups serve the function of providing feedback on the research that is ongoing in the ICOT laboratories. Although working groups have their own discussions which may relate more or less closely to ICOT research, they do not undertake their own research. At times the working groups invite outside speakers who are involved in research that relates to group discussions. In short, therefore, the working groups serve as antennae and sounding boards which channel relevant information into ICOT as well as providing feedback on ICOT research. The composition of the working groups usually includes representatives from universities, some of the electronics companies which are members of ICOT, and research laboratories such as ETL and NTT's Electrical Communications Laboratories (ECL). In addition ICOT members sit on the working groups. For example, the Foundations of Artificial Intelligence Working Group, which has been in existence since 1982, has a respresentative from Hitachi, and others from the universities, ETL and ICOT.

Universities and firms also play the important role of applying and testing hardware and software developed in ICOT. For example, the University of Tokyo, the Tokyo Science University and the Tokyo Institute of Technology are involved in research projects which, though separately funded, apply some of the generic technologies developed in ICOT. (Similar applications-related research done in the firms will be discussed below.) The Tokyo Science University is a private university. About ten years ago the Bioresearch Laboratory was established at this university with the aim of increasing the linkage between university and industrial research. More recently this laboratory has been involved in the construction of applications systems in the areas of medical diagnosis, computer-aided design, and machine scheduling. The programs for these systems are written in Prolog-derived languages developed at ICOT, and the systems run on the sequential inference machine (PSI) designed by ICOT. Similar research is being done at the Tokyo Institute of Technology. Here Prolog-derived languages are being used to develop natural-language processing systems, including machine translation systems and man–machine communications systems using natural language. Some of these systems have been rewritten to run on the PSI which in this way is tested. Accordingly, university research also serves as an applications area and testing ground for the generic hardware and software developed through ICOT research.

It may therefore be concluded that while it is true to say that Japanese universities have not made as great a contribution to the development of artificial intelligence in Japan when compared to American, British and French universities, they nevertheless play an extremely important role in ICOT. Through university participation, ICOT is able to draw on additional expertise, particularly in more fundamental areas or areas which are not closely related to ICOT objectives. Furthermore, since university researchers have an arms-length relationship with ICOT, serving on the working groups but not being involved in the daily research in the ICOT laboratories, they are able to be critical in providing feedback on ICOT research. In addition the universities' research serves as an important applications area and testing ground for the generic hardware and software technologies developed in ICOT. A senior ICOT official summarized the situation in the following way: 'Compared to the British Alvey Programme the role of the Japanese universities in ICOT is relatively small, that I admit, but their role is indispensable for us.'[12]

The role of Japanese firms

The eight member companies of ICOT have played an extremely important role in facilitating the acquisition, assimilation and generation of generic technological knowledge by ICOT. Although in the early stages of the Fifth Generation Project the participating companies were reluctant to send the quantity and quality of researchers that the leaders of ICOT wanted, pressure was brought to bear on them by MITI and ICOT and they eventually succumbed.

At this point it is worth adding a little about MITI's ability to pressurize companies such as occurred in the present instance. This ability, it must be noted, does not stem from any legal right to influence company activities. Rather, it is an example of so-called administrative guidance through which MITI has made industrial policy since 1968 when it lost control over the central allocation of foreign exchange. MITI's present ability to influence company decisions, as in the present case, must be understood in the context of the extremely productive cooperative relationship that has been developed between MITI and the companies in the post-war years. In general MITI programmes and finance have made an important contribution to the growth and international competitiveness of these companies. Therefore, while the companies may not always agree with the decisions and directions proposed by MITI, and while at times they may be successful in dissuading MITI from pursuing particular options, at other times they will be prepared to compromise knowing that they receive significant net benefits from the totality of MITI interventions. Seen in this light, MITI's ability to persuade the stronger firms to take part in projects such as the Fifth Generation and Optical Measurement Projects and allocate an appropriate quantity and quality of researchers is understandable.

The firms have contributed to ICOT activities in at least three important ways. To begin with they have contributed the majority of the almost 100 full-time researchers in ICOT laboratories. While these researchers tend to be relatively young – generally under 35 – all of them have had important experience in their companies in relevant areas of hardware and software production – although when ICOT began they had had no experience in knowledge information processing. In this way ICOT is able to draw on the accumulated stock of technological knowledge that has been developed in the companies.

Secondly, the companies make an extremely important contribution by bringing their substantial experience to bear on the development of hardware which serves as a research tool for the production of software in ICOT. In the case of the three mainframe producers – Fujitsu, Hitachi and NEC – this experience is a function of their position as leaders in the world computer industry. The other five companies also have considerable expertise in the hardware area. One of the great strengths of the ICOT programme is undoubtedly that it brings together complementary innovations on the hardware and software sides in developing fifth generation computers. This is made possible by the ICOT form of organization which integrates the expertise of firms, government research laboratories and universities. In contrast, while many Western university-based research programmes in the area of artificial intelligence might have important strengths in the area of software (which is neither particularly technology- nor capital-intensive), they are usually unable to develop software in conjunction with hardware designed especially for the purposes at hand. As a result it is possible that significant synergies that follow from the interrelated development of software and hardware are lost. In the case of ICOT research, on the other hand, some of these synergies might be captured. According to a senior artificial intelligence researcher in one of the ICOT firms interviewed by the present author an example of the reaping of such synergies is the development of GHC, a Prolog-derived language with possibly important implications in the area of parallel processing. While GHC is from a narrow software point of view simpler than several other Prolog-derived languages that were developed earlier, it is superior to the latter when account is taken of the requirements necessary for the realization of parallel processing. For this sort of reason the integration of hardware and software research into a single unified and focused research system might represent one of the greatest advantages of the ICOT form of organization.

A third important contribution made by the firms to ICOT research arises from the application and testing in the firms of generic technologies developed in ICOT. In this respect the firms play a similar role to that of the universities which was discussed earlier. However, a significant difference is that applications and tests undertaken in the firms are likely to be influenced to a greater extent than in the universities by commercially related criteria. As mentioned earlier, both firms and universities are represented on the working groups organized around ICOT research and in this way both these kinds of organization provide feedback on ICOT research.

In addition, both through the researchers which the firms send to ICOT as well as through their other channels of communications with ICOT researchers, the firms also contribute to ICOT research in the area of software. Here too their experience is valuable.

It may be concluded therefore that the firms make an important contribution to the ability of ICOT to acquire, assimilate and generate generic technological knowledge. They play this role through the provision of researchers to ICOT, through making some of their accumulated experience available by implementing hardware and software designed in ICOT, and through their application and testing of ICOT-related generic technologies.

The acquisition, assimilation and generation of fifth generation computer knowledge by the ICOT member firms

In contrast to the claim made by many Western observers, the aim of ICOT is not to transfer technology to the member firms. Rather the aim is to do generic research on the fifth generation computer. Fuchi, Director of ICOT, has made this clear in an interview with the author:

Fuchi: I am not so much interested in what the firms are doing for themselves in artificial intelligence. We should let them do it their own way. Apart from their cooperation with ICOT, their artificial intelligence activities are becoming broader. [Since I know so little about what is happening in the firms] if you study the firms and write a paper, can I have a copy [*laughter*]?

Fransman: ICOT is primarily interested in generic research. The applications of this research is not your interest – that is for the companies to sort out. Is that correct?

Fuchi: Yes, in principle this is correct. But the firms also do some work on applications for the purpose of getting feedback on the basic research [done in ICOT].[13]

It is clear, therefore, that there is a well-defined division of labour between ICOT, which does the generic research, and the firms which, while helping ICOT under contract by developing various inputs such as hardware, are responsible for the commercialization of fifth generation computer technologies. On the one hand, this division of responsibilities represents a specialization in areas where each type of organization has a relative advantage. On the other hand, as pointed out earlier, the concentration on generic research in ICOT also creates the conditions for joint research cooperation between competing firms. It is for this reason that ICOT leaders have argued that as research progresses it is necessary for ICOT to move forward into new areas of generic research. Any attempt to produce directly commercializable products would run the risk of causing competitive divisions between the firms in turn jeopardizing the research at ICOT. Kunio Murakami of the Knowledge Engineering Department in NTT Communications and Information Processing Laboratories and a laboratory chief at ICOT has expressed this in the following way:

As I see it, the initial stage [of the three stages in the ICOT project] was a period when it was easy to unify our efforts. In the intermediate and final stages where specific things will be built, I think management will become a difficult job. If research results come out as specific ideas aimed at commercial production, there will be rivalry among the companies with their people at ICOT. Even if the people working at ICOT are not aware of it, their company executives will be. That is where management will be difficult. That must be resolved somehow. Since the ICOT people work in a good environment, I don't want that environment hurt by corporate rivalry or the like.[14]

Given this division of labour between ICOT and the firms, how have the latter benefited from ICOT research in terms of their ability to acquire, assimilate and generate technological knowledge in the area of fifth generation computing?

To begin with, some of the firms have benefited from ICOT knowledge when they have developed hardware for ICOT. For example, Mitsubishi Electric was given access to ICOT-related patents in order to develop the personal sequential inference machine (PSI) which was used as a tool for the production of Prolog-related software. In this way Mitsubishi was

able to draw indirectly on some of the skill and experience contributed
by the other firms through the personnel which they seconded to ICOT.
In some instances hardware has been jointly developed in ICOT by
researchers from a number of different member companies. One instance
is the Multi-PSI Development Project which meets once per week with
researchers from Mitsubishi, Oki, Fujitsu, Hitachi and NEC. Here again
firms share in the joint creation of hardware for ICOT. However, in other
cases there has been less joint work as in the example of the development
of the CHI machine by NEC, a more powerful version of PSI.

Through means such as these it is clear that some of the firms which
are relatively weak in the computing area have been able to gain valuable
experience in the field of Prolog-related hardware. (The emphasis on
relative weakness, however, is important since although firms such
as Mitsubishi are not among the three major Japanese mainframe
producers, this firm still has substantial capabilities in the computing
area.) But the stronger firms are also deriving important benefits in the
hardware field. For instance, while Fujitsu and Hitachi were not particularly interested in taking part in the early development of the
sequential inference machine, which was used largely as a software
production tool, they have become far more interested in the parallel
inference machine (PIM). In part this is explained by the prior work that
they had done in the sequential inference area. Fujitsu, for example, had
its Facom Alpha which ran Lisp and was later extended to include
Prolog. In view of the possible future importance of parallel processing
(though there is still a significant degree of technical uncertainty in this
area) the stronger firms in the computing field have become more
involved in developing parallel processing hardware for ICOT.[15]

But if parallel inference machines are to become of significant commercial importance in the future, as expected, then what would motivate one
of the stronger firms to want to enter into a contract with ICOT for the
development of the hardware? Is not a major drawback the fact that all
proprietary rights that result are owned by MITI? In view of the
importance of this question it is worth quoting at length from an
interview that the author held with one of the leading figures in artificial
intelligence from one of the major ICOT-related firms:

A: We hope that in the future ICOT will give us good ideas in the area of
parallel inference machines. . .
Fransman: If all the patent rights on PIM belong to MITI, is it not better
for your company to develop a parallel inference machine entirely in-house
[i.e. without any assistance from ICOT/MITI]?
A: Yes, this is a bit of a problem. . .The patents basically belong to MITI,
but we [i.e. as the innovators] can use them at a lower royalty.
Fransman: But what about [your competitors]? Can they also use the
same patents?

A: Generally speaking, yes.

Fransman: But is this not a problem?

A: There are two explanations [for our interest in doing this research through ICOT]. One is that the patents alone [do not provide enough information] for building [a PIM] – it is a very complex system.

Fransman: You mean some know-how is necessary in addition to the patents and if [your company] works on developing PIM, then you have the know-how. Another company might get the patent rights, but it will not have the know-how.

A: Yes, that is correct. The second reason is that the PIM project is still uncertain. We have not yet solved the architecture of the parallel inference machine...We are still not convinced about the specific way to make PIM. It is still in the research stage.[16]

Two important points emerge from this discussion. The first, which was analysed in greater detail earlier in the present paper, illustrates the significant implications of the *tacitness* that is inherent in the development of technological knowledge. Although MITI owns the technological property rights on the technology that the firms have developed for it under contract, MITI's ability to obtain effective possession of all the relevant technological knowledge is limited by the important degree of tacitness that exists in the creation of this knowledge. A number of implications follow from this. To begin with, the firms retain a degree of effective control over the technological knowledge that they have created under contract. This has both positive and negative implications from the point of view of society as a whole. The positive implication is that, as we have seen, the firm retains an incentive to participate in the joint research exercise even though it is forced to give up *de jure* ownership of the technology it has created. This is a positive implication in view of the important *economies of cooperative research* that may be achieved (and which will be analysed in more detail later). However, the negative implication is that the tacitness inherent in technological knowledge limits the ability of MITI to encourage the *diffusion* of this knowledge among the relevant firms. This point will also be analysed in more detail later.

The second important point to emerge from this part of the interview is that the company was motivated to make a bid for developing a parallel inference machine through the ICOT project, rather than undertaking the project entirely in-house, partly as a result of the substantial amount of uncertainty that exists in this technological area. In the absence of (a) the stock of knowledge in ICOT on which the company could draw in its attempts to develop a parallel inference machine and (b) government funding,[17] it is likely that the company would have undertaken significantly less research in this area. In other words, in this area the ICOT project has produced *additional* knowledge (that is, knowledge in addition to that which would have been created in the absence of the project).

One conclusion that follows therefore from the present discussion is that the ICOT form of organization, together with the tacitness that is inherent in the creation of technological knowledge, has provided the firms with an incentive to participate in the joint creation of technological knowledge. This participation has in turn served as the basis for the realization of important economies of cooperative research.

Having said this, however, it is crucial not to overstress the degree of 'jointness' that is involved in the in-house research that is done in developing hardware for ICOT. While in ICOT laboratories researchers undertake joint research uninhibited by their membership of different institutions, particularly different companies (as is documented more fully later), there is far less cooperation in the ICOT-related in-house research. This important point is made clear in an interview with the same person as in the previous quotation:

> A: So far three companies have joined the research in the PIM area...
> Each company built a 10 processor parallel system. My company will now put more energy into this because we feel that PIM is very important...
> Fransman: Is there much sharing of information between the companies in developing PIM?
> A: There is almost no information sharing between the firms. ICOT contracts *separately* with [the three companies] and so there is no discussion between the firms.
> Fransman: Why is that – you are all working on the same project for ICOT?
> A: In the initial stage – in building the 10 processor parallel system – we had some cooperation because this was the very early stage. But in the second stage, 100 processors is a large system and so we don't like to share knowledge.
> Fransman: And the work is more commercially sensitive now?
> A: Yes, that is correct. This is similar to the super-computer project [i.e. the project discussed in Chapter 5] where there is also very little research cooperation because of the commercial sensitivity. The companies want to do their research inside the company.

This discussion illustrates well the subtle blend of competition and cooperation involved even in the Fifth Generation Project which, compared to other national R & D projects such as the Supercomputer and Optoelectronics Projects, deals with technologies that will be commercialized only in the longer term and which accordingly has a greater degree of research cooperation than these other projects. (While there is no joint laboratory in the Supercomputer Project and all the research is done in-house, in the case of the Optical Measurement Project approximately 36 per cent of the research is done in a joint laboratory.) Japanese electronics firms compete vigorously and this fact produces a constant tension in any attempt made to establish cooperative projects involving the joint creation and sharing of technological knowledge. As will be shown later, within this context the state has a particularly important role to play.

A further benefit that the companies have derived from the ICOT project follows from the opportunity to jointly develop *standardized* software for fifth generation computing. Such joint development has enabled the companies, with state assistance, to overcome a potential failure of the market to generate common software. Such failure might follow from the commercial and technical advantages that may be gained by the individual firm which has its standards accepted as the general standard for the industry as a whole. This might provide some of the other firms with an incentive not to accept the first firm's standards. In the case of ICOT, however, the joint research project is resulting in the development of common software systems. One example is the joint development of GHC, a Prolog-derived language useful for parallel processing.

Apart from the issue of standardization, the Fifth Generation Project has also given the firms the opportunity to develop an integrated hardware/software system. In the case of their existing computer products, the software is largely externally given, derived from the IBM software system. This is true both for companies like Hitachi and Fujitsu which have pursued an IBM-compatible strategy and NEC which, while not IBM-compatible, has been heavily influenced by the IBM system. The technical constraints placed on Japanese computer firms by the dominance of IBM have also limited their opportunities for creativity. However, since the Fifth Generation Project makes a fundamental break with IBM-type computer systems, an opening has been created for experimentation and creativity through the development of new hardware/software computer systems. This point emerged strongly in an interview that the author had with a number of middle-level ICOT researchers as is shown in the following extract:

> B: It is important for hardware researchers to think which software to use and for software researchers to consider what kind of software works well with the hardware developed. The interaction of both sides is necessary to develop a good system.
> Fransman: All of you are involved in hardware. Do you think it has been an advantage for you in developing hardware to be based in ICOT where there is good software–hardware interaction?
> C: I was developing a general purpose computer when I was at [company X]. The system was IBM-compatible for which operating systems were already given. We were developing just hardware without thinking of the software side... However, in developing PSI it was necessary to have good hardware–software interaction. So far Japanese manufacturers have just imported IBM architectures. R & D for the fifth generation computer is the first opportunity for us to develop software as well. In this sense the experience has been personally very meaningful.
> D: I think in a similar way. My boss in [company Y] says to me that the

most important point in developing computers is a sense of balancing. Knowing just one side, either software or hardware, will not make a computer system... As Mr [C] said, I feel that we are trying to make the first indigenous software in Japan, and that is a very good experience for me... [My company] has also been manufacturing IBM compatibles for which the software is given ... we are now developing new indigenous software. The Japanese computer manufacturers have lost the capability to create new technologies [*everyone laughed*]. In my company's case it has been preoccupied with efforts to try to catch up with the technologies of IBM and cannot develop its own new technologies. So it is very useful for the company to have the opportunity to take part in ICOT and this has had a large impact on the firm.

The creation and spreading of the Prolog[18] *culture*

The following is a record of a discussion held on the occasion of a reunion at ICOT of former ICOT researchers who had completed their research at ICOT and returned to their firms:

Hajime Kitakami, Artificial Intelligence Laboratory, Fujitsu Laboratories Ltd: When it comes to the development of Artificial Intelligence (AI) tools, logically there is the problem of what programming language to choose. Controversy is still continuing over the choice of Lisp or Prolog. Since, however, I studied knowledge-base management based on Prolog at ICOT, I have gained a very good understanding of the advantages of Prolog. It has been finally decided that our research will be done on AI tools using Prolog...
Kunio Murakami, Knowledge Engineering Department, NTT Communications and Information Processing Laboratories, and an ICOT laboratory chief: ...how do you feel the fifth generation computer culture is spreading?
Kitakami: I keenly feel there is a great difference between ICOT and the manufacturer in awareness of the Prolog culture, as one might expect. Very few of the manufacturer's people doing programming in Prolog are doing it with a strong awareness of the importance of the language. I feel my experience in building various prototypes at ICOT has refined my Prolog-related programming skills. Back in the company I find it of practical help.
Murakami: Is the Prolog group still in the minority?
Kitakami: I think so. I expect that a steadily increasing number of makers will go to ICOT and return later. They should plan to return with the intention of vigorously spreading the Prolog culture.
Kanae Masuda, New Product Development Department, Computer Works, Mitsubishi Electric Corporation: I feel much the same. Since I work in a development group of the marketing division, I find the over-whelming majority of the group sees Prolog as something alien to them and peculiar to ICOT. Whatever I tell them about Prolog, their usual response is that it will take much more time to take root or that it still remains an unknown. I feel there is a gap between them and us. It seems they regard us as heretics, to may great regret.[19]

A number of important points emerge from this discussion. To begin with, it is clear that the development and spread of Prolog is a *social*, rather than a narrowly technical, phenomenon. In this sense Prolog and its propagation are likened to the spread of a 'culture'. The Prolog supporters are convinced of the superiority of this language in many applications areas. Similarly, Lisp supporters believe that their language is preferable. In the eyes of the Prolog group the Lisp supporters are ill-informed about the details of Prolog and they therefore brand those that favour Prolog as 'heretics'. The social determinants of the development and spread of Prolog are particularly important since both Prolog and its rival artificial intelligence languages like Lisp are still in a flexible evolutionary state. These software technologies are evolving and competition exists between them, at times resulting in attempts to incorporate in the one language some of the attractive features of the other language. At present there is no clear-cut and widely accepted comparison of the efficiency of Prolog and Lisp in different applications areas. Even if there were, the supporters of either language could claim that the comparison is rendered obsolete by the evolutionary changes still occurring in the languages. Under these conditions the spread of the 'Prolog culture' is very much a social matter. Here ICOT has played an extremely important role, by keeping abreast of the latest developments worldwide in these areas of artificial intelligence, by contributing to these developments in doing frontier research, and by creating a 'culture consciousness' which has spread to all of the member firms as well as the associated universities and research institutes. Even if Prolog is not necessarily accepted by artificial intelligence researchers as the superior language, it has become a language to be reckoned with. As a result the relative strengths and weaknesses of each language become more sharply defined and this contributes to the further evolution of these technologies. Japanese researchers in this area, in the universities as well as in ICOT, believe that the tide is turning in favour of Prolog. As evidence they cite factors such as the increasing interest in Prolog on the part of many younger American artificial intelligence researchers, the increasing number of papers of Prolog submitted by American researchers to international conferences, etc. However, even if at the end of the day Lisp wins the competitive battle, ICOT will have played a significant positive role by increasing the level of awareness in Japan about artificial intelligence in general and more specifically about the relative advantages and disadvantages of languages like Prolog and Lisp.

From the last-quoted discussion and from the interview by the present author with middle-level researchers in ICOT it is clear that the firms have been influenced in different ways by the Prolog culture propagated by ICOT. More specifically, a distinction may be drawn between those firms in which artificial intelligence was not well developed before ICOT was established, and those in which it was. In the former case the Prolog culture has tended to dominate, while in the latter support for both Prolog and Lisp coexist in about equal strength. (One of the researchers interviewed suggested that there was also an 'IBM culture' in the major computer-producing firms. 'We also have an "IBM culture" within [my company]... But... I tell my colleagues, "Abandon IBM culture and adopt either Prolog or Lisp culture."')

A number of conclusions may be drawn regarding the influence of ICOT and the Prolog culture at the level of the member firms.

1. The Prolog culture within the firms (and within Japan generally) has developed earlier and at a more rapid pace with the establishment of ICOT, compared to what would have happened without ICOT. According to Fuchi, while artificial intelligence in general and Prolog in particular would have become stronger in Japan in the absence of ICOT, the existence of ICOT has probably accelerated this process by about three years.[20] Representatives of the three main computer companies interviewed by the author, while acknowledging the initial reluctance of their companies to become involved in the Fifth Generation Project, agreed with this estimate. In their view their companies have benefited from the catalytic effect that ICOT has had in this field.

2. While ICOT has chosen Prolog as the kernel language for the Fifth Generation Project, the firms, and in particular the mainframe producers, are giving roughly equal emphasis to Prolog and Lisp.[21] They are therefore covering both options and are accordingly well placed to take advantage of beneficial developments in either or both of these languages.

3. It may also be, in view of the apparent commitment of groups of researchers to either Prolog or Lisp, that ICOT by backing Prolog has also helped stimulate the development of Lisp. This result might follow from competition between these two languages. To the extent that such competition occurs in Japan, ICOT will have also encouraged the further development of Lisp.

ICOT and artificial intelligence within the firms: a case study

In this section both research and commercialized products in the artificial intelligence area are examined in the case of Fujitsu, the largest Japanese computer producer which also holds the largest share of the Japanese computer market. Particular attention is paid to the importance and impact of ICOT-related research.[22]

Research in the area of artificial intelligence began in Fujitsu around 1978 when development work on a machine translation system began. Since then Fujitsu has been involved in the development of both hardware and software related to artificial intelligence.

On the hardware side, Fujitsu in 1980 started development of a Lisp machine. This resulted in the FACOM Alpha which was first marketed around 1986. At first the FACOM Alpha was a dedicated processor for high-speed Lisp processing. The machine does not have its own input/output devices but is connected to a FACOM M-series mainframe computer or S-series minicomputer. The Lisp language processor is based on Utilisp, a dialect of Maclisp. Later, as part of the Fifth Generation Project, a Prolog language processor was added. At present the system allows up to eight users to use Lisp or Prolog at the same time, with 16 Mbytes of memory allocated to each.

Fujitsu has also been involved in the development of a parallel inference machine (PIM). Since substantial inference capabilities are required for information systems with high knowledge levels such as natural language cognition, machine translation, and particular expert systems, Fujitsu has attempted to increase inference performance by developing a PIM. As part of the related research, Fujitsu built an experimental parallel processing machine. This consisted of 16 processing elements (PE) connected by two kinds of dedicated networks, with one of the PEs used for input/output. The next stage is to enlarge this system to 100 processing elements. As part of the first stage of the research Fujitsu proposed a new parallel inference method called KABU-WAKE. The main concept behind the KABU-WAKE method is to reduce communication overhead between processing elements in a parallel processing environment. In order to do this, a parallel inference method was developed based on sequential inference. All of these research activities were undertaken as part of the Fifth Generation Project.

Fujitsu has also been involved in the area of expert systems. One example has been the development of knowledge engineering tools used to reduce the time required to build an expert system and to reduce the level of training required by knowledge engineers. ESHELL is such a knowledge engineering tool. It uses two forms of knowledge representation: production-type representation based on 'If...Then' rules and frame-type representation which describes facts arranged in hierarchical structures. ESHELL has been used by Fujitsu to develop a Personal Finance Adviser which assumes no expert knowledge on the part of its user and which provides advice on matters of personal finance. In addition ESHELL was used to develop a system to assist with the task of job scheduling for basic software development at Fujitsu's Numazu complex. Fujitsu has also developed an expert system based on Lisp designed to assign loads to ships and select particular ships for the purpose of transporting raw materials.

Research has also been done at Fujitsu to develop two knowledge-based logic design systems. The first is a Lisp-based synthesizer that automates gate-level design using random logic for combinational circuits from a functional design. The second is a Prolog-based experimental logic design system. Research on the latter system was carried out in the initial stage of the Fifth Generation Project. One of the purposes of this research was to evaluate Prolog's effectiveness as an implementation language for a new-generation CAD system.

Fujitsu is also doing research aimed at going some way towards a resolution of the so-called 'software crisis'. This crisis has resulted from the rapid rate of technological advance in VLSI technology which, by making available inexpensive microprocessors and VLSI memories, has reduced hardware costs substantially and therefore increased the world demand for software. Using artificial intelligence techniques Fujitsu is developing a number of intelligent software development support systems. These systems are aimed at supporting a designer with design guidelines, design paradigms and other relevant information stored in the system. For example, a software development support system is being researched to assist with the development of software for electronic switching systems. This support system will assist with both the development and the maintenance work involved. The system conforms to CCITT recommendations. It is written in Utilisp and uses the FACOM Alpha Lisp processor. The system uses knowledge gathered from experienced switching system programmers which is stored in a knowledge base. Another knowledge base contains facts about the data structures to be used in the program and rules for converting low-level descriptions into the target language by forward inference.

A related project in the software area involves the development of an intelligent design and verification system for software which supports the entire software development process and aims at increasing the productivity, reliability and maintainability of software based on logic programming languages. The programs developed by the system are assumed to be written in a Prolog-like language. The system is based on knowledge representation and natural language processing techniques. An important function of the system is automatic and semi-automatic program synthesis through the reuse of existing programs. The system is being developed as an R&D activity under the Fifth Generation Project.

Another research area deals with knowledge-based systems and knowledge representation. In this area research is being done on a knowledge-based natural language interface which will free users from having to know about the query languages and data bases and allow them to access data bases in natural languages. The system being developed uses a MINERVA knowledge representation system which is written in Utilisp.

In a similar area, as part of the Fifth Generation Project, research has begun on knowledge representation in Prolog. While Prolog is capable of representing procedural, logical and rule-type knowledge, there is, so far, no clear way of using Prolog to represent object-oriented knowledge. The FLORES (Flexible Logical Object Representation System) project is aimed at remedying this. MINERVA written in Lisp is similar to FLORES written in Prolog in that both systems support multi-paradigm representation, that is procedure-oriented, rule-oriented and object-oriented knowledge representations.

Also in the area of knowledge-based systems, research is being done on a knowledge-base management system. The knowledge represented by a knowledge representation language in an artificial intelligence system is usually stored in a sequential file – a Lisp file when Lisp is used, and a Prolog file when Prolog is used. However, knowledge-base management becomes very difficult if the knowledge base grows to a large size. What is needed when sharing a knowledge base between applications is an effective way of retrieving, updating or deleting a portion of the knowledge base. The knowledge-base management system being developed will provide these facilities.

Fujitsu has long been involved in the area of machine translation. The company has developed two such systems. ATLAS-I is a syntax-based system that was the world's first commercially available English–Japanese translation system. The prototype was completed in 1982. ATLAS-II is a semantic-based system which translates from Japanese to English, although the ultimate aim is the translation of three or more languages. With the current state of development, however, both pre- and post-editing are still required in using these systems.

In the area of image understanding Fujitsu has developed an image processing expert system that helps non-experts construct image processing algorithms. In the same area research is also being done on object representation.

Finally, fundamental research is being done in a number of areas of artificial intelligence. For example, the International Institute for Advanced Study of Social Information Science has chosen knowledge information processing systems (KIPS) as a focusing theme. Many of the research areas under this theme overlap with research being undertaken in the Fifth Generation Project. One research area deals with logic programming languages. For instance, Concurrent Prolog is a logic programming language distinguished by concurrency. By modifying the Concurrent Prolog interpreter developed by E. Shapiro a concurrent logic programming language called Extended Concurrent Prolog (ECP) has been designed and implemented. Research is also being done on the theory of programs, on the theory of data bases and knowledge-based systems and on automated reasoning.

Leading artificial intelligence researchers at the company made the following general comments about their research and its relationship to the Fifth Generation Project:

An increasing number of people hold high expectations for the future of artificial intelligence, but the current state of the art is still far from most people's goals.

Many problems remain to be solved, and a great deal of long-term R & D is necessary. While fundamental research is important, improving real application systems must not be neglected. We would like to coordinate our activities with those of the Next Generation Project. We believe the Next Generation Project will achieve significant results in logic programming language based research in several more years. We also expect to benefit a great deal from the project's more long-term research efforts and will continue to play an active role in the project. Meanwhile, we are continuing our inhouse research using Lisp and other current languages.

Table 7.1 summarizes the eight areas of research in the field of artificial intelligence being undertaken in Fujitsu. As the table shows, there is Fifth Generation Project research being done in five of these eight areas.

A further indication of the impact of ICOT at the level of the firm is provided by data on the number of ICOT-related researchers relative to the total number of artificial intelligence researchers in the company. This example from one of the three mainframe-producing companies is typical of all of these companies. The company currently has 8 researchers at ICOT, while 4 have completed their period at ICOT and have returned to the company. In addition there are approximately 25 further researchers working in the company on ICOT-related research. In total the company has around 200 researchers working in artificial intelligence-related areas. *This implies that about 17 per cent of the company's artificial intelligence-related researchers have had direct experience with ICOT research.*

The diffusion of fifth generation technological knowledge

In general, the economic impact of technical change is a function of the *diffusion*, rather than the generation, of new technologies. To the extent

Table 7.1. *Research areas in Fujitsu in artificial intelligence*

		Some ICOT-funded research in this area?
1.	AI machines	Yes
2.	Expert systems	No
3.	Knowledge-based logic design systems	Yes
4.	Software design support systems	Yes
5.	Knowledge-based systems and knowledge representation	Yes
6.	Machine translation systems	No
7.	Image understanding	No
8.	AI-related fundamental research	Yes

Source: Information supplied to the author by the company.

that government policy is aimed at increasing economic growth, measures should be introduced which will increase the spread of these technologies. However, in some cases such measures may lead to conflict with the private sector firms which have created the technologies. For the latter, profitability may depend on the firm's ability to monopolize technological knowledge. While a more rapid rate of diffusion of this knowledge may favour increased national economic growth, it may simultaneously lead to lower profits in the firm than would occur if the firms were able to limit the spread of the knowledge. In these cases, firms will have an incentive to attempt to minimize diffusion.

MITI has had a good deal of experience in dealing with such conflicts. For example, in the electronics field a number of Japanese firms were able to move from transistor to integrated circuit technology when in the middle 1960s MITI forced NEC to sublicense the planar technology that it had bought from Fairchild.[23] This policy measure enabled these firms to enter the integrated circuit market and their production of ICs soon jumped dramatically.

There have also been conflicts over private and social benefit in the case of the Fifth Generation Project. We saw earlier, for example, that when the idea was first raised, several of the stronger companies were concerned at the prospect of free-riding. However, what appears to an individual firm as a free-riding problem may appear to the government as a socially beneficial spread of technological knowledge. From the point of view of government policy, the objective must be to maximize the diffusion of the knowledge while ensuring the continued participation of the private firms.

It is clear that some diffusion of technological knowledge has taken place from ICOT to the member firms. One example is the assistance given to Mitsubishi in the development of the PSI (personal sequential inference machine). The PSI is now sold commercially by Mitsubishi. Another example is the inclusion of Oki in the group together with Fujitsu and Hitachi to develop PIM (the parallel inference machine). Similarly, in the case of software the firms have been able to draw on the accumulated knowledge of ICOT and in this way software knowledge has been diffused. Nevertheless, it is important to note that only the largest electronics firms, in both the industrial and consumer electronics fields, are members of ICOT. In an interview with the author a senior member of MITI claimed that MITI was aware of this problem and was looking into ways of broadening the participation of Japanese firms in ICOT.

In principle, technological knowledge is diffused not only through the activities of ICOT but also through other means such as the sale of proprietary rights to the technology, as well as through non-commercial channels like the dissemination of technical papers. However, while the latter, constituting a flow of more basic knowledge, might be important, we have already seen that there are important constraints on the diffusion of technological knowledge through the sale of patents. More specifically, we saw that the tacitness that is inherent in the development of technological knowledge constrains MITI's ability to effectively possess and diffuse the knowledge over which it has legal ownership. On the other hand, we also saw that the ability to largely appropriate the fruits of its in-house ICOT-related research has given the firms an incentive to participate in the ICOT joint research, thus facilitating the realization of economies of research cooperation. Unfortunately, figures are not available which analyse the distribution of ICOT-related patents (a) between ICOT member firms, (b) from ICOT member firms to other Japanese firms, and (c) from ICOT member firms to foreign firms. Such data would provide a fuller picture of the diffusion, and therefore the economic effects, of the Fifth Generation Project.

The form of organization of ICOT and the generation of fifth generation technological knowledge: some further points

A number of further interesting points are raised in the ICOT reunion discussion (also quoted earlier) regarding the relationship between form of organization and the creation of generic technological knowledge. These points emerge clearly in the following quotations:

Hideki Hirakawa, Information Systems Laboratory, Toshiba R & D Centre: Personally, I feel my best experience at ICOT was that ICOT's horizontal organization gave me opportunities to do what I could never do in a private company with its vertical organization.

Kanae Masuda, New Product Development Department, Computer Works, Mitsubishi Electric: I am back to development work [in my company] rather close to the operating level. The work itself is something like a continuation of what I did at ICOT. But the work method is entirely different. I strongly feel it is rather tightly controlled, though that is what I was used to before I was sent to ICOT. I may not be allowed to say this... I am convinced that control is not good for leading-edge research such as that done at ICOT. No new ideas come out of an environment where you cannot say or do what you want to. Now I find it difficult to express my ideas. Even when I do take up an idea with someone, it is rejected in the end because it does not make economic sense. On this score, ICOT allowed us a lot of latitude, or 'empty space' as someone called it.

Hajime Kitakami, Artificial Intelligence Laboratory, Fujitsu Laboratories Ltd: The ICOT project, sponsored by government, is very different from research activities conducted by private companies. These activities are very limited because they depend on whether they pay off or not. ICOT can conduct basic research to build fifth generation computers without paying much attention to eventual pay-off. To me as a researcher with a private company, ICOT sometimes looks like God.[24]

A further advantage of the ICOT form of organization is that it clearly provides a conducive environment for the undertaking of more basic or generic research. For firms the generation of profits is a necessary condition for survival. This frequently constrains their ability to undertake more basic or generic research. (One of the largest of the Japanese electronics companies, for example, failed in an initial attempt to set up a new advanced research laboratory for research into twenty-first-century technologies in its existing central research laboratories. Researchers in this laboratory were not sufficiently 'basic research-oriented' as a result of their preoccupation with research with a shorter commercialization period. As a result, a new laboratory was established and located on a different site.) On the other hand, as a government-funded project aiming specifically at the development of generic technologies, ICOT is able to transcend such commerical constraints and create the kind of environment that encourages a longer-term, less commercially fixated, research perspective. This emerges clearly from these statements of young ICOT researchers. ICOT has also attempted to give younger researchers far more research responsibility than they would have in their firms. The underlying rationale here is that younger researchers are better adapted to developing new technologies which often require a rupture with previous ideas and designs.[25]

Summary

Some of the points that have been made in this section on the ICOT form of organization are summarized in Fig. 7.1. This figure was developed by Mr Kiyonori Konishi who, as a secondee to MITI from NTT, was one of those who originally organized the Fifth Generation Project. The figure was used as part of an evaluation of ICOT activities undertaken in 1984 and it was presented at a National Institute for Research Advancement (NIRA) conference in December 1986. The figure shows ICOT as the core surrounded by two further layers. The inner one comprises the eight manufacturers who, as ICOT members, send researchers to the Institute and undertake application research in areas relating to ICOT activities. The outer layer is made up of the 'international, interdisciplinary, collaboration network' which provides input to (and receives in turn input from) ICOT research. In addition the Japanese research community also feeds into this outer layer, as does industry more generally. At the bottom of the figure, ICOT is shown as influencing other similar national and international projects such as Alvey, ESPRIT, MCC and DARPA. The sequencing of ICOT research is portrayed by a spiral movement up the diagram ending with a fifth generation computer in the 1990s containing a highly parallel inference machine and a distributed knowledge base.

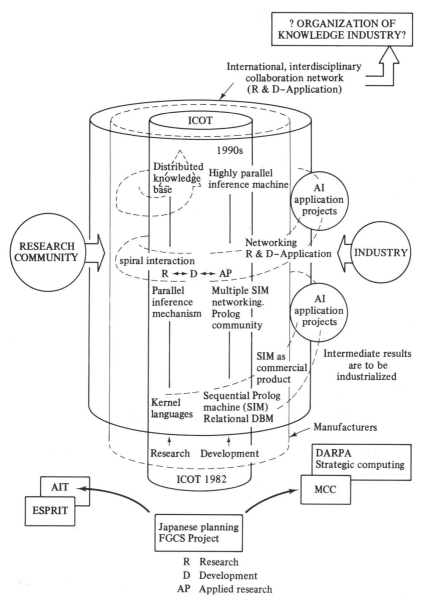

Fig. 7.1. Fifth Generation Project grand design (*Source:* Kiyonori Konishi, see text).

Funding the Fifth Generation Project and the implications

In Table 7.2, figures are given for the funding of the Fifth Generation Project by MITI. As can be seen from this table, in financial year 1987 a sum of 5.6 billion yen was allocated to the project. This is equal to

Table. 2. *Funding the Fifth Generation Project*

	1982	1983	1984	1985	1986	1987
Yen (billions)	0.4	2.7	5.1	4.7	5.5	5.6
Dollars (millions)	2.22	15.00	28.33	26.11	30.55	31.11

Note: An exchange rate of 180 yen = 1 dollar is assumed in conformity with the latest company accounts.

$31.11 million. How significant is this sum from the point of view of the firms? Of the total about 20 per cent goes to ICOT (about $6.2 million for 1987) and the remaining 80 per cent (about $24.8 million to the firms for the subcontracted work done for ICOT. Assuming that the latter sum is distributed equally amongst the eight firms (which it is *not*), this is $3.11 million per firm.

Some idea of the importance of this figure can be obtained by examining the R & D expenditure of the firms. The following example is drawn from one of the largest of these firms. In financial year 1987 this firm allocated 9 per cent of net sales to R & D. However, 3 per cent of net sales was allocated to the company's R & D laboratories, the rest being spent in the operating divisions which are also responsible for some R & D. The amount received by the R & D laboratories was around $890 million. This amount constituted the total budget for these laboratories for research in all areas. The *average* sum of $3.11 million received by the eight ICOT-related firms is 0.35 per cent of this total budget. The latter figure would rise somewhat for the present firm which probably received more than the average amount of the Fifth Generation Project's budget.[26]

As a proportion of the R & D budget for the laboratories the amount received from ICOT is small. However, this should not obscure the facts (a) that as a percentage of R & D devoted to artificial intelligence, the funding received from ICOT is far higher than 0.35 per cent and (b) that a significant degree of uncertainty attaches to research in the area of knowledge processing. If it were not for government funding in this research area it is therefore highly likely that significantly less research would be done in the companies. In terms of the *additionality criterion*, therefore, it is probable that government funding has had an important impact on research in the firms in the area of knowledge processing. This conclusion seems to be supported by the earlier case study of Fujitsu which shows that government funds have been used in most of the areas of this company's artificial intelligence research. In other words, while in overall terms government funding has been fairly limited, at the margin, in the area of knowledge processing where there is a substantial degree of uncertainty regarding future commercial prospects, such funding has had a significant impact.

Evaluation of the Fifth Generation Project

MITI's Machinery and Information Industries Bureau has an evaluation committee which is charged with the evaluation of the Fifth Generation Project. According to interviews that the author has had with some representatives from ICOT member companies, membership of the evaluation committee includes individuals from universities, the computer industry and MITI (including the Agency for Industrial Science and Technology (AIST) and the Electrotechnical Laboratory (ETL)). Each of the ICOT-related companies has members on the committee.

In essence, the method of evaluation involves comparing the objectives of the research undertaken under the project with the realized achievements. If the research objectives are altered during the progress of the research, this is noted and the evaluation adjusted accordingly. In the later stages of the project account is also taken of other evaluation indices such as patents and publications. This method of evaluation might be thought of as an 'internal evaluation' since the evaluation criteria are internal to the project itself.

The internal evaluation method is different to that usually used by economists. For economists it is necessary in any evaluation to take account of the returns that would be earned if the resources were allocated to next-best alternatives. Only the net returns over and above what would be earned in the next-best alternative project may be included as the net social benefit of the project. For this reason an economic evaluation might be thought of as an 'external' evaluation.

In beginning to develop an economic evaluation of the Fifth Generation Project it is necessary to decide on the alternative ways that the resources allocated to this project might have been spent. For the purposes of the exercise the policy judgements are accepted that (a) knowledge processing is an area of potential future importance for Japanese industry and (b) government resources are necessary to stimulate research in this area. (The importance of various forms of *market failure* to account for the necessity for government intervention would have to be taken into account.) The important question then is what are the alternative ways of allocating the resources made available by government for research in the area of knowledge processing. Clearly, that alternative should be chosen which yields the highest net benefit.

It seems reasonable to focus attention on three alternative ways of allocating the available funds. These three alternatives are illustrated in

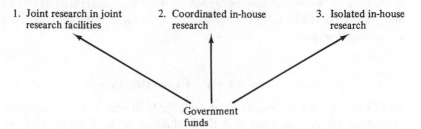

Fig. 7.2   Some alternatives for government high-technology intervention.

Fig. 7.2. The first alternative represents the ICOT case, that is the research is done jointly by the representatives of firms and government research institutes in joint research facilities. This may be referred to as *joint research in joint research facilities*. The second alternative is what might be referred to as *coordinated in-house research*, that is where agreement is achieved between the representatives of firms, government research institutes and, possibly, universities, on the kind of research that is required and on the division of labour in carrying out this research. The research is then done essentially in the institutions (primarily firms) with various kinds of meetings to coordinate the research, ensure interfacing compatibilities, etc. Unlike the first alternative, there is no joint research undertaken in joint research facilities. This basically is the form of organization that has been chosen for the MITI Supercomputer and Future Electronic Devices Projects. The third alternative involves subsidizing the firms to encourage them to do research in this area, but without any government-initiated inter-firm cooperation or coordination, that is *isolated in-house research*.

It will not be possible here to conduct a detailed examination of the net benefits of each of these three alternatives. For one thing, the third alternative in particular is a largely counterfactual case and it will therefore be difficult to estimate net benefits. Nevertheless, some progress can be made through a qualitative analysis of the additional benefits yielded by the first alternative. This additional benefit represents the gain to society from having undertaken the first, rather than the second or third, alternatives.

The main feature that distinguishes the first alternative from the other two is the extra amount of research cooperation that occurs. *Accordingly, the advantage of the first alternative relative to the other two alternatives is simply the additional net benefits that follow from the extra amount of research cooperation that takes place.* Therefore, in producing an economic analysis of the Fifth Generation Project it is necessary to focus on the benefits of this extra research cooperation. These might be referred to as *economies of joint research cooperation*.

The economies of research cooperation in the Fifth Generation Project include the following:

1. Economies of standardization   As pointed out, there has been a significant amount of standardization, particularly in the case of software development. It was noted earlier that the failure to standardize constitutes a special case of market failure. It is unlikely that the same degree of standardization would have been achieved in the other two alternative kinds of research.

2. Economies of scale in research   To the extent that economies of scale in research exist in this area, this will provide additional benefit for the Fifth Generation Project. An institute of the size of ICOT with its almost 100 researchers may be able, through specialization and a more efficient division of labour, to more efficiently acquire knowledge from the international stock of non-proprietary knowledge in the public domain, to assimilate it and to generate further knowledge. Externalities that flow from individual projects may be more effectively captured within an institute of this size. For example, while a researcher in doing research might acquire knowledge that is not particularly relevant for his/her purposes, this knowledge might be drawn on by other researchers working in the same institute.

3. Diffusion economies   As noted, the economic benefits of a project are a function of the diffusion of the knowledge that results. Since in the Fifth Generation Project there is a joint research institute, more of the knowledge is in the semi-public domain than would be the case in either of the other two alternatives. It is therefore more likely that this knowledge will diffuse to the other member companies. (Since there is not an effective inter-firm labour market in Japan, very little of this knowledge will spread via the movement of researchers to non-member companies. As far as the diffusion of knowledge via the distribution of patents is concerned, this method might be used in all three alternatives.)

4. Sharing of distinctive competences   It is likely that additional benefits (over and above what would have occurred in the other two alternatives) have accrued in the Fifth Generation Project as a result of the sharing of distinctive competences located in the companies, the government research laboratories and the universities. The opportunities for sharing are far less in the case of the other alternatives.

5. Benefits resulting from the joint development and sharing of technology   Unlike what would have been possible in the case of the other alternatives, the Fifth Generation Project has benefited significantly from the joint development and sharing of both hardware and software. (While point 4 refers to benefits in creating hardware and software, the present point is concerned with the benefits of using such technology.) For example, in this chapter the benefits of using the personal sequential inference machine (PSI) as a software tool were discussed.

6. Benefits from competition in research   Given the closer proximity of the researchers and the greater degree of cooperation between them, it is likely that the Fifth Generation Project has also achieved additional benefits from a greater amount of competition in research. For example, there is strong competition between the three manufacturers bidding for the production of the parallel inference machine.

It should, however, also be noted that there might be additional costs associated with the first joint research alternative. In view of the reduced degree of control that the firms have over the knowledge which they have contributed to the common project, it may be that there are (a) greater costs in setting up the project and (b) higher costs in administering it. It was noted earlier, for example, that it took over two years of discussion to establish the Fifth Generation Project. It is widely acknowledged by both MITI and company officials that for the reason of diminished control the firms are in general reluctant to enter into joint research projects. MITI, on the other hand, partly in order to increase the social benefit of such national projects and partly in order to more easily justify the expenditure of public funds, attempts wherever possible to encourage joint research. The point, however, is that to the extent that the costs of the joint research option are greater than those of the other two options, this will have to be accounted for in calculating the net benefits of this option.

The discussion of appropriability and control over privately generated technological knowledge, however, raises the important issue regarding the extent to which in practice a choice exists between the three alternatives outlined. In the case of the Supercomputer Project for example (analysed in detail in an earlier chapter) the firms, despite pressure from MITI, were unwilling to establish joint research facilities. This was so regardless of the existence of economies of joint research cooperation, many of which would also have been realized in joint supercomputer research laboratories. The main reason for the reluctance of the firms to establish a joint laboratory in the Supercomputer case was the possibility of early commercialization of the technologies being developed. This in turn suggests that the Fifth Generation Project was ideally suited to joint research, and hence to the realization of the economies of joint research, since a longer period was needed for commercialization. These considerations would have to be taken into account in an economic evaluation exercise. In the Supercomputer case, therefore, it might not be reasonable, for the reasons just given, to think of joint research in joint research facilities as a viable option.

To conclude, it is clear from the evidence considered in the present chapter that important economies of joint research cooperation have been generated by the Fifth Generation Project. These economies have added to the productivity of the research effort. In a recent newspaper interview, Fuchi has attempted to pour some cold water on the fires of enthusiasm that have been fanned by books, such as that by Feigenbaum and McCorduck, on the Fifth Generation Project. Fuchi 'maintains it is not ICOT's aim to construct an intelligent computer: "That will take a hundred years." Rather, when ICOT's 10-year term comes to an end in the early 1990s, Fuchi hopes that they will be able to supply "some tools and ideas and a framework for computer manufacturers to begin tackling the building of Fifth Generation computers"' (*Japan Times*, 12 January 1987). However, whether or not this forecast is accurate, and whether or not ICOT actually succeeds in realizing these goals, an important learning experience will have been generated in the area of knowledge processing for the companies, government research laboratories and universities involved. To a significant extent, this learning experience has been the result of the economies of joint cooperative research discussed in this chapter.

Evaluating the output of the Fifth Generation Project

While in the previous section the advantages of joint research in joint research facilities have been evaluated relative to the other alternative forms of research organization, in this section attention is turned to an evaluation of the research output of the Fifth Generation Project.

As in the case of the Optical Measurement and Control Project examined in an earlier chapter, use is made here of the assessments of foreign academics. Two sources in particular are used. The first is the Japanese Technology Evaluation Program (JTECH) Panel Report on Advanced Computing in Japan, December 1987, a programme supported by the US National Science Foundation, while the second is some of the papers delivered at the ICOT International Conference on Fifth Generation Computer Systems, December 1988.

Some common criticisms of the output of the Fifth Generation Project

Among the criticisms that have been made of the output of the Fifth Generation Project are the following:

a. ICOT has not succeeded in its original objective of contributing to fundamental knowledge in the area of fifth generation computing.
b. ICOT's activities have been too narrowly circumscribed by its choice of logic programming as the kernel language for the Fifth Generation Project.
c. Many other research areas, of potential longer-run importance in the field of artificial intelligence, have been ignored in ICOT research.

These criticisms will now be evaluated.

Evaluation of the criticisms

Denicoff, Chief of Project Development of Thinking Machines Corporation and Chairman of the JTECH panel of seven leading US computer scientists, is unequivocal in his conclusion that to date the Fifth Generation Project has produced no 'fundamental advances': the 'JTECH panelists unanimously concluded that the Japanese effort to date has produced no fundamental advances' (Japanese Technology Evaluation Program, 1987, p. 2).

Leaving aside the issue of the meaning of 'fundamental advance' which was not defined in the JTECH report, the question that arises relates to the significance that must be attached from an evaluation point of view to the absence of such advances from the Fifth Generation Project. Different approaches have been taken in assessing this significance. Some, for instance, have argued that the lack of fundamental advances is not necessarily significant since the Fifth Generation Project does not aim at producing such advances. This is the line taken by Goguen and Hewitt in their contribution to the JTECH report:

We want to address another pervasive myth... which is that ICOT is a second rate research institute because they haven't achieved startling new results...The fact is, ICOT is not doing basic research, and is not supposed to be doing basic research, either in AI or in any other field. Rather, they are doing *innovative long-term applied research.* This means that they want to build prototypes that demonstrate specific progress toward difficult long-term goals. ICOT is focused on developing innovative technology, rather than basic research...Their intention is to develop and validate a new way of designing, programming and using computers, one that can take maximum advantage of VLSI technology, concurrent programming, and ultrahigh level more declarative programming styles, for applications to knowledge processing, and especially to natural language processing (p. 15, emphasis added).

From this point view, a distinction may be drawn between 'fundamental advance' on the one hand and 'innovative long-term applied research' on the other. On the basis of this distinction it would be incorrect to criticize the Fifth Generation Project for failing to produce fundamental advance when its objective is to produce innovative long-term applied research. From an evaluation point of view, therefore, the question is how successful has ICOT been at producing long-term applied innovation, a question to which we shall return shortly.

Others, however, have taken a different line in assessing the significance of the absence of fundamental advances in the Fifth Generation Project. Rosenschein, for example, from SRI International, has argued in his chapter for the JTECH evaluation that the important breakthroughs in AI will come from fundamental conceptual advance, rather than from progress in developing programming languages and systems. Accordingly, If Japan is to benefit from, and contribute to, research in the AI area, a national Japanese research programme in this field should aim at fundamental conceptual advance:

At present, symbolic computation and AI are symbiotic disciplines, but they are by no means co-extensive, and each has its own international dynamic. The assumption that massive investments in symbolic computing will inevitably lead to dramatic progress in AI is naive... Good programming languages and systems are important, especially where they reflect high-level conceptual structures, but in themselves are unlikely to lead to conceptual breakthroughs in AI. These breakthroughs will come (if they do) from sound fundamental work on the substantive problems of representation, reasoning, perception, multiagent communication, planning, and learning. The key ideas will almost certainly be formulated in a way that transcends particular programming idioms, and indeed today's languages and machines are likely to be rendered obsolete by such conceptual breakthroughs. For this reason, a research project on the scale of the Fifth Generation Project should be devoting a substantial portion of its resources to investigating basic conceptual issues (p. 39).

From this point of view the absence of fundamental advances from the Fifth Generation Project constitutes a valid criticism of this project. While not necessarily disagreeing with Goguen and Hewitt that the actual aim of the Fifth Generation Project is to produce innovative long-term applied research, Rosenschein argues that this aim itself is misguided.

At issue in this implicit debate between Rosenschein and Goguen and Hewitt (a debate that is neither made explicit nor resolved in the JTECH report) is whether a linear sequential model operates in this particular area of computer science. Rosenschein implicitly argues that the basic concepts must first be produced followed by attempts to implement these concepts in hardware and software. To the extent that this argument is correct, priority should be given in the first instance to the basic research that will produce the necessary concepts. It is, however, also possible to hypothesize (an argument which is *not* put forward by Goguen and Hewitt) that the process of implementing hardware and software will eventually lead to the development of new basic concepts. In other words, long-term applied research will lead on to fundamental advance. If this is the case, then basic research should not necessarily receive the top priority. It is probably reasonable to conclude that there is not yet sufficient information available on the basis of which to resolve these two alternative hypotheses. Although there is no evidence to suggest that ICOT research has yet led to the development of new fundamental concepts, either within ICOT itself or in the working groups organized around the institute or in the companies where related research is stimulated, it is possible that such concepts will emerge in the future. In this sense Director Fuchi's statement at the ICOT International Conference in December 1988 that 'my evaluation of [the] success [of the Fifth Generation Project] will be based on the verdict . . . five years after the project's completion' is reasonable (*Financial Times*, 7 December 1988).

Although not falling under the heading of 'fundamental advances', there is evidence to suggest that some important and original contributions have been made by ICOT research. Goguen and Hewitt, for example, conclude that the 'development of Flat Guarded Horn Clause by the researchers at ICOT is a significant and original contribution to the state of the art in the design of base languages for concurrent computation' (p. 12). Goto *et al.* (1988) elaborate on the importance of Flat Guarded Horn Clause (FGHC) in the fifth generation programme: 'The research and development of the parallel inference machine (PIM) system is one of the most important targets in the Fifth Generation Computer System project' (p. 208). The PIM system includes the kernel language (KL1), the parallel operating system (PIMOS) and the PIM hardware architecture. The design of KL1 was based on Guarded Horn Clause (GHC). Goto *et al.* (1988) explain that the choice of GHC was based on the suitability of this language for parallel programming. GHC is a logic programming language and the decision had been made to make this the common language for the entire Fifth Generation Project, in this way facilitating effective communication between researchers working on different hardware and software tasks:

One of our most important policies in the R & D of the PIM system is to build up a total system based on logic programming, so that the system designers of the PIM can easily look through all levels of the system in a logic programming framework. This is an important way to solve the so-called *semantic gap* argument: application and implementation are closer, therefore execution is faster.

KL1, the kernel language of the PIM system, was designed based on GHC (Ueda, 1986a). The major reasons for choosing GHC as the basis for KL1 are as follows: GHC has clear and simple semantics as a concurrent logic programming language, by which programmers can express important concepts in parallel programming, such as inter-process communication and synchronization. In addition, GHC is an efficient language, in the sense that we can specify the machine level language [also using GHC] (p. 208).

Goto *et al.* (1988, p. 209) clarify the difference between GHC and Flat Guarded Horn Clause (FGHC): 'KL1 was initially specified as Flat GHC (Ueda, 1986a; Ueda, 1986b), taking efficient implementation into consideration. Flat GHC is a subset of GHC, which allows only built-in predicates as guard goals. This restriction makes language implementation more efficient while retaining most of GHC's descriptive power. Starting from Flat GHC, KL1 has been extended so that it has become a practical language with the features required for the PIMOS design.'

Correcting a common misconception in the United States, Goguen and Hewitt (Japanese Technology Evaluation Program, 1987) point out that 'researchers at ICOT have not been dogmatic about retaining ... Prolog as their base level language for concurrent systems, but instead have shown creativity and taste in developing FGHC, a new base language for concurrent computation that is simple in essence and supports imperative as well as more declarative styles... FGHC should serve ICOT well both in developing higher-level languages and in developing highly concurrent machines' (pp. 8–9).

From the point of view of evaluating the output of the Fifth Generation Project it is important to stress that FGHC, while not as sophisticated as other similar languages, has evolved out of a pragmatic attempt to develop both the hardware and the software for a parallel processing machine and, although not making a 'fundamental advance', represents a creative innovation. *This is one example of innovation in ICOT being shaped by the pragmatic applications-oriented objectives of this institute.* Within this context, sophistication *per se* matters less than effectiveness in contributing to the development of a working prototype fifth generation computer.

A similar case of pragmatic creativity is the work done in ICOT in the area of situation semantics. While the basic theoretical research in the area of situation semantics is being done at the Center for the Study of Language and Information at Stanford University, pragmatic use is being made in ICOT of this research in attempting to implement situation semantics as part of the fifth generation programme. As Goguen and Hewitt put it: 'At the Center for the Study of Language and Information they are axiomatizing situation semantics in a manner rather like that in which set theory has been axiomatized...On the other hand, at ICOT they are implementing situation semantics: Mukai and others at ICOT are doing the implementation in CIL (the Complex Indeterminate Language)...This approach to natural language semantics through situation semantics is really innovative engineering. Also, the differing approaches to situation semantics is an interesting contrast between some research and development styles in the US and Japan' (p. 18). Situation semantics has potentially important applications in areas such as natural language processing which is a major concern in ICOT.

Although the JTECH panel concluded that the Fifth Generation Project has not made any fundamental advances, it also concluded that significant progress had been made in this project in the area of logic programming, relative both to the capabilities that existed in Japan prior to this project and to research in this area in the US. Denicoff therefore concluded that 'All of the panelists grant that the Japanese are performing at the level of, or ahead of, the US in the theory and practice of logic programming' (p. 4). This relative performance must certainly count as one of the major achievements of the Fifth Generation Project, an achievement which is less likely to have been made, or not to the same extent, had ICOT not been established. The reason for this conclusion lies in the advantages of joint research in joint research facilities analysed earlier in this chapter.

Substantive questions were, however, raised by the panel regarding the relevance of this mastery of logic programming. As Denicoff put it: 'The questioning has to do with the importance or value of this achievement to higher level objectives of the AI community and [the] Fifth Generation [Project] itself' (p. 4).

The main reason behind the questioning is doubt regarding the prominent, or even exclusive, role played by logic programming in the Fifth Generation Project. This doubt was expressed, for example, at the 1988 ICOT International Conference by Robin Milner, Director of the Laboratory for the Foundation of Computer Science at Edinburgh University. Milner gave one of four invited papers at this International Conference. Milner stated: 'I think the whole scene of computation is actually rather broader than the particular line that the Japanese have chosen... What I disagree with most is the contention that computing can be reduced to logic. I think it would be more fruitful to treat computing as more basic than logic and to say that logic may be reduced to computing. When one talks about the goal of achieving "logical inference in parallel", to me that should really be the goal of "increasing computing in parallel"... and I think that they have made considerable steps in that direction' (*Financial Times*, 7 December 1988).

Further implicit criticism of the weight given in the Fifth Generation Project to logic programming came at the conference from Herbert Simon, a Nobel Prize laureate who gave one of two invited lectures. It is worth quoting Simon at length here in order to clarify both the rationale behind the emphasis given to logic programming and some of the doubts that have arisen regarding its centrality in the Fifth Generation Project. As Simon (1988, pp. 117–18) expressed it:

Simply put, the idea behind logic programming is that reasoning should be logical, and that programming languages should incorporate from logic the principles and insights that make logic a powerful and rigorous form of reasoning. Underlying any inferential system are principles, some of which are expressed in declarative form, others in procedural form. The former are called axioms, the latter, inference rules. It is an ideal of logic that both axioms and inference rules should be independent of subject matter; that they should give valid results for all possible worlds. When the logic is applied to a particular domain, additional axioms (domain-specific axioms) are supplied to specify what is known about that domain.

Because formal logic has historically been closely connected with questions of rigor in reasoning, systems of logic are usually designed to make verification of proofs as clear and transparent as possible. This is accomplished, first, by separating logical axioms from domain-specific axioms, as already explained, and second, by severely restricting the inference rules (e.g., in the system of Whitehead and Russell they include only substitution and *modus ponens*).

A heavy price is paid for adhering to these principles: the reasoning proceeds by tiny steps, huge numbers of which are needed for even the simplest proofs. Whitehead and Russell paid that price (as attested by the thickness of the volumes of *Principia Mathematica*) because rigor was the name of the game they were playing. But there are many other games that intelligence plays and that we want to play on computers. They do not all have the same requirements...

When we examine human reasoning, especially as it is applied to substantive affairs, it proceeds in quite a different way. There are not just a few inference procedures but many; and these are not all logical rules, but generally incorporate important domain-specific knowledge... Human reasoning is a mixed bag which serves many purposes. It is used to a much greater extent to discover than to verify, and we know that discovery often requires heuristic search, taking long jumps at the expense of guarantees either of completeness or validity. The lack of these guarantees is not a virtue – it is the price we pay for living in a world where completeness and guaranteed correctness of search are computationally infeasible... The principles I have just announced are not laws of logic, but empirical generalizations from human experience. In most real-life situations, human reasoning is, and must be, heuristic search... My problem is not with a programming language. My problem is with what seems to me a misconception of the central principles that underlie intelligence, and that should guide the design of intelligent programs for AI and cognitive science. Among those central principles is the idea that problem solving is heuristic search.

Simon is therefore implicitly critical of the emphasis given in the Fifth Generation Project to logic programming. The JTECH panel concluded that, partly as a result of the concentration on logic programming, the project had omitted research in several areas that were felt to be important:

Along with recognition of the described Fifth Generation Program's progress, JTECH panelists found some research gaps. Little attention, for example, is being paid to developing formal methods for proving the correctness of computer programs. Outside of Japanese efforts in Prolog, JTECH visitors saw general inattention to transformational programming. Compared to American artificial intelligence laboratories, the Fifth Generation Project seems almost to have abandoned substantive research in such fundamental areas as knowledge representation and reasoning, machine learning, fine-grain parallel architectures, connectionism, and *neural modelling* (p. 5, emphasis added).

The concentrated focus on logic programming and the trade-off that this implies in terms of the foregoing of other research areas raises a number of complex issues both for evaluation of the Fifth Generation Project and for the question of optimal organizational design of national research projects such as the present one. In the Fifth Generation Project the decision was made to concentrate resources in one large research institute, ICOT, and in turn, by tightly specifying the output goal for the institute, namely the development of a prototype fifth generation computer, to focus research in a specific, mission-oriented, direction. It is this form of organization which encouraged the choice of one programming approach in order to achieve effective communication between the now almost 100 researchers in ICOT working on different hardware and software tasks. An alternative form of organization would have been the creation of 'distributed research centres', that is to spread the available resources over a larger number of smaller research centres. A major cost of such an alternative form of organization would have been the foregoing of many of the economies of joint research analysed earlier in this chapter. However, an off-setting benefit would probably have been the *greater diversity* of research output that would have resulted from the distributed research centres, each with a degree of autonomy in setting its research agenda.

Leaving aside the unresolvable question of which of these two alternative forms of organization would have yielded greatest net benefit, it is nevertheless incorrect to virtually equate ICOT research with Japanese research in AI as some observers have attempted to do. For example, Rosenschein (Japanese Technology Evaluation Program, 1987, p. 38) notes that 'if one looks at the distribution of research efforts [in the AI area in the United States] as reflected, for instance, in project distribution in major laboratories or papers presented at national conferences, one finds a broad mix of topics, most of which are not being actively pursued in Japan'. He continues:

It might be objected that US activity should not be compared with the Fifth Generation Project, which is, after all, only one project. However, it is the centerpiece of the Japanese national research effort in AI, its priorities have been very influential in setting the overall direction of AI research in Japan, and it has had disproportionate influence in turning funds and attention toward logic programming and away from other topics (p. 38).

While the Fifth Generation Project certainly has had a major impact on AI in Japan, it is incorrect to reduce Japanese AI research to Fifth Generation Project research. To do so is to fundamentally misunderstand the nature of the Japanese Technology-Creating System which is a major object of study in the present book. To take several examples, it was noted earlier in this chapter that ICOT has played an important role in propagating a 'logic programming culture', both in the institute itself as well as in the laboratories of the member companies. However, it was also seen that 'cultural pluralism' exists in the companies. In view of the importance of this point it is worth repeating the quotations from some of the ICOT researchers:

Kunio Murakami, Knowledge Engineering Department.

NTT Communications and Information Processing Laboratories, and an ICOT laboratory head: How do you feel the fifth generation computer culture is spreading?

Hajime Kitakami, Artificial Intelligence Laboratory, Fujitsu Laboratories Ltd: I keenly feel there is a great difference between ICOT and the manufacturer in awareness of the Prolog culture, as one might expect. [As noted earlier, while ICOT first used Prolog as its core language, this was later broadened to include newly developed logic programming languages such as FGHC.] Very few of the manufacturer's people doing programming in Prolog are doing it with a strong awareness of the importance of the language...

Murakami: Is the Prolog group still in the minority?

Kitakami: I think so...

Kanae Masuda, New Product Development Department, Computer Works, Mitusbishi Electric Corporation: I feel much the same. Since I work in a development group... I find the overwhelming majority of the group sees Prolog as something alien to them and peculiar to ICOT. Whatever I tell them about Prolog, their usual response is that it will take much more time to take root or that it still remains an unknown. I feel there is a gap between them and us. It seems they regard us as heretics, to my great regret.

In addition to the 'cultural pluralism' that is evident in the Japanese companies, further diversity is contributed by some of the other institutions that are also an important part of the Japanese System. Here mention must be made of MITI's Electrotechnical Laboratory and NTT's Electrical Communications Laboratories which continue to do research in a wide range of AI-related areas. Similarly, AI research is done in the ATR laboratory near Osaka which is funded by the Japan Key Technology Center, in turn controlled by the Ministry of Post and Telecommunications and MITI. University-based research financed by the Ministry of Education contributes further to a plurality of approach. It would therefore be quite wrong to reduce Japanese AI research to ICOT research. At the ICOT 1988 International Conference, Herbert Simon concluded that 'As far as research programs are concerned, a good philosophy is to "let a hundred flowers bloom"' (p. 117). While diversity in the Japanese System may not quite amount to the flowering of a hundred different approaches to AI, it is clear that the diversity is significantly greater than that present in ICOT.

But perhaps one of the most important 'outputs' of the Fifth Generation Project takes a less tangible form than new programming languages such as FGHC and the parallel inference machine. This 'output' is the creation of a *form of organization* which has proved itself efficient, as argued in detail in this chapter and as the rapid mastery of logic programming demonstrates, in effectively drawing on the international stock of knowledge and in applying this knowledge to pragmatic, mission-oriented and commercial goals. This is one of the major conclusions of the JTECH report:

[The Fifth Generation Project] has scored points in such important areas as: (1) establishing Japan as a full partner in the international community of computer scientists and scholars; (2) demonstrating awareness, beyond that of other countries and most particularly the USA, of the appropriate literature and most recent progress *in the entire field of computer science*; (3) creating AI and software products and tools of high quality, along with an organizational R & D planning mechanism that ensures the timely and efficient transfer of research results into products (p. 2, emphasis added).

As this quotation makes clear, a commitment to logic programming in ICOT has not obscured an awareness of trends and achievements in other areas of AI and computer science in general. Perhaps one of the most flexible and fruitful assets that has been developed in the Fifth Generation Project is its form of organization which can be transferred in the future to other areas of research, both in computer science and elsewhere. For instance, one area in which the JTECH panel detected a 'research gap' in Japanese research was the area of neural computing, as noted earlier. In the same week as the 1988 ICOT International Conference was held, MITI announced that its next high-profile research project in the area of computer-science, to begin in 1990, would be in neural computing (*New Scientist*, 3 December 1988).

Conclusion

From a narrow technical point of view it might seem that the major issue regarding the Fifth Generation Project relates to the degree of success in developing a new kind of computer. The present chapter, however, suggests that there are also a large number of complex issues that are raised by this project about the relationship between competitive and cooperative interactions between firms, about the advantages and disadvantages of different forms of organization, and about the appropriate role for government intervention. A crucial question relates to the bearing that these kinds of factors have on the process of technical change. As the present chapter seeks to illustrate, at least as much research is still required in order to answer this question as is needed to develop the fifth generation computer itself.

8

Cooperation and competition in the Japanese computing and electronic devices industry: a quantitative analysis

Introduction

A major theme of this book is the relationship between competition and cooperation in the Japanese industrial electronics industry. This relationship has been analysed in detail in the previous chapters, largely on the basis of intensive interviews with the representatives of Japanese companies, government and universities. In a number of areas, however, it was felt that greater precision was required. For example, when a respondent said there was 'strong competition' between his firm and another and that this influenced the extent of research cooperation between the two companies it was felt useful to attempt to quantify the degree of competition and to compare it with that existing with other companies. There was a similar need when, for instance, a respondent estimated that the finance provided in a government-initiated national cooperative search project was 'very important' for his company.

Accordingly, a questionnaire was prepared and sent to very senior research managers in four of the major Japanese industrial electronics companies. In order to preserve confidentiality it will only be said that these four companies were drawn from the following group: Fujitsu, Hitachi, Mitsubishi Electric, NEC, Oki and Toshiba. One questionnaire was completed for each of the national cooperative research projects examined in this book (with the exception of the VLSI Project).

The intensity of competition between the companies participating in the national projects

The conventional methods for measuring competition are not particularly helpful in the present case. This applies, for example, to concentration ratios, the Herfindahl index, and market share. There are a number of reasons for this. To begin with, data, when they are available, are often too aggregated. The available data on concentration ratios, for instance, are not sufficiently detailed to indicate those product markets where multi-product companies do and do not compete. While these data may be supplemented by other information on market share available on

243

a more disaggregated basis, there are again important shortcomings for present purposes. One reason for the inadequacy is that the present study is primarily concerned with the development of *technologies* which will only *in the longer run* feed into products which will compete on the product market. The willingness of a company to share knowledge in a particular technology area will depend on its assessment of the effect that the sharing of knowledge will have on its shorter- and longer-run competitiveness. In general, all other things being equal, a company will not be prepared to share knowledge with another company which may use the knowledge to compete more effectively with it on the product market, unless it is compensated adequately for the knowledge which it gives. Data on concentration ratios or market share do not provide sufficient information on the existence of *technological competition*, that is competition between companies to develop the technologies which will support their future product market competitiveness. It is technological competition which will determine a company's willingness to cooperate in research. For this reason companies surveyed were asked directly about the intensity of their technological competition with the other companies participating in the national research project.

The results of the questionnaire are shown in Table 8.1. As can be seen from this table, the firms reported, with only one exception, that there was intense technological competition, measuring 1 on a five-point scale, with at least one other company participating in the national project. The exception is firm C in the Future Electronic Devices Project which reported strong competition, measuring 2 on the scale, with two of the firms. From this data it can be concluded that the firms which participated in the national projects competed intensely in the technologies being developed and advanced in these projects.

Table 8.1. *Intensity of competition between the firms involved in the national cooperative research projects*

Question: How intensely does your firm compete in the relevant technology area with the other firms that are involved in this national project? Assess the intensity of competition with the top three competing firms.

Optical Measurement and Control								High-Speed			
Firm A		Firm B		Firm C		Firm D		Firm A		Firm B	
CF	IC	CF	IC	CF	IC	CF	IC	CF	IC	CF	IC
–	–	1	1	–	–	–	–	B	1	A	1
–	–	2	1	–	–	–	–	C	1	C	1
–	–	3	1	–	–	–	–	–	–	D	3

Key: CF: competing firm (1–3 are unidentified competing firms; A–D are the same as Firm A,..., Firm D). IC: intensity of competition (1 = intense competition ... 5 = no competition).

As noted in chapter 2 and as analysed in more detail in chapter 9, it is this intensity of competition which accounts for the insignificant presence of spontaneous research cooperation, defined as the emergence of research cooperation between companies between whom there is strong technological competition, in the absence of intervention either by government or a large procurer. The main reason for this is high transactions costs involved in establishing agreement to engage in research cooperation. The high transactions costs are themselves the result of attempts to prevent knowledge leakage to other technologically competing firms. By acting as a neutral intermediary, either government or a large procurer like NTT are able to economize on these transactions costs and thus increase the amount of research cooperation between technologically competing companies.

But did the competing companies participating in the national cooperative research projects feel that there was a danger of some of the company's knowledge, possibly important for future competitiveness, leaking to other competing companies through the activities of the project? This question is examined in Table 8.2. A strict comparison between the four national projects is not possible because some ot the firms declined to answer this question for some of the projects. It is, however, possible to compare the High Speed Computer Project with the Future Electronic Devices Project. In the case of the former project three of the four firms estimated a value of 3 on the five-point scale, indicating that there was some danger of knowledge leakage through this project although the danger was not very great. This is of interest for a number of reasons. It was noted in the chapter on the High Speed Computer that there was less inter-firm sharing of knowledge in this project than in any of the others analysed in this book. The main reason was that the major mainframe-producing firms felt that the generic technologies being developed under this project were of great

Computing System				Future Electronic Devices							
Firm C		Firm D		Firm A		Firm B		Firm C		Firm D	
CF	IC	CF	IC	CF	IC	CF	IC	CF	IC	CF	IC
B	1	–	–	–	–	1	1	E	2	–	–
A	1	–	–	–	–	2	1	B	2	–	–
–	–	–	–	–	–	–	–	D	3	–	–

Table 8.2. *Danger of knowledge leakage in the national cooperative research projects*

Question: How do you assess the danger in this national project of some of your company's technological knowledge leaking to other competing companies?

Optical Measurement and Control				High-Speed Computing System				Future Electronic Devices				Fifth Generation Computer			
Firm A	Firm B	Firm C	Firm D	Firm A	Firm B	Firm C	Firm D	Firm A	Firm B	Firm C	Firm D	Firm A	Firm B	Firm C	Firm D
4	2	–	3	3	3	3	4	4	4	2	4	3	–	–	4

Key: 1 = very great .... 5 = unimportant.

Table 8.3. *Opportunism in the national cooperative research projects*

Question: How do you assess the following statement: 'Other Japanese firms, if they could escape detection, would be willing in a joint research project to opportunistically use information from the other cooperating firms while keeping private as much of their information as possible'?

Optical Measurement and Control				High-Speed Computing System				Future Electronic Devices				Fifth Generation Computer			
Firm A	Firm B	Firm C	Firm D	Firm A	Firm B	Firm C	Firm D	Firm A	Firm B	Firm C	Firm D	Firm A	Firm B	Firm C	Firm D
3	3	–	5	2	3	5	5	4	5	5	5	3	–	–	–

Key: 1 = fully agree .... 5 = totally disagree.

potential importance for their long-run competitiveness. It was for this reason that the suggestion for a joint laboratory was rejected. It is of interest that, despite the limited inter-firm flows of information in this project, as documented in the earlier chapter, three of the participating firms still felt there was some danger of knowledge leakage. This provides further support for the suggestion that the technologies in this project were regarded as sensitive by the participating companies.

The contrast with the Future Electronic Devices Project is also of interest. Here three of the four firms concluded that there was little danger of knowledge leakage. In the chapter on this project, it was noted that this case involved a process of joint search and that there was a good deal of knowledge exchange between the companies involved, particularly those located in the Kansai area. Furthermore, the research itself on three-dimensional devices and superlattices was regarded as somewhat academic and not of immediate consequence for the competitiveness of the companies. In this sense there was seen to be little danger from the relatively free exchange of knowledge between the companies.

Are Japanese companies likely to behave *opportunistically*, exploiting the fruits of joint research for private benefit? This question derives additional meaning from the significance which has been attached in some of the economic theory literature to opportunistic behaviour on the part of companies. (For an early statement of the importance and implications of opportunism, see Williamson, 1975.) This question is examined quantitatively in Table 8.3. A number of points emerge from this table. For all of the four national projects, firms C and D either totally disagreed with the statement that other Japanese firms would be willing to behave opportunistically, or they did not answer the question. On the other hand, the answers of firms A and B varied by project. Firm A felt there was some chance that other firms would behave opportunistically in the Optical Measurement, High-Speed Computing and Fifth Generation Projects, but that there was little chance in the Future Electronic Devices Project where, as just explained, the companies were fairly free in their exchange of information and knowledge. Firm B, on the other hand, felt that there was a very strong chance (measured by 2 on the five-point scale) of opportunistic behaviour in the High-Speed Computing Project, the most 'sensitive' of all the projects, but totally disagreed that there was a chance of such behaviour in the Future Electronic Devices Project. The average score over all the projects was 4.0. To the extent that is meaningful to aggregate over the four projects (which is a little doubtful since the answers suggest that opportunistic behaviour is project related), the score of 4.0 suggests that in general the firms felt that opportunistic behaviour was not a major problem in the national cooperative research projects. This is supported by the fact that there is only one score of 2 in the table and none of 1. It is, however, not possible to detect from this question whether the relative absence of opportunism was the result of little opportunity for opportunism, of a high chance of opportunism being detected, or of a culturally-determined low propensity for opportunism.

The role of government in facilitating research cooperation

It was stated earlier that government, as a result of its ability to be neutral with respect to the conflicting interests of competing companies, is able to economize on the transactions costs involved in getting agreement on research cooperation. While this emerged qualitatively in many of the author's interviews, it was felt desirable to get further quantitative data on this question. The results are shown in Table 8.4 and indicate that the most important way in which government facilitated cooperative research was through the provision of subsidized funding. The average score over all three projects on which answers were obtained was 2.00. Subsidized funding served to complement the funds allocated by the company to the particular research area, possibly to free some of the company's resources previously

Table 8.4. *Role of government as a facilitator of national cooperative research*

Question: How important are the following forms of government involvement in facilitating cooperative research?

	Optical Measurement and Control							
	Firm A		Firm B		Firm C		Firm D	
	R	S	R	S	R	S	R	S
Provision of subsidized funding for the co-operative research	–	2	1	2	–	–	1	3
Bearing part of the translation costs of establishing cooperative research (e.g. providing officials who arrange and run meetings, etc.)	–	2	3	4	–	–	3	5
Government acting as a neutral arbitrator so that firms do not need to be concerned about the leakage of sensitive knowledge	–	2	2	2	–	–	2	4
Other (please specify)	–	–	–	–	–	–	–	–

Key: R rank, S score (1 = very important . . . . 5 = unimportant).

allocated to this area to be used in other activities of the company, and to compensate the company for knowledge-leakage to other companies. Table 8.4 also shows that the companies felt the government played an important role in facilitating research cooperation by acting as a neutral arbitrator so that firms did not need to be concerned about the leakage of sensitive knowledge. The average score over the three projects for this factor was 2.63. Far less important, however, was the bearing by government of part of the transaction costs of establishing cooperative research, for example by providing the officials to organize the project. For this factor, the average score was 4.25.

The benefits of the national cooperative research projects

But how important, relative to one another, were the various benefits received by the participating companies from the national cooperative research projects? Data on this question are provided in Table 8.5. Companies were asked to score the importance of the benefit received on a

High-Speed Computing System								Fifth Generation Computer							
Firm A		Firm B		Firm C		Firm D		Firm A		Firm B		Firm C		Firm D	
R	S	R	S	R	S	R	S	R	S	R	S	R	S	R	S
1	1	1	1	–	–	1	3	1	1	–	–	–	–	1	3
3	5	3	3	–	–	3	5	3	5	–	–	–	–	3	5
2	2	2	2	–	–	2	4	2	2	–	–	–	–	2	3
–	–	–	–	–	–	–	–	–	–	–	–	–	–	–	–

Table 8.5. *Benefits received from the national cooperative research projects*

Question: How important are the following benefits for your company?

	Optical Measurement and Control								High-Speed			
	Firm A		Firm B		Firm C		Firm D		Firm A		Firm B	
Benefit Received	R	S	R	S	R	S	R	S	R	S	R	S
1. Funds received from MITI	–	2	1	1	–	–	2	2	1	1	1	1
2. Access to knowledge contributed by other firms	–	3	4	2	–	–	6	3	–	5	3	2
3. Access to knowledge contributed by MITI/ETL	–	3	9	4	–	–	5	2	–	3	6	3
4. Access to knowledge contributed by universities.	–	4	7	4	–	–	4	2	–	3	7	4
5. Access to international sources of knowledge	–	4	8	4	–	–	7	3	–	–	8	4
6. Avoiding overlapping research	–	4	5	3	–	–	9	4	–	5	4	2
7. Reducing research costs by sharing equipment	–	3	6	3	–	–	8	4	–	5	–	–
8. Increasing research competition	–	2	3	2	–	–	3	2	–	5	5	3
9. Devoting additional corporate research attention to the project's technologies	–	3	2	1	–	–	1	1	2	2	2	2
10. To share uncertain search[a]	–	–	–	–	–	–	–	–	–	–	–	–

Key: R rank, S score (1 = very important ... 5 = completely unimportant).
Notes: In some instances, firms provide data on score but not on rank.
[a] Additional benefit cited by respondents but not listed on questionnaire form.

five-point scale and then to rank the benefits in order of importance. The results of this question were computed in two ways: by computing the average score over all the firms and then ranking the average score; and by doing the same with the average rank.

Over all four national cooperative research projects the average score and the average rank yielded the same answer for the three most important benefits. These, in order of importance, were: (1) funds received from MITI; (2) devoting additional corporate research attention to the project's

Computing System				Future Electronic Devices								Fifth Generation Computer			
Firm C		Firm D		Firm A		Firm B		Firm C		Firm D		Firm A		Firm D	
R	S	R	S	R	S	R	S	R	S	R	S	R	S	R	S
3	3	1	1	–	2	2	2	1	1	2	3	1	1	2	2
7	4	–	–	–	3	–	5	–	–	8	4	7	3	8	4
4	3	–	–	–	3	–	5	–	–	6	3	2	2	5	3
6	4	–	–	–	4	–	5	–	–	5	2	3	2	4	2
8	4	–	–	–	4	–	5	–	–	7	2	6	3	7	4
5	4	–	–	–	3	4	4	–	–	4	4	5	2	6	4
9	5	–	–	–	2	–	5	–	–	9	5	–	5	9	5
2	3	4	3	–	3	1	2	3	3	3	3	–	5	3	2
1	1	2	2	–	3	3	3	2	2	1	1	4	2	1	1
–	–	3	1	–	–	–	–	–	–	3	1	–	–	–	–

technologies; and (3) increasing research competition between the participating companies. The average scores for these three benefits were 1.69, 1.85 and 2.92 respectively. (On the five-point scale, 1 indicated that the benefit was very important, 5 that it was completely unimportant.)

The importance of MITI funding in Table 8.5 corroborates Table 8.4 where it is shown that the companies felt that the provision of subsidized funding was the most important role played by government. This serves to highlight the point, stressed again in the concluding chapter, that *although the proportional contribution by the Japanese government to total R & D is very low relative to other Western governments, government subsidization of R & D is nevertheless very important for the longer-run development of particular technology areas.*

It is of interest that the devotion of additional attention to the project's technologies was felt by the companies to be the second most important benefit from the cooperative project. The implication is that not as much attention would have been given to these technologies in the absence of the project. This point is taken up and elaborated upon in the concluding chapter with the aid of the concept of *bounded vision*. There it is shown that organizations differ systematically in terms of their 'field of vision' with regard to areas of science and technology. *The data provided in Table 8.5 suggest strongly that participating companies have derived significant benefit from the blending of the bounded visions of different companies, government laboratories and universities that has been brought about through the organization of the national cooperative research projects.*

In terms of access to knowledge contributed through the national project from sources outside the participating company itself, a different result was obtained according to whether account was taken of the average score or the average rank. According to the average score, access to knowledge contributed by MITI/ETL was the fourth most important benefit, with an average score of 3.09 on the five-point scale. In terms of the average rank, however, this was the sixth most important benefit. Access to knowledge contributed by universities was the fifth most important benefit in terms of average rank. Access to knowledge contributed by the other participating firms was generally not felt to be a very important benefit, being the sixth most important benefit in terms of average score (3.46) and the seventh most important benefit according to average rank. Access to international sources of knowledge was regarded as the eighth most important benefit in terms both of average score (3.70) and average rank. Avoiding overlapping research was the seventh most important benefit according to average score (3.55) and the fifth most important in terms of average rank. The least important benefit was the reduction of research costs by the sharing of equipment, ninth in terms of average score (4.20) and similarly ninth according to average rank.

Interestingly, when the importance of benefits received from the national project is disaggregated by project, the same result is achieved for the first and second most important benefits as is achieved with all four projects taken together. Thus in all projects the first or second benefit is the funding received from MITI or the devoting of additional corporate research attention to the project's technologies. There is disagreement regarding the third most important benefit (according to average score). In the Optical Measurement and Control Project the third most important benefit was access to knowledge contributed through the national project by other participating companies (with an average score of 2.67). In the High-Speed Computing System Project the third most important benefit was access to knowledge contributed by MITI/ETL (3.0). This is unsurprising since, as mentioned in the chapter on this project, important niobium technology used in the development of Josephson junctions was developed in ETL and transferred to the companies involved in this project. In the Future Electronic Devices Project five benefits received the third highest score in terms of average score (3.67), while in the Fifth Generation Project the third most important benefit was access to knowledge contributed through the project by universities (2.0). Again the latter is unsurprising since an important contribution is being made by the universities to the Fifth Generation Project in terms of the role they play in the working groups around ICOT and in the development and testing of ICOT-generated technologies on both the hardware and software sides.

Other consequences of the national projects

An important ingredient in any evaluation exercise is the estimation of *additionality*; that is, the additional effects that occurred as a result of the project which would not have taken place in the absence of the project. It is always extremely difficult to estimate such additional effects. To begin with, the estimate rests on a counterfactual set of assumptions and this makes the exercise inherently problematical. Furthermore, companies may not have an incentive to give an accurate indication of additionality since, in order to justify the receipt of public funds, they may have a vested interest in exaggerating the additional benefits received from the project. Despite these difficulties it was felt important to get company estimates of additionality. These are shown in Table 8.6 for three of the national projects. There is consistency across both projects and companies that between 25 per cent and 75 per cent of the research done in the technology area would have been done in the absence of the national project. In other words, the national projects have tended to supplement existing corporate research, rather than bring into existence entirely new research that would not otherwise have received any attention. Looked at the other way round, *as a result of the national projects, between 25 per cent and 75 per cent additional research was undertaken.* In terms of projects the average score (3.0) was highest for the Optical Measurement and Control Project, indicating that in this project between 25 and 50 per cent of the research in this area would have been done without the national project. For the other two projects, the High-Speed Computer and the Future Electronic Devices Projects, the average score (2.5 in both cases) indicated that between 50 and 75 per cent of the research would have been done.

The success of the national projects from the point of view of the participating companies is shown in Table 8.7. In the case of three projects,

Table 8.6. *Amount of research occurring in the absence of the national cooperative research projects*

Question: How much research would have occurred in your company in this technology area had MITI not established this project?

Optical Measurement and Control				High-Speed Computing System				Future Electronic Devices			
Firm A	Firm B	Firm C	Firm D	Firm A	Firm B	Firm C	Firm D	Firm A	Firm B	Firm C	Firm D
c	c	–	c	b	c	b	c	c	b	b	c

Key: Letter denotes percentage of the company's existing research that would have been done in the absence of the project.

a = 75–100
b = 50–75
c = 25–50
d = 0–25
e = none

Table 8.7. *Evaluation of success of the national cooperative research projects*

Question: How do you rate the success of this project to date from your company's point of view?

Optical Measurement and Control				High-Speed Computing System				Future Electronic Devices				Fifth Generation Computer			
Firm A	Firm B	Firm C	Firm D	Firm A	Firm B	Firm C	Firm D	Firm A	Firm B	Firm C	Firm D	Firm A	Firm B	Firm C	Firm D
2	3	–	1	2	3	2	2	2	1	3	2	2	2	–	2

Key: 1 = very successful . . . 5 = completely unsuccessful.

the Optical Measurement, Future Electronic Devices and Fifth Generation Projects, the average score was 2.0 indicating that the projects were successful. The average score was not much different for the fourth project, the High-Speed Computer Project, with a score of 2.25. In two instances companies rated the project as very successful (1) while in three cases the project was rated as fairly successful.

9

Conclusions and theoretical
implications

In this final chapter, the analysis of the cooperative research projects and the history of the Japanese computing and electronic devices industry is linked to the broader concerns of this book. These concerns relate to the process of technical change as one of the main determinants of differences between national economic performances.

The chapter begins with a discussion of one of the important determinants of Japanese international competitiveness in the computing and electronic devices industry, namely the process of incremental technical change brought about within a given production process. It is shown that in Japan forms of organization have evolved which have facilitated the effective mobilization of information flows, which in turn have been utilized as an important input for innovation.

These forms of organization have been highly effective in bringing about incremental changes, the cumulative significance of which has in some cases outweighed the importance of more radical changes. In this way a successful process of technical change 'for tomorrow' has occurred in Japan. Furthermore, it is important to stress that these forms of organization have been developed primarily by the Japanese companies with little or no influence from government.

However, qualitatively different problems occur in attempting to create technologies for 'the day after tomorrow', even where the country in which the technologies are being created is a follower in the process of trying to catch-up with the international leaders. The main reason for the qualitative difference is the existence of uncertainty which injects special problem into the decision-making environment. The problem of uncertainty is therefore discussed, first theoretically, and then in connection with the way in which uncertainty has been dealt with in Japan. Here three periods are distinguished, the Early Catching-Up Period, 1945–65; the Late Catching-Up Period, 1966–79; and the Frontier-Leading Period (except for basic research), 1980–present. It is shown that the problem of uncertainty in the earlier periods related to the difficulty of staying in the competitive game while ensuring an adequate rate of return on the investments in innovation required to do so. In the last period, however, with the international technology frontier having been reached, uncertainty related more to the technologies themselves and necessitated the undertaking of a significantly increased amount of what is referred to as *oriented-basic research.*

In the discussion of uncertainty it is shown that the Japanese government played an important role in reducing some of the effects of uncertainty, thereby increasing the investment in innovation that was required to become, and remain, internationally competitive. However, it is also stressed that uncertainty reduction is not necessarily socially beneficial. A case in point is industries in some of the semi-industrialized countries which have been protected from international competition and which as a result have become permanent infant industries. In Japan, however, the uncertainty-reducing effects of government intervention have gone together with a significant degree of pressure for innovation exerted by the competitive interactions of Japanese companies. The role of competition in the Japanese computing and electronic devices industry is examined in the following section.

Competition, however, is not an unmixed blessing. Particular attention is paid to two of the difficulties raised by competition. The first is the negative effect exerted on the possibilities for research cooperation. Since research cooperation is one of the major themes of the present book, this issue is examined in detail and it is concluded that the Japanese government (and Nippon Telegraph and Telephone (NTT) as an important procurer) have played important roles in economizing on the transaction costs involved in establishing research cooperation between competing firms, thus increasing benefits derived from the economies of research cooperation. The second problem posed by competition which is examined here is the negative effect exerted on the diffusion of technological knowledge. Here again it is shown that the Japanese government has played an important role in increasing diffusion beyond what otherwise would have taken place.

An important theme that threads its way through this concluding chapter is the development of the concept of a *Japanese Technology-Creating System.* This system contains the major Japanese organizations and institutions which individually and in interaction have shaped the process of technical change in Japan. One important function which the system has played is to *blend the various bounded visions* of the different organizations, thereby improving the ability of the system to acquire, assimilate, create and diffuse new technologies.

Finally, a few concluding notes deal with the comparison of the Japanese industrial electronics and consumer electronics sectors, the role of government financing of investment in innovation for 'the day after tomorrow', economics and technical change, and the continued evolution of the Japanese System.

International competitiveness and technical change

Japanese economic performance in particular industries and in aggregate is easily enough described. Far more difficult, however, is the task of *explanation*. The explanations that are the main concerns of the present book deal primarily with the process of technical change. We begin with a discussion of some of the kinds of technical change that have been brought about mainly by the Japanese companies themselves and which have had an important impact on their achievement of international competitiveness.

Incremental technical change and the linear model

Technical change lies at the heart of the achievement of international competitiveness. In order to become, and remain, internationally competitive, a firm will have to acquire, assimilate and create new technologies. The rate of acquisition, assimilation and creation must be particularly rapid in those industries where the science and technology base is undergoing a quick transformation, such as in the case of the industry under study, the computer and electronic devices industry.

The Japanese experience in areas such as computers and electronic devices, however (not to mention other discrete products industries such as motor cars, consumer electronics, cameras, etc.), has taught us that the acquisition, assimilation and creation of technological knowledge, and correspondingly the achievement of international competitiveness, does not necessarily require the mastery of basic or fundamental science or quantum leaps in knowledge. The Japanese experience thus confirms the results of detailed studies done in areas such as petrochemicals (Enos, 1962) and shipbuilding (Gilfillan, 1935) which concluded that over time the cumulative effect of incremental technical change can be more significant than that of radical technical change.

Reflecting on the Japanese example, many researchers have stressed the need to break with a so-called linear model of technical change which emphasizes the sequence: basic research—applied research—development—marketing; for a recent rejection see Aoki and Rosenberg (1987). Since, it is argued, Japanese international competitiveness has been based on strength in the 'downstream' areas, this sequential model does not hold. While it is correct to criticize the linearity of the model and insist that it be replaced by a more complex model with feedback loops linking the activities from basic research to marketing, it is worth remembering that in most areas Japanese companies have tended to begin with the 'downstream' areas and have gradually moved further 'upstream' into areas of oriented-basic and basic research. In many cases this has meant that the latter kinds of research have been more closely tied to the commercialization of goods and services.

Intra-firm forms of organization that facilitate innovation

Recent research on international competitiveness and technical change in the discrete products industries in Japan has stressed the importance of forms of organization which have evolved within Japanese firms which facilitate innovation through the effective mobilization of flows of information and the utilization of these flows as an input for innovation. The following serve as examples of these forms of organization:

Just-in-time production, the elimination of buffer stocks and total quality control

The organizational practices of just-in-time, the elimination of buffer stocks, and total quality control may be analysed as forms of organization designed to mobilize information flows and use them for innovation. For instance, if components are to be produced and delivered just-in-time to be used in the assembly process, it is necessary that they meet the required quality control standards. In turn this requires that sufficient information be assembled to ensure adequate quality. The elimination of buffer stocks, by creating a costly shutdown of the production line when defective components are discovered, serves also to generate what may be referred to as high-priority information on defects, while at the same time creating a strong incentive to take immediate measures to correct such defects. (This point is elaborated upon and stressed by Schonberger (1982).) Total quality control, which has been extended to areas such as management practices and software quality control, similarly serves to mobilize feedback flows of information which are used as an input to improve quality. Such feedback flows, for example, are mobilized from customers and other users, and from company employees working in small groups to consider self-consciously how to improve quality in their particular segment of the total set of the company's activities. (See, for example, the NEC diagram on total quality control reproduced as Appendix 1.)

Decentralization

Reinforcing the organizational practices discussed above, are a number of characteristics that typify Japanese corporations. According to Aoki and Rosenberg (1987) and Aoki (1988), the first characteristic is the reliance upon on-site information. 'Instead of the systematic approach to problem-solving through the centralization of information and direction, problem-solving in the Japanese organizational context is typically decentralized and relegated to the lowest possible level of the formal hierarchy. Politically, this dispersed problem-solving provides considerable autonomy to the operating subordinate unit' (Aoki and Rosenberg, 1987, p. 11) The second characteristic is semi-horizontal communications. 'When problem-solving must be dealt with co-jointly by multiple functional units, direct communication among the relevant units, without the clear direction of a common superordinate, is typical ... Politically the Japanese organization may appear as a coalition of semi-autonomous component units rather than as a coherent whole directed by the visible authority of the central office' (p. 12). The final characteristic is the ranking hierarchy that exists in Japanese organizations. Personnel 'are ranked according to seniority and merit ... [and] are evaluated by their contributions to collective, semi-autonomous problem-solving rather than by some more abstract measure of their individual skills. Promotion often takes the form of transfer to other departments ... the cross-jurisdictional transfer of personnel facilitates and reinforces the semi-horizontal communications among functional subunits' (p. 12)

Information flows between the R & D laboratories and the production divisions

Effective flows of information between the R & D laboratories and the production divisions smooth and blend the interface between these two specialized parts of the Japanese corporation. Various organizational practices facilitate these effective flows of information. One example is the usual practice of recruiting new R & D workers with master's degrees rather than PhDs – in about 80 per cent of cases in some of the large electronics corporations. Advanced research training then tends to be provided within the companies rather than in the universities (the companies having an incentive to do so by the institution of lifetime employment which eliminates the externality resulting from the turnover of labour). One important implication of this practice is that R & D workers tend to lack the 'academicism' and 'professionalism' of many of their doctoral colleagues in Western countries, are more easily moulded to the needs of the corporation such as the need for research to be part of a process of value creation and commercialization rather than being an end in itself, and tend to be able to communicate more effectively with those specializing in production divisions. Frequent transfer of staff in both directions between research laboratories and production divisions (a transfer from the former to the latter often constituting a promotion), further lubricates the interface. The difficulty of exit from the Japanese corporation as a result of lifetime employment further facilitates the 'mouldability' of R & D workers.

A further practice which facilitates effective information flows between R & D laboratories and production divisions is that involving the funding of the laboratories. According to this practice, a substantial proportion of the budget of R & D laboratories (usually around 50 per cent) comes from production divisions, tied to demands that they express for particular research topics to be undertaken. In this way production divisions are able to 'pull' the research done in the laboratories in the direction of their needs. The other 50 per cent of the budget usually comes from central company resources, thus ensuring that there is also a 'seeds-push' element in the research of the laboratories. It is only relatively recently that basic research laboratories, receiving 100 per cent of their budget from central resources, have been established in Japanese electronics companies and it is still too early to assess how these laboratories will interface with the production divisions.

Vertical integration

Frequently referred to, but less frequently carefully analysed, are the advantages that follow from the vertical integration of core technological activities. These advantages may also be analysed from the point of view of mobilizing, and utilizing, effectively flows of information.

A significant difference between the form of organization of many of the large Japanese electronics corporations and some of their Western counterparts, is the degree of vertical integration of such core technological activities. Vertical integration is defined here as the possession in-house of core technological capabilities in the areas of devices, stand-alone systems incorporating these devices (e.g. computers, digital switches, etc.), and broader systems integrating the stand-alone systems (e.g. communications systems). In this sense, Japanese electronics firms, at least the largest amongst them, are highly vertically integrated, even though they also depend on a network of subcontractors for the production of technologically simpler components. (There is, of course, also a degree of inter-firm specialization in the production of capital goods, equipment and materials for the electronics industry.)

The economics of information flows suggests that this form of vertical integration may have efficiency properties exceeding that of the alternative of vertical disintegration. One example to make this clearer is that of the relationship between the semiconductor division and the computer division in a technologically vertically integrated company (as discussed earlier in this book in the quotation from Taiyu Kobayashi of Fujitsu).[1] In the case of Fujitsu, the decision was made to merge the activities of these two divisions. This was done so that the designers of semiconductors could interact closely with the designers of computers, sharing information so that the needs of one group would be taken into account as an influence on the activities of the other group. In Kobayashi's view, Fujitsu had an advantage over other technologically vertically integrated computer-producing companies where the semiconductor division was not similarly integrated with the computer division and where the former division produced semiconductors for consumer products as well as for computers. The reason, according to Kobayashi, is that in these cases the semiconductor division is 'pulled' by the incompatible needs of the consumer goods and computer divisions, resulting in semiconductors that are not optimally designed and produced for the purpose of computer performance.

Can such information flows occur effectively between distinct companies interacting through the market? In other words, would the flow of information be as effective if Semiconductor Company and Computer Company were two autonomous profitmaking entities? If this were the case there would be a number of hurdles that would have to be overcome before an efficient flow of information could occur between the companies.

To begin with, Computer Company would have to provide Semiconductor Company with the necessary information that will enable the latter to design and produce semiconductors that are particularly well suited in terms of computer cost and performance. However, once this information is provided, Computer Company will have limited control over the way in which it is used by Semiconductor Company. For example, Semiconductor Company may find profitable opportunities for selling the semiconductors also to other computer companies which compete with Computer Company. This difficulty could be overcome by the specification of a written or verbal contract between the two companies limiting the use of the information provided by Computer Company. In practice, however, it might be extremely difficult to specify in contractual form the relevant information provided by Computer Company and distinguish it from that possessed by Semiconductor Company. Furthermore, there is the possibility that Semiconductor Company might opportunistically exploit the situation once it has effective possession of the information provided by Computer Company. Difficulties such as these might imply high transaction costs in reaching an agreement.

Further problems arise from the existence of what might be referred to as *bounded vision*. By and large, companies (more specifically, the people working in the companies) 'see' and 'know' things that are closely related to what they do. Accordingly, the employees of Computer Company may not 'see' the potential importance of information, which they either have or could acquire, which might be useful for the employees of Semiconductor Company in their design and production of semiconductors suited for the design and development of computers. Likewise, Semiconductor Company employees might not see the importance of information that they could provide to Computer Company. This information gap created by the bounded vision of the companies could be overcome by a closer interaction of the relevant employees of both companies. This, however, would create further difficulties. For example, the company may fear a leakage of knowledge – as a result, say, of visits from the engineers of the other company – which may negatively affect profitability or market share. Furthermore, the company might want to be compensated for the time of employees taken up as a result of their interactions with staff of the other company. Yet it would be difficult to decide *ex ante* on the magnitude of this compensation without knowing the value of the information flows that would result and would be harnessed by the company.

These sorts of difficulties are less likely to arise in a technologically vertically integrated company. As we saw above, decentralization in Japanese companies has facilitated effective intra-corporate information flows.

The Japanese Technology-Creating System

The forms of organization which have just been analysed are to be found in most of the large Japanese electronics companies. This suggests that there are *national characteristics* which distinguish the Japanese case from that of other countries and which have an influence on the international competitiveness of Japanese companies. In turn these characteristics, the outcome of the historical evolution of the Japanese political economy, suggest that it is meaningful to develop a conceptualization of a Japanese Technology-Creating System, or Japanese System for short. The usefulness of the system concept is that it requires (1) an identification of the components of the system, (2) a specification of the interrelationships between these components, and (3) an analysis of the ways in which the interrelationships affect the system as a whole. As will be seen later, in developing the concept of a Japanese System it will be necessary to take account of the transformations of this system over time and the relationship of this national system to that of other national systems which together comprise a global system. Since the present objective is an analysis of technical change in the Japanese computer and electronic devices industry, not a purely theoretical objective, the concept of a Japanese System will be developed in a relatively concrete way through an analysis of this particular industry.

The intra-firm forms of organization which have just been analysed, forms of organization which evolved over time for complex reasons, have had an important influence on the comparative international performance of the Japanese System. The reason is that these forms of organization have facilitated primarily incremental technical changes which have positively affected the international competitiveness of Japanese electronics companies. The results can be seen in the pattern of trade in electronics-related products between Japan and its trading partners.

The mobilization of information flows in order to effect incremental improvements can provide an important source of beneficial change once the production process and the associated technologies have been established. Under these circumstances, innovation may be seen as a process of incremental change for 'tomorrow'. However, problems of a qualitatively different kind arise in innovation for 'the day after tomorrow'. The reason is that *uncertainty* (as opposed to risk for which a probability distribution can be derived in order to assist the making of decisions) becomes a key factor in the decision-making environment. As the empirical chapters of the present study have shown, one of the distinctive characteristics of the Japanese System has resulted from the way in which various types of uncertainty have been confronted in order to facilitate the long-term acquisition, creation and diffusion of technological knowledge. To grasp this important feature of the Japanese System, it is necessary to go beyond the analysis of intra-firm forms of organization.

The problems posed by uncertainty: a general analysis

Investment in innovation can be negatively affected by uncertainty with consequent negative implications for the performance of the national system. It is necessary to distinguish here two types of uncertainty. *Type I uncertainty* refers to the inherently uncertain outcome of research: if the outcome were certain, it would not be necessary to do the research since the results would be known in advance. This uncertainty exerts a negative influence on the incentive to undertake research. This negative effect is particularly strong in organizations which depend on the generation of profit. *Type II uncertainty* refers to the uncertain ability of an investor in innovation to reap an adequate rate of return from the investment. This uncertainty is the result of the 'public good' nature of technological knowledge which implies that the knowledge may be acquired by others at a cost significantly lower than that incurred by the creator of that knowledge. Type II uncertainty also reduces the incentive to invest in research.

Under some circumstances, type I and type II uncertainty may be responsible for 'market failure': that is, the inability of private companies acting and interacting in the absence of government intervention, to produce an appropriate amount of investment in innovation. This then creates a dilemma which different national systems deal with in different ways.

It should be noted, however, that uncertainty does not always result in market failure. To begin with, in some cases the expected return from a successful innovation may be so high as to more than outweigh the negative effects of type I uncertainty. Secondly, firms have a number of strategies available to them with which to attempt to reduce type II uncertainty. One possibility is for a firm to apply for a patent which will for a time legally restrict the ability of others to use the technology. This strategy is, however, subject to the limitation of others illegally using the technology, or using the information disclosed in the patent records to assist in 'innovating around' the patent. Another possibility is for the firm to keep the technology secret. A further possibility is for the firm to seek 'first mover' advantages by immediately commercializing the technology and establishing a head-start by progressing down the learning-curve, achieving a lower cost structure and higher market share, and perhaps customer loyalty. To the extent that one or more of these strategies are successful, type II uncertainty will be reduced and market failure may not occur.

A third reason why uncertainty may not result in market failure is that the degree of uncertainty involved may be too small to significantly reduce the incentive to invest in innovation. This may be the case in many incremental innovations (which, as noted earlier, may be more important cumulatively than major breakthroughs).

This third point suggests, in turn, that, in examining the effects of uncertainty, it is important to distinguish between the creation of new technologies for 'tomorrow' and for the 'day after tomorrow'. In the former case, the degree of uncertainty may sometimes be relatively low with the result that disincentive effects are not problematical. When creating technologies for the day after tomorrow, however, the degree of uncertainty is likely to be far more significant, raising the problem of the incentive to invest in innovation. In general, the longer term the research, all other things being equal, the greater the problem of type I uncertainty. This is a major dilemma confronted by all capitalist national systems.

A related dilemma results from the existence of type I uncertainty. As a result of this kind of uncertainty, it is necessary for the long-term international competitiveness of national systems that they generate *diversity* in innovation. Since it is unclear which research areas will become commercially important, it is necessary to ensure that a fairly wide range of alternatives are covered in order to reduce the overall probability of picking losers. However, the need for diversity on the one hand, and the incentive system which guides investment in innovation on the other, may often be in conflict. The greater is the expected type I uncertainty in a research area, the less likely is it that resources will be allocated to research in this area, thus reducing the likelihood of diversity resulting from research in this field. Once again this raises questions regarding the ways in which national systems have coped with this dilemma.

(In passing it is worth pointing out that, from the point of view of the global system as a whole, it is diversity which underlies the evolutionary process of technical and economic change. The market process acts as a selection mechanism, akin to natural selection in the biological model, selecting those innovations which meet its criteria and resulting in an expansion of those firms and organizations which are the 'bearers' of the selected innovations. From the point of view of the national system, however, the dilemma is how to generate the necessary degree of diversity.)

Uncertainty and the Japanese System

At different stages in the development of the Japanese computer and electronic devices industry, different kinds of uncertainty-related problems were confronted. In order to analyse these problems and the way in which they were tackled in the Japanese System it is helpful to periodize the evolution of the industry. The following three periods (which are derived from the historical chapter in this book) may be distinguished:

a. Early Catching-Up Period, 1945–1965
b. Late Catching-Up Period, 1966–1979
c. Frontier-Leading Period (except for basic research), 1980–present.

The ways in which uncertainty was dealt with in each of these three periods will now be analysed.

Early Catching-Up Period, 1945–1965

In the early years of this period, several key innovations occurred which gave birth to the new information technology industry, namely the development of the first computers and transistors. Significantly, the companies which were to become the 'bearers' of the new pervasive information technologies were in these years heavily committed to neighbouring technologies. In chapter 2, these companies were divided into two groups, the one involved in the telecommunications field and consisting of NEC, Hitachi, Fujitsu and Oki, and the other involved largely in the area of heavy electrical equipment. This second group included Hitachi, Toshiba and Mitsubishi Electric.

It is significant that until around 1959 or 1960 none of these companies played a leading role in Japan in assimilating, further developing and diffusing the new information technologies. The case of Fujitsu is a particularly significant example, because this company was the first among both groups of companies to seize the initiative and develop its own computer, the FACOM 100, a relay-based computer completed in 1954. Fujitsu was later to become the leading Japanese computer company in terms of market share in Japan. However, although the 'computer seed' emerged at an early stage in Fujitsu, it lay dormant for a long time in the company. It was only after 1959 when Kanjiro Okada became President of Fujitsu, a time when the computer market both in Japan and in Western countries was beginning to grow and a number of Western companies had already committed themselves to this market, that computers were given high priority in the company. The FACOM 100 was developed in Fujitsu on the basis of a grant received from the Ministry of International Trade and Industry, rather than from the company's own resources. In 1960 a new Electronics Department was established in Fujitsu to produce computers; until then computers were produced in the wing of a factory making communication equipment.

It is important to understand why Fujitsu took so long to seize the opportunity presented by the emergence of the new information technologies. Taiyu Kobayashi, who was one of the main pioneers of computer development in Fujitsu and who later became Chairman of the company's Board, provides an important insight into this question. Noting that the computer group in Fujitsu was until 1959 'still viewed with the bias accorded a step-child' by most of the company's directors, Kobayashi recalled that 'more than half of the directors preferred a more cautious course of action which dealt with known quantities. Rather than attempting some unknown . . . if we stuck to contract work for Nippon Telegraph and Telephone [NTT], it had the advantages a long and steady relationship offers, as well as the prospect of assured profitability' (T. Kobayashi, 1986, pp. 44–75).

Several important points emerge from this account. The first is that at this time the majority of the directors of Fujitsu were deciding, under conditions of type I and type II uncertainty, not to prioritize the production of computers. As a result of type I uncertainty, they were unsure whether investment by Fujitsu in computer research would produce the necessary technological capabilities for competitive computer production. The existence of type II uncertainty meant that they were also unsure whether Fujitsu, as a result of the activities of competing firms, would be able to appropriate an adequate rate of return from its investment in innovation (that is, innovation at the level of the company). The second point is that this decision was made against the background of Fujitsu's existing relationship with NTT. As part of the so-called Den Den family of supplying firms, Fujitsu was involved in a long-term, stable and relatively certain relationship with NTT as a supplier of telecommunications equipment. The uncertainty of the computer market, together with the relative certainty of NTT's telecommunications purchases, resulted in a disincentive for Fujitsu, a for-profit organization, to enter the field of computers. Similarly, the other companies that were to become the leaders of the Japanese electronics industry were at this time also preoccupied with their major markets in telecommunications and heavy electrical equipment with the result that they too failed to take the initiative and lead the development in Japan of the new information technologies.

During the first part of the Early Catching-Up Period, it was government research institutes and universities, rather than the for-profit companies, which played the leadership role in the Japanese System, acquiring, further developing and diffusing the new technologies. As shown in chapter 2, there is evidence to suggest that by 1953 or 1954 computing had become a priority area for development in the Ministry of International Trade and Industry's Electrotechnical Laboratory, beginning to rival energy research which had been its main *raison d'être*. A little later, NTT's Electrical Communications Laboratories, also a government organization, entered the computing field with the development of the Musashino-1 computer in 1957 which was based on the parametron developed at Tokyo University. Both the Musashino-1 and the ETL IV, ETL's second transistorized computer introduced also in 1957, were transferred to the Japanese companies at a subsidized cost and became their first commercially significant computers.

This sequence of events has a number of implications for the functioning of the Japanese System during the first part of the Early Catching-Up Period. The most important implication is that as a result of uncertainty, a situation of market failure arose and the companies failed to take the initiative in acquiring, developing and diffusing the new information technologies. In the absence of the activities of government institutions, the most important being ETL and ECL, it is indisputable that the companies would have taken significantly longer to enter the computer market and that of related electronic devices. In the event, however, the cost of entry was subsidized by these government institutions, whose research activities had the consequence of reducing the uncertainty that the firms confronted, since proven working models developed in these institutions were made available at very low cost to the companies. Although less important than the government research institutions, several universities also played a significant role through the computer research which they did, some of which also had the effect of reducing the entry cost of the private companies.

It may be concluded, therefore, that the roles played in the Japanese System by the two kinds of organization, for-profit companies and government research institutions, were highly complementary. While the existence of uncertainty deterred the for-profit companies from entering the computer market at this early stage, the government research institutions, having access to government funding which was not contingent upon the generation of commercial profits, and having as one of their primary briefs assisting the development of technological capabilities in Japanese companies, were able to compensate for this area of weakness in the Japanese System.

The job of dealing with uncertainty in the area of computers, however, was not undertaken solely by the government research institutions. MITI and NTT also played an extremely important role, similarly reducing the negative effects of uncertainty. Here mention must be made of measures such as the protection of the domestic market for computers which, by excluding more efficient foreign producers of computers, had the effect of reducing type II uncertainty confronting the computer-producing firms. Likewise, the Ministry of Education, by ensuring that the universities would only purchase Japanese-made computers, guaranteed that this extremely important market in the early stages of the computer industry would be reserved for Japanese companies. By helping to establish the Japan Electronic Computer Company, MITI and the Japan Development Bank further expanded the potential market for computers in Japan while alleviating the possible cash-flow difficulties of the companies. NTT, as a rapidly increasing market for large computers, also helped to reduce the uncertainty facing its suppliers, Fujitsu, Hitachi and NEC. As a result of the extremely important role played by NTT, both as a significant market for the Den Den firms and as a central source for the creation of generic and long-term technologies in the Electrical Communications Laboratories, NTT and ECL constituted key components of the Japanese Technology-Creating System in the electronics area.

In the early 1960s, MITI and the firms, realizing that a significant technology gap remained *vis-à-vis* other Western computer producers, took steps to reduce this gap while at the same time reducing the degree of type I uncertainly, by licensing technology from the major American computer companies (with the notable exception of IBM). Only Fujitsu failed to enter into a licensing agreement. At the same time, efforts were increased to enhance in a complementary way the technological capabilities of the Japanese companies. In part, these efforts took the form of national cooperative research projects that will be considered in more detail later. In this way, the import of foreign technology and the strengthening of domestic technological capabilities through the promotion and protection of the Japanese computer and electronic devices industry, went hand-in-hand.

Late Catching-Up Period, 1966–1979

By 1966 the locus of research activity in the area of computers and electronic devices had shifted firmly to the companies. Fujitsu, Hitachi, NEC, Toshiba, Mitsubishi Electric and Oki were now firmly committed to the new information technologies. While ETL continued to play an important role both in the direct undertaking of research and in the coordination of many of the MITI-initiated cooperative research projects (which are considered in more detail below), its activities served primarily as a complement, rather than a substitute, for research initiatives undertaken in the companies. Nevertheless, ETL made a significant contribution by serving as part of MITI's 'technical antennae', making assessments independently of the firms of areas of strength and weakness in the Japanese electronics industry and taking steps to initiate national research programmes in order to redress the weaknesses. For example, it was ETL researchers who in the 1960s first identified the memory area as a critical bottleneck in computer technology and who emphasized the importance of research in this field in a number of MITI-initiated national research projects. ECL, on the other hand, as the research arm of NTT, which had responsibility for the management and development of the national telecommunications network, played a slightly different role. Together with NTT planners who were concerned with the quantitative and qualitative improvement of the telecommunications network, ECL researchers played an even more directive role, initiating numerous cooperative R&D projects together with researchers from the Den Den firms.[2]

Uncertainty was also injected into the Japanese System as a result of the unpredictable actions of competitors. Two important examples were the introduction by IBM, the company that had a dominant lead in world markets, of its System 360 in 1964 and System 370 in 1970. It is illuminating to analyse the responses of the various components of the Japanese System to these moves by IBM.

System 360, which was based on hybrid integrated circuits, constituted a major breakthrough allowing a significant reduction in both the cost and size of mainframe computers. In Japan, System 360 was extremely successful, being used in the 1964 Tokyo Olympic Games and being purchased by a number of Japanese banks. The organizations which constituted the Japanese System responded in several ways to the introduction of System 360. To begin with, those Japanese corporations which had technology licensing agreements with American counterparts soon introduced System 360-compatible models. This was done by Hitachi, NEC and Toshiba which had technology agreements with RCA, Honeywell and General Electric, respectively. For these companies, licensing provided one way of reducing the uncertainty resulting from a rival's major breakthrough. In 1965 Fujitsu began to modify its existing 230 series, culminating in the FACOM 230-60 which was influenced by System 360 and was introduced in 1968. According to the company, the FACOM 230-60 was a 'strategic turning-point' for Fujitsu, allowing it to move past NEC and Hitachi into first place in 1968 with the largest market share amongst the Japanese computer-producing companies.

Important steps were also taken by MITI to help the firms reduce the technology gap with their foreign competitors and therefore decrease the uncertainty which they confronted. A notable example is the Very High Speed Computer System Project, 1966–72, which MITI initiated. Since this project is analysed at length in chapter 2, the detailed conclusions of the analysis will not be repeated here. It is simply noted that it was concluded that, while it is likely that the Japanese computer and related electronic devices industry would have continued to grow and narrow the technology gap in the absence of the VHSCS Project, this project nevertheless contributed to the strengthening of the Japanese industry largely through the resources that were made available for research, although these were not particularly large, and the process of inter-firm specialization that was encouraged by the project. In this way government assisted in reducing some of the effects of uncertainty.

Far more serious, however, than System 360 was the introduction by IBM of System 370 in 1970. This event injected a substantial dose of uncertainty into the international computer industry, including that in the United States and Japan. As a result of System 370, General Electric, RCA and TRW of the United States terminated their mainframe computer activities. In turn this had knock-on effects for Toshiba, Hitachi and Mitsubishi which had signed technology agreements with these firms in the early 1960s. In addition to coping with System 370, Japanese computer producers also had to contend with the gradual removal of restrictions on foreign trade and investment which implied increasing competitive pressures on the domestic market.

There were a number of responses in the Japanese System to these uncertainty-raising events and these are analysed in detail in chapter 2. To summarize, the firms themselves renewed their efforts to upgrade their models in order to compete with System 370. However, these efforts were strongly supported by government organizations. In order to reduce the technology gap which had widened significantly with the introduction of System 360 and strengthen the technological capabilities of the Japanese companies, MITI pursued a strategy consisting of three components. Firstly, *substantial* financial support, detailed in chapter 2, was given to the companies. In view of the magnitude of this support, it is clear that the Japanese government played an extremely important role in significantly reducing some of the deleterious short-term effects of uncertainty. Without this financial support it is highly likely that several of the Japanese companies would have immediately exited from the mainframe computer market. Secondly, MITI set up a number of cooperative research projects with the major Japanese companies involved in the computer industry. These included the Mainframe Computer Project (or the 3.5 Generation Project as it was commonly referred to) 1972–76 which aimed at the development of Japanese models that would compete with System 370. Thirdly, MITI attempted to encourage merger or closer inter-firm coordination amongst the Japanese computer-producing companies. While attempts to merge firms failed, three couplings of firms were established: Fujitsu–Hitachi which concentrated on the production of IBM-compatible models; NEC–Toshiba which produced non-IBM-compatible computers; and Mitsubishi–Oki which produced the COSMOS series of computers. Through this arrangement the Japanese System as a whole was able to further reduce uncertainty by pursuing simultaneously the two major strategies that computer companies worldwide had developed to cope with the hugely dominant IBM, namely the IBM-compatible and the independent strategies.

MITI, however, was only partly successful in its attempt to encourage inter-firm coordination. While MITI aimed at encouraging a degree of inter-firm specialization by getting the firms to produce different computer models with different characteristics, the firms soon introduced directly competing models. Furthermore, MITI support for the computer industry was insufficient to enable the survival of all of the Japanese participants in this industry. While Toshiba, Mitsubishi and Oki benefited greatly from the various electronics-related MITI projects in some of their activities, by the end of the 1970s they had all made the decision to exit from the mainframe computer market. Ironically, the objective that MITI had identified of bringing about a greater concentration amongst Japanese mainframe producers was achieved, not through government pressure or negotiation, but through the market process. Some of the Japanese companies were more able to survive than others.

However, this market process in part bore some of the distinctive characteristics of the Japanese System. Thus it was no random event that the three companies which survived in the mainframe market were Fujitsu, Hitachi and NEC. As noted earlier, these three companies were the most important members of the so-called Den Den Family which supplied NTT. As late as 1981, for example, at a time when its international sales had increased significantly, NEC still depended on NTT for 12 per cent of total company sales. In 1968, in the wake of the introduction of IBM's System 360, NTT had established, with Fujitsu, Hitachi and NEC, the DIPS Project (Dendenkosha Information Processing System) designed to produce mainframe computers for use in the telecommunications network. This project, which has continued producing upgraded models to the present day, drew on the results of some of the MITI-initiated projects such as the Very High Speed Computer System Project, 1966–72. However, access to the lucrative NTT market was highly restricted as Fujitsu itself had discovered when in the early 1960s, when the company was behind NEC and Hitachi on the Japanese computer market, it had tried to enter this market. As Fujitsu's Taiyu Kobayashi later recalled:

Nippon Telegraph and Telephone [was] one of Fujitsu's main customers – primarily for telephone switching equipment. We also ... tried to sell them computers ... However, they had an unwritten policy that worked against us. Regardless of how hard we strove, as a manufacturer late to the market, we were not able to displace NEC which was there first. A friend of mine at Nippon Telegraph and Telephone told me, 'If you want to obtain a lion's share of the orders from us, you have to become the undisputed leader so well known in markets outside NTT's sphere of influence, that everyone will be asking why we are not buying Fujitsu equipment (T. Kobayashi, 1986, p. 46).

As this quotation makes clear, the 'market process' in the telecommunications area in the Japanese System at this stage, a process that helped to ensure the survival in the mainframe computer market of Fujitsu, Hitachi and NEC, was qualitatively different from the corn market envisaged by Marshall and other economists.

Frontier-leading period (except for basic research), 1980–present:
the importance of oriented-basic research

By the end of the 1970s Japanese companies had reached the international technology frontier in many areas of computers and related electronic devices. Some indicators of this state of affairs, discussed in more detail in chapter 2, are the achievement of performance levels comparable to those of IBM computers by the middle to late 1970s, and the increasing share of the international memory semiconductor market attained by Japanese companies.

Having reached the international technology frontier in these areas, however, the Japanese System now had to deal with a qualitatively different type of uncertainty. In the catching-up period, uncertainty related not so much to the technologies themselves, since it was clear from observing the products of the leaders which technologies were viable. In this sense Japanese companies benefited from being IBM-followers. During the catching-up period uncertainty related more to the ability of the follower to master the existing technologies in order to remain in the game and earn reasonable rates of return on the investments required to do so. *However, once the technology frontier had been reached, uncertainty related more to the technologies themselves* since it was no longer possible to assess viable technologies by following the leader.

From the late 1970s, high priority was given, both by the Japanese companies and by MITI and NTT, to the undertaking of what may be called *oriented-basic research*. While this research differed from what is usually understood by the concepts of 'basic', 'scientific' or 'curiosity-oriented' research, it also differed from conventional applied or developmental research. Although the aim of oriented-basic research was the development of technologies that would, as the end result of the development process, be commercialized, this kind of research necessitated delving more deeply into the technologies themselves so that they might be further advanced. These characteristics of oriented-basic research will become clearer when some of the technologies that were chosen for development are discussed.

There were a number of related reasons for the rapidly growing importance of oriented-basic research in the Japanese System:

(i) The fact of having caught up meant that there was less to learn from the leaders and that more research had therefore to be done in the Japanese System.

(ii) The possibility, and the increasing reality, of being denied technology by competing companies and their governments already at the technology frontier made it more important to further deepen Japanese technological capabilities.

(iii) The evolution of what may be referred to as a 'reverse linear sequence', that is the progression from production to development to applied research, resulted in an increasing 'compulsion' to undertake oriented-basic research. Through the undertaking of developmental research, problems and puzzles were thrown up which required more oriented-basic research for their resolution.

(iv) A combination of 'science push', that is the availability as a result of scientific research of new potentially commercially important technological opportunities, and government efforts to reduce the effects of type I uncertainty by heavily subsidizing the early costs of exploiting these opportunities, also influenced the increasing importance of oriented-basic research. Although these technological opportunities existed before in the Catching-up Period (a) the capabilities did not exist for undertaking oriented-basic research, and (b) the priorities of both companies and government did not emphasize the importance of this kind of research; they preferred to concentrate efforts on more practical developmental research. (An exception to this statement is probably the PIPS Project, which, as noted in chapter 2, was more concerned with what is referred to here as oriented-basic research.)

(v) Finally, growing international pressure on Japan, as an important beneficiary from the 'international stock of public scientific and technological knowledge', to increase its contribution to this stock also contributed to the greater importance of oriented-basic research.

As a result of a combination of these factors, a number of projects were initiated by MITI in the late 1970s which were analysed in detail in the empirical chapters of this book. Here these projects will be discussed from the point of view of the question of dealing with uncertainty. Later the issue of research cooperation will be examined. Table 9.1 provides a summary of the oriented-basic research done in the projects analysed in this book. A number of important conclusions follow from these projects:

(i) In all cases, the research areas chosen stressed potentially important

Table 9.1. *Oriented-basic research areas in five MITI-initiated projects*

Project	Research areas
VLSI	Electron-beam lithography
Optical Measurement and Control	Optoelectronic integrated circuits; GaAs-based optoelectronic devices; optoelectronic systems
High-Speed Computing System	Josephson junctions; GaAs-based high-speed devices (HEMTs, GaAs FETs); parallel processing
Future Electronic Devices	Three-dimensional devices; superlattices; environmentally resistant devices; biochips
Fifth Generation Computer	Logic programming-based hardware and software

future technologies, rather than technologies currently in use in Japanese firms. The choice of projects shows that an implicit assumption guiding the choice was that the firms themselves were capable of further developing their current technologies and in this task did not require government assistance. The partial exception to this conclusion is the VLSI Project, the earliest of the projects examined in detail in this book, which began in 1976. In this project, one of the technologies which received attention was optical lithography. However, great stress was placed in the project on electron-beam technology in the (mistaken) belief that this technology would become important in the near future in VLSI production. In the event, however, while optical lithography technology was further developed so that it could be used to deal with sub-micron circuit widths, an event not anticipated by the organizers of the project, electron-beam technology for the direct writing of circuits, as opposed to its use in mask production, is likely to soon become important in the era of ultra-large-scale integration, or ULSI. Hitachi, for example, in 1988 announced the development of an electron beam lithography system for the direct drawing of circuit patterns onto silicon wafers with a 0.1 micron line width. Hitachi expects this system to be used in the development of 256 Mbit and 1 Gbit dynamic random access memories (DRAMS). Interestingly, the research on which this system was based was done under the VLSI research programme initiated by NTT in 1974, two years before the MITI VLSI project began, involving Fujitsu, Hitachi and NEC.[3]

The fact that the technologies chosen were future technologies, not well developed at the time of their choice, is a further justification for the term oriented-basic research, used to describe the technologies developed under these MITI-initiated projects.

(ii) *In all cases an important degree of uncertainty surrounded the commercial viability of the technologies chosen, with the result that the firms probably would have allocated significantly less resources to research in these areas in the absence of the MITI-initiated projects.* This central point is analysed in detail in each of the projects examined in this book and the reader is referred to the relevant chapter.

(iii) Taken as a whole, the technologies chosen for development in these projects represent many of the 'core' technologies that may, on the basis of present knowledge, be important in the computer and electronic devices industry until the end of the century. Again this point is examined in detail in each of the projects.

(iv) In most of the projects it was MITI/ETL officials who initiated the proposals for research, rather than representatives from the Japanese companies. This observation raises an important question since there was nothing which prevented company representatives from making their own proposals for research projects; through the many MITI-related policy fora this could have been readily done. Why did it tend to be MITI/ETL officials, rather than company employees, who first identified potentially commercially important future technologies, that is, technologies for 'the day after tomorrow'? This important question will be examined later with the development of the concept of 'bounded vision'.

It may therefore be concluded that MITI officials in this period played an important role in reducing the effects of uncertainty by identifying and subsidizing areas for longer term oriented-basic research, that is research for 'the day after tomorrow'.

Competition and the Japanese System

The benefits and costs of competition

In the previous section it has been stressed that an important role has been played in the Japanese System by government organizations which have acted in order to reduce some of the negative effects of uncertainty. *It must be emphasized, however, that uncertainty reduction per se is not necessarily socially beneficial.* A good example in this connection is the introduction in some developing countries of trade protection as an instrument designed to encourage industrialization. While in some cases this measure had the effect of reducing uncertainty by removing the threat of foreign competition, it also had the consequence of removing much of the pressure to innovate. The result in these cases was the emergence of 'permanently infant industries' that failed to become internationally competitive.[4] This example serves to underscore the point that Schumpeter made so lucidly, namely that competition acts as a powerful motive force, 'compelling' innovative change, while at the same time destroying obsolete technologies, capital goods and skills.[5]

While competition has beneficial consequences as a result of the compulsion which it generates for the creation and diffusion of innovation, it has, as Schumpeter also noted, destructive effects too. In this book we have been particularly concerned with two of the negative effects of competition and with the way in which the Japanese System has dealt with these effects. The first effect results from the way in which competitive relations between firms limit their ability to cooperate in research, thus preventing the realization of economies of research cooperation. (While it is also possible that firms could agree to cooperate in research as part of a broader agreement to collude and restrict competition, this has not been the tendency in the Japanese computing and electronic devices industry.)

The second negative effect of competition discussed in this book is the restrictions placed by competing firms on the diffusion of the technological knowledge which underlies their competitiveness. This technological knowledge (not all the technological knowledge under the firm's control) tends to be privatized and monopolized in an effort to protect competitiveness. The result is that the diffusion of this technological knowledge is limited, leading to less social benefit from the use of this knowledge than would be derived if the knowledge were more widely spread. The way in which these negative effects have been dealt with in the Japanese System in the case of the computer and electronic devices industry will be analysed in more detail in this section.

Competition in the Japanese System

For the purposes of this book, competition may be defined as the processes which accompany the offering without collusion by two or more firms of substitutable products (including services) to one or more users who exercise choice between the alternative products.

A central feature of the Japanese Technology-Creating System in the area of computers and electronic devices is the intense competition that exists between Japanese companies, that is both between Japanese-owned companies and between them and the Japanese subsidiaries of foreign-owned companies such as IBM Japan. The intensity of the competition has meant that Japanese companies have been *compelled* to innovate at the same time as they have benefited from government policies which have reduced some of the negative effects of uncertainty. In this way the competitive process has served the Japanese System well, ensuring particularly that downstream manufacturing processes would be efficiently carried out and improved by the Japanese companies. On the other hand in those areas where the market process has been less effective, and where accordingly it has been felt necessary by those managing the major institutions in the Japanese System to go beyond the market, in areas such as the creation and diffusion of technologies for the 'day after tomorrow', the market mechanism has been complemented by other state-initiated measures.

There has been strong competition between Japanese companies in the computer and electronic devices industry. Two indicators of this competition have been given in the present study. The first is the change in the ranking of the industrial electronics companies in terms of Japanese market share. Thus in 1968, for example, Fujitsu replaced NEC and Hitachi as the leading Japanese firm in the computer market. The second indicator comes from the extreme lengths to which Japanese industrial electronics companies have gone, documented in great detail in the present study, to prevent the leakage of knowledge to competing companies. This competition, à la Schumpeter, has meant that the Japanese companies have been under intense pressure to innovate and improve their products. In this way competition has been an important influence on the process of technical change in the Japanese System.

Competition, however, has also influenced the process of technical change in a less positive way, by inhibiting the possibilities of research cooperation between competing firms. It is to this question that attention is now turned.

Research cooperation in the Japanese System

Spontaneous inter-firm exchange of research knowledge

A senior researcher in one of the Japanese industrial electronics firms, when interviewed, told of an occasion when he was invited to an IBM laboratory to present a paper. After giving the paper he was invited into the room of an IBM researcher. The researcher showed him an IBM research paper, marked 'confidential', that dealt with a similar research topic and asked whether the Japanese researcher would like a copy. The Japanese researcher expressed surprise that he had been offered the paper, remarking on the recentness of the paper and its confidential classification. 'Oh, don't worry about that', said the IBM researcher, 'this paper deals with more basic research, but it is knowledge about how to turn this into products that really counts. Besides, you have just given us the benefit of some of the research done inside your company.'

This story illustrates the fact that companies often spontaneously give away some of the knowledge which has been created with the use of company resources. Other examples include research papers published and distributed by the company, and papers presented by company researchers at conferences and in other public fora. Such spontaneous inter-firm exchange of research knowledge may occur for a number of reasons. First, the knowledge may be made public in order to elicit feedback on the research. Comments made by conference participants, further research stimulated by the original company's research, etc., may provide important feedback which facilitates additional learning. Secondly, knowledge made public may be part of an implicit exchange. A company sending researchers to a conference may be implicitly exchanging knowledge with the other companies which do likewise. A failure to provide sufficient knowledge may result in a firm not being invited to the next conference, or to other firms withdrawing their participation. In this way, there may be a tendency over time towards what the companies regard as a fair exchange of information. Thirdly, knowledge may be made public in order to enhance the firm's reputation which in turn may provide the firm with other benefits such as increased sales. Fourthly, and related to the third point, a firm may make some of its research results public in order to recruit researchers attracted by the quality of research in the area.

For these reasons large firms usually spontaneously exchange some of their research knowledge. However, the existence of such spontaneous forms of inter-firm exchange of research knowledge should not be taken to imply that firms find it equally easy to engage in inter-firm research cooperation. In order to elaborate on this point it is necessary first to clarify the social benefits that follow from inter-firm research cooperation.

The economies of research cooperation

In the present book a number of social benefits have been identified which follow from inter-firm research cooperation. These include the following:

  (i) Blending of firm-specific distinctive competences.
 (ii) Avoiding duplication in research.
(iii) Improving 'industrial system coherence', that is inter-firm user–producer relationships, by encouraging specialization and information flows.
 (iv) Pooling information, and specializing in the collection of information, regarding the technologies concerned.
  (v) Enhancing research competition between the cooperating firms.
 (vi) Sharing expensive, non-divisible, equipment.

These benefits are examined in detail in the analyses of the various cooperative research projects and the reader is referred to the relevant chapters for further information.

The relative absence of spontaneous inter-firm research cooperation

In the Japanese computer and electronic devices industry the author was able to discover only two examples in the post-war period, involving the large industrial electronics companies discussed in this book, of spontaneous inter-firm cooperation; that is, cooperation arranged privately between the cooperating firms without the intervention of government agencies or a large procurer.

The first example is that of Nippon Peripherals Ltd, set up by Fujitsu and Hitachi to develop high capacity magnetic disks and memory devices which automatically exchange magnetic cartridges. As discussed in chapter 2, this company was felt to be beneficial for the founding companies, providing several of the economies of research cooperation referred to here. However, the company is very small, and the market for the products which it produces is also small. It therefore cannot be claimed that this is a particularly significant example of research cooperation. The second example is that of cooperation between Fujitsu, Hitachi and Mitsubishi Electric to develop the Global family of 32-bit microprocessors. This project was set up against the background of dominance of the microprocessor market by American producers. However, as stated by Hitachi Technology (1988, p. 9), 'compatibility was the only field in which Hitachi, Fujitsu and Mitsubishi collaborated. In all other aspects of the design process, each company developed its product entirely independently'. Accordingly, it cannot be claimed that this project represents a significant example of research cooperation involving the joint creation and sharing of knowledge.

A puzzle is presented by the coexistence of potentially important economies of research cooperation and the relative absence of spontaneous research cooperation. If research cooperation may be beneficial for private companies, why then do they not spontaneously cooperate more frequently?

The main reason for the lack of spontaneous research cooperation is the transactions costs involved in setting up inter-firm cooperative research. For private Japanese electronics firms these costs have been sufficiently high to significantly inhibit the establishment of spontaneous cooperative research agreements.

A major cause of high transactions costs is the cost of knowledge leakage from the firm. Knowledge leakage refers to events such as the leakage to competing firms of technological knowledge which a company judges is important for its competitiveness, and the leakage of information about the company's strengths, weaknesses and strategies. Even preliminary discussions with competing companies about the possibilities and areas for research cooperation may entail knowledge leakages of these kinds. High transaction costs may result from the incurring of two different types of costs. Firstly, in view of the dangers of knowledge leakage, substantial costs may be incurred in long, complex negotiations as steps are taken to minimize the outflow of knowledge and information. Secondly, further costs may result from the consequences for the firm of its knowledge and information having leaked to competing firms.

Transaction costs also arise from attempts to prevent opportunistic behaviour. As discussed in the empirical chapters, each of the cooperating firms have an incentive to minimize the knowledge it contributes to the cooperative research venture, while maximizing the knowledge it receives from the venture. For example, by sending bright but inexperienced researchers to a joint laboratory, a firm may ensure that it gives little knowledge away, while maximizing the input it receives from the jointly created knowledge. Costly negotiations and measures may be required to guard against such opportunistic behaviour, pushing up transactions costs.

Government and the economizing of the transactions costs involved in research cooperation

For all these reasons, transactions costs have tended to be high, resulting in minimal spontaneous inter-firm research cooperation. *However, an important conclusion of the present book is that government or a large procurer is able to economize on transactions costs thus reducing the costs of research cooperation and ensuring that a greater amount of research cooperation takes place, which in turn facilitates the realization of economies of research cooperation.*

Government or a large procurer is able to play this role primarily by acting as a neutral intermediary, facilitating research cooperation between the competing firms by ensuring that inappropriate knowledge leakages do not occur and preventing the emergence of opportunistic behaviour. For example, companies contemplating cooperative research may be able to disclose to government officials some knowledge of their technologies and information about their strengths, weaknesses and strategies which determine their priorities for cooperative research themes, while being unwilling to divulge this to the representatives of competing companies. Acting as a go-between, government representatives can search for common ground between the firms willing to participate in cooperative research, while maintaining the privacy of knowledge and information which individual companies regard as sensitive. As shown in detail in this book, it is this kind of role which MITI/ETL employees played. A similar role, facilitating and coordinating cooperative research, was played by NTT/ECL personnel.[6] Through the economizing of transactions costs, these officials have reduced the costs of research cooperation, thus increasing the extent of cooperative research between competing Japanese electronics companies.

Kinds of research cooperation

In the present book, two kinds of research cooperation have been distinguished, namely coordinated in-house research (CIHR) and joint research in joint research facilities (JRJF). CIHR involves the coordination by government, or a large procurer, of research among competing companies, with the research being done inside the participating companies. While there may be some exchange of knowledge and information between the participating companies, possibly taking the form of a joint search or a constrained joint search for new technologies, such exchanges will tend to be limited. On the other hand, JRJF, with the cooperative research being done in joint research facilities, involves the joint creation and sharing of knowledge and information. The degree of research cooperation may therefore be thought of as being significantly higher in the case of JRJF. CIHR and JRJF are to be distinguished from isolated in-house research (IIHR) where government subsidizes research but makes no attempt to coordinate this research or establish research cooperation. While the Japanese government has sponsored IIHR (see, for example, the R & D subsidies that have been given[7]) attempts have been made, as shown in the present book, to encourage JRJF, where a priority area involving oriented-basic research has been identified and where the participating firms have been willing to establish joint research facilities, or, failing that, CIHR.

The limitations on JRJF

Another of the important conclusions to emerge from the present book is that JRJF, involving the highest degree of research cooperation, with the joint creation and sharing of knowledge, has been extremely limited in the Japanese computer and electronic devices industry. While three of the five MITI-initiated projects examined in the present book involve some JRJF, in only one, the Fifth Generation Computer Project, has the majority of research resources been allocated to this form of research cooperation. And even in this project some of the research, notably the production of hardware to the specifications drawn up by the joint researchers in ICOT (the Institute for New Generation Computer Technology), has been done in-house. In the case of the Optical Measurement and Control Project, as shown in this book, only 36 per cent of the resources went to the joint laboratory, while in the VLSI Project, often held up as *the* example of Japanese research cooperation, the figure was only 15 to 20 per cent. In the Supercomputer Project and the Future Electronic Devices Project there was no JRJF, although it was argued in the case of the latter project that, while there could have been joint research in joint research facilities, in the event this was prevented by the paucity of resources allocated to the project.

A further conclusion which emerged from this book was that it was the expected *direct* impact of the knowledge to be created through research cooperation on the competitiveness of the firm which determined its willingness to participate in JRJF. *This conclusion runs counter to that which has been put forward arguing that it is basic or generic research which can be undertaken jointly in joint research facilities.* It was argued in the case of the Supercomputer Project, for example, that while areas of basic or generic research could be identified, the refusal of the main participating firms to undertake JRJF must be explained in terms of the expected possible direct impact of the research on the long-run competitiveness of the firm. *This example suggests, furthermore, that in some circumstances the concept of pre-competitive research is misguided.* If research is to be judged to be worth undertaking by a for-profit company, it must be expected, even with uncertainty, to eventually yield competitive advantage. From this point of view, the notion of pre-competitive research in for-profit companies is a contradiction in terms. Competing firms may be willing to enter into JRJF where the expected direct impact of the research on the firm's competitiveness is judged to be insignificant. One example that emerged from both the VLSI and the Optoelectronics Projects is research on the characteristics of materials. Such research could be done through JRJF, not because it was 'pre-competitive', but because the *direct* impact of this research on the competitiveness of the companies was not great. *Additional know-how*, such as that contained in processing techniques, is required before knowledge about the characteristics of materials can be transformed into commercial value. Such research was therefore a good candidate for JRJF.

On the basis of the information analysed in this book and the summary of research cooperation in the Japanese System presented in the present chapter, it may be concluded that the Japanese government has played an important role in facilitating research cooperation between competing Japanese corporations. While this cooperation has taken the form primarily of CIHR, in some cases JRJF has also been established. The social benefits accruing from these cooperative research projects are analysed in detail in the individual chapters of this book in the sections providing evaluations of the projects and the reader is referred to these chapters for further information.

Diffusion of knowledge in the Japanese System

A working definition of 'diffusion'

The notion of the diffusion of knowledge used in this book differs somewhat from the usual one. Conventionally, diffusion refers to the adoption of new technologies. In the present book, however, diffusion is used in a more limited sense to refer to the spread of knowledge between competing firms which use that knowledge as part of the competitive process.

Diffusion of knowledge in the government-initiated cooperative research projects

The analyses of the cooperative research projects contained in this book reveal that *government intervention results in a significantly wider diffusion of knowledge than would have occurred in the absence of such intervention*. The major way in which a wider diffusion of knowledge was brought about was through the inclusion of relatively weaker firms in the cooperative research projects. In a number of cases documented in the present book, there was initial opposition from the stronger firms to the inclusion in the project of weaker firms as a result of worries about the possibilities of free-riding (or, more accurately, low-cost riding). However, as a result of government insistence, motivated by a desire to strengthen the national system as a whole, on the one hand, and generous government financial subsidies which tended to compensate the stronger firms for low-cost riding, on the other, agreement was reached on including the relatively weaker firms. As a result of the participation of the latter firms, the technological knowledge created under the cooperative research projects was more widely spread than would otherwise have been the case.

Through the analysis of the diffusion of government-owned patents generated under the cooperative research projects it was also concluded that the sale of such patents did not constitute an important channel for the diffusion of knowledge. While in most cases the Japanese government retained *de jure* ownership of the intellectual property rights generated under the project, *de facto*, as a result of the significant degree of tacitness of the knowledge generated, the companies in some cases maintained effective control of the knowledge. Rather than attempting to increase its control over the knowledge created under the cooperative research projects, and to diffuse this knowledge to other Japanese firms, MITI seems to have been content to increase diffusion through the fairly wide inclusion of the major industrial electronics companies. However, as shown in the detailed studies in this book, MITI holds the rights to a large number of patents created under the cooperative research projects and makes these rights available both to Japanese and foreign firms.

Bounded vision and the Japanese System

The present study also suggests that the different kinds of organization which have made up the Japanese System, namely for-profit corporations, government technology planning bodies, government research institutions and universities, differ systematically in terms of their technological 'vision', that is their ability to perceive particular areas of science and technology as being important for their purposes, and to acquire and develop the knowledge in these areas.

For example, the vision, in this sense, of for-profit corporations is bounded by their current activities in product and factor markets, in production, and in R & D, as well as by their need to generate sufficient profits in the short to medium term. This need implies that corporations frequently attach lower priority to areas of science and technology where the degree of commercial uncertainty is expected to be high. Since the longer is the time period required for the commercial application of scientific and technological knowledge the greater tends to be the associated degree of uncertainty, for-profit corporations frequently tend to be 'near-sighted'. A number of important examples of such near-sightedness were analysed in the present book. These included the failure of the Japanese corporations in the areas of telecommunications and heavy electrical equipment to enter the field of computers and related electronic devices until the late 1950s. A further example was the failure of IBM to remain strongly committed to the development of Josephson junctions immediately after 1983 and the desire of the Japanese companies similarly to de-emphasize such research after this IBM decision.

The vision of the other kinds of organizations comprising the Japanese System, was also bounded, but was limited by different factors. Thus, for example, the vision of ETL was bounded by its objective, as part of the Ministry of International Trade and Industry, to develop technologies that were not being adequately developed by the private corporations, and to help strengthen the capabilities of Japanese firms in these technologies. Since it was not a commercial organization, and since its budget was unaffected by the commercialization of the technologies which it developed,

ETL was able to develop technologies that remained beyond the vision of the for-profit companies. One example was the development of the first relay and transistor computers in ETL and their subsequent transfer to the companies. Other examples include some of the technologies that began to be developed in the Japanese System in the late 1970s such as artificial intelligence, gallium arsenide-based devices, and optoelectronic integrated circuits. While in some cases significant research in these areas first began in ETL, the initiative was taken by ETL to establish national cooperative research projects to further develop these technologies with the participation of companies and with government funding. Although over time the significance of ETL, with a relatively constant number of researchers and budget, decreased relative to that of the rapidly growing industrial electronics companies, this organization has continued to contribute a different bounded vision to the Japanese System. A similar role, analysed in more detail in a forthcoming companion volume by the present author, has been played by NTT's Electrical Communications Laboratories. Similarly, while Japanese universities, for reasons touched on in the chapters dealing with the Supercomputer Project and the Future Electronic Devices Project, have not played as important a role in the creation of technology in the Japanese System as their counterparts in the major Western countries, they have at times also contributed their own particular bounded vision to the total perspective of the Japanese System. In the present book, for example, the role of the Japanese universities in the early computing and electronic devices industry was examined.

It is significant that particular institutional practices, aimed at instilling a broad (though still bounded) vision, have become routine in MITI, thus enabling MITI officials to 'see' weaknesses, strengths and opportunities that may not be as clear to the employees of the other major kinds of organization that comprise the Japanese System. Thus it is standard practice that the relatively small number of MITI officials who have passed the top entry examination become generalists moving frequently between the different divisions of the Ministry. A distinction is drawn between the *jimukan*, or administrative official, and the *gikan* or technical official. While the *jimukan* is recruited from a non-technical background, frequently from the best-known law faculties in Japan, the *gikan* has a scientific or technical background. However, both these kinds of official rotate frequently, although the *gikan* tend more often to go to more technical departments. While such moves may be dysfunctional in terms of the negative impact which they have on specialization, they provide the benefits of a broad vision which allows these officials to understand the Japanese System as a whole, including its international role. Furthermore, the practice also strengthens horizontal communication between these officials involved in the different divisions. At the same time, other officials with a scientific and technological background, such as those employed in the various laboratories under the control of MITI's Agency for Industrial Science and

Technology, specialize more narrowly in their own areas of expertise. From this specialized base they are able to act as MITI's antennae, tracking developments in the scientific and technological areas and contributing to MITI's vision of the weaknesses, strengths and opportunities that face the Japanese System. Numerous examples of the way in which MITI officials have acted on the basis of the Ministry's vision built up in this way have been given in the present book.

It is also significant that a number of very senior company research managers have, at least implicitly, also pointed to the importance of the blending of bounded visions brought about in the Japanese System. In interviews with the author, these managers were convinced of the important contribution that has been made to long-term economic performance by MITI officials and ETL researchers as a result of their ability to compensate for the shortsightedness and blind spots of the companies. There was, however, debate about the future role of ETL in view of considerations such as the increasing average age of ETL researchers as a result of the fixed complement of research staff in the laboratory and the low turnover rate, and the increasing size and research strength of the companies together with their growing involvement in longer-term oriented-basic research.

Before leaving the question of bounded vision, it is worth making clear the distinction between this concept and that of 'bounded rationality' developed by Herbert Simon. Simon's concept refers to the limitations on the ability of individuals to acquire, store, retrieve and process information due to the constraints of the human brain and language. For Simon the 'rationality' of human decisions is bounded by these considerations. Since the concept of bounded rationality operates at the level of the individual, any organization, by definition comprised of a collection of individuals, must be constrained by such bounds on rationality. The concept of bounded vision, on the other hand, goes beyond that of bounded rationality to suggest that different kinds of organizations (a) receive different kinds of information as a result of their primary activities and (b) are limited in what they search for and 'see' by the overall objectives of the organization. Types of organization therefore differ in terms of the factors which bound their vision. At the same time it is also accepted that the vision organization will be influenced by the limitations on their ability to handle information. In this sense, therefore, the concepts of bounded vision and bounded rationality are complementary.

Some additional notes

Industrial electronics and consumer electronics in the Japanese System compared

It is important to stress that the present study has been concerned solely with the industrial electronics sector and with the largest industrial electronics companies and their suppliers. The Japanese Technology-Creating Systems in the areas of industrial electronics and consumer electronics have fundamentally different features. *Most significantly, the Japanese government and Japanese government research institutions have played a substantially smaller role in the development of consumer goods-related technologies than in the case of industrial technologies* (including computers, telecommunications and related electronic devices). The reason is simply that government officials have believed that generally speaking Japanese consumer electronics companies have been capable of developing themselves the technologies that they require. For this reason very few of the national cooperative research projects have dealt centrally with consumer goods technologies. *It would be highly misleading, therefore, to attempt to generalize about the Japanese electronics sector as a whole on the basis of an analysis of industrial electronics.* Many of the conclusions drawn in the present chapter, therefore, apply only to the case of the more complex industrial technologies. It is true, however, that there is some overlap between consumer and industrial technologies and this tends to blur somewhat the distinction made here. Nevertheless, it remains the case that the Japanese companies specializing in consumer electronics have been far more independent of the Japanese government in the postwar period than have their industrial electronics counterparts. Further information is provided in Appendix 2 on the relative specialization of the major Japanese companies in the area of industrial and consumer goods.

Government subsidies and the creation of new technologies

A number of writers have shown that the amount of funding allocated by the Japanese government for the creation of new technologies is small relative to what has been allocated to other areas such as agriculture and energy, and relative to what has been spent in the United States and Europe. This illustration is, of course, important and redresses a misconception that large amounts have been spent by the Japanese government to encourage the adoption and development of new technologies. It is now well known that the Japanese government is responsible for a far smaller proportion of total national R & D than is the United States or United Kingdom government.[8] However, it would be a mistake to conclude from these figures that the Japanese government has not played an important role in the development of new technologies in the Japanese System. Quite apart from the role of the Japanese government in areas such as uncertainty-reduction and facilitating research cooperation, which have been considered in detail here, in strictly financial terms the Japanese government has played an important role in financing the development of many core technologies with longer-run commercial prospects. The present book, for example, documents for one of the leading Japanese industrial electronics firms that *approximately 20 per cent of research resources spent on projects with a time horizon of 10 years or more came from MITI*. Similarly, figures were given for the development of the HEMT electronic device, showing that a similar proportion of the development costs of this uncertain technology also came from MITI. In this way, by underwriting the research and development costs of developing uncertain but core technologies of potentially great significance for the computing and electronic devices industry, MITI has played an important role. At the same time, it must be stressed that the present study has also shown that MITI has tended to leave the further development of current technologies to the firms themselves. Thus, for example, since the VLSI Project which ended in 1980, there has been no MITI project dealing with current silicon device technologies. This contrasts strongly with the Sematech project in the United States and the JESSI project in Europe.

Economics and technical change

A brief word is also in order regarding some of the implications of the discussion in the present chapter for economic theory.

The analysis of the process of technical change in the Japanese System has revealed the key importance of *time, uncertainty* and *knowledge*. Over time, things become other than what they were so that time in this sense is irreversible. In order to grasp the process of change a time dimension is needed in the analysis. But the introduction of an irreversible time dimension adds formidable problems for theoretical analysis. One reason is the qualitative distinction that separates that part of the time dimension called the past from that called the future. An irreducible degree of uncertainty relates to the future, since the future may not be the same as the past. And the further that it is necessary to go into the future in order to make a decision, the greater is the degree of uncertainty that is confronted. It is for this reason that it was found necessary in the present study to stress the distinction between technologies created 'for tomorrow' and 'for the day after tomorrow'. It is here that expectations enter the picture, expectations about the shape of things to come. In this world of uncertainty, probability distributions, based on *past* data, are not necessarily of help in decision-making. But the expectations of different 'rational' people may differ, and even be inconsistent. This results not only from their different bounded rationalities, from their different abilities to acquire, store and process information, but also from the fact that the future is uncertain, with the implication that current information is not necessarily a guide to the future.

In such a world, the world of longer-run technical change, the development of rational, optimizing models has little meaning. To take an important illustration from the present study, was IBM rational to allocate the amount of resources it did to the development of Josephson junctions and was it rational to substantially de-emphasize its research effort in this area in 1983? Were the Japanese firms and their government rational when they made the decision to include Josephson junctions in their Supercomputer Project, and when they decided to remain in this research area even after IBM had pulled out? From the vantage point of 1983 IBM could not foresee the dramatic breakthroughs in superconductivity that, ironically, originated from their own laboratories in Zurich some three years later. The meaninglessness of such questions quickly becomes apparent. This emphasizes the importance of a correct handling of the concepts of time, uncertainty and knowledge in any theoretical treatment of the process of technical change and its relationship to economic change. The problem with the bulk of the current body of economic theory is that it is not well adapted to the adequate handling of concepts such as these. Yet, as the present study shows, these concepts are crucial for the analysis of the process of technical change, and therefore crucial for an understanding of the related process of economic change.

The continued evolution of the Japanese System

As shown by the periodization of the Japanese System above, the system has been in a constant state of evolution, altering its institutions and forms of organization and the role they have played in the process of technical change. At the present time the Japanese System is undergoing an important transformation and it is fitting to end this chapter with a brief outline of some of the main features of change.

Perhaps the most important has been the internationalization of Japanese organizations. While there are several causes of this internationalization, including the high savings rate in Japan, the strong yen, and the threat and reality of protectionist measures in the major Western markets, there are important implications of this phenomenon for the process of technical change in Japanese companies, government research institutions and universities. Increasingly what has been referred to here as the Japanese System is becoming less national and events outside Japan are exerting a greater influence on the process of technical change in these organizations. This change is, of course, an evolutionary one. The importance, for example, of scientific and technological interactions with other national systems throughout the whole of the postwar period has been stressed in many of the chapters of the present book. At the present time, however, Japanese science and technology is becoming increasingly international. There are two indicators of this striking change. The first is the substantial increase in the last few years in the number of foreign scientists and engineers either visiting or based for longer periods in Japanese company, government and university laboratories. The second indicator is the recent move by Japanese companies to internationalize their research base by opening laboratories, particularly in more fundamental areas of research, in Western countries. In many cases these laboratories are staffed primarily by Western researchers.

These trends towards internationalization are extremely important since they imply that Japanese companies, government laboratories and universities are to a greater extent becoming more closely integrated into world science and technology. Does this mean, however, that the concept of a Japanese System as propounded in this book is losing its analytical value?

There are a number of reasons for suggesting that the concept of a Japanese System still retains its analytical use. The main reason is that despite the internationalization of Japanese companies, as measured, for example, by the role they play in international markets and science and technology, the major companies still have their main activities located in Japan. These include activities such as overall strategic decision-making and the bulk of research and development. The vitality and growth of the Japanese market has reinforced the tendency to retain these kinds of activities in Japan. Although the relationship between Japanese companies on the one hand and government policy-makers, government laboratories and universities on the other is changing in ways that have been discussed in this book, the interactions between these institutions are still sufficiently close to justify the application of a concept of a national system to analyse them. For this reason an understanding of the Japanese System remains essential for an understanding of Japanese technological and economic performance.

Appendixes

Appendix 1
NEC's total quality control

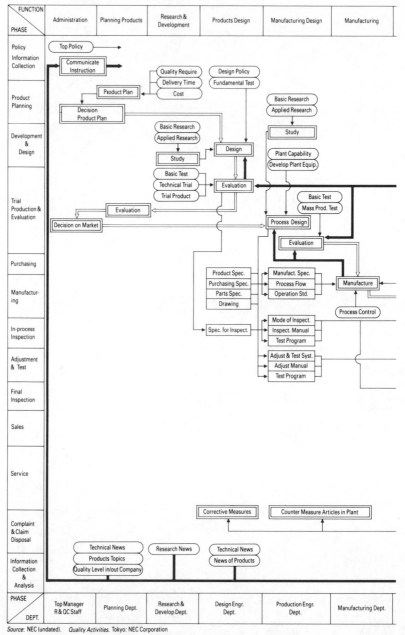

Fig. A.1   NEC's total quality control (*Source*: NEC, undated).

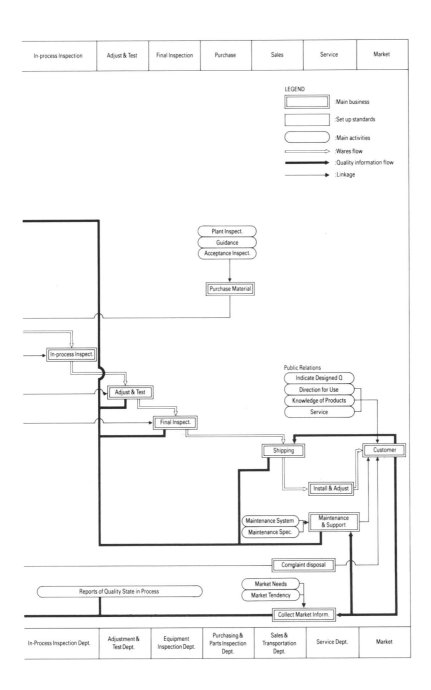

Appendix 2
Specialization in industrial and consumer electronics by Japanese electronics companies

The Japanese electronics industry is highly concentrated. In 1984 there were twenty-one companies among the top hundred in the electronics sector with net sales in excess of a billion dollars. Of these twenty-one companies nine had net sales in excess of a trillion yen (equivalent to about 4 billion dollars at the exchange rate then prevailing). These companies were: Hitachi, Matsushita, Toshiba, Nippon Electric (NEC), Mitsubishi Electric, Fujitsu, Sanyo, Sony and Sharp. These nine companies produced about one-third of the total output of the electronics sector and accounted for a greater proportion of the sector's exports.

The biggest of these companies in terms of total net sales are diversified companies producing both electronic and electrical products. For example, Hitachi in 1986 had net sales of 5.01 trillion yen (or 27.83 billion dollars[1]). The largest single product division in the company was Information and Communication Systems and Electronic Devices which accounted for 29.0 per cent of net sales. In descending order the other product divisions were Consumer Products (21.6 per cent), Wire and Cable, Metals, Chemicals and Other Products (17.6 per cent), Industrial Machinery and Plant (16.7 per cent) and Power Systems and Equipment (15.2 per cent). In 1986 Toshiba's net sales were 3.37 trillion yen (18.72 billion dollars). The most important product division was Industrial Electronics and Electronic Components (33 per cent of net sales), followed by Consumer Products (31 per cent), Heavy Electrical Apparatus (26 per cent), and Materials, Machinery and Other Products (10 per cent).

The relative size of the nine Japanese companies compared to other large international companies is shown in Table A.1. This demonstrates that only IBM and General Electric of the United States were larger than Hitachi and Matsushita, the two largest of the Japanese companies.

Further information is given in Table A.2 on the specialization in the nine companies according to the three major product divisions in the electronics industry: consumer electronics, industrial electronics and electronic components. From this table it can be seen that a major division exists between those companies that have specialized in the consumer electronics sector and those in the industrial electronics sector. The companies that have specialized most highly in consumer electronics are Sony (with 81 per cent of total 1984 sales in consumer electronics), Sanyo (52 per cent), Matsushita (48 per cent) and Sharp (45 per cent). In terms of absolute size of consumer electronics sales, Matsushita was the largest (1,914 billion yen) followed by Sony (900 billion yen), Hitachi (655 billion yen), Sanyo (585 billion yen), Toshiba (569 billion yen) and Sharp (458 billion yen).

Table A.1. *Size of Japanese and other international electronic/electrical companies*

Company		FY 1979 Sales (US $ million)	AAG (%)	FY 1983 Sales (US $ million)	Index Hitachi, Ltd. = 100 FY 1984
Hitachi[a]		12,237	10	18,196	100
Matsushita		9,844	14	16,619	91
Toshiba[a]		7,940	9	11,279	62
NEC[a]		3,592	20	7,341	40
Mitsubishi[a]		4,956	10	7,253	40
Fujitsu[a]		2,498	19	5,041	28
Sanyo		3,142	11	4,690	26
Sony		2,681	15	4,629	25
Sharp[a]		2,145	19	4,239	23
IBM	(USA)	22,863	15	40,180	221
GE	(USA)	22,461	5	26,797	147
Philips	(Netherlands)	11,646	9	16,181	89
Siemens	(West Germany)	10,975	9	15,459	85
ITT	(USA)	17,191	–	14,155	78
Général d'Elec.	(France)	5,327	23	10,009[b]	55
Westinghouse	(USA)	7,332	7	9,533	52
GEC	(UK)	4,369	26	8,646[b]	48
Samsung Group	(S. Korea)	3,077	24	7,167	39
Thomson-Brandt	(France)	4,565	16	7,156[b]	39
AEG-Telefunken	(West Germany)	4,672	–	4,515	25
Foreign firms in Japan		3,149	10	4,605	25

Key:
FY 1979 Financial year ending 31 March 1979.
AAG   Average annual growth.

Notes:
[a] FY 1980 – FY 1984.
[b] FY 1982.

Source: Dodwell Marketing Consultants (1989).

On the other hand, Fujitsu is the most specialized in the industrial electronics sector which accounted for 77 per cent of its total 1984 sales. In terms of industrial sector specialization Fujitsu was followed by NEC (66 per cent), Mitsubishi (29 per cent), Sharp (20 per cent), Toshiba (19 per cent) and Sony and Hitachi (15 per cent each). In terms of absolute size of industrial electronics sales, NEC was largest with 1,163 billion yen, followed by Fujitsu (931 billion yen), Hitachi (655 billion yen), Toshiba (514 billion yen), Mitsubishi (505 billion yen), Matsushita (319 billion yen) and Sharp (203 billion yen).

In the electronic components sector NEC and Fujitsu were the most specialized with 24 per cent and 18 per cent respectively of their total 1984 sales in such products. In terms of absolute size, however, Hitachi led with sales of 611 billion yen followed by NEC (423 billion yen), Toshiba (379 billion yen) and Matsushita (360 billion yen).

From these tables it is clear that the four largest Den Den firms, Fujitsu, Hitachi,

Table A.2. Sectoral specialization by major Japanese electronics companies

	Electronics total (billion yen) (% of total sales)			Consumer electronics (billion yen) (% of total sales)		Industrial electronics (billion yen) (% of total sales)		Electronic components (billion yen) (% of total sales)	
	FY 1980	AAG(%)	FY 1984	FY 1980	FY 1984	FY 1980	FY 1984	FY 1980	FY 1984
Hitachi	913 (31)	20	1,921 (44)	324 (11)	655 (15)	383 (13)	655 (15)	306 (7)	611 (14)
Matsushita[a]	1,182 (50)	22	2,593 (65)	922 (39)	1,914 (48)	165 (7)	319 (8)	95 (4)	360 (9)
Toshiba	781 (41)	17	1,462 (54)	343 (18)	569 (21)	286 (15)	514 (19)	152 (8)	379 (14)
NEC	819 (95)	20	1,709 (97)	60 (7)	123 (7)	578 (67)	1,163 (66)	181 (21)	423 (24)
Mitsubishi	595 (50)	16	1,079 (62)	155 (13)	313 (18)	321 (27)	505 (29)	119 (10)	261 (15)

Fujitsu	599 (100)	19	1,210 (100)	36 (6)	61 (5)	497 (80)	931 (77)	84 (14)	218 (18)
Sanyo[a]	407 (54)	14	676 (60)	392 (52)	585 (52)	– –	68 (6)	15 (2)	23 (2)
Sony[a]	643 (100)	15	1,111 (100)	547 (85)	900 (81)	84 (13)	167 (15)	12 (2)	44 (4)
Sharp	361 (70)	23	814 (80)	191 (37)	458 (45)	103 (20)	203 (20)	67 (13)	153 (15)
Total	6,300	19	12,575	2,970	5,578	2,399	4,525	931	2,472

Key:
FY 1980 Financial Year ending 31 March 1980.
AAG   Average annual growth.
Note:
[a]FY 1979 – FY 1983.
Source: Dodwell Marketing Consultants (1989).

Table A.3. *The importance of communications products in the four main NTT-supplying companies*

	Fujitsu (billion dollars) (%)		Hitachi (billion dollars) (%)		NEC (billion dollars) (%)		Oki (billion dollars) (%)	
	1985	1986	1985	1986	1985	1986	1985	1986
Net sales[a]	8.679	9.399	29.490[b]	29.473[b]	12.547	13.116	2.320	2.181
	(100)	(100)	(100)	(100)	(100)	(100)	(100)	(100)
of which:								
Communications	1.171	1.412			3.666	4.197	0.523	0.551
	(14)	(15)			(29)	(32)	(23)	(25)
Computers and industrial electronic systems	5.320	6.202	3.861[c]	4.444[c]	4.751	4.804	1.131	1.093
	(61)	(66)	(13)	(15)	(38)	(37)	(49)	(50)
Electronic devices	1.708	1.253	2.333	2.139	3.311	2.479	0.555	0.456
	(20)	(13)	(8)	(7)	(26)	(19)	(24)	(21)
Consumer electronics	0.325	0.366			1.047	1.006	0.106[d]	0.092[d]
	(4)	(4)			(8)	(8)	(5)	(4)

Notes:

[a] As in company reports, an exchange rate of 1 US dollar = 180 yen is assumed.

[b] Of which: Information and Communication Systems and Electronic Devices amounting to 8.863 billion dollars (1985) and 8.539 billion dollars (1986), which constitute 30% and 29% of net sales respectively, and comprises the largest product category.

[c] Refers to computers only and is therefore *not* necessarily strictly comparable with data for the other firms.

[d] In the Oki report this is 'other, including consumer electronics'.

Source: Compiled from company Annual Reports.

NEC and Oki, are amongst those Japanese firms that have specialized most heavily, both in terms of absolute sales and in terms of proportional significance, in industrial electronics. The notable exception is Oki which in 1984 was the eighteenth largest company in the Japanese electronics industry. Its inclusion in the Den Den family is for historical reasons.

Further information is provided in Table A.3 on the importance of communications products in the four Den Den firms. As can be seen from this table, Hitachi is by far the largest of the Den Den firms with 1986 net sales of 29.5 billion dollars compared to the second firm, NEC, with 13.1 billion dollars. However, as already noted, Hitachi is a more diversified electrical and electronics firm. Net sales from Hitachi's Information and Communication Systems and Electronic Devices Division, the company's largest division responsible for 29 per cent of total net sales in 1986, amounted to 8.5 billion dollars in this year. Since this division roughly corresponds to the product range of Fujitsu, NEC and Oki, this would make Hitachi the third largest Den Den electronics firm after NEC and Fujitsu. Oki comes last with net sales about 25 per cent of Hitachi's sales in the information technology area.

Table A.3 also shows that NEC has been most dependent on telecommunications among the firms for which data are available.[2] In 1986 communications equipment accounted for 32 per cent of NEC's net sales, amounting to 4.2 billion dollars. Of the three firms for which there is comparable data, Oki was second in terms of communications dependence with communications sales equal to 25 per cent of net sales. However, these sales amounted to 0.6 billion dollars compared to Fujitsu's 1.4 billion dollars, which accounted for 15 per cent of this firm's net sales.

In terms of computers and industrial electronic systems, Fujitsu was the largest company in 1986 with sales of 6.2 billion dollars, amounting to 66 per cent of the net sales. The corresponding figures for the other companies were NEC, 4.8 billion dollars (37 per cent of the net sales), Hitachi, 4.4 billion dollars (15 per cent of net sales), and Oki 1.1 billion dollars (50 per cent of net sales).

NEC was also the largest producer of electronic devices with sales in this product area of 2.5 billion dollars in 1986 (19 per cent of the company's total net sales). The corresponding figures for the other companies were Hitachi, 2.2 billion dollars (7 per cent of the net sales), Fujitsu, 1.3 billion dollars (13 per cent), and Oki, 0.5 billion dollars (21 per cent).

Notes

1. Introduction

1. For an example of this view see, for example, Johnson (1982).
2. For an example of this view see, for example, Komiya *et al.* (1988) and Trezise (1987).
3. Two recent papers considering this issue are Boltho (1985) and Flaherty (1987).
4. For a recent analysis of this end and related issues see McNulty (1984).

2. A periodization of the development of the computer and electronic devices industry in Japan, 1948–1979

1. Johnson, 1982, p. 211.
2. Ibid., p. 220. This was in the special category for poor countries.
3. In terms of the concept introduced in the concluding chapter of this book, computing and the other new information technologies lay outside the 'bounded vision' of these companies.
4. T. Kobayashi, 1986, p. 40.
5. Flamm, 1985, Table 7.4, p. 7-13A. For Flamm's later published work, see Flamm (1987, 1988).
6. T. Kobayashi, 1986, pp. 44–5, emphasis added. The implications of the long-term and relatively certain relationship between NTT and its supplier companies are considered in a companion volume on telecommunications in Japan (Fransman, forthcoming).
7. A major shortcoming in Chalmers Johnson's interesting account of MITI and the growth of industrial policy from 1925 to 1975 is his failure to take account of the role of ETL which, as will be shown in this chapter, made a significant contribution to the growth of the Japanese electronics and computing sectors. Neither ETL nor ECL are mentioned in the index to his book (Johnson, 1982).
8. A detailed account of the contemporary organization of ETL is to be found in Strauss (1986). Information is provided there on the decision-making processes that take place in the selection of research topics, which involve interaction between ETL, AIST, and MITI's Industrial Technology and Industrial Structure Councils.
9. In the concluding chapter the concept 'bounded vision' is introduced in order to analyse these differences between for-profit companies and government research laboratories.
10. For more details on the relationship between ECL and NTT's group of

supplying firms see Fransman (forthcoming) on telecommunications in Japan.

11. The concept of 'bounded vision' is used in the concluding chapter to explain the difference in the perspective of university research.
12. K. Kobayashi, 1986, p. 36.
13. Koji Kobayashi (1986), later Chairman of the Board and Chief Executive Officer of NEC, suggests that two NEC engineers published essentially the same results as Shannon two years before the latter in the area of switching circuit network theory. 'In 1938, two years after they [Akira Nakashima and Masao Hanzawa] first made known their switching theory in Japan, C. E. Shannon of Bell Telephone Labs. in the United States presented almost identical research results and gained widespread recognition for his achievement.' The first Japanese computer 'was the relay-type ETL Mark I, developed in [1953] by the Electro-technical Laboratory of the Ministry of International Trade and Industry. It was constructed under the supervision of Mochinori Goto, and according to Hidetoshi Takahashi, a professor at the University of Tokyo at that time, it was based on the design theory derived from the Nakashima-Hanzawa theory' (pp. 13, 14).
14. Interview with a central researcher in ETL at the time who has subsequently been regarded as an influential university-based leader of the Japanese computer industry.
15. The following is an extract from an interview with a senior member of the Japanese computer establishment who was a computer researcher in ETL in the 1950s:

> Fransman: It is interesting that MITI and NTT often developed different technologies.
> Informant: Yes. They negotiated with each other – how NTT would do research on parametrons [and ETL on transistors].
> Fransman: Oh, that was explicitly agreed, was it?
> Informant: Yes, in order to promote domestic technology [while also developing foreign technology].
> Fransman: Why did NTT choose parametrons and ETL transistors?
> Informant: I am not sure. But Wadasan [who became head of ETL's electronics division in 1954] always said that parametrons would not be promising. So he decided to choose transistors. His judgment was reasonable. Wadasan had good researchers under his control.

16. In NEC, for example, currently the world's largest producer of memory integrated circuits, although research on transistors began in 1950, it was only in 1958 that the company opened a transistor manufacturing factory in its Tamagawa plant. By 1961 the volume of semiconductor devices produced exceeded that of transistors (NEC, 1984, pp. 42–4).
17. See note 15 for the source of this information.
18. K. Kobayashi, 1986, p. 36.
19. The FACOM 202's 'electrical power consumption was high however, and it generated a tremendous amount of heat. Consequently, not only did the cost of cooling equipment become excessive, but the oil that was used as a coolant would sometimes leak from odd places' (T. Kobayashi, 1986, p. 42).
20. 'Mitsubishi Electric...asked Wada for support from ETL. But Wada refused. He said to me that Mitsubishi Electric would not have enough power to develop such a complicated computer system.' See note 15 for source.
21. Based on information supplied by a current senior member of ETL.
22. Ibid.
23. For a detailed account of the Machinery Industry Promotion Special

Measures Law (number 154 of 5 June 1956) and subsequent related interventions by MITI, see Fransman (1986a, pp. 190–6).

24. For an account of how these measures related to more general MITI policies at the time see Johnson (1982, pp. 226, 237).
25. Flamm, 1985, p. 10-35.
26. Calculated from Flamm (1985, table 7.4, p. 7-13A).
27. Johnson, 1982, p. 228.
28. '. . . a long term vision for the industrial structure was developed in 1963. In this vision two criteria for an optimum industrial structure were spelled out: (1) the "Income Elasticity Criterion" focussing attention on demand and (2) the "Productivity Increase Rate Criterion" focussing on supply. On the basis of these criteria the path towards heavy and chemical industries development was chosen as the most desirable' (MITI, 1983; quoted in Freeman, 1987, p. 38).
29. In the 1930s, for example, twenty-six industries were designated as 'important industries', including silk thread, rayon, paper, cement, iron and steel, and coal (Johnson, 1982, p. 110).
30. For a more detailed discussion of the general issues see Fransman (1986b, chapters 8–9). Apparently in the 1950s a number of Japanese loan applications to the World Bank were turned down on the grounds that the industries in question did not enjoy a comparative advantage (discussion with a current member of the World Bank).
31. Speech delivered to OECD Industrial Committee, 24 June 1970. Quoted in Abegglen and Stalk (1985, p. 71, emphasis added).
32. For example, in December 1955 the Japanese Government introduced the Five-Year Plan for Economic Independence (*Keizai Jiritsu 5 ka-nen Keikaku*) which aimed at 'four principal policy objectives: (1) modernization of industrial plant and equipment, (2) promotion of international trade, (3) raising the degree of self-sufficiency, and (4) curtailment of consumption. The second and third themes would appear contradictory to those who have ever studied the standard theory of international trade. The authors of the national economic plan and the policy-makers at the time did not seem to understand fully the notion of the gains from free trade based upon comparative advantage and efficient resource allocation through international trade and the competitive price mechanism. It seemed that the persistent tendency of Japan's balance of payments to run large deficits in the 1950s and up to the mid 1960s was behind these two apparently contradictory policy objectives. . .The Government did not seem to have considered the use of an overall price adjustment measure, namely . . . exchange rate depreciation for achieving the balance of its international payments. In general, the policy-makers in the Government and the leaders in the business community in this period did not much believe in the role of [the] price mechanism for equalizing demand for and supply of any type of goods or service' (Komiya and Itoh, 1986, pp. 4, 5).

    For a more detailed criticism of the Japanese government's industrial policy, see Komiya, Okuno and Suzumura (1988).
33. Komiya and Itoh, 1986, p. 14, emphasis added. In 1961 the tariff on computers was increased from 15 to 25 per cent (Flamm, 1985, p. 7-19).
34. Johnson (1982) notes that 'It is hard to recapture today the crisis atmosphere that existed in Japanese industrial circles during 1961' largely as a result of the pressure put on Japan to liberalize following Eisenhower's November 1960 promulgation calling for US–Japan negotiations over trade restrictions on cotton textiles. He suggests that 'the most important bureaucratic

response to liberalization was MITI's invention of the concept of "industrial structure" and the creation on 1 April 1961 of the Industrial Structure Investigation Council...The concept was simply a shorthand term for comparisons of Japanese industries with those of North America and Western Europe' (pp. 250–3). While concessions to the pressure to liberalize were made in areas such as textiles, the pursuit of what MITI regarded as a desirable industrial structure led to the protection and promotion of selected industries such as the computer and electronic devices industry.

35. Komiya and Itoh, 1986, pp. 14, 15.
36. See, for example, Welke (1982, p. 38). Flamm (1985, p. 7-65) notes that 'IBM computers manufactured in Japan were treated as foreign computers.'
37. The following is an extract from an interview between the present author and a senior figure in the Japanese computer Establishment. Informant: 'At the beginning of the computer age the government closed the Japanese market and kept it for Japanese firms. [For example,] universities could not buy IBM machines...'. Fransman: 'In retrospect, was this good for Japanese long-run development?' Informant: 'I think at an early stage of the technology it was a good way of promoting domestic technology... Furthermore, the Ministry of Education paid 50 per cent of the price of [domestically produced] computers used in universities.' Foreign penetration of the public sector market for computers was significantly less than of the private sector market. For example, Welke (1982, p. 39) notes that in 'the restricted markets for ministries, agencies, local governments, universities, etc., the market share of foreign computer manufacture is much less than in the open market (only about 14 per cent in comparison to over 50 per cent) because public users were urged to buy domestic products. But in January 1978 the Cabinet made a decision to give foreign manufacturers the same chance as domestic manufacturers in this market.' Taiyu Kobayashi (1986, p. 51), who became Chairman of the Board of Fujitsu in 1981, states that in the mid 1960s 'universities were the most important customers among mainframe computer users' in Japan.
38. See Fransman (1986b), Chapter 8.
39. Johnson, 1982, p. 263.
40. Quoted in Johnson (1982, p. 247).
41. Flamm, 1985, pp. 7-15–7-17.
42. Flamm, 1985, table 7.4, p. 7-13A.
43. T. Kobayashi, 1986, pp. 45–6.
44. For a comprehensive history of the use of engineering research associations in Japan after their 'import' from Britain see the first part of Sigurdson (1986).
45. Interview between the author and a senior manager in the Hitachi Central Research Laboratory.
46. T. Kobayashi, 1986, p. 46.
47. Ibid., p. 51.
48. Ibid., p. 80.
49. 'The Fujitsu 230-60 had not yet been completed when Tokyo University installed a Hitachi 5020 built with technology from RCA. To make up for this humiliation at Tokyo University, we concentrated our efforts on Kyoto University... Since there were Kyoto University alumni like myself from other companies who were using their network of associations to help their sales effort, I encountered friends from my college days. We joked and kidded with each other outwardly, but inside each was fiercely determined to "bring home this order"' (Ibid., pp. 51, 53).

50. Tatsuno, 1986, p. 11.
51. Calder, 1983.
52. Flamm, 1985, p. 7-23.
53. Interview with a senior device researcher at Tokyo University.
54. Interview with a NEC Vice-President. The VHSCS project was the first national project to use LSI technology.
55. Flamm, 1985, p. 7-24 and footnote 7-66/7.
56. AIST, 1986b, p. 7. No reliable figures exist for the company expenditures, partly because it is difficult to draw the line between the company's project-related research and the other work it is doing in the computing area. However, it is probably not unreasonable to double the MITI expenditure figure on the project to get an estimate of total expenditure on project-related research.
57. AIST, 1986b, p. 7.
58. Data given to the author by MITI.
59. This may be referred to as the 'isolated in-house research' option.
60. This may be referred to as the 'coordinated in-house research' option.
61. This important point was corroborated in a number of interviews with senior research personnel involved in the VHSCS project in NEC, Hitachi and ETL.
62. The patent data referred to in this paragraph were derived from information on patents given to the present author by MITI officials. Of the thirty-nine patents there were two on which there was insufficient information to judge whether there was joint research.
63. For a detailed account of the development of the DIPS computer see Fransman forthcoming).
64. Based on an analysis of data supplied to the author by MITI. The figure of sixty-eight patents for the VHSCS project is inconsistent with that of thirty-nine patents referred to earlier in this section. The figures come from different MITI divisions. One possible explanation is that the larger figure is more up to date, including an additional one or two years to 31 March 1987. It is not clear from the data whether the two firms that purchased the licences included firms that had created the technology under the VHSCS project.
65. Johnson, 1982, pp. 290–1.
66. See Fransman (forthcoming).
67. Johnson, 1982, p. 302.
68. Welke, 1982, p. 39. Restrictions were also removed on the inflows of foreign capital. In November 1979 the Diet passed MITI's liberalization of the Foreign Exchange and Foreign Trade Control Law of 1949 and the Foreign Capital Law of 1950.
69. From the late 1970s 'the dominant philosophy among Japan's economic policy authorities and public has been changing considerably. The philosophy that free trade is basically most desirable for the Japanese economy, although there could be exceptions such as agricultural protection, has gained common recognition among policy-makers, leading businessmen and knowledgeable people in Japan. Japan's trade policy, which in the past tended to have the mercantilist tendencies of promoting exports and restricting imports, began to change towards freer trade' (Komiya and Itoh, 1986, p. 42).
70. T. Kobayashi, 1986, p. 79.
71. 'Word of Dr Amdahl's troubles with IBM was passed along to me. The information was supplied to us by a person named Rodriguez of Litton

Industries through Hanzo Omi, a Fujitsu director. Later, when Dr Amdahl founded Amdahl Corporation, Mr Rodriguez became one of the partners' (Ibid., p. 82).

72. Ibid., p. 85

73. 'When we heard Dr Amdahl was going to leave IBM to form his own company, we approached Hitachi with the suggestion they join us in establishing a relationship with Amdahl. Thinking it was an excellent opportunity *because of Amdahl Corporation's LSI technology*, we established a connection with them, but Hitachi for some reason declined' (Ibid., p. 95, emphasis added).

74. Ibid., p. 84.

75. Ibid., p. 85.

76. Ibid., p. 87.

77. It might prove difficult to draw up a contract between the semiconductor and computer companies governing the generation of, and payment for, these information flows, as a result of factors such as uncertainty regarding the kind of information that will be relevant (only by having the information will the computer company know whether it is relevant, but then it would have acquired the information without paying for it) and uncertainty regarding the value to the computer company of using the information.

78. T. Kobayashi, 1986, p. 115.

79. Ibid., p. 116.

80. This has been argued by Taiyu Kobayashi: 'Semiconductor and computer manufacturing at Hitachi were separate divisions. Their surprise at our success may – this is just my conjecture – have been due to the fact [that] their semiconductor people, interested in the bottom line of their own operation, were unwilling to put much effort into producing the complicated and initially unprofitable semiconductors requested by their computer division... Hitachi's semiconductor division at the time had already grown too big for them to incorporate it into their computer division... Instead, they drew the best of their engineers from each and set up a "device development centre"' (1986, p. 118).

81. See T. Kobayashi (1986, chapter V) for an interesting and illuminating account.

82. Johnson, 1982, pp. 290–1.

83. Johnson, 1982, pp. 267, 268, 277, 278. The success in bringing about mergers in these other six industries was patchy. For example, while successful merger occurred in the case of Yawata and Fuji in the steel industry, the Nissan–Prince merger was the only one in the automobile industry.

84. In October 1986 the members of the Japanese Technology Evaluation Program panel on advanced computing in Japan (a programme sponsored by the United States National Science Foundation) were made aware of the disadvantages that some Japanese companies see in their relatively small size in terms of computer output: 'We were told repeatedly (at NEC and Fujitsu) that not only was IBM larger than all of the Japanese computer industry put together, but that the largest Japanese exporter of computer products was IBM Japan' (Japanese Technology Evaluation Program, 1987, p. 49).

85. The concluding chapter contains a more detailed theoretical analysis of the importance of uncertainty and the way in which it has been dealt with in the Japanese System.

86. For a more detailed discussion of the impact of the 1971 Law on the computer numerically controlled (CNC) machine tool industry in Japan, see Fransman (1986a, pp. 190–6).

87. The term '3.5 generation' derived from the notion that the IBM System 370 constituted only a half generation advance over the System 360 which was regarded as a third generation computer system (Flamm, 1985, p. 7-69).

88. Currency conversion: Yen 330 = $1.

89. Nihon Denshikikai Kogyokai, 1979, pp. 134–6. See also Mirai Kogaku Kenkyujyo (1983).

90. 'With trade liberalization in 1971 ... when the industry was facing competition with the IBM 370 series ... a system of subsidies [was] established. Although in effect for only a limited period, the subsidies were a powerful measure, providing 50 per cent of development costs for new machines from three groups of producers. In doing this, *MITI was trying to force mergers in the [computer] industry, but the companies resisted*' (Imai, 1986, p. 143, emphasis added).

91. T. Kobayashi, 1986, p. 94.

92. Ibid., p. 95

93. 'The grouping of Fujitsu and Hitachi was of course accomplished due to the administrative guidance of MITI. At the same time, the fact that my predecessor, President Seimiya and Hitachi Executive Vice President Kubo were classmates and drinking companions also was a factor. That discussions moved along so smoothly, and the cooperation of both companies yielded such fine results, can be attributed to their close friendship' (Ibid., p. 97).

94. For a more detailed history of NEC see the author's research on telecommunications in Japan (Fransman, forthcoming).

95. For more details on the Den Den family see the author's research on telecommunications in Japan (Fransman, forthcoming).

96. AIST, 1986b, p. 7.

97. It is possible that this took somewhat longer in the case of software which is discussed in more detail below.

98. One example is the kind of innovation that occurred in Fujitsu (referred to earlier) which followed from the integration of the semiconductor and computer divisions of the company.

99. It is not intended to suggest here that MITI was the sole arbiter regarding the choice of computer strategy. For example, there is strong evidence as shown above that Fujitsu had already decided on an IBM-compatible path before the MITI programmes from 1971. Nevertheless, through the coordinated decision-making process involving MITI and the firms, the Japanese System as a whole was able to reduce the uncertainty involved in the choice of any single computer strategy.

100. T. Kobayashi, 1986, p. 97.

101. Ibid., pp. 97–8.

102. Present author's interview with a senior research official from Fujitsu.

103. As suggested above, in practice there was very little joint creation and sharing of technological knowledge by Fujitsu and Hitachi.

104. Flamm, 1985, p. 7-31.

105. These data were calculated by the present author by examining each of the 365 PIPS patents. The original list of patents was given to the author by a MITI official.

106. In all seven cases the firms involved in the joint patent were Hitachi and Hitachi Metal, both part of the Hitachi group.

107. Strictly speaking, joint patents only provide an indication of joint research involving the creation of patentable knowledge. It is possible that there were other forms of joint research, although it must be added that there is no evidence that these other forms occurred in the PIPS project.

108. The complexities surrounding this point are examined in detail later in this book.
109. The data referred to in this paragraph were obtained from a different MITI office from those contained in the last paragraph, and are not strictly compatible.
110. Interview with a senior MITI official involved in the establishment of several subsequent research projects.
111. For example, 'In 1981, NTT's procurement budget came to about 2.7 billion dollars. For NEC, NTT's largest and most important supplier, procurements exceeded 500 million dollars, representing 12 per cent of total company sales' (Okimoto, 1986, p. 82).

3. The VLSI Research Project, 1976–1980

1. United States Congress, 1984, p. 1.
2. It is possible that the views of Mitsubishi Electric were different from those of the other four participating companies. Mitsubishi was apparently initially excluded from the VLSI project on the grounds of its relative weakness in the associated technologies. However, using the political muscle of the Mitsubishi group, the company eventually gained access to the VLSI Project. As something of a 'free rider' Mitsubishi might have had different views on the desirability of joint research.
3. Okimoto, Sugano and Weinstein (1984, p. 19) are therefore incorrect when they say of the VLSI project in their useful book on semiconductors that 'in the various cooperating laboratories, each research team included engineers from all [the five] member companies'. See Sigurdson's (1986) excellent account of the VLSI Project for a more accurate indication of the corporate membership of the Joint laboratories (p. 49). As will be shown below from our analysis of joint patents, the membership of the first three laboratories was somewhat different from that suggested by Sigurdson.
4. For introductory accounts of semiconductor technologies see Scace (1981) and Oldham (1980).
5. See also Scace (1981, pp. 10–11).
6. Interview with a senior Toshiba researcher.
7. Sigurdson (1986, pp. 88, 92) notes that after the VLSI Project Hitachi began producing optical steppers.
8. An exception to this conclusion is where the 'success rate' is significantly different between laboratories, that is the proportion of joint research which results in patents applied for and/or granted. Insufficient information in the case of the VLSI Project makes it impossible to check on the differences between success rates across the six laboratories.
9. These data were given to the author by the VLSI Research Association.
10. The direct impact refers to the effect of that knowledge itself, unsupplemented by additional knowledge, on competitiveness, etc.
11. It will be recalled that evidence was presented earlier suggesting that while there was strong competition between Hitachi, Fujitsu and Toshiba in the area of lithography equipment, this was not true to the same extent for NEC or Mitsubishi.
12. Imai, 1984, p. 14.
13. Imai, 1984, p. 14: 'of the whole project ... about 20 per cent was carried out in a Joint Research Institute [i.e. the VLSI Joint Research Laboratory]'. Imai, 1986, p. 143: 'Only about 15 per cent of the research (in terms of cost) was carried out in the Joint Research Institute .'

14. See Elster (1983).
15. It may also be that the costs of running the project will also be higher under JRJF as a result of the joint laboratories that will have to be set up.

4. The Optical Measurement and Control System Project, 1979–1985

1. The author is grateful to Professor James L. Merz for access to an unpublished paper from which this table is derived.
2. The economies of joint research were analysed in detail in chapter 3 dealing with the VLSI Project.
3. See p. 102
4. See chapter 3 on the VLSI Project.
5. Merz (1987, p. 14) notes that 'It was decided that the first application would be to an oil refinery plant for a number of reasons: (1) Such plants tend to be extremely large and yet closed systems, so that an optical system would be appropriate; (2) There is a need for a large number of sensors for process control, and these sensors could be optical devices; (3) The use of electrical energy for measurement and control raises very serious safety issues; and (4) not insignificantly, there was funding available to MITI though the tax base provided by the oil companies. [The] total system ... was actually introduced in the Mizushima oil refinery plant of the Japan Mining Co. (Nihon Kogyo), located about one hour from Osaka, during the month of January 1986.'
6. See pp. 65, 66.
7. Interview with a senior official from Fujitsu with responsibility for the Optical Measurement Project.
8. Interview with senior officials from Toshiba with responsibility for the Optical Measurement Project.
9. This, the previous three, and the following two quotations are from the same senior executive referred to above.
10. This discussion has abstracted from possible differences in the quality of researchers sent to the joint laboratory. Such differences, as discussed earlier, may influence the benefit that a company derives from its participation in the joint research. This is considered in the following paragraph.
11. See United States Department of Defense (1987).
12. The author, as mentioned earlier, is grateful to Professor Merz for access to his circulated but unpublished paper (Merz, 1987).
13. Regarding the choice of indium phosphide (InP) for the new optoelectronics project, Merz has the following to say: 'It is not clear that InP-based materials should be totally excluded from consideration. Although the emphasis of OJL's activities have to do with optoelectronic integrated circuits rather than optical communications (and hence do not require the very low losses available in optical fibers at longer wavelength), InP may have advantages even for the short-haul systems envisioned for OEICs because of the zero-dispersion characteristics of some fibers at these wavelengths, which would lead to higher bandwidth applications. In the final year of OJL some attention is being given to InP [which has a higher wavelength than GaAs] ... and the next ... optoelectronics project will have more to do with InP' (p. 40).
14. It should be noted that the opposite may not be true, that is JRJF may not be an alternative to CIHR. As pointed out earlier in this section, in some areas the propensity to share knowledge is too low to allow for JRJF. In these cases it is incorrect to see JRJF and CIHR as alternatives.

15. In order to calculate the net social benefit it is necessary to take account of the *additional* costs of JRJF as compared to CIHR. This is considered in more detail later in this section.
16. This may be correct even if their backgrounds were similar. The effects of varying backgrounds are discussed under the preceding heading.
17. It should be noted that, in commenting on the present chapter, several MITI officials strongly disagreed with the interpretation offered in this paragraph.
18. While this information is not available, there is evidence of some diffusion to non-participating companies. Thus Merz (1987) suggests that one of the 'best examples of technology transfer' achieved by the Joint Laboratory is the case of an infra-red topograph system which was developed through close cooperation between the characterization group (group 6) and the bulk growth group (group 1). 'The infra-red topograph system developed for the inspection of gallium arsenide wafers for internal defects was made available to Hamamatsu Photonics Co. (*not* a member company [of the Joint Laboratory]). The system is now commercially available, selling for about $33,000. As of the first of the year, five of these units had been sold, and 20 other sales were expected. MITI receives a royalty of about 1 per cent of the price of each machine' (p. 30).
19. The shortcomings of joint patents as a perfect indicator of joint research were examined earlier, in the chapter dealing with the VLSI Project.

5. The High-Speed Computing System for Scientific and Technological Uses Project (The Supercomputer Project), 1981–1989

1. An idea of the narrowness of the supercomputer market is given by figures for the number of supercomputers in use in Japan in 1987. These figures assumed significance when, as part of the US–Japanese trade conflict, attention was focused on the US share of the Japanese supercomputer market. According to Japanese figures, there were in 1987 about 60 supercomputers in use in Japan, of which approximately 20 were being used in the public sector (*Japan Times*, 23 January 1987, p. 6).
2. See Sigurdson (1986, pp. 42, 44).
3. Agency for Industrial Science and Technology, 1986a, p. 6.
4. *Financial Times*, 19 November 1987, p. 36.
5. Ibid.
6. The author is extremely grateful to the Thomas J. Watson Research Centre for this information.
7. See Pugh *et al.* (1980–1983).
8. Correspondence between the author and an official at the Thomas J. Watson Research Centre.
9. This and subsequent quotations are from Pugh (1985).
10. *Financial Times*, 19 November 1987, p. 36.
11. Bednorz and Mueller, 1986.
12. Jane Rippeteau, *Financial Times*, 4 November 1987.
13. Ibid.
14. *Financial Times*, 19 November 1987, p. 36.
15. *Japan Times*, 16 April 1987.
16. *Japan Times*, 14 June 1987.
17. Even if the MITI decision was motivated by 'irrational' factors such as a desire to avoid 'losing face' by the abandonment of a research project that it had previously selected, or pressures to continue the research by ETL researchers

who had developed a vested interest in the work, the fact remains that there was a greater flexibility and degree of pluralism in the Japanese research agenda because of the *limited* influence exerted by the commercially motivated decisions of private companies.

18. This project is discussed in detail on page 32 *et seq.*
19. Fujitsu, *Annual Report*, 1986, p. 17.
20. Fujitsu, *Annual Report*, 1987, p. 27.

7. The Fifth Generation Computer Project, 1982–1991

1. Examples of knowledge representation procedures include 'is – a hierarchies' (e.g. an Alsatian is – a kind of dog; a dog is – a kind of animal that has four legs). The knowledge-base management system must be able to generate the deduction that Alsatians have four legs. Another example is 'if – then statements', for example, *if* a person has consumed more than x amount of alcohol, *then* attempting to drive within a period of y hours will be dangerous and resorting to other means of transportation is recommended.
2. The implications of this are analysed in the concluding chapter with reference to the concept of 'bounded vision'.
3. As discussed below, Prolog was later replaced by another logic programming language, Flat Guarded Horn Clause, which had some similarities to Prolog.
4. These economies of cooperative research were examined in the earlier chapters and are analysed in more detail below.
5. It should be noted that ICOT officials, in commenting on the present chapter, strongly disagreed with this interpretation of the implications of tacit knowledge.
6. ICOT, 1985a, p. 21.
7. Ibid., p. 22.
8. Interview by the author with four researchers at ICOT, 21 April 1987.
9. At times 'under the table' payments do supplement personal incomes. The author has come across instances of this in other academic areas in Japan.
10. Interview with the author.
11. Interview with the author.
12. Interview with the author.
13. This interview was conducted in 1987.
14. ICOT, 1985b, p. 17.
15. Fujitsu, Hitachi and Oki have been involved in the initial research on parallel processing.
16. This interview was held in 1987. It should be noted that ICOT officials who commented on this chapter strongly disagreed with A's account and with the present interpretation of A's statement.
17. Government funding is examined in greater detail below.
18. In this section, as elsewhere in this chapter, Prolog should be read as referring more broadly to logic programming.
19. ICOT, 1985a, pp. 15–16.
20. Interview with the author.
21. This emerged clearly in the interviews with middle-level researchers at ICOT.
22. This section is based on information given to the author by a representative of Fujitsu.
23. Tatsuno, 1986, p. 11.

24. ICOT, 1985a, pp. 18–20.
25. In the final chapter this difference in approach between ICOT and the firms is explained in terms of the concept of 'bounded vision'.
26. These data are based on information supplied by the company to the author.

9. Conclusions and theoretical implications

1. See p. 42.
2. The Den Den relationship will be analysed in more detail in a forthcoming companion volume on telecommunications.
3. Hitachi Technology, 1988, p. 11.
4. For a detailed elaboration, see Fransman (1986b)
5. The quotation from Schumpeter is given on p. 5
6. See Fransman (forthcoming).
7. Goto and Wakasugi, 1988, pp. 190–6.
8. See, for example, Trezise (1983).

Appendix 2. Specialization in industrial and consumer electronics by Japanese electronics companies

1. All yen figures for 1986 are converted into dollars at an exchange rate of 180 yen, in accordance with majority company practice in the corporate accounts for that year.
2. Unfortunately Hitachi's sales data are not strictly comparable with those for the other firms.

Bibliography

Abegglen, J. C. (ed.) 1970. *Business Strategies for Japan.* Tokyo: Sophia University.

Abegglen, J. C. and Stalk, G. 1985. *Kaisha, the Japanese Corporation.* Tokyo: Charles E. Tuttle.

Abernathey, W. J. *et al.* 1983. *Industrial Renaissance.* New York: Basic Books.

Agency for Industrial Science and Technology 1986a. *1986.* Tokyo: Ministry of International Trade and Industry.

1986b. *Research Planning for AIST Research Projects.* Shiken Kenkyusho Kenkyu Keikakiu.

Allen G. C. 1972. *A Short Economic History of Modern Japan, 1867–1936.* London: Allen and Unwin.

1987. *How Japan Competes: An Assessment of International Trading Practices with Special Reference to 'Dumping'* London: Institute of Economic Affairs.

1980. *Japan's Economic Policy.* London: Macmillan.

1981. *The Japanese Economy.* London: Weidenfeld and Nicolson

Anchordoguy, M. 1988a. Mastering the market: Japanese government targeting of the computer industry, *International Organization* 42: 509–43.

1988b. The public corporation: a potent Japanese policy weapon, *Political Science Quarterly* 103: 707–24.

Anderson, M. A. 1984. *Science and Technology in Japan.* London: Longman.

Aoki, M. 1984. *The Cooperative Game Theory of the Firm.* Oxford: Clarendon Press.

1988a. *Information, Incentives and Bargaining in the Japanese Economy.* Cambridge: Cambridge University Press.

1988b. The Japanese bureaucracy in economic administration. In *Government Policy Towards Industry in the USA and Japan,* ed. J.B. Shoven, pp. 265–300. Cambridge: Cambridge University Press.

Aoki, M. and Rosenberg, N. 1987. *The Japanese Firm as an Innovating Institution.* Paper prepared for International Roundtable Conference, 'Institutions in a New Democratic Society – Search for a New Frontier', Tokyo, 15–17 September 1987.

Beasley, W. G. 1973. *The Modern History of Japan,* 2nd ed. London: Weidenfield and Nicolson.

Beckmann, G. M. and Genji, O. 1969. *The Japanese Communist Party, 1922–1945.* Stanford: Stanford University Press.

Bednorz, G. and Mueller, K. A. 1986. Possible high tc superconductivity in the

Ba–La–Cu–O system, *Zeitschrift für Physic B,* condensed matter.

Bernstein, G. L. 1976. *Japanese Marxist.* Cambridge, Mass.: Harvard University Press.

Bisson, T. A. 1976. *Saibatsu Dissolution of Japan.* Westport, Connecticut: Greenwood Press.

Boltho, A. 1975. *An Economic Survey, 1953–73.* Oxford: Oxford University Press.

1985. Was Japan's industrial policy successful?, *Cambridge Journal of Economics* 9: 187–201.

Borrus, M. 1982. *US–Japanese Competition in the Semiconductor Industry.* Berkeley: University of California, Institute of International Study.

1988. *Competing for Electronics.* Cambridge, Mass.: Ballinger.

Borrus, M. and Zysman, J. 1986. Japan. In *National Policies for Developing High Technology Industries,* eds. F. W. Rushing and C. G. Brown, pp. 111–42. Boulder, Colo.: Westview Press.

Borrus, M., Tyson, L. and Zysman, J. 1987. Creating advantage: how government policies shape international trade in semiconductor industry. In *Strategic Trade Policy and New International Economics,* ed. P. Krugman, pp. 91–114. Cambridge, Mass.: MIT Press.

Bronfenbrenner, M. 1970. Japan's Galbraithian economy, *Public Interest* 21: 149–57.

Calder, K. E. 1983. Computer industry. In *Kodansha Encyclopedia of Japan,* p. 346. Tokyo: Kondasha.

Caves, R. E. and Uekusa, M. 1976. *Industrial Organization in Japan.* Washington, D.C.: The Brookings Institute.

Chan, S. C. 1974. The Japanese motor vehicle industry: a study of the history of the Japanese motor vehicle industry and the impact of Japanese motor vehicles on the US market. Ph.D. dissertation, American University, Washington, D.C.

Cang, C. S. 1981, *The Japanese Auto Industry and the US Market.* New York: Praeger.

Chokki, T. 1986. History and structure of the Japanese machine tool industry. In *Machinery and Economic Development,* ed. M. Fransman. London: Macmillan.

Christopher, R. C. 1984. *The Japanese Mind.* London: Pan Books.

Clark, R. 1979. *The Japanese Company.* New Haven: Yale University Press.

Cole, R. E. 1979. *Work, Mobility and Participation.* Berkeley: University of California Press.

(ed.) 1982. *Industry at the Crossroads,* Ann Arbor: University of Michigan Press.

Davidson, W. H. 1984. *The Amazing Race.* New York: John Wiley.

Denison, E. F. and Chung, W. K. 1976. *How Japan's Economy Grew so Fast.* Washington, D.C.: The Brookings Institute.

Dodwell Marketing Consultants. 1989. *The Structure of the Japanese Electronics Industry,* 2nd ed. Tokyo: Dodwell.

Doi, T. 1973. *The Anatomy of Dependence.* Tokyo: Kodansha International.

Dore, R. P. 1959. *Land Reform in Japan.* London: Oxford University Press.

1973. *British Factory – Japanese Factory.* London: Allen and Unwin.

1978. *Shinohata.* New York: Panther Books.

1983. *A Case Study of Technology Forecasting in Japan.* London: The Technical Change Centre.

Eads, G. C. and Nelson, R. R. 1986. Japanese high technology policy: what lessons for the United States? In *Japan's High Technology Industries: Lessons and Limitations of Industrial Policy*. Seattle: University of Washington Press.

Elster, J. 1983. *Explaining Technical Change*. Cambridge: Cambrdige University Press.

Ends, J. L. 1962. Invention and innovation in the petroleum refining industry. In *The Rate and Direction of Inventive Activity: Economic and Social Factors*. Princeton: Princeton University, Press.

Eto, H. and Matsui, K. (eds.) 1984. *R & D Management Systems in Japanese industry*. Amsterdam: North Holland.

Feigenbaum, E. A. 1983. *The Fifth Generation*. London: Addison Wesley.

Feigenbaum, E. A. and McCorduck, P. 1983. *The Fifth Generation*. London: Pan Books.

Flaherty, M. T. 1987. Discussion on Suzumura, K. and Okunu-Fujiwara, M., 'Industrial policy in Japan: Overview and evaluation'. In *Trade Friction and Economic Policy*, eds. R. Sato and P. Wachtel. Cambridge: Cambridge University Press.

Flamm, K. 1985. *Targeting Technology*. Washington, D.C.: The Brookings Institute (mimeo).

1987. *Targeting the Computer*. Washington, D.C.: The Brookings Institute.

1988. *Creating the Computer*. Washington, D.C.: The Brookings Institute.

Fodella, G (ed.) 1983. *Japan's Economy in a Comparative Perspective*. Tenterden, Kent: Paul Norbury.

Fox, G. C. and Messina, P. C. 1987 Advanced computer architectures, *Scientific American* 257: 44–53.

Francks, P. 1984. *Technology and Agricultural Development in Pre-war Japan*. New Haven: Yale University Press.

Frank, I. (ed.) 1975. *The Japanese Economy in International Perspective*. Baltimore: The Johns Hopkins Press.

Fransman, M. 1982a. Learning and the capital goods sector under free trade: the case of Hong Kong, *World Development* 10(11) 991-1014.

(ed.) 1982b. *Industry and Accumulation in Africa*. London: Heinemann.

1984a. Explaining the success of Asian NICs: incentives and technology, *IDS Bulletin* (University of Sussex) 15(2).

1984b. Promoting technological capability in the capital goods sector: the case of Singapore, *Research Policy* 13: 33–54.

(ed.) 1986a. *Machinery and Economic Development*. London: Macmillan.

1986b. *Technology and Economic Development*. Brighton: Wheatsheaf.

1986c. International competitiveness, technical change and the State: The machine tool industry in Taiwan and Japan, *World Development* 14(12): 1375–96.

1988. Corporate strategy and technology transfer in Japanese biotechnology – creating a system. In Biosymposium Tokyo '88: Communication for Advancement of Biotechnology. *Proceedings*. Tokyo: BIDEC.

forthcoming. *Japanese Telecommunications*.

Fransman, M. and King, K. (eds.) 1984. *Technology Capability in the Third World*. London: Macmillan.

Freeman, C. 1987. *Technology Policy and Economic Performance: Lessons from Japan*. London: Pinter.

1988. Information technology and the new economic paradigm. In *Strategic Issues in Information Technology*, ed. H. Schutte, pp. 159–76. Maidenhead: Pergamon Infotech.

Friedman, D. 1988. *The Misunderstood Miracle: Industrial Development and Political Change in Japan*, Ithaca: Cornell University Press.

Fukutake, T. 1982a. *Japanese Society Today*, 2nd ed. Tokyo: University of Tokyo Press.

1982b. *The Japanese Social Structure: Its Evolution in the Modern Century*, translated by R. P. Dore. Tokyo: University of Tokyo Press.

Gamota, G. and Frieman, W. 1988. *Gaining Ground*. Cambridge, Mass.: Ballinger.

Gibney, F. 1982, *Miracle by Design*. New York: Times Books.

Gibson, R. W. 1981. *Japanese Scientific and Technical Literature: A Subject Guide*. Aldershot: Gower.

Gilfillan, S. 1934. *Inventing the Ship*. Chicago: Follet.

Goldsmith, R. W. 1983. *The Financial Development of Japan, 1868–79*. New Haven: Yale University Press.

Goto, A. and Wakasugi, R. 1988. Technology policy. In *Industrial Policy of Japan*, eds. R. Komiya, M. Okuno and K. Suzumura, pp. 183–204. Tokyo: Academic Press.

Goto, A., Sato, M., Nakajima, K., Taki, K. and Matsumoto, A. 1988. Overview of the Parallel Inference Machine architecture (PIM). In *Proceedings of the International Conference on Fifth Generation Computer Systems, 1988*, Tokyo, 28 November – 2 December, pp. 208–29.

Gregory, G. 1985. *Japanese Electronics Technology: Enterprise and Innovation* Tokyo: The Japan Times.

Grupp, H. and Gundrum, U. 1988. National science systems and science indicator systems, *Problems of Measuring Technological Change*, ed. H. Grupp, pp. 3–12. Cologne: Verlag TUV Rheinland.

Hadley, E. M. 1970. *Antitrust in Japan*. Princeton: Princeton University Press.

Halliday, J. 1975. *A Political History of Japanese Capitalism*. New York: Pantheon Books.

Han, K. 1971. *Sources of Growth Rates in Japan and Korea*. Tokyo: Asia Productivity Organization.

Hecht, J. 1987. Computing with light, *New Scientist* 116: 45–8.

Higashi, C. 1983. *Japanese Trade Policy Formulation*. New York: Praeger.

Hirschmeier, J. 1964. *The Origins of Entrepreneurship in Modern Japan*. Cambridge, Mass.: Harvard University Press.

Hirschmeier, J. and Yui, T. 1981. *The Development of Japanese Business*. London: Allen and Unwin.

Hitachi Technology, 1988. *Hitachi Review*, special issue.

Ho, A. K. 1973. *Japan's Trade Liberalization in the 1960s*. New York: International Arts and Sciences Press Inc.

ICOT 1985a. *ICOT Journal* no. 10.

1985b. *ICOT Journal* no. 11.

1986. *Outline of the Fifth Generation Computer Project*. Tokyo: Institute for New Generation Computer Technology.

Imai, K. 1984. Japan's industrial policy for high technology industries, Discussion Paper No. 119, Institute of Business Research, Hitotsubashi University, Tokyo.

1986. Japan's industrial policy for high technology industry. In *Japan's High Technology Industries. Lessons and Limitations of Industrial Policy*, ed. H. Patrick. Tokyo: University of Tokyo Press.

Imai, K., Nonaka, I. and Takeuchi, M. 1985. Managing the new product development process: how Japanese companies learn and unlearn. In *The Uneasy Alliance*, ed. K. B. Clark, R. H. Hayes and C. Lorenz, pp. 337–76. Cambridge, Mass.: Harvard Business School Press.

Instiue of East Asia Studies, 1982. *The Japanese Challenge and the American Response: A Symposium*. Berkeley: University of California.

Irvine, J. and Martin, B. R. 1984. *Foresight in Science*. London: Frances Pinter.

Itoh, M. 1980. *Value and Crisis:* New York: Monthly Review Press.

Japan Economic Almanac 1985. Published by the *Japan Economic Journal*, international weekly edition of the *Nihon Keizai Shimbun*.

Japan Science and Technology Agency 1985. White Paper on Science and Technology 1985. Towards creation of new technology for the 21st century (summary). Foreign Press Centre, January 1985, W–84–20.

Japanese Technology Evaluation Program 1987. *JTECH Panel Report On Advanced Computing In Japan*. McLean, Va.: Science Applications International Corporation.

JMA Consultants Inc. 1982. Management and productivity improvement in Japan. Tokyo.

Johnson, C. 1978. *Japan's Public Policy Companies*. Washington: American Enterprise Institute.

1982. *MITI and the Japanese Miracle*. Stanford: Stanford University Press.

Kagono, T., Nonaka, I., Sakakibara, K. and Okumura, A. 1985. *Strategic versus Evolutionary Management*. Amsterdam: North Holland.

Kamata, S. 1983. *Japan in the Passing Lane*. London: Allen and Unwin.

Kaplan, E. J. 1972. *Japan: The Government–Business Relationship*. Washington, D.C.: U.S. Dept. of Commerce.

Karube, I. 1986. Trends in bioelectronics research, *Science and Technology in Japan* 5(19).

Kellman, M. and Landau, D. 1984. The nature of Japan's comparative advantage, *World Development* 12: 433–8.

Kikuchi, M. 1983. *Japanese Electronics: A Worm's Eye View of its Evolution*. Tokyo: The Simul Press.

Klein, L. and Ohkawa, K. (eds.) 1968. *Economic Growth: The Japanese Experience since the Meyi Era*. Homewood, Ill.: Richard Irwin.

Kobayashi, K. 1986. *Computers and Communications*. Cambridge, Mass.: MIT Press.

Kobayashi, T. 1986. *Fortune Favors the brave: Fujitsu – Thirty Years in Computers*. Tokyo: Toyo Keizai Shinposha.

Kodansha Encyclopedia of Japan, 1983. Tokyo: Kodansha.

Kojima, K. and Ozawa, T. 1984. Japan's general trading companies: *Merchants of Economic Development*. Paris: OECD Development Centre.

Komiya, R. and Itoh, M. 1986 *International Trade and Trade Policy of Japan: 1955– 1984*, Discussion Paper, Research Institute for the Japanese Economy. Faculty of Economics, University of Tokyo.

Komiya, R., Okuno, M. and Suzumura, K. (eds.) 1988. *Industrial Policy of Japan*. Tokyo: Academic Press.

Kondo, Y. 1988. Quality in Japan. In *Quality Control Handbook*, ed. J.M. Juran, pp. 35F. 1–35F. 30. New York: McGraw-Hill.

Kono, T. 1984. *Strategy and Structure of Japanese Enterprises*. London: Macmillan.

Krause, L. B. 1982. *US Economic Policy Toward the Association of Southeast Asian Nations: Meeting the Japanese Challenge*. Washington, D.C.: The Brookings Institute.

Langlois, R. N., Pugel, T. A., Haklisch, C. S., Nelron, R. R. and Egelhoff, W. G. 1988. *Microelectronics: An Industry in Transition*. London: Unwin Hyman.

Levine, S. B. and Kawada, H. 1980. *Human Resources in Japanese Industrial Development*. Princeton: Princeton University Press.

Lockwood, W. W. 1968. *The Economic Development of Japan: Growth and Structural Change*. Princeton: Princeton University Press.

(ed.) 1970. *The State and Economic Enterprise in Japan*. Princeton: Princeton University Press.

Lynn, L. 1982. *How Japan Innovates: A Comparison with the US in the Case of Oxygen Steelmaking*. Boulder, Colo.: Westview Press.

McLean, M. (ed.) 1982. *The Japanese Electronic Challenge*. London: Pinter.

(ed.) 1983. *Mechatronics: Developments in Japan and Europe*. London: Pinter.

(1985). *The Information Explosion*. London: Pinter.

McMillan, C. J. 1984. *The Japanese Industrial System*. Berlin: Walter de Gruyter.

McNulty, P. J. 1984. On the nature and theory of economic organization: the role of the firm reconsidered, *History of Political Economy* 16.2: 233–53.

Magaziner, I. C. 1980. *Japanese Industry Policy*. London: Policy Studies Institute.

Masanor, M. 1982. *Japanese Technology*. Tokyo: The Simul Press.

Mathieson, R. C. 1979. *Japan's Role in Soviet Economic Growth*. New York: Praeger.

Meindl, J. D. 1987. Chips for advanced computing, *Scientific American* 257: 54–63.

Merz, J. L. 1987. The Optoelectronics Joint Research Laboratory: light shed on cooperative research in Japan, Department of Electrical and Computer Engineering, University of California, Santa Barbara (mimeo.).

Milward, R. S. 1979. *Japan: The Past in the Present*. Tenterden, Kent: Paul Norbury.

Mirai Kogaku Kenkyujyo 1983. *NIRA Output – Erekutoronikusu no hatten katei ni kansuru bunseki*. Tokyo: Sogo Kenkyu Kaihatsu Kiko. [*Translated* Future Engineering Laboratory 1983. *NIRA Output – An Analysis of the Development Process in Electronics*. Tokyo: NIRA.]

Mizisno, S. 1981. *Early Foundations for Japan's Twentieth Century Economic Emergence*. New York: Vantage Press.

Moore, J. 1982. *Japanese Workers and the Struggle for Power 1945–1947*. Madison: University of Wisconsin Press.

Morishima, M. 1982. *Why has Japan 'Succeeded'? Western Technology and the Japanese Ethos*. Cambridge: Cambridge University Press.

Moritani, M. 1982. *Japanese Technology*. Tokyo: The Simul Press.

Morley, J. M. (ed.) 1971. *Dilemmas of Growth in Prewar Japan*. Princeton: Princeton University Press.

Moto-oka, T. and Kitsuregawa, M. 1985. *The Fifth Generation Computer: The Japanese Challenge*. Chichester: John Wiley.

Moulder, F. 1979. *Japan, China and the Modern World Economy*. Cambridge: Cambridge University Press.

Myers, R. H. and Peattie, M. R. (eds.) 1984. *The Japanese Colonial Empire, 1895–1945*. Princeton: Princeton University Press.

Najita, T. and Koschmann, J. V. (eds.) 1982. *Conflict in Modern Japanese History: The Neglected Tradition*. Princeton: Princeton University Press.

Nakagawa, K. (ed.) 1979. *Labour and Management*. Tokyo: University of Tokyo Press.

Nakamura, G. 1986. Strategic management in major Japanese hightech companies, *Long Range Planning* 19: 82–91.

Nakamura, T. 1981. *The Postwar Japanese Economy: Its Development and Structure*. Tokyo: University of Tokyo Press.

1983. *Economic Growth in Prewar Japan*. New Haven: Yale University Press.

Nakjayama, I. 1975. *Industrialization and Labour–Management Relations in Japan*. Tokyo: The Japan Institute of Labour.

National Economic Development Office 1983. *Transferable Factors in Japan's Economic Success*. London: National Economic Development Office.

National Institution for Research Advancement (NIRA) 1985. *Comprehensive Study of Microelectronics 1985*. Tokyo: NIRA.

NEC 1984. *The First Eighty Years*. Tokyo: NEC.

undated. *Quality Activities*. Tokyo: NEC.

Nihon Denshikikai Kogyokai 1979. *Denshikogyo Sanjunen-shi*. Tokyo: Nihon Denshikikai Kogyokai. [*Translated* Electronic Industry Association of Japan 1979. *Thirty Year History of the Electronics Industry*. Tokyo: EIAJ]

OECD 1972. *The Industrial Policy of Japan*. Paris: OECD

OECD *Economic Surveys*, Japan (annual).

Ohkawa K. 1957. *The Growth Rate of the Japanese Economy since 1878*. Tokyo: Kinokuniya Bookstore Company.

1972. *Differential Structure and Agriculture*. Tokyo: Kinokuniya Bookstore Company.

1983. Capital formation, productivity and employment: Japan's historical experience and its possible relevance to UDCs. International Development Centre of Japan, Tokyo.

Ohkawa, K. and Rosovsky, H. 1973. *Japanese Economic Growth*. London: Oxford University Press.

Ohkawa, K. and Shinohara, M. (eds.) 1979. *Patterns of Japanese Economic Development: A Quantitative Appraisal*. New Haven: Yale University Press.

Okimoto, D. I. (ed.) 1982. *Japan's Economy: Coping with Change in the International Environment*. Boulder, Colo.: Westview Press.

1986. Regime characteristics of Japanese industrial policy. In *Japan's High Technology Industries. Lessons and Limitations of Industrial Policy*, ed. H. Patrick. Tokyo: University of Tokyo Press.

Okimoto, D. I., Sugano, T. and Weinstein, F. B. (eds.) 1984. *Competitive Edge*. Stanford: Stanford University Press.

Okita, S. 1980. *The Developing Economies and Japan*. Tokyo: University of Tokyo Press.

Oldham, W. G. 1980. The fabrication of microelectronic circuits. In *The Microelectronic Revolution*, ed. T. Forester. Oxford: Basil Blackwell.

Olsen, E. A. 1978. *Japan: Economic Growth, Resource Scarcity and Environment Constraints*. Boulder, Colo.: Westview Press.

Ozaki, R. S. 1972. *The Control of Imports and Foreign Capital in Japan*. New York: Praeger.

Ozawa, T. 1966. Imitation, innovation and trade: a study of foreign licensing operations in Japan. Columbia University.

1974. *Japan's technological challenge to the West 1950–1974: Motivation and Accomplishment*. Cambridge, Mass.: MIT Press.

1979. *Multinationalism, Japanese Style*. Princeton: Princeton University Press.

Patel, P. and Pavitt, K. 1987. Is Western Europe losing the technological race?, *Research Policy* 16: 59–85.

Patrick, H. (ed.) (1976). *Japanese Industrialization and its Social Consequences*. Berkeley: University of California Press.

1980. The postwar economic history of Japan. Discussion Paper 349, Economic Growth Center, Yale University.

1982. Japanese financial development in historical perspective, 1868–1980. Discussion Paper 398, Economic Growth Center, Yale University.

Patrick, H. and Rosovsky, H. (eds.) 1976. *Asia's New Giant*. Washington, D.C.: The Brookings Institute.

Peck, M. J. 1983. Government coordination of R & D in the Japanese electronic industry. Yale University (mimeo.).

Peck, M. J. and Tamura, S. 1976. Technology. In *Asia's New Giant*, eds. H. Patrick and H. Rosovsky. Washington D.C.: The Brookings Institute.

Pohl, H. (ed.) 1982. Innovation, know-how, rationalization and investment in the German and Japanese economies, 1868/1971–1930/1980. *Proceedings of the German–Japanese Symposium*, Siemens Training Centre, Berlin, 20–23 March 1979.

Porter, M. E. 1987. Changing patterns of international competition. In *The Competitive Challenge*, ed. D. J. Teece, pp. 27–57. Cambridge, Mass.: Ballinger.

Pugh, E. W. 1985. Technology assessment. *Proceedings of IEEE* 73: 1756–63.

Pugh, E. W. *et al.* 1980. Josephson extendability study. IBM Technical Report.

1983. Josephson–semiconductor extendability study. IBM Technical Report.

Rappa, M. A. 1985. Capital financing strategies of the Japanese semiconductor industry, *California Management Review* 27: 85–99.

Reischaugh, E. O. and Craig, A. M. 1979. *Japan: Traditions and Transformation*. Cambridge, Mass.: Harvard University Press.

Roberts, J. G. 1973. *Mitsui*. New York: Weatherhill.

Rosenberg, N. and Steinmüller, W. E. 1982. The economic implications of the VLSI revolution. In *Inside the Black Box*, ed. N. Rosenberg. Cambridge: Cambridge University Press.

1988. Why are the Americans such poor imitators, *American Economic Association Papers* 78: 229–34.

Rosenbloom, R. S. and Cusumano, M. A. 1987. Technological pioneering and competitive advantage, *California Management Review* 29: 51–76.

Rosovsky, H. 1961. *Capital Formation in Japan, 1868–1940*. New York: Free Press of Glencoe.

1972. What are the 'lessons' of Japanese economic history? In *Economic Development in the Long Run*, ed. A. J. Youngson. New York: St Martin's Press.

Santora, J. C. 1982. *Japanese Management, 1970–1981: A Selected Guide to Periodical Literature*. Monticello: Nance Bibliographies.

Sato, K. (ed.) 1980. *Industry and Business in Japan*, London: Croom Helm.

Sato, K. and Hoshino, Y. 1984. *The Anatomy of Japanese Business*. London: Croom Helm.

Scace, R. I. 1981. *Semiconductor Technology for the Non-Technologist*. Washington, D.C.: National Bureau of Standards, U.S. Department of Commerce.

Scalapino, R. A. 1967. *The Japanese Communist Movement, 1920–1966*. Berkeley: University of California Press.

Schonberger, R. J. 1982. *Japanese Manufacturing Techniques*. New York: The Free Press.

Schumpeter, J. A. 1966. *Capitalism, Socialism and Democracy*. London: Allen and Unwin.

Scott, B. R., Rosenblum, J. W. and Sproat, A. T. 1980. *Case Studies in Political Economy: Japan 1854–1977*. Cambridge, Mass.: Harvard Business School.

Sethi, S. P. 1975. *Japanese Business and Social Conflict*. Cambridge, Mass.: Ballinger.

Shimada, H. 1985. The perceptions and the reality of Japanese industrial relations. In *The Management Challenge*, ed. L. C. Thurow, pp. 42–66. Cambridge, Mass.: MIT Press.

Shinohara, M. 1970. *Structural Change in Japan's Economic Development*. Economic Research Series no. 11, Institute of Economic Research, Hitotsuluski University. Tokyo: Kimokuniya Bookstore.

1982. *Industrial Growth, Trade and Dynamic Patterns in the Japanese Economy*. Tokyo: University of Tokyo Press.

Shulman, F. K. 1982. *Doctoral dissertations on Japan and on Korea 1969–1979: an Annotated Bibliography of Studies in Western Languages*. Seattle: University of Washington Press.

Sigurdson, J. 1983, Japan's high technology race: the information technologies. Report no. 8, Research Policy Institute, University of Lund.

1986. *Industry and State Partnership in Japan. The Very Large Scale Integrated Circuits (VLSI) Project*. Lund: Research Policy Institute.

Simon, H. A. 1988. Prospects for Cognitive Science. In *Proceedings of the International Conference on Fifth Generation Computer Systems, 1988*, Tokyo, 28 November–2 December, pp. 111–19.

Sinha, R. 1982. *Japan's Options for the 1980s*. London: Croom Helm.

Smith, R. J. 1983. *Japanese Society: Tradition, Self and the Social Order*. Cambridge: Cambridge University Press.

Sobel, R. 1986. *IBM v. Japan*. New York: Stein and Day.

Steven, R. 1983. *Classes in Contemporary Japan*. Cambridge: Cambridge University Press.

Strauss, M. M. 1986. The organization of research in the information sciences. Case studies in Japan and the US. Master of Science dissertation submitted to the Massachusetts Institute of Technology.

Sumiya, M. and Koji, T. (eds.) 1979. *An Outline of Japanese Economic History 1603–1940. Major Works and Research Findings*. Tokyo: University of Tokyo Press.

Suzumura, K. and Okuno-Fujiwara, M. 1987a. Industrial policy in Japan: overview and evaluation. In *US–Japanese Economic Relations: Co-operation, Competition and Confrontation*, eds. R. Sato and P. Wachtel. New York: Pergamon Press.

Suzumura, K. and Okuno-Fujiwara, M. 1987b. Industrial policy in Japan: overview and evaluation. In *Trade Friction and Economic Policy*, eds. R. Sato and P. Wachtel. Cambridge: Cambridge University Press.

Tarui, Y. 1982. *Talking about ICs – From Transistor to VLSI* (IC no hanasu – Toranjista kara cho ISI made), NHK 411, Tokyo.

Tarui, Y. and Takeishi, Y. 1981. Basic technology for VLSI. In *Semiconductor Silicon 1981*, pp. 6–19.

Tatsuno, S. 1986. *The Technopolis Strategy*. New York: Prentice Hall.

Trezise, P. H. 1983. Industrial policy is not the major reason for Japan's success, *The Brookings Review* 1:13–18.

Tsurumi, Y. 1979. *Japanese Business: A Research Guide with Annotated Bibliography*. New York: Praeger.

1980. *Technology Transfer and Foreign Trade*. New York: Arno Press.

Turner, L. 1987. *Industrial Collaboration with Japan*. London: Routledge and Kegan Paul.

Ueda, K. 1986a Guarded horn clauses: a parallel logic programming language with the concept of a guard. TR 208, ICOT.

1986b Introduction to guarded horn clauses. TR 209, ICOT.

Uenohara, M. 1982. Japanese social system for technological development – its merits and demerits. Manuscript of the Holst Memorial Lecture, 8 December 1982. Technische Hogeschool, Eindhoven, The Netherlands (mimeo.).

1985. Increased reliance of modern industrial technology on scientific outcomes. In *Transforming Scientific Ideas into Innovations*, eds. B. Bartocha and S. Okamura. Tokyo: Japan Society for the Promotion of Science.

United States Congress 1982. Joint Economic Committee. *The Japanese financial system in comparative perspective*. Report of the Joint Economic Committee. Washington D.C.: Government Printing office.

1984. Japanese technological advances and possible United States responses using research joint ventures. Report prepared by the Subcommittee on Investigations and Oversight and the Subcommittee on Science, Research and Technology transmitted to the Committee on Science and Technology, US House of Representatives, October.

United States Department of Defense 1987. *Report of Defense Science Board Task Force on Defense Semiconductor Dependency*. Washington, D.C.: Office of the Under-Secretary of Defence for Acquisition.

Urabe, K. 1988. Innovation and the Japanese management system. In *Innovation and Management*, eds. K. Urabe, J. Child and T. Kagono, pp. 1–25. Berlin: Walter de Gruyter.

Uyehara, C. H. (ed.) 1982. *Technological Exchange: The US–Japanese experience*. Proceedings of a symposium held on 21 October 1981, sponsored by the Japan–American Society of Washington. Washington, D.C.: University Press of America.

Vogel, E. F. (ed.) 1975. *Modern Japanese Organization and Decision-making*. Berkeley: University of California Press.

Waswo, A. 1977. *Japanese Landlords: The Decline of a Rural Elite*. Berkeley: University of California Press.

Watawabe, S. 1983. Market structure, industrial organization and technological development: the case of the Japanese electronics-based NC-machine tool industry. WEP 2–22/WP.111, International Labour Organization, Geneva.

Welke, H. J. 1982. *Data Processing in Japan.* Amsterdam: North Holland.

Williams, R. 1988. UK science and technology: in search of a marriage of convenience, *Financial Times*, 3 February, p. 23.

Williamson, O. E. 1975. *Markets and Hierarchies.* New York: The Free Press.

Woronoff, J. 1981. *Japan's Wasted Workers.* Tokyo: Lotus Press.

Yamamura, K. 1967. *Economic Policy in Postwar Japan.* Berkeley: University of California Press.

(ed.) 1982. *Policy and Trade Issues of the Japanese Economy: American and Japanese Perspectives.* Seattle: University of Washington Press.

Yamazaki, M. 1980. *Japan's Community-based Industries.* Tokyo: Asia Productivity Organization.

Yanaga, C. 1968. *Big Business in Japanese Politics.* New Haven: Yale University Press.

Yoshimara, K. 1979, *Japanese Economic Development.* Tokyo: Oxford University Press.

Yoshino, M. Y. 1968. *Japan's Managerial System.* Cambridge, Mass.: MIT Press.

Young, A. K. 1979. *The Sogo Shosha.* Boulder, Colo.: Westview Press.

Index

3-D devices, *see* three-dimensional devices

Agency for Industrial Science and
    Technology, 17, 102, 178
    bounded vision, 285–6
    ICOT evaluation committee, 229
AI, *see* artificial intelligence
Aiso, H., 197
AIST, *see* Agency for Industrial Science
    and Technology
aluminium gallium arsenide, 180, 187
Alvey programme comparison, 209
Amdahl, G. 40–3
Amdahl Corporation, 41–3
America, *see* United States
array processor technology, 195
artificial intelligence, 195
    Fifth Generation Project, 198, 219–23, 241
    parallel inference machines, 213–14
    universities' role, 207–9
ATLAS (machine translation system), 222

basic research, 282
basic technology knowledge, 110–11, 201,
    209
Bednorz, G., 166
Bell Laboratories, HEMT research, 159
bio-sensors proposal, 179, 181
biochip research, 177, 181, 185–6
'bounded rationality' concept, 286
'bounded vision' concept, 3, 12, 252, 257,
    262–3, 276
    Japanese System, 284–6

Canon, VLSI Project participant, 71–2
CAP, *see* cellular array processor
CDL, *see* Computer Development
    Laboratory
cellular array processor, 157
chip technology

biochip research, 177, 181, 185–6
environmentally resistant, 179, 181
CIHR, *see* coordinated in-house research
CIL, *see* Complex Indeterminate Language
Colmeraur, G., 195
commercializable products, VLSI Project,
    83–5
company specialization, 294–9 (App. 2)
competition
    cooperative research analysis, 243–55
    IBM computers, 7
    industrial electronics corporations, 2
    international competitiveness: decentrali-
    zation practice, 259–60; information
    flows, 260–1; just-in-time production,
    259; technical change, 258–9; total
    quality control approach, 259; vertical
    integration, 261–3
    Japanese System 12, 276–84; benefits and
    costs, 276–7; central features, 277–8;
    government role, 280–1; JRJF
    limitations, 282–3; knowledge
    diffusion, 283–4; research
    cooperation, 278–81
    research and development, 257
Complex Indeterminate Language, 237
compound electronic devices, 99–100,
    103, 108
Computer Development Laboratory, 80
computer industry
    American links, 28, 39, 42–3
    commercial sector research, 103–4
    cooperation and competition, 243–55
    development of (1948–79): cooperative
    research, 23–38; government subsidies,
    44–5; research institutions, 13–23;
    tariff protection, 25–7; trade
    liberalization, 38–56
    domestic market protection, 268
    IBM world dominance, 40

323

joint research issues, 103–7, 129
mainframe market, 55–6
market share, 43, 49, 52, 98
memory technology, 32
mergers, 47
protected status, 23, 24–5, 26–7
R&D, 31, 44, 49–51, 131–3
technology periods, 266–73
VHSCS Project, 33
computer languages
CIL, 237
Concurrent Prolog, 222
Extended Concurrent Prolog, 222
Flat Guarded Horn Clause (FGHC),
197, 236, 237
Guarded Horn Clause (GHC), 211
Lisp, 195, 199, 213, 220
Prolog, 193, 195–6, 209, 213, 222
Utilisp, 221
computers
development, 13–23
ETL IV, 267–8
ETL series, 19–20, 22–3, 31
FUJIC development, 20
Hep supercomputer, 147
IBM compatibility, 216–17
IBM System 360, 30, 31–2
IBM System 370, 39, 45
mainframe development, 55–6
mainframes, 271
Musashino-1, 267
optical, 176
parametron development, 18–19, 31,
38
parametron-based, 267–8
planar technology, 31
relay-based, 266
semiconductor design, 41–2
Supercomputer Project 145–76
transistor development, 19, 101
von Neumann 145, 198
Concurrent Prolog, 222
consumer electronics
industrial specialization, 294–9
(App. 2)
Japanese System, 286–7
cooperative research
benefits, 279
electronic devices, 243–55, 256–90
government role, 248–9, 251–2
inter-firm, 279–80
Japanese System, 278–83
knowledge diffusion, 283–4

national projects, benefits, 249–55
types of, 281
cooperative research agreements, 1–3, 8
coordinated in-house research (CIHR)
conclusions, 281
FED Project, 177–91
Fifth Generation Project, 230
Optical Measurement Project, 109, 133–4
Supercomputer Project, 154–8, 170–2
VLSI Project, 89–95
corporate research resources, Optical
Measurement Project, 131–3
costs/funding
FED Project, 182, 186
Fifth Generation Project, 227–9
ICOT, 194, 227–9
Optical Measurement Project, 133,
141–2, 144
summary, 280, 281
Supercomputer Project 145, 151–2, 160–1
VLSI Project, 58, 80–1
cryogenic technology, 148–9, 180
crystal technology
growth techniques, 116, 123–4
VLSI Project, 78–9, 84
Czochralski technique, 124

DCL Josephson devices, 164
decentralization practice, 259–60
Den Den family, 14, 20, 47, 55–6
Catching-Up Periods, 267, 268, 269–72
Optical Measurement Project, 107, 128
Dendenkosha Information Processing
System (DIPS computer), 38, 272
Denelcor, Hep supercomputer, 147
DIPS computer, *see* Dendenkosha
Information Processing System
DRAMS, *see* dynamic random access
memory
dynamic random access memory, 275

Early Catching-Up Period (1945–65),
256, 266–9
ECL, *see* Electrical Communications
Laboratories
economics
CIHR economies, 170–2
competitiveness, 258–63
electronics specialization, 294–9
(App. 2)
Fifth Generation Project, 231–3
industrial policy debate, 2
joint research issues, 59–63

market processes, 4–6
Optical Measurement Project, 134–7
R & D economies, 279–81
VLSI Project evaluation, 81–97
wealth causes, 4
ECP, *see* Extended Concurrent Prolog
Electrical Communications Laboratories
   (ECL), 268–72
   development history, 17–23, 56
   developmental role, 8
   Japanese System role, 4
   VLSI Project participant, 75
electron-beam technology, 69, 71, 84, 275
electron-drift mobility, 148
electronic devices industry
   cooperation and competition, 243–55
   development, 24
   importance, 147–50
   tariff rates, 26
electronics industry
   cooperative research, 256–90
   Japanese System, 287–90
   specialization, 294–9 (App. 2)
Electrotechnical Laboratory (ETL)
   background, 16–23
   bounded vision problem, 284–5
   computer developments, 18–20
   computer series, 19–21
   developmental role, 2, 8
   FED Project, 179
   ICOT evaluation committee, 229
   Japanese System role, 4
   joint research projects, 59, 118
   Josephson junction research, 162–7
   Late Catching-Up Period, 269–72
   OJL membership, 119
   Optical Measurement Project, 98–144
   Prolog working group, 198
   research role, late 1970s, 101–2
   Supercomputer Project, 150, 168–9
   transistor technology, 13
   VHSCS project, 32
employment, lifetime practice, 61
Engineering Futures Laboratory, 177
Engineering Research Association for
   Optoelectronics Applied System, 109
environmentally resistant chips, 179,
   181
epitaxial growth, 116, 124
Esaki, L., 159, 179–80
ESHELL (expert system), 220
ETL, *see* Electrotechnical Laboratory
Europe, Japanese rival, 9

expert systems, Fujitsu research, 220
Extended Concurrent Prolog, 222

FACOM series
   Catching-Up Periods, 266, 270
   computers, 15, 31, 40, 47, 213, 220
Fanuc, 19
FED, *see* Future Electronic Devices
   Project
FGHC, *see* Flat Guarded Horn Clause
FIBI, *see* focussed ion beam implanter
field effect transistor, 148
Fifth Generation Computer Project
   (1982–91), 1, 10, 38, 55, 193–242
   background, 194–6
   benefits, 231–2
   competition/cooperation blending, 215
   evaluation, 229–42; criticisms of output,
      233–42; economies obtained, 231–3;
      output, 233
   funding, 227–9
   ICOT establishment, 197–200
   ICOT organization, 200–27
   introduction, 193–4
   JRJF, 282
   membership, 197–8
   objectives, 196–7
   origins, 177–9
   Prolog/Lisp cultures, 219
   research objectives, 147, 151
   subsystems, 196–7
Fifth Generation Computer Survey
   Committee, 197
fine-line lithography, 74–5
Flat Guarded Horn Clause, 197, 211, 236,
   237, 241
Flexible Logical Object Representation
   System, 221–2
FLORES, *see* Flexible Logical Object
   Representation System
focussed ion beam implanter, 116, 124–5,
   135
FONTAC project, 29–30
   research policy, 59, 60
for-profit corporations, 3, 12
   resource constraints, 176
fortified devices, 177
free-riding, 177–18, 120–1, 140, 142
Frontier-Leading Period (1980–present),
   256, 272–6
Fuchi, Kazuhiro, 195–9, 211, 233
FUJIC computer, development, 20
Fujitsu

Amdahl link, 40–3
artificial intelligence research, 219
Catching-Up Periods, 266–9, 269–72
computer commitment, 15–16
cooperative research analysis, 243–55
designs, 20, 33, 49
FACOM project 15, 31, 40, 47
FED Project, 185–6
FONTAC project, 30
HEMT research, 159–61, 168, 169, 172
IBM compatibility strategy, 47
ICOT member, 202, 210, 213
inter-firm research cooperation, 279
market leader, 15, 43, 49
OJL project member, 119
Supercomputer Project, 151–2, 154–5,
    156–7, 159–61
vertical integration, 261
VLSI Project participant, 66, 75–80
funding, *see* costs
Fuqua, D., 58
Furukawa, OJL project member, 119
Future Electronic Devices Project (1981–90),
    1, 10, 177–92
  background, 177–9
  conclusion, 191–2
  costs/funding, 182, 186
  devices selected, 177, 179–81
  evaluation, 186–91; CIHR benefits, 188–9;
    knowledge benefits, 187–8, 189–91;
    uncertainty effects, 189; universities'
    role, 191
  government role, 182, 186
  High Speed Computer Project
    comparison, 245–7, 255
  in-house research decision, 182, 186
  joint research proposal, 181–2
  JRJF possibility, 282
  participants, 183
  research organization, 182–6
'Future Systems' codename, 57

GaAs, *see* gallium arsenide
gallium arsenide
  III-V compounds 99–100
  electronic ICs, 116, 123–6
  Optical Measurement Project, 108
  silicon comparison, 148
  silicon substrates, 140
  Supercomputer Project, 148–61, 164,
    167
  superlattices research, 180, 187
  suppliers, 107

'generic research-push' determinant
  FED Project, 184
  optoelectronics, 108, 112, 120, 126–8
  Supercomputer Project, 165
generic technology
  joint research issue, 66
  knowledge, 110–11
GHC computer language, 211
gikan (technical official), 285
Global family, 32-bit processors, 279
Gore, A., 57–8
government
  AI research funding, 228
  computer industry, 1, 26–7
  cooperative research role, 248–9,
    251–2
  FED Project, 182, 186
  industrial policy, 2
  involvement, 271, 280–1
  MITI finance, 33–4, 45–50
  Optical Measurement Project, 105, 115,
    133, 141–3
  research cooperation, 1, 4
  research institutes, 3–4, 13–23,
    267, 268
  research support alternatives, 230
  subsidies commitment, 287–8
  Supercomputer Project, 145, 151–2

Hatoyama, G.M., 13
Hayashi, I., 119
HEMT, *see* high electron mobility
    transistor
Hep supercomputer, 147
Herfindahl index, 243
high electron mobility transistor, 126, 187
  electron-drift feature, 148
  government research, 168
  Supercomputer Project, 153–7,
    159–61, 168, 171
High-Speed Computing System Project,
    see Supercomputer Project
Hirakawa, H., 225
Hirano, M., 119
Hitachi, 53
  Catching-Up Periods, 266–9, 269–72
  cooperative research analysis, 243–55
  ETL Mark IV technology, 21
  FED Project, 185–6
  first computer, 16
  HEMT research, 161
  ICOT member, 202, 210, 213
  inter-firm research cooperation, 279

OJL project member, 119
Supercomputer Project, 151–2,
154–5, 161
VHSCS Project, 32, 33
VLSI Project participant, 66, 75–7
hojokin (conditional loan), 29
Hokushin company, 21
hybrid integrated circits, 270

IBM
computer compatibility, 47, 51
computer industry dominance, 40, 196
Fifth Generation project, 194
Japanese competition, 7, 9, 38–56
Josephson junctions research, 149,
151, 162–8
Late Catching-Up Period, 270
research knowledge, exchange, 278
Supercomputer Project stimulus, 145–7,
150
superconductivity research, 166, 289
System 360 computers, 30, 31–2
System 370 computers, 9, 39, 45
VLSI Project stimulus 58–9
IBM Japan, 27, 49
ICOT, *see* Institute for New Generation
Computer Technology
IC, *see* integrated circuit
IIHR, *see* isolated in-house research
Iizuka, T., 119
in-house research, types, 281
industrial electronics
Japanese System, 286–7
specialization, 294–9 (App. 2)
Industrial Problems Research
Association, 44
Industrial Structure Council, 178
industrial system benefit, 128–9
information flows
FED Project, 183–5, 187–8
ICOT researchers, 204
innovation factor, 256
mobilization & utilization, 261, 263
Prolog development, 138–9, 205
quality control, 259
R & D laboratories, 260–1
technical change effects, 5
VLSI Project, 62, 73–80
information technology
computers, R & D, 49, 50
development, 8, 14
Information Technology Promotion
Agency, 31

innovation, uncertainty factor, 265
Institute of Fifth Generation
Computing, 55
Institute for New Generation Computer
Technology, 55, 193–242
benefits, 215–16
criticisms, 233–42
establishment, 197–200
evaluation committee, 229
membership, 199–200, 202
organization form, 200–27; AI case
study, 219–23; basic knowledge
resource, 203–4; knowledge assimilation, 211–17; knowledge diffusion,
223–5; member firms' role, 209–11;
Prolog culture development, 217–19;
summary, 226–7; universities' role,
205–9
private sector role 209–29
universities' role 205–9
Institute of Physical and Chemical
Research, 206
integrated circuit
development, 31, 59
environment-proof, 179, 181
optoelectronic, 99–101, 108, 112,
116, 123–7
intellectual property rights, 62–3
computer industry, 53–4
state ownership, 137, 139–41
international implications
competitiveness, 258–63
government subsidies, 287–8
Japanese system, 263–4, 289–90
uncertainty features, 264–76
isolated in-house research (IIHR), 89–95
conclusions, 281
Fifth Generation Project, 230
itakuhi (contract research), 29

Japan Development Bank, 14, 23, 46, 268
Japan Electronic Computer Company, 26,
268
Japan Electronic Industry Development
Association, 23
VLSI Project, 57, 59, 63
Japan Information Processing Development
Centre, 38, 197, 198
Japan Key Technology Center, 128, 137
Japanese System, *see* Japanese Technology-
Creating System
Japanese Technology Evaluation Program,
55, 233–5

Supercomputer Project, 175
Japanese Technology-Creating System,
  1, 3, 8
  bounded vision, 284–6
  competition, 276–84
  computer development, 20, 21–2
  concept, 6
  development, 257
  ETL/ECL contribution, 21–2,
    38, 56
  evolution, 289–90
  Frontier-Leading Period, 273
  Late Catching-Up Period, 269–72
  mainframe development, 271–2
  national characteristics, 263–4
  universities, research role, 175–6
JEIDA, see Japan Electronic Industry
  Development Association
  jimukan (administrative official), 285
JIPDEC, see Japan Information Processing
  Development Centre
Jisedai Programme, 177–9
JJ, see Josephson junction
joint research
  Fifth Generation Project, 231–2
  Optical Measurement Project, 98–144
  Supercomputer Project prospect, 152–4
joint research in joint research
  facilities (JRJF)
  conclusions, 281–3
  FED Project, 182–3, 188–9, 192
  Fifth Generation Project, 230, 282
  Optical Measurement Project, 109, 133–4
  VLSI Project, 89, 93–5
Josephson, B., 149
Josephson junction 6
  development, 162–8, 176
  explanation, 149–50
  HEMT application, 160
  IBM research, 149, 151, 164-6
  Supercomputer Project, 145, 154–5
JRJF, see joint research in joint
  research facilities
JTECH, see Japanese Technology
  Evaluation Program
just-in-time production, 259

KABU-WAKE method, 220
Kansai companies, FED project, 183–4
Karatsu, H., 198
Karube, I. 181
Kitakami, H., 204, 217, 225, 241
Kleinsasser, A., 166

know-how
  socialized knowledge factor, 63
  state ownership, 137
  Supercomputer Project, 169
  VLSI Project, 73–80
knowledge (*see also* know-how,
  technological knowledge)
  basic resource, 201, 209
  engineering, 220
  FED Project, 187–8, 189–91
  Fifth Generation Project, 195–6,
    198–9, 200–5, 222–6
  ICOT resource, 200–5
  leakage danger, 245–6, 248–9,
    262–3, 280
  Optical Measurement Project, 105–6,
    110–12, 117–18, 120, 130
  representation systems, 196, 221
  sharing, 2, 9, 105–6, 110–12, 143
  sharing/diffusion, 223–6
  Supercomputer Project, 157–8, 168–70
  VLSI Project, 62–3, 73–80
knowledge-based logic design systems,
  220, 221
Kobayashi, T., 15, 30, 40, 61, 160, 261–2,
  266–7, 272
Komagata, S., 13
Konishi, K., 197, 226
Kowalski, R., 195
kōza (research unit), 207
Kubo, Dr, 13
Kurakami, K., 240–1
kyōju (professor), 207

LAN, see local area network
LANDSAT data test, 157
laser diodes, 100
Late Catching-Up Period (1966–79), 256,
  269–72
LEC, see liquid-encapsulated
  Czochralski technique
lifetime employment policy, 61
light-emitting diodes, research, 99, 100
liquid-encapsulated Czochralski
  technique, 123
Lisp, 195, 199, 213, 218–20
lithography, VLSI Project, 69–80, 84
local area network, Optical Measurement
  Project, 129
logic programming (*see also* Prolog), 203,
  238–9, 241–2

machine translation systems, 219, 222

Machinery and Information Industries
  Bureau, 57, 179, 199
Maeda, N., 197
mainframe computers
  DIPS project, 272
  hybrid integrated circuits, 270
  Late Catching-Up Period, 271
  market, 55–6
market processes, 3, 4–5
market share
  electronic devices industry, 243
  joint research influence, 66
  specialization, 294–9 (App. 2)
  VLSI Project success, 82–3
maskless ion implantation, 116, 124
Masuda, K., 225, 241
materials analysis, 116
Matsushita
  FED project, 183–4
  ICOT member, 202
  OJL project member, 119
MBE, *see* molecular beam epitaxy
MECS, *see* Ministry of Education, Culture
  and Science
Meindl, J.D., 148–9
memory devices, 32, 269
mergers
  computer industry, Japan, 47
  strategic industries, 44–5
Merz, J. L., 109, 115, 123–6
MESFET, *see* metal-semiconductor
  field-effect transistor
Metal Organic Chemical Vapor
  Deposition, 124
metal oxide silicon field-effect transistor,
  180
metal-semiconductor field-effect
  transistor, 148–9, 151, 153–5, 157
MIMD, *see* multiple instruction,
  multiple data-stream technology
MINERVA (knowledge representation
  system), 221
Ministry of Communications, 14
Ministry of Education, Culture and
  Science, 141, 206
Ministry of International Trade and
  Industry (*see also* Electrotechnical
  Laboratory)
  computer industry, 43, 45–50, 146
  Fifth Generation Project, 193–242
  Five Year Programmes, 29
  integrated circuit development, 31
  intellectual property rights, 53–4

inter-firm coordination, 271–2
  Optical Measurement Project, 98–144
  PIPS project (1971–80), 48
  R & D, 47–8, 55
  research options, 10
  strategic industries criteria, 24
  Supercomputer Project, 145–76
  technology development, 2
  VHSCS Project, 32–7, 44
  VLSI Project funding, 58
Ministry of Post and
  Telecommunications, 14
MITI, *see* Ministry of International
  Trade and Industry
Mitsubishi
  exits mainframe market, 55
  ICOT member, 202
  OJL project member, 119
  VLSI Project participant, 67, 75–80
Mitsubishi Electric 21
  Catching-Up Periods, 266–9, 269–72
  cooperative research analysis, 243–55
  FED Project, 183–4, 186
  inter-firm research cooperation, 279
  Supercomputer Project, 146, 154–5, 157
Miyazaki, N., 204
Mizushima oil refinery, 108, 109
MOCVD, *see* Metal Organic
  Chemical Vapor Deposition
MODFET, *see* modulation-doped field-
  effect transistor
modulation-doped field-effect transistor, 148,
  149, 157
molecular beam epitaxy, 124, 156, 157,
  160, 169
superlattices 180, 187
MOSFET, *see* metal oxide silicon field-
  effect transistor
Moto-oka, T., 195, 197
Mueller, K. A., 165, 166
multiple instruction, multiple data-stream
  technology, 157, 195
Murakami, K., 212, 217, 241
Musashino-1 computer, 20, 267

Nakano, M., 197
Nakayama, S., 44
National Institute for Research
  Advancement, 226
Nebashi, M., 64–5
NEC
  3-D devices research, 180, 181
  Catching-Up Periods, 266–72

cooperative research analysis, 243–55
designs, 20–1
FED Project, 183, 184, 186
first computer, 16
HEMT production, 161
IBM competition, 30–1
ICOT member, 202, 210, 213
memory devices, R&D, 32
OJL project member, 119
semiconductor memories, 171
Supercomputer Project, 151–2, 154–5,
    168
Toshiba link, 39, 47
total quality control, 259, 292–3 (App. 1)
VLSI Project participant, 67, 75–80, 88
NEC–Toshiba Information Systems, 80
Next Generation Base Technologies Devel-
    opment Programme (Jisedai), 177–9,
    190
NGS (no government support), 89–95
Nikon, VLSI Project participant 71–2
niobium technology, 162, 167
Nippon Electric Company, *see* NEC
Nippon Peripherals Limited, 52, 53, 279
Nippon Telegraph and Telephone
    (*see also* Electrical Communications
        Laboratories)
    cooperative research agreements, 1–2
    Early Catching-Up Period, 267
    ETL research comparison, 18
    formation and development, 14
    research cooperation, 6
NIRA, *see* National Institute for
    Research Advancement
NTIS, *see* NEC–Toshiba Information
    Systems
NTT, *see* Nippon Telegraph and Telephone

OJL, *see* Optoelectronics Joint Research
    Laboratory
Okabe, Y., 167
Okada, K., 15–16, 266
Okamura, A., 119
Oki
    Catching-Up Periods, 266–9, 269–72
    cooperative research analysis, 243–55
    exits mainframe market, 55
    FED Project, 183, 184
    ICOT member, 202
    OJL project member, 119
    Supercomputer Project, 146, 152,
        154–5, 156–7
optical computers, 176

optical fibre cables, 107, 127, 130
Optical Measurement and Control System
    Project (1979–85), 1, 10, 98–144
    conclusions, 142–4
    cooperative research, 252–3, 255
    crystal growth technology, 116, 123–4
    evaluation: competence blending benefits,
        134; industrial system benefits, 128–30,
        information gain benefits,
        136–7; joint research benefits, 133–4;
        knowledge diffusion benefit, 137–41;
        large-size advantages, 134–6; output,
        121–8; research resources allocation,
        131–3
    funding, 133, 141–2, 144
    government influence, 143
    introduction, 98–9
    JRJF, 282
    NTT/MITI/ECL representation, 107
    OJL, 115–21
    origins, 99–107
    research design, 107–14
Optical Measurement System, 113 (fig. 4.2)
optical sensors, 108, 112
Optoelectronic Industry and Technology
    Development Association, 130
optoelectronic technology, 98–144
Optoelectronics Joint Research
    Laboratory, 115–21
    output evaluation, 121–8
organization form
    innovation factor, 256
    intra-firm, 259–63
    Japanese System, effect, 263–4
    vertical integration, 287–8
oriented-basic research, 9–11, 257
    Fifth Generation Computer Project, 274
    Frontier-Leading Period, 273–5
    Future Electronic Devices Project, 274
    High-Speed Computing System Project,
        274
    Optical Measurement and Control
        Project, 274
    VLSI Project, 274

parallel inference machine, 201, 213–14,
    220, 226, 241
parallel processing system, 146, 154,
    156, 157, 174, 195
parametron, 18–19, 20, 31, 38
patents
    FED Project, 189–91
    Jisedai Programme, 190

Optical Measurement Project, 137–41
research output measure, 81–2
socialized knowledge factor, 63
state ownership benefits, 137–9
Supercomputer Project, 169, 172
technology comparisons, 33, 36, 53–4
VLSI Project, 73–80
Pattern Information Processing System project, 33, 48, 53-5
oriented-basic research, 274
personal sequential inference machine 209, 212–13
personnel, staff recruitment, R & D, 260–1
photolithography, 69
UHV system, 125
PIM, *see* parallel inference machine
PIPS, *see* Pattern Information Processing system project
planar technology, 31, 124
pressure incentive, technical change effects, 5
production policies, 259, 279
profits, generation, 3
Prolog, 193, 197
ICOT applicatons, 209, 222–3
introduction, 198–9
kernel AI language issue, 199–200
language choice, 195–6
novel features, 205
parallel processing, 213
Prolog culture discussion, 217–19
PSI, *see* personal sequential inference machine

quality control, 259, 292–3 (App. 1)

R & D, *see* research and development
Reactive Ion Beam Etching, 125
research cooperation, 1–2, 6, 8
benefits, 9, 12
market processes, 6
oriented-basic research, 9
research and development
artificial intelligence, 228
benefits question, 58
bounded vision effect, 3
Catching-Up Periods, 266–72
cooperation/competition analysis:
benefits, national projects, 249–53;
competition intensity, 243–8;
evaluation, 253–5; government role, 248–9; introduction, 243
FED Project: background, 177–9;

conclusion, 191–2; devices selected, 177, 179–81; evaluation, 186–91;
joint laboratory proposal, 181–2;
research organization, 182–6
Fifth Generation Project: background, 194–6; conclusion, 242;
evaluation, 229–42; funding, 227–9;
ICOT establishment, 197–200;
ICOT organization form, 200–27;
objectives, 196–7
Frontier-Leading Period, 272–6
government finance, 21, 22–3, 37–8, 45–50
information flows, 260–1
integrated circuits, 31
joint schemes, 53
memory device technology, 32
MITI-initiated cooperation, 33, 44
Optical Measurement project:
conclusions, 142–4; costs/funding, 133, 141–2, 144; evaluation, 124–41;
large size advantages, 134–6; OJL, 115–21; origins, 99–107; research design, 107–14
oriented-basic research, 9, 257, 273–5
private sector, 22, 31, 37–8
research cooperation, types, 281
staff recruitment policies, 260–1
Supercomputer Project: background, 145–50; company interest, 150–2;
design, 154–8; evaluation, 158–76;
government funding, 145, 151–2;
joint laboratory question, 152–4
Temporary Measures Law 1971, 45
universities' role, 175–6
VLSI Project: background, 57–8;
company opposition, 63–4; economic issues, 59–63; evaluation, 81–96;
laboratories structure, 64–73; shared knowledge, 73–80
workers, 4
resonant hot electron transistor, 187
RIBE, *see* Reactive Ion Beam Etching
RIKEN, *see* Institute of Physical and Chemical Research

Sahashi, S., 27
Sakurai, Dr, 101–7
Sanken, 44
Sanyo, FED Project, 183–4
satellite imaging, 157
semiconductors
design, 41–2

fabrication technology, 116, 124–5
memories, NEC, 171
Optical Measurement Project, 99–100, 103, 121–8, 137
research history, 58
superlattices, 179–82, 185
vertical integration approach, 261–2
Sharp
FED Project, 183–4
ICOT member, 202
silicon, transistor, 148, 149, 157
Simon, H., 238–9, 241, 286
single-phase yttrium barium copper oxide, 166–7
social aspects
CIHR joint research benefits, 188–9
joint research benefits, 93, 137–8
research cooperation, 279–81
software, (see also computer languages)
AI systems, 221
standardization factor, 216, 231
Sony, FED Project, 185
Space Industries Office, 179, 181
SPYDER software system, 55
standardization, software, 216, 231
state ownership, Optical Measurement Project patents, 137
strategic industries, funding, 14
subsidies, 45, 64–5
Sumimoto, OJL project member, 119
Sumimoto Electric, FED Project, 185
Supercomputer Project (1981–89), 1, 10, 145–76
background, 145–50
CIHR examples, 156–8
companies' response, 150–2
conclusion, 176
costs/funding, 145, 151–2, 160–1
design, 154–6
evaluation, 158–76; CIHR benefits, 170–2; HEMT story, 159–61; Josephson junction story, 162–6; knowledge sharing benefits, 168–70; project output, 172–5; some conclusions, 167–8; uncertainty, 148–9, 158–9, 176
FED Project comparison, 245–7, 255
government role, 145
IBM factor, 146–7
initiation, 150
joint research proposal, 152–4
knowledge sharing, 157–8, 168–70
membership, 151

new electronic devices, 147–50
objectives, 146–7, 159
patents and know-how, 169, 172
research allocation, 155
universities' role, 175–6
superconductivity, 149, 166, 167, 289
superlattice semiconductors, FED Project, 177, 179–81, 182, 185, 187
System 360, 30, 31, 32
System 370, 39, 45

Takahashi, S., 19
Tanaka, S., 60, 63, 181
tariff
liberalization, 1970s, 38–9
protection policy, 25–7
Tarui, Y., 64–5
technical change, 258–63
technological knowledge
cooperative research, 201–2, 211
diffusion, 35–7, 223–5, 283–4
ICOT organization, 203–5, 225–7
Japanese contribution, 274
leakage danger, 245–6, 248–9, 262–3, 280
MITI ownership, 172
ownership question, 214–15
patents, ownership issues, 36–7
sharing, private companies, 34–5
sharing/competition issue, 244
social benefits, 37, 54
socialization factor, 62–3
spontaneous inter-firm exchange, 278–9
technology agreements
Early Catching-Up Period, 269
US links, 8, 15, 28, 32–3, 39, 47
telecommunications, history, 14
Temporary Measures Law 1971, 45
three-dimensional devices, FED Project, 177–91
Tokyo University of Technology, 177
Toshiba
Catching-Up Periods, 266–9, 269–72
cooperative research analysis, 243–55
exits mainframe market, 55
FED Project, 183, 184
ICOT member, 202
NEC link, 39, 47
OJL project member, 119
Supercomputer Project, 146, 151, 154–5, 157
VLSI Project participant, 66, 75–80
total quality control, 259, 292–3
(App. 1)

trade, liberalization, 1970s, 38–56
transistors
　ETL IV computer, 267–8
　FED Project, 180, 185, 187
　gallium arsenide, 148–61, 164, 167
　niobium technology, 162–7
　superconductivity experiments, 166–7
　US invention, 13
　TROPIX architecture, 55
Tsu, R., 159, 179–80

Uenohara, M., 61
UHV, *see* ultra-high vacuum system
ultra-high vacuum system, 124, 125, 135
uncertainty
　decision-making factor, 256–7
　FED Project, 189
　general analysis, 264–5
　government role, 268
　Japanese System, 265–76; Early
　　Catching-Up Period, 266–9;
　　Frontier-Leading Period, 272–6;
　　Late Catching-Up Period, 269–72
　MITI role, 276
　Supercomputer Project, 148–9, 158–9,
　　176
United States
　cooperative agreements, 8, 15, 28,
　　32–3, 39, 47
　Japanese market rival, 9
universities
　computer purchasing policy, 269
　Early Catching-Up Period, 267, 268
　early computer research, 18
　FED Project role, 177, 191
　Fifth Generation Computer Project
　　role, 193
　ICOT role 205–9
　research role, 4, 8, 102, 141
　Supercomputer Project role, 175–6
　technology development, 2, 13
University of Tokyo, 195, 197, 208–9
'use-pull' determinant

FED Project, 185
optoelectronics, 108, 112, 121, 126–8
Supercomputer Project role, 156
Utilisp, 221

variable processor pipeline, 157
vertical integration practice, 261–3
Very High Speed Computer System
　Project (1966–72), 32–7, 44, 270
Very Large Scale Integration technology,
　195, 197
VHSCS, *see* Very High Speed Computer
　System Project
VLSI Research Association, 64, 71
VLSI Research Project (1976–80), 1, 10
　background, 57–8
　commercializable products, 83–5
　conclusions, 96–7
　establishment, 58–9
　evaluation: general considerations,
　　89–92; market share growth, 82–9;
　　patents and papers measure, 81–2;
　　summary, 92–6
　funding, 80–1
　joint research: company opposition,
　　63–4; difficulties, 66, 85–9;
　　economic issues, 59–63; laboratories
　　allocation, 64–73
　NEC management system, 88 (fig. 3.5)
　shared knowledge analysis, 73–80;
　　laboratories 1, 2 and 3, 74–7;
　　laboratories 4, 5 and 6, 77–8
von Neumann computer, 145, 198
VPP, *see* variable processor pipeline

Wada, Dr, 19
Walgren, D., 57
war, Japanese electronics industry, 7
wealth, causes, 4
Working Party (Jisedai Programme),
　177–9

X-ray lithography, 69